# THE
# TEXTILE MANUFACTURES
# AND THE
# COSTUMES OF THE PEOPLE OF INDIA

# THE TEXTILE MANUFACTURES AND THE COSTUMES OF THE PEOPLE OF INDIA

**John Forbes Watson**

GYAN

*Published by*

Gyan Publishing House
5, Ansari Road
Daryaganj, New Delhi-110002
Phone: 011-47034999, 9811692060
E-mail: books@gyanbooks.com

*Distribution Network*
gyanbooks.com
India, USA, Canada, UK, Australia, France



ISBN : 978-81-212-2886-2 (HB)
First Published, 1866

2nd Impression 2021

*Printed at:* Gyan Press, Delhi.



**The**
**Textile Manufactures**
**and the**
**Costumes of the People of India**
Author: John Forbes Watson

# CONTENTS.

**INTRODUCTION :—**

LOOM-MADE GARMENTS.—SAREES—*continued.*



## II. KERCHIEFS FOR HEAD AND SHOULDERS.

## PIECE GOODS.

PIECE GOODS—*continued.*

PIECE GOODS—*continued.*

PAGE

## COLOURED COTTON GOODS.



## PRINTED COTTON GOODS.



## COTTON.—MISCELLANEOUS.

PIECE GOODS—*continued.* PAGE

## SILK.



## WILD SILKS.



## LOOM EMBROIDERY,—GOLD AND SILVER.

PIECE GOODS—*continued.* PAGE

WOOLLEN GOODS—*continued.* PAGE

WOOLLEN GOODS—*continued.*

PAGE

FABRICS FROM CENTRAL ASIA AND RUSSIA.

# LIST OF ILLUSTRATIONS.

## LIST OF ILLUSTRATIONS—*cont.*

THE

# TEXTILE MANUFACTURES AND COSTUMES

OF THE

# PEOPLE OF INDIA.

## INTRODUCTION.

SPECIMENS of all the important Textile Manufactures of India existing in the stores of the India Museum have been collected in eighteen large volumes, of which twenty sets have been prepared, each set being, as nearly as possible, an exact counterpart of all the others. The eighteen volumes, forming one set, contain 700 specimens, illustrating, in a complete and convenient manner, this branch of Indian Manufactures. The twenty sets are to be distributed in Great Britain and India—thirteen in the former and seven in the latter—so that there will be twenty places, each provided with a collection exactly like all the others, and so arranged as to admit of the interchange of references when desired.

Each sample has been prepared in such a way as to indicate the character of the whole piece from which it was cut, and thus enable the manufacturer to reproduce the article if he wishes to do so. In other words, the eighteen volumes contain 700 *working samples or specimens.*

The twenty sets of volumes may thus be regarded as *Twenty Industrial Museums,* illustrating the Textile Manufactures of India, and promoting trade operations between the East and West, in so far as these are concerned.

To make this series of Museums, however, accomplish more fully and properly the end in view, it was felt that *something* was needed beyond the mere bringing together of specimens, and this something the present volume is intended to supply.

The interests of the people in India, as well as those of the people at Home, are concerned in this matter, and *both interests must be considered.* Our remarks in the first instance, however, will apply more particularly to the latter.

About two hundred millions of souls form the population of what we commonly speak of as India ; and, scant though the garments of the vast majority may be, an order to clothe them all would try the resources of the greatest manufacturing nation on earth. It is clear, therefore, that India is in a position to become a magnificent customer. She may still be this, and yet continue to seek her supplies in part from herself ; for to clothe but a mere per-centage of such a vast population would double the looms of Lancashire.

This is what might and may be ; but *that which is,* is greatly otherwise, for, in point of fact, India buys but sparingly of our manufactures.

Many things probably combine to bring about this result, and it is not our purpose here to inquire into them all. But there are some which are important and apparent, and to these allusion should be made.

If we attempt to induce an individual or a nation to become a customer, we endeavour to make the articles which we know to be liked and needed, and these we offer for sale. We do not make an effort to impose on others *our own tastes and needs,* but we produce what will please the customer and what he wants. The British manufacturer follows this rule generally ; but he seems to have failed to do so in the case of India, or to have done it with so little success, that it would almost appear as if he were incapable of *appreciating* Oriental tastes and habits.

There are probably few things beyond the understanding of our manufacturers, but it will be admitted that some education in the matter is necessary, and that without it the value of certain characteristics of Indian ornament and form will not be properly realized. This supposes the means of such education to be readily accessible, which hitherto has not been the case, simply because manufacturers have not known with any certainty what goods were suitable.* To attain to skill in meeting Eastern tastes and Eastern wants will require study and much consideration even when the means of study are supplied; but up to the present time the manufacturer has had no *ready opportunity* of acquiring a full and correct knowledge of what was wanted.

The deficiency here alluded to will, we believe, be supplied by these local Museums, and the object of the present work is to give further aid to those who consult them. If the manufacturer should still encounter difficulties, when exceptional points are in question, these can be got over by reference to the parent and more elaborate collection in the India Museum; and there also full information on doubtful matters can be obtained. In fact, it is but reasonable to expect that this will occasionally be necessary.

The 700 specimens (and we again point out that they are all what is called *working samples*) show what the people of India affect and deem suitable in the way of textile fabrics, and if the supply of these is to come from Britain, they must be *imitated* there. *What is wanted, and what is to be copied to meet that want,* is thus accessible for study in these Museums.

It was thought, however, that something more than mere specimens was needed to enable the manufacturer to do this intelligibly. It was necessary that he should know how the garment was worn, by which sex, and for what purpose —how, in short, the people were clothed, as well as the qualities of the fabrics they used. It was further necessary that he should know why certain arrangements of ornamentation were adopted, as well as the styles of ornamentation and the materials employed.† Information on these points, and on many other similar ones, the present volume is also intended to supply.

---

* We are quite aware of the efforts which of late years have been made, more particularly by Glasgow and Manchester, to manufacture *Sarees* and some similar loom-made articles of clothing; the result, however, has been insignificant when we remember the extent of the consumption of such articles.

† The steadiness of Indian taste and fashion is a point to which the manufacturers' attention should be directed. Among the people of India there is not that constant desire for change in the material and style of their costume which is so noticeable in Europe. Some patterns which are now favourites, have been so for centuries, and certain articles of dress were ages ago very much what they now are. It is not, however, to be understood from this that new styles of ornamentation have not been occasionally introduced by the native manufacturer in recent times. What this note is intended to convey is simply that there is a much greater fixity of fashion in India than in Europe, and it is not necessary to point out that this has a very direct bearing on the operations of trade.

It is shown that a very large proportion of the clothing of the people of India, whether Hindu or Mahomedan, consists of articles which are untouched by needle or scissors. These articles leave the loom in a state ready to be worn, and have their analogues in our Shawls, Plaids, and Scarfs. The principal of these are the Turbans, Loongees, and Dhotees worn by men, and the Sarees worn by women.

The Dhotee is nothing but a scarf folded round the loins and brought up between the legs, and this constitutes the whole clothing of a large number of the lower and poorer classes. The Loongee, again, is a similar but larger scarf or plaid, worn over the shoulders and upper part of the body. The Turban is a longer and narrower scarf, which is folded round the head to form a head-dress. The Saree, or woman's plaid, is used to cover both the body and the head.

Loongees, Dhotees, Sarees, and Turbans have each different functions, and the quality of the fabric must fulfil these; they have appropriate lengths and breadths, and these must be considered; they have suitable modes or styles of ornamentation, and these too must be kept in view.

In order to enable the manufacturer to do this easily and successfully, the 700 specimens have in the present work been arranged in groups—thus Turbans have been considered separately, and then Loongees, and so on. These large groups have been again subdivided, and the basis of this subdivision has been the quality of the body of the garment, the material of which it is made, the mode of ornamentation, &c. Thus Loongees made of cotton are not associated with those made of silk; nor are those in which gold thread is used for their decoration conjoined with those in which coloured cotton or silk is so employed.

This work, therefore, may be regarded as an analysis of the contents of the eighteen volumes, and a classification of them according to function, quality, material, and decoration.

Many important facts stand saliently out as the result of this analysis; such, for instance, as that by far the larger proportion of the clothing of the people of India is made of cotton; that there are certain colours or tones of colour which are favourites; that gold is largely used in the ornamentation of all sorts of fabrics—cotton as well as silk; and that in the decoration of every garment regard is always had to the special purpose which that garment is intended to fulfil.

Indeed, the modes of ornamentation are so peculiar and so characteristic, that it will often be found that nothing beyond a difference in this respect separates one group from another. Too much attention cannot be given to this point. A piece of cloth may be offered for sale whose length and breadth and quality may fit it admirably for a Turban or a Loongee, yet it may prove utterly unsaleable because its decoration is unsuitable and injures its usefulness; or because it is not in good taste from the Indian's point of view; or, farther, because its colours are not fast and will not admit of the constant and rough washing to which his clothing is subjected.

It must not be thought that the Taste of India takes delight in what is gaudy and glaring.

No one will study the contents of these volumes and come to that conclusion. On the contrary, there will be found there good evidence that Indian taste in decoration is, in the highest degree, refined. Such combinations of form and colour as many of these specimens exhibit *everyone will call beautiful;* and this beauty has one constant feature—a quietness and harmony which never fail to fascinate. This also can be said of it—there is no waste of ornamentation, which is present where it should be, and absent where it should not be. The portions which are concealed when the garment is on the wearer are rarely decorated; nor is there any of that lavish expenditure of ornament which so often purchases *show* at the expense of *comfort.* It is in obedience to this principle that the decoration of these loom-made garments is nearly always confined to one or both ends, or to one or both borders, according to circumstances.

We trust that the importance of this class of Indian garments has been made as clear as it should be. We refer to *those garments which leave the loom ready for wear*—the Turbans, Loongees, Dhotees, and Sarees, which bear a certain resemblance to our Shawls, Plaids, and Scarfs, though they by no means serve the same purposes. The photographs interspersed throughout the work illustrate fully the various modes of wearing them. It cannot be too often repeated that they constitute a large portion of the whole clothing of the people;

and it is clear that the nation which desires to supply that clothing can only be successful in doing so by offering garments of this character for sale.

But while they constitute a large portion they by no means constitute the whole. In all times—past and present—Mahomedans have worn vestments made out of Piece-goods by the aid of scissors and needles, and Hindus have been long and increasingly following them in this respect. Jackets, Coats, and Trousers are worn by men; and Bodices, Trousers, and Skirts or Petticoats, by women. These are not made as they are with us in Europe, but, nevertheless, they may appropriately enough go by these names.

Many of the photographs are inserted to show the various styles of these vestments, and the volumes contain numerous specimens of the piece-goods out of which they are made.

Like the loom-made garments, these also consist chiefly of cotton, and among them appear the beautiful muslins of Dacca. These are so exquisitely fine that we have dwelt at considerable length on the mode of their manufacture, and on the question of comparative fineness as raised between them and the most delicate muslins hitherto produced in Europe. A careful consideration of all the evidence which has yet been brought to bear on this question leads clearly to the conclusion, that the weavers of Dacca can and do produce a fabric which, *for fineness, as well as for all other good qualities, has nowhere been equalled.* While on this subject we have taken occasion to speak of the character and extent of Sizing used by the native weaver. This is a point of great practical importance, as it has been thought, and probably correctly so, that the Size used by the British manufacturer is often the cause of that *mildewing* which is so destructive to the cotton goods sent from this country to India.

Among the piece-goods also occur a number of specimens of the loom-made Brocades and of the Hand-Embroideries of India. There may be little hope of Europe ever being able to make these cheaper than India herself can; but, as a mere lesson in taste, the study of them may prove useful to the Home manufacturer.*

* Those who may wish to acquire an extended knowledge of the variety and beauty of these exquisite productions will have to consult the Collection at the India Museum as now attached to the Department of the Reporter on the Products of India.

This leads us to remark that there are certain fabrics which will probably always be best, and most cheaply manufactured by hand. It is found to be so even in this country, where the powers of machinery have been pushed to their utmost. The hand-loom weaver still exists amongst us, nor is it likely that he will ever cease to do so. Less likely still is it that machinery will ever be able to drive him from the field in India. The very fine and the richly decorated fabrics of that country will probably always require the delicate manipulation of human fingers for their production.

In such manufactures the foremost place will be taken by that country which can most cheaply supply labour, intelligence, and refined taste—all three combined. This being the case, it is not probable that England will ever be able to compete successfully with the native manufacturer in the production of fabrics of this sort. The reverse, indeed, is in every sense probable, and the native looms will continue to yield the Embroideries, the Shawls, and the Carpets, for which they are already so famous. They will continue to do this for the customer in India, and it is quite possible, when the beauty of some of their productions is better known and appreciated, that they will find profitable customers in the far West as well. Such a hope is not without something to rest on, and it may be the sooner realized now that these collections have been made.

In the meantime the British manufacturer must not look for his customers to the upper ten millions of India, but to the hundreds of millions in the lower grades. The plainer and cheaper stuffs of cotton, or of cotton and wool together, are those which he has the best chance of selling, and those which he would be able to sell largely, if in their manufacture he would keep well in view the requirements and tastes of the people to whom he offers them.

This naturally brings us to the more special consideration of the manner in which the interests of India are concerned in the matter.

We know India now-a-days as a country whose Raw Products we largely receive. We pay for these partly in *kind* and partly in *money;* but India never buys from us what will repay our purchases from her, and the consequence is that we have always to send out the large difference in bullion, which never comes back to us, disappearing there as if it had been dropped into the ocean.

We buy her Cotton, Indigo, Coffee, and Spices ; and we sell her what we can in the shape of Textile and other Manufactures. It must not be forgotten, however, that there was a time when India supplied us largely with Textiles. It was she who sent us the famous Longcloths, and the very term *Calico* is derived from *Calicut* where they were made. She may never resume her position as an exporting manufacturer of goods of this sort,—though what the extension of the mill-system in India may eventually lead to it is difficult to say, and her friends would most unwillingly see its development fettered by restrictions of any sort. This is clear, however, that it will be a benefit to the masses of the people of India to be supplied with their clothing at the cheapest possible rate—let this be done by whom it may. If Great Britain can give Loongees, Dhotees, Sarees, and Calicoes to India which cost less than those made by her own weavers, *both* countries will be benefited. In a great productive country like India it is certain that *she* will gain ; for if supplies from Britain set labour free there, it will only be to divert it at once into other and perhaps more profitable channels. It might be otherwise if India were not a country whose strength in raw products is great and far from developed ; but as it is, her resources in this direction are known to be capable of a vast expansion and to be sufficient to occupy the energies of her whole people.

The machinery and skill of Britain may thus do a present service to India, by supplying her with material for clothing her people at a cheap rate—an end to which these *collections* must certainly lead by showing the home manufacturer what it is that the natives require. But they may also show that certain fabrics can be produced at a lower cost than in Europe, and make India *both buy and sell* her textiles. Those which she would offer for sale would in all probability be her Carpets and Embroideries, which, as already stated, can be made by hand with a greater perfection and beauty than by any machinery hitherto invented.

There are other reasons which make it desirable that a few of these twenty sets should be placed in India. For instance, as each set is a copy of all the others, they may prove useful in *facilitating* trade operations. They will enable the agent in India to refer the merchant or the manufacturer at home to a certain specimen, and ask him to produce an article as like it as possible, or with such alterations as he may see fit to suggest. And so, in like manner, they may enable the merchant of one part of India to deal with the merchant of another, when, through an examination of these volumes, he learns that an article is made there which will suit his customers. This aspect of their usefulness gives these collections a title to be called *Trade Museums* in a fuller and broader sense than belongs to any which have yet been established.

It is not desirable, however, that the *scheme* should stop with the textile manufactures. It is hoped, indeed, that it may yet be greatly extended and in various directions, to the advantage alike of Britain and of India, whose common interest it certainly is in every way to cultivate intimate commercial relations. A large amount of information has been drawn together regarding all classes of Indian manufactures and of Indian products, and it is clearly of immense advantage to this country and to India that this knowledge should be so disseminated as to prove *practically* useful—in other words, so as to influence directly the interchange of commodities. No way, we think, could so effectually accomplish this as the one which, with the sanction and support of the Secretary of State for India in Council, has been chosen in the case of the Textile Manufactures; and it is satisfactory to know that the resources of the Department would enable future efforts in the same direction, having regard to other manufactures or products, to be made with less labour and with increased economy.

NOTE.—A Memorandum, submitted to the India Office, regarding the distribution in Britain and India of the Collections of Specimens, to which this work forms the key,—the enumeration of the places in this country where they have been deposited, and the statement of the conditions attached to the gift by the Secretary of State for India in Council, will be found in an Appendix at p. 149.

# COSTUME OF THE PEOPLE OF INDIA.

It will be convenient to consider the Textile Manufactures of India as divided into two classes :—the first comprehending the various scarf or plaid-like articles of dress which leave the loom ready for wear, and the second consisting of piece goods for the conversion of which into clothing the scissors and needle are required.

It would appear that before the invasion of India by the Mahomedans, the art of sewing was not practised there.*

Anterior to that period, therefore, it is probable that nearly the whole clothing of the people consisted of loom-made articles coming strictly under the first head.

Strict Hindus may yet be found to whom a garment composed of several pieces sewn together is an abomination and defilement. Throughout India generally, however, they have now begun to wear various made-up articles of dress such as were formerly used only by the Mahomedans.

On the other hand, the Mahomedans of our day frequently content themselves with the simpler covering which is more peculiarly the dress of the Hindu.

This partial assimilation of the costumes of the two great races of India has been brought about in various ways. For instance, under the old Mahomedan rule, Hindu men of rank in the employment of the Government were obliged to present themselves on state occasions dressed in the same fashion as their conquerors. The element of compulsion in this was at first distasteful. The innovation was accordingly resisted, and on their return to their homes they discarded the costume they had been forced to assume, and reverted to that to which they had been accustomed, and which they regarded as belonging to their race. Indeed, the wearing of the Mahomedan costume would at first be looked on as an emblem of defeat and vassalage, and a despotic interference with customs almost sacred from their age. It must be remembered, however, that this change of costume was only imposed upon those who were *in office* under the new rule—on those, in short, who were placed in some sort of authority ; and hence, in course of time, the change of costume came to be regarded as an evidence of power in those who adopted it, and to be valued accordingly. It is not difficult to see how this would bring the matter eventually within the influence of fashion, which has its rule in India as elsewhere. The new costume, in fact, became an evidence that its wearer occupied a position of more or less importance, and this reconciled him to a change which pride of custom and religious feeling would have led him to resist.

* Buchanan, in Montgomery Martin's "Eastern India," Vol. II., p. 699.

Of course this reconciliation was the more readily accomplished, because the made-up articles of dress were after trial found to be convenient and suitable to the climate. Nor was there anything in the *style* of the new costume to make a Hindu desire to discontinue its use after he had once got accustomed to it, whilst there was much to recommend it.

As regards the Hindu women, however, for a long period they scrupulously adhered on all occasions to their native costume. Indeed, even yet the petticoat is not regarded as a legitimate garment; and in some parts of the country in which it is used, women of rank, when they eat, cook, or pray, lay it aside and retain only their under wrapper which has been made without the use of scissors or needle.* In a few districts also, even to the present day, the bosom is left uncovered by respectable women:—the use of the *Cholee*, or bodice, being reserved for the impure.

There was thus a tendency, in the first instance, to resist the adoption of those new forms of costume which necessitated the use of the needle, and this tendency cannot yet be regarded as altogether extinct. But though the great bulk of the articles of clothing worn by the native population of India still consists of scarfs, or of simple pieces of cloth of dimensions suited to the purposes which they are intended to fulfil, a considerable quantity of textile materials is now made up into various convenient forms of dress, such as coats and jackets for men, and skirts and bodices for women—alike among Hindus and Mahomedans.

The class of plaid or scarf-like articles of dress, as a speciality of Oriental costume, assumes a position as regards extent which in Europe we do not easily understand. It constitutes by far the larger proportion of the textiles used for clothing, and is, therefore, the most important and the one most worthy of attention, *especially from a commercial point of view.* It is, moreover, the class which has given scope for the introduction of those forms of decoration, which so admirably display the powers of the native weaver in producing beautiful combinations of form and colour, and in arranging these in the way best calculated to set-off and adorn the garment when it is looked at on the person of the wearer.

The articles of dress which come under the first group are naturally divided into those used by men and those used by women, and we shall accordingly proceed to describe these separately. The object will be to make the reader understand the manner in which they are worn, and to indicate the qualities which experience has shown to be suitable, and the patterns which have proved pleasing to the people:—in short, to illustrate what may be called the *fashions* of India.

---

* The use of the petticoat among Hindu women is confined to Northern India, Rajpootana, &c. South of the Nerbudda it is almost entirely unknown, the Saree in all its forms being the only garment worn in conjunction with the Cholee or bodice.

# LOOM-MADE ARTICLES OF MALE ATTIRE.

In describing the various articles of male attire in this group, we shall not start with those fulfilling the purpose for which clothing was probably first adopted, but rather begin with those which have to do with the protection and adornment of the head.

After these we shall proceed with the description of those articles in the scarf form which are employed to envelope the shoulders and upper portions of the body; next, those which are used as a covering to the loins and lower extremities; and, lastly, those which are employed simply to encircle the waist.

## I.—TURBANS.

The Turban is in almost universal use throughout India.

As its chief function is the protection of the head from the heat of the sun, it is usually of a fine muslin-like texture which, when folded, is at once light, bulky, and porous—thus admirably fulfilling its main purpose.

Of the materials employed in the manufacture of turbans, cotton occupies the first place. Besides being the cheapest and most abundant, it has the merit of being a good non-conductor and of permitting at the same time the free escape of perspiration. It is farther recommended by the fact that it admits of the ready introduction of other materials for the purposes of adornment.

Silk, however, is used to some extent by the higher classes:—several places (like Seringapatam in olden times) being famous for the manufacture of silk turbans.

Wool is not often used in the manufacture of turban pieces; when it is used, they are generally in the form of small shawls, those of embroidered Cashmere cloth being good illustrations.

The tribe or caste to which the wearer belongs frequently determines the size and shape of the turban, and there are numerous varieties which take special names from their forms or from the materials of which they are made.*

* The following are some of the names by which the Turban, or Pugri, is known :—

*Puttee-dar pugri.* A compact, neat turban, in very general use both by Hindus and Mahomedans.

*Joore-dar pugri.* Similar to the Puttee-dar, but has a knot on the crown. Worn also by Hindus and Mahomedans.

*Khirkee-dar pugri.* Full-dress turban of Hindu and Mahomedan gentlemen attached to native courts, and with the *Goshwara*, or band of brocade, is portion of an honorary dress presented on certain state occasions to persons of rank by native princes. In the lower provinces this is, however, worn by Hindus only.

*Nustalik.* A full dress turban of the finest plain muslin, used with the court dress of Mahomedan Durbars, as at Delhi in olden times, and at Hydrabad, &c., in the present day. This form is very small, and fits closely to the head.

*Chakreedar.* A form of turban used by Mahomedans of Mysore and South of India. The court form of the ancient Beejapore monarchy, continued by Tippoo Sultaun.

*Séthi.* Used by bankers, &c. A small form not unlike the Nustalik.

*Mundeel.* Turban of muslin, with gold stripes, spots, and ends. Usually worn by military officers.

*Surbund.*, *Surbuttee.*, *Buttee.* } Derived from *Sur* the head and *Bandhna* to bind—*Buttee* signifying twisted or coiled round.

*Morassa.* A short turban.

*Umamu.* A loose turban.

*Dustar.* A fine muslin turban.

*Shumla.* A shawl turban.

In the mode of folding and wearing the turban an opportunity is often taken for the display of style and taste.

The Costume illustrations which accompany this work show the multitude of forms which the turban may be made to assume by a little ingenuity in the mode of folding or making up. Although the subject in Plate I.—opposite—and Plate II.—facing p. 18—have been specially chosen to illustrate this, most of the male figures in Plates III. IV. VII. and VIII. also afford illustrations.

Among these will be found turbans ranging from the neat compact head-dress which adorns the Mussulman in figure 2 of Plate I, to the wisp of calico which envelopes the head of the last figure of Plate VIII.—facing p. 118; —while in figure 50, Plate VII.—facing p. 140, —the turban piece not only envelopes the head but leaves enough to pass across the chest and over the shoulder.

With regard to the colours employed and the principles observed in the ornamentation of turbans, a few words may be said before proceeding more specifically to indicate their characteristics.

Turbans are to be found in India presenting every colour and hue in the rainbow, but white naturally takes by far the most prominent position. Red comes next, then yellow, and after them green, blue, purple, and, occasionally, even black; the darker colours being almost invariably relieved by embroidery.

Among turbans made of silk, we find buffs, shots, and greys; and in those made of cotton, printing is frequently employed to produce patterns suited to the tastes of particular consumers.

As regards what may be called the special ornamentation of fabrics designed for making up into turbans—its peculiarity—one founded upon true art as well as economy—is that the decoration is, as much as possible, confined to those portions of the material which in wear are exposed to view. The introduction of ornamentation, in undue proportion, would not only involve an unnecessary consumption of comparatively expensive materials, but would actually interfere with the function which the turban is intended to fulfil.

The native artist thus affords evidence of skill in avoiding an infringement of what may be called a first principle in art.

Nor is this confined to native work as it is seen in what we are presently speaking of, for the same compliment may be broadly paid to the productions of the Indian artisan, who is always careful to avoid a useless or wasteful ornamentation, and who never allows himself to forget the purpose which the article he is adorning is designed to fulfil. But it is not in these respects alone that the excellency of the native artisan is to be seen. He continually displays an admirable skill in the arrangement of form and colour—producing those beautiful and harmonious combinations which are to the eye what chords in music are to the ear. The subdued elegance which characterizes Indian decoration never fails to please. It marks a pure and refined taste, and whether it be the result of cultivation or of instinct it certainly exhibits a charming obedience to the great principles of art.

The turban in its unfolded condition ordinarily consists of a strip of cloth varying in breadth from 9 to 12 inches, and in length from 15 to 25 yards. In some cases, however, the breadth extends to 36 inches, while the length occasionally reaches to 60 yards.

In the process of making up, the outer end is usually left free to hang down a little, or is turned up over the folds at the back when the tying is finished. In the simpler and more common forms, coloured thread is introduced into this free end as an ornament,

TURBANS. PLAIN AND COLORED.

while in others gold in stripes, varying in breadth from one-eighth of an inch to several inches, is introduced.

Sometimes the gold, or other decorative medium, in addition to running across the end is made to extend longitudinally a little way up from the end, so as to be seen on the side of one or two of the last folds of the turban. In some instances, again, the embellishment is carried so far up that all the outer folds of the turban present it to view. In Pl. II. the standing figure in the group represents the first of these styles; the sitting figure to the left in the same group the second; while the turban on figure 10 shows the more copious ornamentation last alluded to.

For the assistance of those who may wish more precise information regarding this class of manufacture, we shall now refer in detail to the *working samples* shown in the volumes to which allusion has been made.

The turbans are divisible into two groups, consisting of long and square turban pieces. In describing these, a classification founded upon the quality of the material and the style of ornamentation will be adopted.

## A.—TURBAN-PIECES ;—LONG.

### 1. TURBAN PIECES.—COTTON ; PLAIN, BLEACHED AND UNBLEACHED.

Nos. 1 and 7, Vol. 1, are examples of a plain material, the only difference between them and ordinary piece goods being that they are specially manufactured of the requisite length and width.

It will be observed that, like the vast majority of the India fabrics, they are undressed ; the employment of size to the extent of stiffening the material being objectionable from its interfering with the lightness and openness of the article. This is a remark which applies with equal force both to scarf-like and to other fabrics designed for wear next the skin in hot climates. The use of size interferes with the pleasant *feel* of the fabric, and impedes free transpiration from the body.

No. 1 (bleached) is 15 yards long, 12 inches wide, and weighs 6 ounces. No. 7 is 24 yards long, 12 inches wide, and weighs $8\frac{1}{2}$ ounces.

The only other example coming under this head is No. 9, in the same volume, which affords a specimen of a thick unbleached material from Arracan. Its length is only 3 yds. 18 in., its width 9 inches, and its weight 11 ounces. Being a thicker and bulkier material, it does not require to be so long.

### 2. TURBAN PIECES.—COTTON ; PLAIN, WITH COLOURED ENDS.

Of these Nos. 3 and 4, from Lahore, are examples. In both of these the ornamental effect is produced by the introduction across their ends of a yellow stripe, about an inch wide, with double pink stripes on each side.

No. 3 is $6\frac{1}{2}$ yards long, 1 yard wide, and 15 ounces in weight. No. 4 is $8\frac{1}{2}$ yards long, 1 yard wide, and of weight proportional to No. 3, both being about the same in quality. These two, it will be observed, are much shorter than Nos. 1 and 7 in the former group, but here increased breadth is made to supply the necessary bulk.

### 3. TURBAN PIECES.—COTTON ; PLAIN, WITH GOLD THREAD IN ENDS.

The subjoined table embraces the examples of the class of ornamentation in this important group.

The pieces shown are of various degrees of fineness, and some (Nos. 13, 14, and 18, for instance) are excellent examples of muslins from both bleached and unbleached thread. As already indicated, the finer qualities (such as Nos. 7 and 9) require a greater length in the piece and a greater number of folds round the head, to give the necessary protection against the effect of the sun's rays.

Besides being examples of the material used for turbans, these specimens exhibit the extent to which gold thread is used for decorating the principal or free end of the turban-piece. A stripe of gold thread nearly 4 inches wide, as in No. 15, is of course very effective, but the turban with merely a $\frac{1}{8}$ or a $\frac{1}{12}$-inch stripe of the same material, as in No. 16, when seen on the head, is felt to be far from destitute of ornament.

It is of importance that the metal thus introduced should be of a quality which will stand the process of washing. Nos. 2, 8, and 12 are instances in which inferior gold thread has been used, while No. 15 shows a better quality.

A marginal stripe of red cotton thread (as in No. 6) constitutes a favourite combination, and adds considerably to the ornamental character of the plain gold stripe.

Nos. 15 and 18 are beautiful examples of fine muslin-like materials used for turbans, and in these the gold thread is seen to be of excellent quality. The first of these comes from Chundeyree, long celebrated for its muslins, and the last from Hyderabad in the Deccan, having been probably manufactured at Dhanwarum or Nandair, places famous for fabrics of this kind.

| Vol. | No. | Description. | Measurement of piece. | | Weight of piece. | Place of manufacture or where obtained. |
|---|---|---|---|---|---|---|
| | | | Length. | Width. | | |
| | | | yds. ins. | yds. ins. | lbs. oz. | |
| I. | 2 | Cotton, bleached. Common material, with two narrow gold stripes in end. | 23 0 | 0 12 | 0 12 | Bhurtpore. |
| ,, | 5 | Cotton, bleached. Thin texture; narrow ($\frac{1}{8}$-inch) stripe of gold thread in end. | 16 0 | 1 3 | 0 14 | Kangra. |
| ,, | 6 | Cotton, bleached. Fine texture. Two-inch stripe of gold thread in end, with small double lines of red on each side. | 20 0 | 0 11 | 0 8 | Cashmere. |
| ,, | 8 | Cotton, bleached. Medium texture. In common use among the higher classes. Wide ($2\frac{1}{4}$ inches) stripe of gold thread, with two smaller ones nearer to end. | 23 18 | 0 13 | 1 2 | Sind. |
| ,, | 10 | Cotton, bleached. Made in India, of English thread. One-inch gold stripe in end. | 22 0 | 0 $13\frac{1}{2}$ | 0 9 | Benares. |
| ,, | 11 | Cotton, bleached. Made at the same time as the last sample, but of Indian thread. 2-inch stripe of gold thread in end. | 22 0 | 0 $13\frac{1}{2}$ | 0 12 | Benares. |
| ,, | 12 | Cotton, bleached. Fine, light texture. $\frac{1}{4}$-inch stripe of gold thread in end. | 17 0 | 0 12 | 0 7 | Hoshiarpore. |
| ,, | 13 | Cotton, bleached. Fine texture. $\frac{3}{4}$-inch stripe of gold thread in end. | 33 0 | 0 10 | 0 9 | Hyderabad, Deccan. |
| ,, | 14 | Cotton, bleached. Fine texture. $\frac{1}{4}$-inch stripe of gold thread in end. | 20 0 | 0 9 | 0 9 | Hyderabad, Deccan. |
| ,, | 15 | Cotton, unbleached. Fine texture. Broad ($2\frac{3}{4}$ inches) stripe of gold thread, and three narrow stripes of same closer to end. | 29 0 | 0 $12\frac{1}{2}$ | 0 $7\frac{1}{2}$ | Chundeyree. |
| ,, | 16 | Cotton, unbleached. Gauze, of good texture. Very narrow ($\frac{1}{12}$-inch) stripe of gold thread in end. Price 4*s.* 8*d.* | 21 0 | 0 9 | 0 6 | Madras. |
| ,, | 17 | Cotton, unbleached. Favourite texture. $1\frac{1}{2}$-inch stripe of gold thread, with three narrow stripes nearer to end, and one narrow stripe on inner margin. A narrow stripe ($\frac{1}{12}$-inch) of gold thread is also introduced into the other end of this turban-piece. | 21 0 | 0 $10\frac{1}{2}$ | 0 10 | Hyderabad, Deccan. |
| ,, | 18 | Cotton, unbleached. Gauze-like texture. $\frac{3}{4}$-inch stripe of gold thread across end. | 33 0 | 0 13 | 0 9 | Hyderabad, Deccan. |

4. Turban Pieces.—Cotton; dyed or printed.

**Nos. 20, 30, 31, 32, and 34 are the examples given.**

Of these No. 34 is the one which, in point of material and colour, is the most worthy of attention.

No. 20 is interesting as a specimen of what, next to colouring by hand, may be considered the simplest way of producing an ornamental effect,—namely, that of using a stamp to lay a body color on the surface of the material. In the specimen in question a star pattern, in white and black, has been thus stamped on a dull red ground. This mode of ornamentation is not uncommon, but it is not an economical one, as the material cannot be cleaned or washed. In the specimen referred to (No. 20) it will be observed that the white stands out from the dull red ground on which it is placed in a way which has a good effect.

It is said that in the making up of this turban padding is employed, a mode of construction which is not uncommon in some parts of the country. The turban piece in question (No. 20) is 14 yards long, 10 inches wide, and weighs 7 ounces. It was manufactured at Bhurtpore.

No. 30 is a rather coarse material with a small close pattern in dark-red and black on a pinkish-white ground. About 3 inches of the end is dark-red with a pattern in black printed on it. Length 15 yards, width 9 inches, and weight 9½ ounces. Manufactured at Sydapet, and stated to be worn by the Lubbays, an industrious class of Mahomedan fishermen and merchants on the Madras coast.

No. 31, an ordinary calico material. Pattern, a small zig-zag stripe of red on a white ground. Six inches of the principal end are dark-red, with an ornamental pattern in black printed on it. Length, 12 yards; width, 11 inches; weight, 1 lb. Manufactured at Pomady but bought in Madras bazaar. Price in 1854, 2*s.* 7½*d.**

No. 32, quality similar to last example. Pattern a small black and white check. Six inches of principal end dark red, with pattern in black and white. Length, 16½ yards; width, 9 inches; weight, 15½ ounces. From Pomady, in Madras, price 3*s.* In this, and in No. 31, the fabric is sized or stiffened in an unusual degree, but this would probably be removed before making up the piece for use.

No. 34 shows a favourite style of pattern, and although very inferior in texture, is otherwise not unlike the specimens from Jeypore—Nos. 23 to 28 included under group 6. The pattern may be described as a double zig-zag. Three inches of the principal end is of the main colour of the piece, viz. purple. When made up, the whole would form a turban similar in appearance to that shown in figure 8, Pl. II. Length, 16½ yards; width 10 inches; weight, 15½ ounces. Obtained in Madras. Price 3*s.* 1½*d.*

5. Turban-Pieces.—Cotton; dyed, coloured, or printed; Gold Thread in Ends.

The subjoined table contains the examples coming under this head.

Nos. 23 to 29 inclusive are admirable specimens both of material and of style. They are from Jeypore, a native state, which in other branches of art shows evidence of skill in manipulation and in management of colour.

* The prices given here and elsewhere throughout this work, and which are the same as those on the labels in the Fabric Books, must not be taken as a correct guide to present values. They simply represent the sums paid in 1854 by the various Committees appointed by the Government in India to collect specimens for the Paris Universal Exhibition of the following year. Although on the main reliable for the period named, the prices attached to some of the articles are clearly inaccurate.

The turban in fig. 9, of Plate II. shows the peculiar zig-zag pattern, which is a favourite in many parts of Rajpootana, and is employed in other garment pieces besides turbans. Some of the examples are so soft and fine to the touch, that it is at first difficult to believe that they are composed of cotton unmixed with silk.

No. 33, made at Madura in Madras, a place long celebrated for its manufactures and for its excellent dyes, is a good example of a useful material and of a favourite dark-red colour which shows the gold thread to much advantage.

In this piece it will also be observed that a little gold thread is worked into the end of the turban which is usually next the head. In the folding and tying up of such turbans the wearer manages to show both ends.

| Vol. | No. | Description. | Measurement of piece. | | Weight of of piece. | Place of manufacture or where obtained. |
|---|---|---|---|---|---|---|
| | | | Length. | Width. | | |
| | | | yds. ins. | yds. ins. | lbs. oz. | |
| I. | 23 | Cotton, printed. Fine texture. Red and white zig-zag pattern. $1\frac{1}{2}$-inch stripe of gold thread in principal end. | 18 18 | 0 9 | 0 4 | Jeypore, Rajpootana. |
| „ | 24 | Cotton, printed. Fine texture. Zig-zag striped pattern, in variegated colours. $1\frac{5}{8}$-inch gold stripe in end. | 17 18 | 0 9 | 0 $3\frac{1}{2}$ | Ditto |
| „ | 25 | Cotton, printed. Fine texture. Pattern, small zig-zag stripes, of crimson and yellow. About 3 inches of end plain red, with $1\frac{3}{4}$-inch stripe of gold thread. | 18 18 | 0 $8\frac{1}{2}$ | 0 4 | Ditto |
| „ | 26 | Cotton, printed. Fine texture. Pattern, zig-zag stripes, $\frac{5}{8}$ inch wide, in variegated colours. Principal end, plain red with $3\frac{1}{4}$-inch stripe of gold thread. | 18 18 | 0 9 | 0 4 | Ditto |
| „ | 27 | Cotton, printed. Fine texture. Zig-zag stripes, of a dotted pattern, in variegated colours, on a scarlet ground. Principal end, plain scarlet, with $2\frac{3}{8}$ inch stripe of gold thread. | 24 0 | 0 11 | 0 8 | Ditto |
| „ | 28 | Cotton, printed. Fine texture. Zig-zag stripes in red and white. Principal end, plain red, with gold thread stripe $1\frac{1}{2}$ inches wide. | 17 0 | 0 9 | 0 $3\frac{1}{2}$ | Ditto |
| „ | 29 | Cotton, printed. Fine texture. Figured pattern dotted in colours. 2 inch stripe of gold thread in principal end. Favourite pattern in Rajpootana. | 21 0 | 0 10 | 0 $5\frac{1}{2}$ | Ditto |
| „ | 33 | Cotton, printed. Useful material. Pattern, a small white spot on a deep chocolate red ground. Principal end ornamented with 1-inch stripe, and three smaller ones of gold thread. The other end has also four gold threads introduced into the fabric. Price 10*s*. | 23 0 | 0 12 | 0 13 | Madura, Madras. |

## 6. Turban-Pieces.—Cotton ; dyed, coloured, or printed ; Gold Thread in Ends, Borders, &c.

In these we have examples of the more profuse application of the gold thread for ornamental purposes. Nos. 19, 22, 36 and 37, are illustrations of the method by which, in addition to the stripe *across* the principal end, the external folds become an ornamental portion of the turban when in wear. To accomplish this, one or more stripes of gold thread are carried to a considerable distance down the piece from the free end ; in one case indeed it extends throughout the whole length of the piece.

TURBANS. ORNAMENTED, &c.

The extent to which this method is adopted varies considerably. A bulky turban, like that which No. 36 would make up, requires a larger amount of this kind of ornamentation to produce the effect shown in figure 10, Pl., II. than would be needed by one of smaller dimensions.

Nos. 36 and 37, like No. 33 referred to under the last head, are from Madura in Madras, and afford additional examples of that dark red which is so favourite and so suitable a colour for this class of turbans.

The following details apply to each of the four examples in this group:

No. 19. Length, 19½ yards; width, 13 inches. A light red colour. Cross stripes and figures in gold thread of a poor quality occupy 20 inches of the principal end, and two stripes, each of about half an inch in breadth, extend four yards down centre of piece. From Oodeypoor in Rajpootana.

No. 22. Length, 13 yards; width, 17 inches, weight 12 ounces. Red. Three ¼-inch wide stripes of gold with black margins run throughout the whole length of the borders and centre of piece. Four and a half yards of the principal end are ornamented with gold spots somewhat of a *pine* shape, and it is finished off with a figured and striped pattern also in gold thread. From Hoshiarpore, Punjab.

No. 36. Length, 26½ yards; width, 15 inches; weight, 1 lb. 3½ oz. Price £4. Favourite red colour. Stripes of gold thread extend for 10 yards down the centre from the principal end, and for 4½ yards from the other end. About 20 inches of the principal end are enriched with cross stripes and figures in gold From Madura, Madras.

No. 37. Length, 23 yards; width, 12 inches; weight, 13 oz. Price £2. Favourite colour, like the last, and from the same place of manufacture. In addition to an inch-wide stripe of gold in centre, this specimen has a narrow stripe of the same extending 6 yards down from the principal or free end, and a 3-inch wide cross stripe, with 10 smaller ones in three rows, completes the ornamentation.

## 7. Turban-Pieces.—Cotton; dyed; Gold printed.

The specimen No. 21, although imperfect in execution, affords an illustration of a kind of ornamentation which is not uncommon, and which can be adopted with considerable advantage in the embellishment of fabrics not requiring to be washed nor likely to be exposed to wet.

The process by which this mode of decoration is accomplished is by stamping the desired pattern on the cloth with glue. The gold or silver leaf, as the case may be, is then laid on, and adheres to the glue. When dry, what has not rested on the glue is rubbed off.

The turban piece No. 21 is 14½ yards long and 7 inches wide. The ground is crimson. A gold printed figured stripe, 3¼ inches wide, extends the whole length of the centre of the piece. Padding is used in making up this turban, and, in this case, there is no special ornamentation across either end. From Bhurtpore.

Such gold printed turbans are used for marriage ceremonies and other household or family festivals, and not for ordinary wear.

### 8. Turban-Pieces.—Silk, &c.

As before indicated, silk, although not nearly so common as cotton, is nevertheless frequently employed in the manufacture of turbans.

The example given (No. 38) is of silk and cotton, and affords an illustration of a fabric fairly suited for its purpose, such mixtures of the two materials being, in some respects, better calculated to fulfil the functions of the turban than silk alone.

It is probable that some of the beautiful silk materials, of the *mousseline de soie* or gauze class, would, if manufactured into proper turban-pieces, form an attractive article with the richer natives, always supposing that suitable colours and styles of end ornamentation were adopted.

The example given (No. 38) is $20\frac{1}{2}$ yards long, 10 inches wide, and weighs $8\frac{3}{4}$ ounces. Price 11*s.*

The warp is a dark purplish red silk, and the weft is a dark cotton. The end is decorated with a $\frac{3}{4}$-inch stripe, with two smaller ones on each side.

## B.—TURBAN-PIECES ;—SQUARE.

The class of turbans, or *roomals*, to which we have now to refer, are those composed of large squares, or pieces nearly square. When made up they present an appearance somewhat like that shown in fig. 12, Pl. II., and fig. 24, Pl. IV., which illustrate the *Shumla*, or shawl turban.

These squares vary in size from one and a half to four yards per side—three, and three and a half yards constituting a useful size. Yarns of the quality of English 60$^s$ (warp) and 80$^s$ (weft) would produce articles of suitable texture.

These squares are sometimes worn over the shoulders as well as used for head-dresses. No. 43, Vol. II. is said to be used both ways. It is a tolerably fine plain *book-muslin*, with a gold stripe in the borders. Length, 2 yards ; width, 2 yards ; weight, 6 ounces. Price 11*s.* Manufactured at Arnee, Madras.

No. 35, Vol. I., is 96 inches square, and its weight is 12 ounces. It is a moderately fine muslin of the favourite deep-red colour before alluded to. On two sides it has a black border, $1\frac{1}{2}$ inches wide, with a figured gold pattern in it of $1\frac{3}{8}$ inches. The other two sides have each a stripe consisting of a few black and gold threads. Manufactured at Madura, Madras. Price 13*s.*

No. 40, Vol. I., is a fine muslin, scarlet, with deep ($3\frac{5}{8}$ inches) gold borders set off with black. It is not quite square, the length one way being 1 yard 22 inches, and the other 1 yard 16 inches. Its weight—$6\frac{1}{2}$ ounces—appears heavy, when its fineness is considered, but this is due to the amount of gold thread which it contains. Manufactured at Bhurtpore, near Agra.

No. 39 Vol. I., affords an example in which silk and gold together are employed for the decoration of a cotton fabric, a combination of which we shall find many illustrations in the other classes of wearing apparel. Form nearly square, the length one way being $3\frac{1}{2}$ yards, and the other $3\frac{1}{4}$ yards ; weight 1 lb. 11 oz. Price £2 15*s.* 3*d.* Colour, a deep blue. Has a figured border, $1\frac{1}{8}$ inch wide, of gold and silk on two borders, and of silk alone on the other two.

In the foregoing descriptions of the modes of ornamenting turbans, it will be observed that silver thread has not been mentioned as in use for that purpose. In some parts of the country, however, it is employed, as for instance in the Dharwar district, where a kind of turban called the *Mondasa* is manufactured, and is said to be worn by the poorer classes on festival days. The use of silver thread is not common, on account of its liability to tarnish; and perhaps also because the difference between the cost of the small quantity of gold and of silver thread, which proves sufficient for the embellishment of a turban, is too small to render it an important element in the calculation, whilst the greater beauty of the former secures for it the preference.

## II.—LOONGEES AND DHOTEES.

Before the introduction of the art of sewing, the dress of the male Hindu, in addition to the head-cloth, consisted of two scarf-formed pieces, one of which was worn over the shoulders and upper part of the body, and the other was used as covering for the loins and legs. The first of these is called a Loongee * and the second a Dhotee.†

At the present time the usual dress of the poorer classes of Mahomedans and Hindus, whilst at home or at work, consists simply of the piece of cloth called a Dhotee wrapped round the loins. The end of this, after a couple of turns round the waist, is passed by the Hindu between the legs, and thrust under the folds which cross behind. Occasionally, however, the end is passed from behind and fastened in front. Amongst the Mahomedans again, the loin-cloth, after being folded two or three times round the waist, is usually allowed to hang down:—that is, it is not tucked up between the legs as with the Hindus.

The standing figure in group 4, Pl. I., and other figures in Plates III. and IV., afford illustrations of the manner in which this article of dress is worn. The simpler form consists of a small piece of calico, ‡ with its ends turned over a string tied round the haunches, while the more elaborate forms are nearly as copious as a woman's petticoat. Figures 22 and 23, Pl. IV., show this.

Although piece-goods of a suitable breadth are largely cut up into dhotees, as well as into shoulder-scarfs, it is to the Loongee and Dhotee manufactured of the proper length and width, that is, in separate pieces, that we have here more particularly to refer.

The first class of articles, viz. the Loongees, or scarfs, for wearing over the body and shoulders, are of the more importance, because they afford greater scope for the introduction of those decorations which we have seen to be so successfully employed in turbans.

* This term has come to be generally applied to the shoulder or upper cloth worn by males. The majority of the specimens forwarded from India, and inserted in the Fabric Books, were so designated, and although not precisely correct, this name (Loongee) is here adopted as affording, for trade purposes, a convenient distinction between shoulder and loin cloths. Strictly speaking, the Loongee is worn by Mahomedans, and has the same function as the Dhotee of the Hindu.

† *Dhotee;* derived from *dhona*, to wash, and so named from being washed daily at the time of bathing. Every *Dhotee*, however, has not this daily washing, for in its more elaborate form it is embellished with ornamental borders, and, by the rich as well as the poor, on festival occasions, is doffed after the ablutions for the day have been finished.

‡ *Langgoti* is the name used when the *Dhotee* is very small. (Buchanan, in Martin's "Eastern India," Vol. III., p. 103.)

As we proceed it will be observed that these scarfs are frequently manufactured in pairs,* with a fag between for convenience of separation; the longer portion being used to wrap round the upper part of the body, and the shorter piece round the loins, as already described.

The Loongee is worn over the shoulder in a variety of ways. Plates III. and IV., and more particularly the latter, show some of these.

It will be observed, also, that most of the male figures represented in Plates I and III. have a cloth of some sort thrown over the shoulder, ready to be adjusted as circumstances may require. The same cloth, when of plain material, acts not only as a plaid during the day, but as a sheet at night.†

These scarfs vary in length from 3 to 6 yards, and in breadth from 1 or 1½ to 3 yards; two breadths being often joined to form a wider garment.‡

The materials (cotton, silk, and sometimes wool, or combinations of these) of which the Loongees and Dhotees are made, are fully illustrated by the examples, upwards of ninety in number, to be seen in the Textile Work itself.§

The remark made under the head of Turbans, as to the character of the special ornamentation adopted, applies equally to the loom-made garment pieces presently to be described; the principle, as already stated, being to employ the decoration in the manner best calculated to set off the articles *when in wear*. For this purpose, not only are the ends ornamented, but the borders also, as may be seen in the scarfs over the shoulders of the figures in Pl. IV. In the case of these men's scarfs, the two ends as well as the borders receive the same amount of ornamentation because both are seen when in use. As in the case of turbans, however, we find that the scarfs worn by women have only one ornamented end, the opposite one being usually concealed in the process of folding round the person.

The introduction of special borders and ends into the parts not seen would not only be wasteful, and therefore objectionable, but from the character of the materials employed, it would increase the thickness of the fabric in a way which would interfere with the comfort of the wearer.

We now proceed to afford specific information regarding this class of native manufacture.

An arrangement similar to that adopted in the case of turbans will be followed; that is, we shall speak of them according to quality and character of ornamentation, beginning with the inferior and proceeding upwards to the more elaborate specimens.¶

---

* A cloth of this sort, of which two pieces form a dress, is called *Jore*, from *Jora*, a pair.

† The calico sheet called *Dohar* is in the cold weather doubled and worn over the shoulders. (Buchanan, in Martin's "Eastern India.")

‡ A scarf consisting of two such pieces or breadths stitched together, is called *Doputta* (literally two breadths); the single piece, or width, *Ecputta* (one breadth) is also used without being joined; but those who can afford it prefer the more ample garment supplied by the *Doputta*.

§ Silk and wool loin cloths, or combinations of both, are called *Pitambur*, and are worn by Brahmins and other high class Hindus exclusively at meal times, when cotton garments of any kind are impure. At meals the Brahmin or other strict Hindu ought to wear no other garment than a *Pitambur*, the head and body to the waist being uncovered.

¶ The only inconvenience which may be experienced from this arrangement is that the reader who wishes to refer to the samples themselves will have occasionally to turn from one volume to another. This arises from three causes. As originally grouped the examples most worthy of attention were inserted first: in other instances an effort was made to keep together the manufactures of a particular district; and, lastly, in order to render the work as complete as possible, two or three of the volumes were prepared after the others were finished.

MALE ATTIRE. COTTON.

## A. LOONGEES, INCLUDING DHOTEES WHEN MANUFACTURED TOGETHER.

### 1. Cotton.—Plain; coloured ends; no borders.

This group, in its simplicity, approaches the class of piece goods which have merely to be cut across to form scarfs of suitable dimensions.*

Nos. 79 and 80 (Vol. II.) afford illustrations of the commonest material of which this garment is made.

No. 79 is a rag for a boy, and is 1 yard 3 inches in length, 19 inches in width, and weighs 2 ounces. It has a few chocolate-coloured threads across each end close to the edge. From Biekul (now Carwar) N. Canara.

No. 80. A coarse, thick, unbleached cotton, having two red stripes and one blue at each end. Worn by the Burghers, an aboriginal Hill-tribe in Southern India. Length, 5 yards 9 inches; width, 1 yard; weight, 3 lbs. 1 oz. From Coimbatore, Madras.

### 2. Cotton.—Plain; coloured borders and ends.

Nos. 46, 47, 50, and 54, Vol. II., in the subjoined Table afford examples of the *Jore* or complete dress of two pieces, the longer forming the *Loongee* for wear round the shoulders and upper part of the body, and the shorter, which is of the same pattern, being the loin cloth or *Dhotee*. These are woven with a *fag*, to allow of their being readily separated.

No. 75 is an instance of an unusually wide border.

Nos. 76, 77, and 78 are illustrations of what may be called the minimum of ornamentation under this head—slight, however, as it is, it adds materially to the attractiveness of the piece.

No. 52 is a plain muslin material with simple borders and ends. Although entered as a *man's garment*, it would be much more frequently used as a woman's *Saree*.

Nos. 109 and 110, Vol. III., although received from Bombay, and stated to have been made at Surat, are probably of English manufacture. The borders are good, but the few stripes which form the end pattern are too poor, in proportion, to be effective. So far as we have observed, this is a remark which applies to almost all the attempts hitherto made in this country to manufacture this class of goods for the Indian market.

The light, open texture of the fabric, required for ordinary wear in India, is well shown in this group; but further on we shall find illustrations of the thicker cotton materials which

---

It will be observed that the numbers on the right-hand corner of the labels run through the different volumes consecutively—from 1 upwards—an arrangement which affords facility of reference. In each example the utmost care has been taken to give a sufficient number of portions to show the whole pattern, and so to constitute what is called a *working sample*.

In cases which show only one specimen of a border or end pattern, it is to be understood that the two ends or borders are alike.

* The greater proportion of the *grey*, and the inferior qualities of the bleached piece-goods exported from this country to India, are employed in this manner.

are employed during the cold season of the year, and the manufacture of which has as yet, we believe, been entirely confined to India itself.

| Vol. | No. | Description. | Measurement. Length. | Measurement. Width. | Weight. | Cost.* | Place of manufacture, or where obtained. |
|---|---|---|---|---|---|---|---|
| | | | yds. ins. | yds. ins. | lbs. oz. | £ s. d. | |
| II. | 46 | Cotton, plain. One-inch border. Coloured stripes, $\frac{2}{3}$ inch wide, in each end, in yellow and chocolate. | Loongee 5 20 Dhotee 2 27 | 1 2 | 1 4 | 0 2 6 | Ganjam, Madras. |
| II. | 47 | Cotton, plain. Gauze-like texture. Green and yellow striped border, $\frac{2}{3}$ inch wide. At each end, one $1\frac{1}{8}$ inch, red and green stripe, and one $\frac{1}{4}$-inch red stripe, $1\frac{1}{2}$ inch apart. | Loongee 5 4 Dhotee 2 27 | 1 6 | 0 14 | 0 2 3 | Nagang, bought in Madras. |
| II. | 50 | Cotton, plain. A blue and yellow stripe, $\frac{1}{3}$ inch wide in border, and two similar stripes across each end. | Loongee 3 9 Dhotee 2 18 | not given | 1 6 | 0 3 9 | Nellore, Madras. |
| II. | 54 | Cotton, plain, unbleached. One-inch border of reddish brown, striped with two blue lines. At each end, two red and yellow cross stripes, one $1\frac{7}{8}$ inches, and one $\frac{5}{12}$ inch wide. | Loongee 4 18 Dhotee 2 27 | 1 6 | 1 $2\frac{1}{4}$ | 0 2 $1\frac{1}{2}$ | Congeveram, Madras. |
| II. | 75 | Cotton, plain, unbleached. Seven-inch border (unusually wide), red, yellow, and white stripes. Stripes of same colours in $6\frac{1}{2}$ inches of the principal end. At opposite end $\frac{1}{2}$-inch stripe of red and white. | 5 28 | 1 4 | 1 7 | 0 3 3 | Ganjam, Madras. |
| II. | 76 | Cotton, plain. $\frac{1}{3}$-inch brown stripe in border (badly marked). Two $\frac{1}{12}$ inch, and one $\frac{1}{3}$-inch red stripes across each end. | 3 0 | 1 3 | 0 $8\frac{1}{2}$ | 0 1 3 | Candapoor, N. Canara. |
| II. | 77 | Cotton, plain, unbleached, $\frac{1}{8}$ inch chocolate colour stripe in border, and two similar ones across each end. | 8 9 | 1 5 | 1 10 | 0 2 $4\frac{1}{2}$ | Vencata-gorry, Madras. |
| II. | 78 | Cotton, plain, unbleached. $\frac{1}{12}$-inch chocolate colour line in border. At each end, one $\frac{1}{3}$ inch, and, at 2 inches distance, two $\frac{1}{12}$-inch stripes of red. | | | | | |
| III. | 109 | Cotton, plain. A $2\frac{1}{3}$-inch border, figured in red, green, and yellow thread. Three lines of red thread across each end. | 2 9 | 1 3 | 0 $6\frac{1}{2}$ | 0 1 0 | Surat, Bombay. |
| III. | 110 | Cotton, plain. Two-inch chequered border, in red, green, and yellow. $\frac{1}{2}$-inch stripe of five red lines across each end. | 4 8 | 1 5 | 0 $12\frac{1}{2}$ | 0 1 $7\frac{1}{2}$ | Surat, Bombay. |
| II. | 52 | Coarse muslin. Yellow stripe ($\frac{5}{12}$ inch wide) in border. One $\frac{7}{12}$ inch, and one small double stripe of yellow across principal end. | 7 27 | 1 9 | 0 $13\frac{1}{2}$ | 0 3 0 | Nagang, bought in Madras. |

* See note, page 17.

### 3. Cotton.—Plain ; silk in borders and ends.

In this class the ornamentation is accomplished by the use of silk.

In No. 45 the silk is inserted in the border only, and in No. 48 in the end only; but in the other examples given in the table below, both ends and borders are of silk.

Nos. 44, 45, 48, afford examples of the pleasing effect produced by making the pointings (called *Kutaree*, from *Kutar*, a dagger) seemingly unite the inner side of the border to the body of the garment.

**It will be observed that the whole of the examples under this head, with the exception of the boy's garment (No. 48), are woven in two pieces to form a *Jore*, or dress.**

| Vol. | No. | Description. | Measurement. Length. | Measurement. Width. | Weight. | Cost. | Place of manufacture, or where obtained. |
|---|---|---|---|---|---|---|---|
| | | | yds. ins. | yds. ins. | lbs. oz. | £ s. d. | |
| II. | 45 | Cotton, plain. Common texture: figured border, $\frac{5}{8}$ inch wide, of coloured cotton, with a little *Moonga* silk used in imitation of gold thread. The *Kutar* pattern introduced in the inner edge of border. Two coloured stripes (yellow and chocolate) at each end, one $\frac{7}{12}$ inch and one $\frac{1}{8}$ inch wide, and $3\frac{1}{4}$ inch apart. Woven in two pieces, with a fag between.* | Loongee 5 18<br>Dhotee 3 4 | 1 10 | 1 9 | 0 3 0 | Ganjam, Madras. |
| II. | 48 | Cotton, plain. Boy's garment. Borders $2\frac{1}{4}$ inches wide, of variegated stripes. In ends, two coloured stripes of cotton and silk; one $2\frac{1}{2}$ inches and one $\frac{1}{2}$ inch wide, and $1\frac{3}{8}$ inches apart. In this instance the borders are of different colours. This variation adds to the attractiveness of the piece, so long as both colours are kept in harmony. | 1 34 | 0 27 | about 0 $2\frac{1}{2}$ | 0 1 4 | Congeveram, Madras. |
| II. | 44 | Cotton, plain. Figured border, with *Kutar* edge of coloured silk $1\frac{3}{4}$ inches wide; one 3-inch silk and cotton, and one 1-inch cotton coloured stripe in end. Woven in two pieces, with a fag between.* | Loongee 5 9<br>Dhotee 3 9 | 1 9 | 1 8 | 0 8 0 | Salem, Madras. |
| II. | 49 | Cotton, plain, unbleached. Narrow stripe of deep plum-coloured silk, $\frac{1}{12}$ inch wide, along border. Cross stripes of same colour at each end, viz., one $\frac{2}{3}$ inch wide, and narrow double stripe, $1\frac{3}{4}$ inch wide nearer to end. Woven in two pieces, with a fag between.* | Loongee 3 0<br>Dhotee 2 27 | 1 18 | 1 11 | 0 8 6 | Woozzoor, Madras. |
| II. | 53 | Cotton, plain, unbleached. Good texture. Figured silk border (with *Kutar* edge), $1\frac{1}{2}$ inch wide, white silk being used in it in imitation of silver thread. At each end one 3-inch and one $\frac{3}{4}$-inch coloured stripe of silk and cotton. Woven in two pieces, with a fag between.* | Loongee 5 9<br>Dhotee 3 0 | 1 9 | 1 11 | 0 8 0 | Salem, Madras. |
| II. | 55 | Cotton, plain, unbleached. Good texture. $\frac{1}{2}$ inch reddish brown silk stripe in border. Two similar stripes, one $2\frac{1}{4}$ inches and one $\frac{2}{3}$ inch wide, at each end. Woven in two pieces, with a fag between.* | Loongee 4 27<br>Dhotee 2 27 | 1 4 | 1 6 | 0 5 6 | Congeveram, Madras. |

* The *fag* here alluded to as dividing the piece into two portions, that is, into the Loongee, or body garment, and the Dhotee, or loin cloth, is introduced in order to allow of the two garments being easily separated.

### 4. Cotton.—Plain; Coloured borders; Gold in ends.

Example No. 51, Vol. II. A plain muslin with narrow deep purple-coloured borders, and at each end a half-inch cross stripe of crimson and gold thread. This sample is another illustration of the manner in which, by a judicious use of a small amount of material, a pleasant effect is produced. Length, 3 yards; width, 1 yard 9 inches; weight, 1 lb. 3 oz. Price 10*s.* 6*d.* From Arnee, Madras.

### 5. Cotton.—Plain; Gold and coloured Cotton in borders; Gold in ends.

No. 42, Vol. II. Bleached. Figured borders of gold and of black cotton thread. Has two stripes of gold at each end. Two pieces in one length with *fag* between. Length of Loongee 5 yards 27 inches, and of Dhotee 3 yards 4 inches; width, 1 yard 13 inches; weight, 1 lb. 3 oz. Price 1*l.* 10*s.* From Woopparaddy, Madras.

### 6. Cotton.—Plain; Gold and coloured Silk in borders; Gold in ends.

No. 41, Vol. II., is an excellent example both of texture and style. Material, unbleached cotton. Flowered borders of black silk and gold $1\frac{1}{4}$ inches wide. Gold stripe ($2\frac{1}{4}$ inches wide) at each end. Length, 8 yards 21 inches; width, 1 yard 19 inches; weight, 1 lb. Price 3*l.* 12*s.* From Madura, Madras.

Having shown the manner in which a plain white cotton fabric is rendered attractive, by the ornamentation of its ends and borders, we come next to the instances in which colour is employed in the body of the piece, as well as in the ends and borders.

In the three groups which follow, the classification has not, as in the previous groups, been strictly founded upon the character of the border and end patterns, since the quality or thickness of the material has been also taken into consideration.

In group 7, the texture, although a little closer, will be found to be not unlike that of examples already dealt with. In No. 8 group, however, we find a stouter and softer material; whilst in group 9 the fabric is as thick as many of the slighter woollen cloths made in England.

It is an error to suppose that thick and warm fabrics are not required in India. Throughout a great portion of that country the suffering of the poor from cold during certain seasons, particularly at night, is as great as with us in Europe. The temperature in many parts of India falls occasionally during the cold season to the freezing point or below it. But even when the temperature does not go down so low as 32°, a fall from 90° during the day to 60° at night—a by no means uncommon occurrence at certain seasons—produces a very decided sensation of cold and a consequent demand for warm clothing.

The thicker materials now under consideration are durable as well as warm, and of their commercial importance as a class, evidence is afforded by the fact that during the recent cotton famine in England and the consequent rise in price of the raw material in India, the native goods retained their position in the market more firmly than the English ones did, though the price of the native-made goods rose to a much greater extent than did that of the European. The report of the Sudder Board of Revenue to the Government of the North-Western Provinces "regarding the slackness of demand for European cotton goods" (dated Allahabad, 16th March 1864) so well illustrates this point that we give in a foot-note the portions which specially refer to the subject.*

---

* "The extraordinary rise of price" (of the raw material) "has affected, though unequally, the demand both for native and for European stuffs. The same money only buys half, and often less than half, the quantity of cloth it used to." . . . . . . . "The enhanced prices have diminished the consumption both of English and of native pieces; but, at least in the western districts, they have affected the English more than the native. This is remarkable, seeing that the native goods have advanced in price in a higher ratio than the European—the increase in the former

The man who could afford to purchase only one garment piece in the year found it true economy to buy one which would both last long, and give him a proper protection against cold.*

We may here remark that many of the mixed cotton and woollen fabrics now manufactured in this country would probably be suitable substitutes in the Indian market for the thick and warm cotton stuffs which the native makes; all that is wanted being skill in turning out goods of the proper lengths and breadths, and with a style of ornamentation like that which the native adopts and likes; an important necessity, however, being that they should be of good washing material, both as to quality and dye: without this qualification they would be useless.

It would be well if a thicker class of cotton goods could be supplied at a price which would suit the ordinary Indian consumer; but there is no doubt that mixtures of cotton and wool of a fine soft description, would suit a large class of the people. Indeed, we actually find that in India, where the supply of the finer kinds of wool is as yet but limited, the high price of cotton during the past three years considerably increased the use of woollen manufactures, which in some districts were more than doubled in price.†

## 7. Cotton.—Coloured Thread; Borders and Ends formed by Modifications of Pattern.

The subjoined table indicates the examples which come under this head.

It will be observed that with the exception of Nos. 117, Vol. III., and 129, Vol. IV., the whole of the illustrations given have been manufactured by the Lubbays of Madras, to whom reference has already been made. Some of the specimens show expertness in the imitation of foreign‡ patterns, and their skill in suiting these to the requirements of the

being cent. per cent., and in some cases rising even to near 200 per cent., while the latter have risen only from 50 to 100 per cent."

"One chief reason for this difference is, no doubt, that the native fabrics are heavier and contain more cotton: the cost of production remaining the same, the rise in the price is of course greater in the heavier than in the lighter stuffs." . . . . . . . . "What is strange is, that while they have increased in price so much more than English goods, they should still maintain themselves in the market better than English goods can do. Yet the tenor of the evidence contained in the returns leaves no doubt on this head."

"The consumption of the native goods has diminished in consequence of the increased price, but the consumption of English goods has diminished in far greater measure. In this view the native goods have, to some extent and in a certain sense, taken the place of the English; yet this has been, not in consequence of increased, but in spite of very considerably diminished production. The reasons assigned are various. It is alleged that, notwithstanding the relatively greater increase of its price, the cost of the coarse native article is still considerably less than that of any English stuffs that would answer the same object. It is held that the native article is more durable, thicker, warmer, and better suited to the wants of the people in these provinces; and that Lancashire must produce a coarser, thicker, and cheaper article than it does at present before it can compete in this department of manufacture with the native weaver."

In the appendix to the same report, Mr. W. A. Forbes states that the *Markeen*, a stout warm kind of English cloth, somewhat like the stout native variety, became doubled in price, whereas the ordinary light English goods increased in price to the extent of only one-third.

* The inconvenience which would arise from wearing the thicker material during the hot period of the year is simply avoided by not putting it on.

† Mr. H. D. Robertson (in Appendix to the Report already quoted) states this with reference to the Saharunpore districts, and the remark applies to other places as well.

‡ Is it certain that the checks and other patterns here alluded to are *foreign* to India? Our knowledge of the fact that these Lubbays are reputed to have devoted themselves very much to the manufacture of such imitations seems to indicate the probability that the patterns in question are of exotic origin, and we are inclined to believe that some of the more Tartan-looking ones must be so. On the other hand we have, from parts of India with which our communications have been of recent date, patterns clearly of Indian origin, yet very similar to our Tartans.

**Indian market. It will be observed that in the checks which have been imitated, the ends and borders, which constitute the article a separate and special garment, have been produced simply by a modification of the body pattern.**

| Vol. | No. | Description. | Measurement. Length. | Measurement. Width. | Weight. | Cost. | Place of Manufacture, or where obtained. |
|---|---|---|---|---|---|---|---|
| | | | yds. ins. | yds. ins. | lbs. oz. | £ s. d. | |
| II. | 63 | Cotton. Pattern, green, red, white, and yellow check. Borders 1 inch, and ends 7 inches, formed by modification of pattern. | 3 27 | 1 3 | 0 10½ | 0 3 6 | Conathoor, Madras. |
| II. | 65 | Cotton. Pattern, black and white check, on crimson ground. Borders 1 inch wide, and ends 8 inches, formed by modification of pattern. | 3 18 | 1 2 | 1 1 | 0 3 0 | Pulicat, Madras. |
| II. | 66 | Cotton. Pattern, large blue and white check. Borders and ends formed by modification of pattern. | 3 27 | 1 6 | 0 12 | 0 2 9 | Mylapore, Madras. |
| II. | 67 | Cotton. Pattern, blue and white (½ inch) check on scarlet ground. Borders and ends formed by modification of pattern. | 4 9 | 1 2 | 0 14 | 0 8 0 | Pulicat, Madras. |
| II. | 68 | Cotton. Pattern, large (2½ inch) blue and white check. Blue ground. No special border. Yellow cross stripes in each end. | 3 27 | 1 2 | 1 3 | 0 5 3 | Pulicat, Madras. |
| II. | 69 | Cotton. Pattern, green, yellow, and white (¾ inch) check on a red ground. Border and ends formed by modification of pattern | 7 12 | 1 2 | 1 6 | 0 7 0 | Mylapore, Madras. |
| II. | 71 | Cotton. Pattern, a small blue (¼ inch) check on crimson ground. Border 1½ inch wide, formed by modification of pattern. Cross stripes of red and white introduced into each end. | 2 9 | 1 4 | 0 7½ | 0 2 0 | Coonathoor, Madras. |
| II. | 72 | Cotton. Pattern, small crimson check (9 lines to an inch) on a black ground. The weft stripe withdrawn in 40 inches of each end, and cross stripes of red and white are introduced. | 6 27 | 1 3 | 1 6 | 0 8 0 | Coonathoor. Madras. |
| II. | 73 | Cotton. Pattern, blue, crimson, and white check. 1 inch border and 6 inch ends, formed by modification of pattern. | 3 18 | 0 34 | 0 9 | 0 2 7½ | Coonathoor, Madras. |
| III. | 117 | Cotton. Pattern, small blue and white check to within 12 inches of each end. 2½-inch blue stripe border. Cross stripes of blue at each end. | 4 18 | 1 22 | 1 4 | 0 4 6 | Loodiana, Punjab. |
| IV. | 129 | Cotton. Pattern, red and white check. 3¼-inch border and 7 inches of each end marked by modification of pattern. | 4 30 | 1 8 | 1 0 | 0 6 0 | Shikarpore, Sind. |

8. COTTON.—COLOURED THREAD; STRIPES AND CHECKS; SPECIAL BORDERS AND ENDS.

In this group it will be observed that although some of the patterns are similar to those in the last one, the borders have a more special character.

As regards thickness of material some of the examples in it are intermediate between the last group and that which is to follow. No. 111, Vol. III., shows a soft material, pleasant to wear, and is worthy of careful examination.

| Vol. | No. | Description. | Measurement. Length. | Width. | Weight. | Cost. | Place of Manufacture, or whence obtained. |
|---|---|---|---|---|---|---|---|
| | | | yds. ins. | yds. ins. | lbs. oz. | £ s. d. | |
| II. | 59 | Cotton. Deep rose colour, with black stripes, 11 to the inch. Borders (¾-inch) green and black stripes. At each end two yellow and green stripes, one ⅝ inch and one ½ inch wide. | 4 9 | 1 0 | 0 13 | 0 4 0½ | Mylapore, Madras. |
| II. | 60 | Cotton. Dull yellow and chocolate-coloured check. (12 to the inch), 6 inches of each end being darker in pattern than body of piece. Borders (2½-inch) dark chocolate colour stripes. Made and worn by the Lubbays. | 2 9 | 1 9 | 0 10½ | 0 2 3 | Karikal, Madras. |
| II. | 62 | Cotton. Small black line check (10 to an inch) on dark blue ground. Coloured stripes in borders 3¾ inches wide. In about a yard of each end of the piece the check pattern is discontinued and cross stripes of various colours and widths introduced. Worn by the Lubbays.* | 6 0 | 1 4 | 1 5½ | 0 7 9 | Coonathoor, Madras. |
| II. | 64 | Cotton. Deep rose colour ground, with narrow black stripe, 10 to the inch. Same as No. 59, but without the border. Worn by the Lubbays. | 2 9 | 1 4 | 0 4 | 0 2 6 | Karikal, Madras. |
| III. | 100 | Cotton. Red. Borders. 2-inch stripes, chiefly green. A green, red, and white 3¾-inch stripe across each end. | 5 28 | 0 32 | 1 2 | 0 4 0 | Shikarpore, Sind. |
| III. | 105 | Cotton. Check of narrow blue lines ⅙-inch apart. One inch border striped in colours. Cross stripes (5 inches) at each end, in orange, green, and crimson. A common pattern. | 6 12 | 1 4 | 1 14 | 0 6 0 | Shikarpore, Sind. |
| III. | 111 | Cotton. Plain twilled. 1-inch borders, red stripe, and dotted margin. Across each end a 3-inch stripe in yellow, blue and red, and ¼-inch stripe, in red and blue. | 2 30 | 1 18 | 1 7 | 0 7 3½ | Nurrapore, Sind. |
| III. | 113 | Cotton. Twilled, chrome yellow colour. Borders, ¾-inch stripe of green with white line edges. At each end cross stripe 1⅔ inches wide, same pattern as borders; and near the extreme end a ⅙-inch stripe of green and white. | 2 27 | 1 14 | 1 7 | 0 4 0 | Shikarpore, Sind. |

## 9. Cotton.—Coloured Thread; Checks and Stripes; Figured Diaper Body; Borders and Ends formed generally by modification of Pattern.

The subjoined table includes the first examples given of the thick material* to which reference has been made, and to which the remarks regarding the probable advantages of employing a mixture of wool and cotton apply.

Nos. 119, Vol. III., and 126 and 127, Vol. IV., are good examples of intermediate qualities. Nos. 479 and 480, Vol. XII., given under the head of Cloths for Domestic Purposes, afford illustrations of a still stouter and warmer fabric, which would prove saleable at certain times and places.†

* Called *Kass* or, more properly, *Khes.* Loodiana *Khes* is said to be the best kind of cotton fabric made in the Punjab. It is exported in some quantity to Leh and Chanthan in Chinese Tartary.

Buchanan in "Martin's Eastern India," Vol. I. p. 353, defines *Khes* to be a cotton diaper used by natives as a dress, but in demand by Europeans for table-linen purposes. The prices of the specimens from Sind, although representing what they actually cost, can scarcely be regarded as representing their real value in the market.

† So also do some of the thicker materials used for trouserings shown amongst the piece-goods.

| Vol. | No. | Description. | Measurement. Length. | Measurement. Width. | Weight of Piece. | Cost. | Place of Manufacture, or where obtained. |
|---|---|---|---|---|---|---|---|
| | | | yds. ins. | yds ins. | lbs. oz. | £ s. d. | |
| III. | 102 | Cotton. Figured, diaper pattern. Two-inch borders, dark umber and green stripes ; main stripe of light umber. 2¾-inch green stripe across each end. A soft and thick fabric, much used. | 5 4 | 1 20 | 3 6 | 0 4 7 | Nurrapore, Sind. |
| III. | 112 | Cotton. Figured, diaper pattern in red and white. Two-inch borders formed by variation in colour, and absence of the white stripe of the check pattern. Each end for 6 inches marked in similar way. Not so soft and thick as No. 102. | 2 32 | 1 10 | 1 6 | 0 8 0 ? | Nurrapore, Sind. |
| III. | 114 | Cotton. Figured pattern in blue and white. Borders 4½ inches, and ends 10½ inches, formed by adaptation of body pattern. | 2 27 | 1 14 | 1 14 | 0 9 9 ? | Nurrapore, Sind. |
| III. | 115 | Cotton. Figured pattern in blue and white, checked with crimson. Border and ends formed by adaptation of main pattern. | 2 33 | 1 22 | 2 1 | 0 15 4½? | Nurrapore, Sind. |
| III. | 116 | Cotton. Blue and white, ½ inch, checkered pattern. Borders 1¼ inch, of blue stripes. Stripe 1¾ inch wide, and of same pattern as border across each end. | 2 34 | 0 26 | 2 1 | 0 9 9 ? | Nurrapore, Sind. |
| III. | 118 | Cotton. Figured pattern, blue and white. Border 1½ inch, and ends 5 inches, formed by modification of body pattern. | 2 13 | 1 4 | 1 12 | 0 5 0 | Runeeporeim, Sind. |
| III. | 119 | Cotton. Small blue and red checkered pattern, on a white ground. An inch border of similar pattern, but still smaller. Blue and white cross stripes at each end, in keeping with general design. | 2 27 | 1 20 | 1 5 | 0 12 0 ? | Runeeporeim, Sind. |
| III. | 120 | Cotton. Dark blue, with broad white stripes. Special modification of pattern to form borders and ends. Used as a covering for the body, and also as horse cloths. | 3 12 | 1 10 | 2 2½ | 0 3 6 | Shikarpore, Sind. |
| IV. | 121 | Cotton. Dark blue. Large blue and white check. Striped 1½-inch borders, and one 2¾-inch stripe across each end in accordance with pattern of piece. | 3 11½ | 1 10 | 1 13¼ | 0 2 0 | Shikarpore, Sind. |
| IV. | 122 | Cotton. Blue and white stripe. 1 inch coloured stripe in border. 1½-inch red stripe across each end. | 2 27 | 1 4 | 1 4 | 0 1 1½ | Shikarpore, Sind. |
| IV. | 125 | Cotton. Somewhat like a small diaper pattern. The only attempt at ornamentation is in the narrow fringe at the end of the piece, in which red cotton is introduced at intervals of 1 inch. | 3 0 | 1 18 | 1 5 | — | Sylhet. |
| IV. | 126 | Cotton. Bleached. Somewhat like the "duck" used for military summer trowsers. No special borders or ends. Good example of a favourite plain warm material. | 2 18 | 1 9 | 1 3 | — | Cachar. |
| IV. | 127 | Cotton. Bleached, coarse. Borders 3¼ inch stripe of pink. Similar stripes across each end. Soft and thick material. | 8 0 | 1 2 | 1 14 | 0 2 0 ? | Shikarpore, Sind. |
| XII. | 479 | Cotton. *Soojney.* A thick material of *unbleached* cotton, with large diaper pattern in *bleached* cotton woven in the unbleached material. Used as a counterpane. | 2 9 | 1 4 | 2 0 | 0 4 6 | Kurnool, Madras. |
| XII. | 480 | Cotton. *Soojney.* A thick material of dark red cotton, with large diaper pattern in bleached cotton woven in the coloured material. Used as a counterpane. In this and the previous example, the design towards the end is varied from the diamond shape or diaper pattern into zig-zag cross stripes, also in bleached cotton on the red ground, and an inch and a half of the extreme end is plain white, with a slight fringe. | 2 9 | 1 4 | 2 0 | 0 4 6 | Kurnool, Madras. |

### 10. Cotton.—Dyed; Borders and Ends printed.

No. 58, Vol. II. and No. 130, Vol. IV., afford illustrations of printing brought to bear upon the production of garment pieces of the class now under notice. No. 58, 8 yards 9 inches long, 1 yard 10 inches wide, weighing 1 lb. 11 oz. and costing 7*s.*, is a badly dyed pale pink with narrow (½ inch) figured borders in chocolate and black. At each end there are two cross stripes, one similar to the border, the other narrower and entirely chocolate colour. From Masulipatam, Madras.

No. 130, though poor in execution, shows tolerably well how printing may accomplish a desired effect.

The body is the dull but favourite red,* with squares of white spots. The borders (1¾ inch wide) are black with white dotted pattern. There are two cross stripes at each end (one 3½ and the other 1½ inches) of the same pattern as the border, but separated to the extent of 6 inches by a pattern of flowered pines. Length, 2 yards 3 inches; width, 1 yard 6 inches, weight 4½ ounces, price 1*s.* From Surat, Bombay.

We come now to the coloured cotton Loongees and Dhotees in which silk is introduced into the ends and borders in order to add to their attractiveness. In manufacturing this class of goods it is important that the borders should be stiff and thick, and that the weft should not appear through the silk.

### 11. Cotton.—Coloured or dyed; Silk Ends; no Borders.

Nos. 97 and 99, Vol III., are from Kohat, an important wool-producing district.

The first is dark blue without a border, but plain and figured stripes, in coloured silk and cotton, are woven across each end to a depth of 9 inches. This piece is 10 yards long by 37 inches wide, and weighs 1 lb. 12 oz.

No. 99 is of a similar character, except that across each end the stripes are of red and yellow silk and 2½ inches wide. The dimensions of this sample are; length 3 yards, width 1 yard 2 inches, and weight 1 lb. 1 oz.

These are examples of a garment which is extensively used by both sexes in the valleys west of Kohat.

### 12. Cotton.—Coloured or dyed; Silk Borders; coloured Cotton Ends.

No. 103, is also from Kohat, and is of dark blue cotton, with a plain 1-inch stripe of red along the border. Each end is marked by a weft of white thread for a depth of 9 inches. The length is 4 yards 17 inches, width 1 yard 6 inches, weight 1 lb. 15 oz. Commonly worn by the men of the Ayrore valley in the Kohat district.

The body pattern of No. 108 is a small check of red and white on a green ground. It has a 2¼-inch stripe of crimson silk in the border, and the ends are varied by a narrow stripe pattern crossed by faint stripes of green. This piece, which is 2 yards 3 inches long by 1 yard 6 inches wide, and weighs 8 ounces, is from Surat in Bombay. The price in 1854 was 4*s.*

---

* The favourite reds, as a rule, are dark ones. The *Turkey reds* and other variations of pure madder dye colours are extremely popular, not merely on account of the colour, but because that colour is a fast one—a most important consideration with the native customer, owing to the very frequent washing of a rough character.

### 13. Cotton.—Plain dyed; Silk Borders and Ends.

Nos. 95 and 98, Vol. III., are the examples under this head. No. 95 is dark blue (a favourite colour) with 1½-inch border of dark crimson silk. About 42 inches of each end is decorated with plain and figured cross stripes, in silk and cotton, of various colours.

This specimen is interesting, not merely because so considerable a portion of each end is ornamented, but also because the border is sewn on.*

Length of piece, 5 yards 24 inches; width, 1 yard 8 inches; weight, 3 lb. 4 oz. From Kohat.

No. 98 is a soft material worthy of notice. The pattern, which is a kind of diaper, in crimson, deserves attention. The border in this instance is a stripe of yellow silk (probably in imitation of gold lace) with margins of coloured cotton thread. Across each end is a coloured and figured stripe of silk and cotton 3½ inches wide.

Length 3 yards, width 1 yard 8 inches, weight, 1 lb. 8 oz. It cost 11*s.* 6*d.* From Nurrapore, Sind.

### 14. Cotton.—Check; Silk Borders and Ends.

No. 96 is an example of a favourite pattern in the Punjab. The body pattern is a very small dark blue check, with a border formed by a 2½ inch stripe of red silk. In each end, for 15 inches, cross stripes of yellow, green, and crimson silks are introduced. Length 4 yards, width 1 yard 17 inches, and weight 1 lb. 5½ oz. Price 12*s.* From Leiah, in the Punjab.

The pattern of No. 101, Vol. III. is a wide open check of narrow crimson lines, 1 inch apart, on a white ground. Border, a 2-inch stripe of crimson silk, with ¾-inch edging on the inner side of the *Kutar* pattern. Across each end, a 3¾-inch stripe of crimson silk and white cotton. Length 3 yards 7 inches. Width 1 yard 8 inches. Weight 11½ ounces. Price in 1854, 4*s.* 10*d.* From Pind Dadun Khan.

No. 104, Vol. III. This is a check pattern, formed by faint crimson lines $\frac{5}{12}$ths of an inch apart on white ground. The border consists of a plain 2-inch crimson silk stripe, and across each end are a 4⅓-inch stripe of crimson, green, and yellow silks, and four supplementary stripes of crimson and yellow silks ⅙ inch wide. Length 3 yards 22 inches, width 1 yard 16 inches, weight 1 lb. 3 oz. Price 11*s.* 6*d.* From Lahore in the Punjab.

### 15. Cotton.—Plain Dye; Cotton and Silk Borders; Gold Ends.

No. 56, Vol. II., is a further illustration of the method in which the two garment pieces, viz., the Loongee and Dhotee, are woven in one piece with a *fag* at the point of separation. The material is a rose-coloured muslin with a 1¼-inch border, "Kutar" pattern. Moonga silk is introduced, apparently in imitation of gold thread. At each end is a ¾-inch cross stripe of gold and black thread.

The length of the longer piece, or Loongee, is 5 yards 27 inches, and of the shorter, or Dhotee, 2 yards 18 inches, the width 1 yard 11 inches, and the weight 1 lb. 2 ozs. From Rajahmundry, Madras, where, in 1854, the piece cost 14*s.* 6*d.*

---

* This is occasionally done; and borders made for the purpose might be so employed to a greater extent than they are.

MALE ATTIRE. COTTON AND SILK.

### 16. Cotton.—Plain Dye; Gold Borders and Ends.

**No. 57, Vol. II., is a pink coarse muslin or light cotton fabric. The special border in this instance is of the *Kutar* pattern already described. It is stamped in black on the piece, and is figured with gold thread. At each end are a $\frac{3}{4}$-inch and a $\frac{5}{12}$-inch stripe of dark brown, relieved by lines of gold thread.**

**Length 8 yards 18 inches. Width 1 yard 11 inches. Weight 1 lb. 3 oz. Price 1*l*. 4*s*. 6*d*. From Madura, but purchased in Madras.**

### 17. Silk and Cotton Check.

No. 61. Vol. II., is of a deep rose-coloured ground, in which is woven a faint check of yellow silk thread. The borders and ends are a modification of the main pattern. Manufactured by the Lubbays, and obtained from Mylapore, Madras. Length 3 yards 27 inches, width 1 yard 2 inches, weight 10 ounces. Price 4*s*. 6*d*.

### 18. Silk and Cotton.—Silk Borders and Ends.

Nos. 92 and 93, Vol. III., in this group, are worthy of attention as affording examples of a thickish material formed by a combination of silk and cotton.

| Vol. | No. | Description. | Measurement. | | Weight. | Cost. | Place of Manufacture, or where obtained. |
|---|---|---|---|---|---|---|---|
| | | | Length. | Width. | | | |
| | | | yds. ins. | yds. ins. | lbs. oz. | £ s. d. | |
| III. | 92 | Light blue cotton weft, and silk warp, with $\frac{1}{2}$-inch coloured and figured stripes, $\frac{1}{6}$ inch apart. Border $2\frac{5}{8}$ inches wide, laced pattern, in yellow and other coloured silks. At each end a broad ($4\frac{2}{3}$ inches) cross silk stripe, one crimson and the other yellow. Edged with two $1\frac{3}{4}$-inch figured stripes. | 4 $7\frac{1}{2}$ | 1 18 | 1 14 | — | Hyderabad, Sind. |
| III. | 93 | Coloured stripes, alternately $\frac{1}{3}$ inch and $\frac{1}{4}$ inch wide. $2\frac{3}{4}$-inch border of blue and coloured silks, laced pattern. At each end a broad silk cross stripe of yellow on one side, and crimson on the other, edged with two $1\frac{1}{4}$-inch figured stripes in coloured silks. Total width of cross stripes in ends, 8 inches. | 4 0 | 1 20 | 2 0 | — | Hyderabad, Sind. |
| III. | 94 | Green, with $\frac{1}{2}$ inch check of crimson silk. 4 inch stripe of yellow silk at each end, and a faint stripe of the same colour in the border. | 6 20 | 1 6 | 1 1 | 0 16 0 | Runeepore, Sind. |

### 19. Silk and Cotton.—Gold in Borders and Ends.

No. 86, Vol. III., Cotton weft and silk warp. Pattern, a white ground checked with crimson silk lines $\frac{1}{6}$ inch apart. Rich laced border ($1\frac{1}{4}$ inch wide) in gold and blue and white thread.

Deep ($9\frac{1}{2}$ inch) cross stripes of gold and crimson at each end. Length 7 yards 15 inches. Width 1 yard 18 inches, weight 1 lb. 1 oz. Price 1*l*. 12*s*. From Jhelum, in the Punjab.

No. 218, Vol. VI., is a gauze-like fabric of green cotton warp and crimson silk weft. Border ($\frac{5}{6}$ inch wide) of crimson silk figured with gold lace. At each end a laced pattern of gold thread $1\frac{3}{4}$ inches wide. Length 3 yards $4\frac{1}{2}$ inches. Width, 1 yard 15 inches, weight, 9 ounces. Price 18*s*. From Bombay.

### 20. Silk.—Gold Borders and Ends.

The specimens described in the following table afford some excellent examples of the extent to which ornamentation of the class of garments under notice is carried. These rich Loongees are only manufactured in a few places in India, and all of them display a remarkable similarity in the patterns of their borders and ends.

| Vol. | No. | Description. | Measurement. Length. | Measurement. Width. | Weight of Piece. | Cost. | Place of Manufacture, or where obtained. |
|---|---|---|---|---|---|---|---|
| | | | yds. ins. | yds. ins. | lbs. oz. | £ s. d. | |
| III. | 81 | Yellow corded silk. Rich laced border $2\frac{1}{6}$ inches wide, of gold and crimson and black silk. $7\frac{1}{2}$-inch cross stripes at each end of gold and crimson silk. Woven in half widths, each having the border on one side only. Two of such widths being sewn together, a complete garment with two borders is formed. | 3 25 | 0 29 | 0 $14\frac{1}{4}$ | — | Bhawulpore. |
| III. | 82 | Deep crimson ground, checked with narrow green lines $\frac{1}{3}$ of an inch apart. Rich laced borders $1\frac{3}{4}$ inches wide in gold and coloured silks. Cross stripes at each end of green and crimson silk and gold. This example, unlike No. 81, is woven in one piece, with a border on each side. | 3 10 | 1 16 | 1 $4\frac{3}{4}$ | — | Jhelum, Punjab. |
| III. | 84 | Plain, light cinnamon-coloured silk. Rich laced border (2 inches wide) of gold and coloured silks. Each end has also a 3-inch cross stripe of gold lace in the same colours, but of different pattern. Woven in half widths, two pieces sewn together forming one garment. | 4 3 | 0 $28\frac{1}{2}$ | 0 $9\frac{1}{2}$ | — | Bhawulpore. |
| III. | 85 | Deep crimson ground, with a check of narrow white lines $\frac{1}{3}$-inch apart. Richly laced border (2 inches wide) of gold and silver threads and coloured silks. Cross stripe $4\frac{1}{3}$ inches wide in gold and colours at each end. | 3 34 | 1 18 | 1 $12\frac{3}{4}$ | 7 19 $7\frac{1}{2}$ | Lahore, Punjab. |
| III. | 87 | Crimson ground. Border ($1\frac{3}{4}$ inches wide) of gold and blue. At each end a cross stripe, $2\frac{3}{4}$ inches wide, of gold and coloured cotton threads.* | 3 18 | 1 14 | 1 $1\frac{1}{2}$ | 4 0 0 | Goodaspore, Punjab. |
| III. | 89 | Figured stripes alternately yellow and green, and crimson and white. Richly laced 2-inch border of gold and coloured silks. At each end a $3\frac{1}{2}$-inch cross stripe, in design and material similar to border. | 4 8 | 1 18 | 1 $8\frac{1}{2}$ | — | Bhawulpore. |
| III. | 90 | Deep red silk with small yellow check (6 lines to an inch). $2\frac{1}{4}$-inch border of crimson silk, crossed by $\frac{1}{3}$-inch stripes of gold thread, 1-$\frac{1}{2}$inch apart. In 19 inches of each end cross stripes of crimson and green silks with gold. | 7 0 | 1 14 | 1 $13\frac{1}{4}$ | 2 6 0 | Buttala, Goodaspore. |
| III. | 91 | Yellow silk, with small crimson check (six lines to an inch). $2\frac{1}{2}$-inch border of crimson silk, crossed by $\frac{1}{3}$-inch stripes of gold thread, $1\frac{1}{4}$ inches apart. Ends (20 inches) cross stripes of crimson, green, and yellow silk, and gold. | 7 5 | 1 20 | 1 $14\frac{1}{2}$ | 4 0 0 | Buttala, Goodaspore. |

* This peculiar use of gold and coloured cotton thread for the ornamentation of silk fabrics is very effective.

### 21. Silk.—Gold and Silver figured Stripes.

**No. 88, Vol. III., is an example of a piece said to be suitable for a Loongee. The pattern, however, is more like that employed for trowser pieces. The specimen in question has neither borders nor ends, and to make it into a loongee, these would have to be added. From Bhawulpore.* Length, 5 yds. 15 in.; width, 31 inches; weight, 1 lb. 3¾ oz.**

### 22. Silk.—Silver Ends; Silk Borders.

No. 83, Vol. III. Crimson checked by narrow green lines; borders green with the *Kutar* pattern; ends, for 18 inches, ornamented with cross stripes of green, yellow, black and silver. Length, 6 yds. 24 ins.; width, 1 yd. 14 ins.; weight, 1 lb. 1 oz. From Rawul Pindee, Punjab.

### 23. Wool.—Variously Ornamented.

In the Table below will be found a description of the examples in which wool is the material employed. It will be observed that these have in the Table been grouped according to the mode in which their borders and ends are decorated.

| No. of Vol. | No. of Sample. | | Description. | Measurement. Length. | Measurement. Width. | Weight of piece. | Cost. | Place of Manufacture, or where obtained. |
|---|---|---|---|---|---|---|---|---|
| | | | | yds. ins. | yds. ins. | lbs. oz. | £ s. d. | |
| XVI. | 628 | Striped Ends. | Deep end (16 inches) formed by cross stripes of various colours and widths. | 6 12 | 0 30 | 1 11 | — | Hyderabad, Sind. |
| XVI. | 636 | Striped Ends. | Large double line check of blue on plain uncoloured ground. 3 inches of end dark crimson, with blue and white cross stripes. | 3 13 | 0 28 | 4 0 | — | Kooloo, obtained from Kangra. |
| XVI. | 642 | Striped Ends. | Plain, uncoloured. Close to end a $\frac{1}{10}$ inch coloured stripe. | 3 19 | 1 16 | 3 4 | 0 5 3 | Beejapoor. |
| XVII. | 644 | Striped Borders and Ends. | Plain, uncoloured, coarse texture. ¾-inch stripe of yellow in border. Fringed end, with narrow cross line of yellow. Sewn together in centre to form complete loongee. | 3 0 | 1 14 | 2 5 | 0 3 7½ | Bangalore, sent from Madras. |
| XVIII. | 677 | Striped Borders and Ends. | Red ground, with small yellow check; border (¾-inch wide) is a long stripe of a flowered pattern, woven in coloured wools and silk, sewn on to the garment piece. A similar stripe is inserted across the end of the loongee. | 5 9 | 1 34 | 2 0 | 5 4 0 | Cashmere. |
| XVI. | 637 | Striped Borders and Ends. | Crimson, with 1-inch stripe in border of uncoloured cotton. Two sewn together form one garment piece. | 3 0 | 1 14 | 2 4 | 0 3 0 | Bangalore, sent from Madras. |

* The specimens from Bhawulpore were presented by the Nawab, and their cost is consequently unknown. As already stated, it would not be safe in any instance to regard the prices attached to the articles as the present value. They merely represent the amount known to have been paid for them when they were bought in 1854.

| No. of | | | Description. | Measurement. | | Weight of piece. | Cost. | Place of Manufacture, or where obtained. |
|---|---|---|---|---|---|---|---|---|
| Vol. | Sample. | | | Length. | Width. | | | |
| | | | | yds. ins. | yds. ins. | lbs. oz. | £ s. d. | |
| XVIII. | 687 | Silk Borders. | Plain uncoloured material. Border ($1\frac{1}{2}$ inch wide) consisting of a $1\frac{1}{8}$-inch stripe of green silk, and an inner $\frac{3}{8}$-inch silk stripe of crimson, with yellow centre. Also called a "Dhoosa," or wrapper. | 3 6 | 1 9 | 1 2 | 1 14 0 | Lahore. |
| XVIII. | 688 | Silk Borders. | Plain, dark, uncoloured material. Border (2 inches wide) consisting of a $1\frac{6}{10}$-inch stripe of crimson silk, and a $\frac{4}{10}$-inch inner silk stripe of white with green centre. Woven in two lengths with fag between. | Single piece. 3 4 | 1 17 | 1 $12\frac{1}{2}$ | 1 14 0 | Lahore. |
| XVIII. | 689 | Silk Borders. | Plain, light drab, uncoloured material. Border, $1\frac{1}{2}$ inches wide, of crimson silk, plain. Woven in two lengths with fag between. | Single piece. 3 14 | 1 9 | 1 $1\frac{1}{2}$ | 1 6 0 | Lahore. |
| XVIII. | 690 | Silk Borders. | Plain, uncoloured, brown material. Border, $1\frac{3}{8}$ inches wide, consisting of an inch stripe of crimson silk, and an inner $\frac{3}{8}$-inch silk stripe of white and green. | 2 30 | 1 6 | 0 $14\frac{1}{2}$ | 1 6 0 | Lahore. |
| XVIII. | 691 | Silk Borders. | Plain, uncoloured, white material. Border ($1\frac{1}{2}$ inches wide), consisting of $1\frac{1}{6}$ inch stripe of green silk, and a $\frac{1}{3}$-inch stripe of crimson and yellow silk in the inner side. | 3 5 | 1 12 | 1 $5\frac{1}{4}$ | 1 15 0 | Lahore. |
| XVII. | 652 | Silk Border & Ends. | Plain, dark grey body. Border, $1\frac{1}{2}$-inch stripe in crimson, green and yellow silks. Across end a 3-inch stripe with figured centre in crimson, yellow and green coloured silks. Used for body clothing in cold weather, also for bed covers and saddle-cloths. Sewn together in centre to form one garment. | 5 12 | 0 25 | 3 14 | About 0 4 0 | Hyderabad Sind. |

No. 676, Vol. XVIII., from Cashmere, is an example of a woollen Loongee with silk and silver borders. The colour is orange yellow, and the pattern a small diaper. The borders, which are of the same pattern, have a silver thread warp. They are upwards of 5 inches in width, and have green silk and woollen stripes on either side, with an additional stripe of green silk between them and the extreme edge of the piece.*

This concludes what we have to say of the important class of Loongees and Pitamburs, and of Loongees and Dhotees manufactured in one piece.

* The dimensions, weight, &c., of this garment piece are unknown, as it came to hand in an uncomplete state. For this reason also, in cutting it up for insertion in the collection under description, it was found possible to show the border in a certain number only of the examples, and even these are arranged across the page, instead of vertically, as usual.

## B.—DHOTEES;—SINGLE.

Of the Dhotees or loin-cloths manufactured separately a brief notice will suffice, the general character of this garment having already been pointed out.

In these there is not so much room for variety as in the case of the articles employed for the protection or adornment of the upper portions of the person. In a garment, indeed, so much of which is concealed in consequence of the mode of wearing it, the opportunity for ornamentation is limited. The use of such a material as metal would be apt to interfere with the comfort of the wearer. The necessity for its being frequently washed is, perhaps, the principal reason for avoiding much decoration.

The following table comprehends the whole of the examples of Dhotees uncombined with Loongees which we have considered it necessary to give. The examples from Santipore, Nos. 289, 290, and 291, Vol. VIII., are perhaps the most worthy of attention.

Nos. 106 and 107, Vol. III., are similar to many of the loongees in having silk borders, the chief difference being that the end pattern in the dhotee is reduced to a few cross stripes.

No. 124, Vol. IV., received from Surat, shows the kind of article which is occasionally manufactured in England for export, and No. 123 illustrates a yellowish colour which would, in some districts, prove an attraction if adopted for *grey shirtings*.

| Vol. | No. | Description. | Measurement. | | Weight of piece. | Cost. | Place of Manufacture, or where obtained. |
|---|---|---|---|---|---|---|---|
| | | | Length. | Width. | | | |
| | | | yds. ins. | yds. ins. | lbs. oz. | £ s. d. | |
| III. | 106 | Cotton, plain. Border, 4-inch figured crimson silk stripe. Three faint red cotton stripes across each end. | 3 22 | 1 8 | 0 11½ | 0 5 0 | Surat, Bombay. |
| III. | 107 | Cotton, plain. Border, 2½-inch stripe, chiefly of crimson silk. Faintly marked 1 inch stripe of red across each end. | 4 6 | 1 2 | 0 13½ | 0 4 0 | Surat, Bombay. |
| IV. | 124 | Cotton, plain, with ¾-inch coloured stripe *woven* in border. Three narrow red lines across each end. | 3 30 | 0 34 | 0 12½ | 0 1 5 | Surat, Bombay. |
| IV. | 123 | Cotton, plain. 1-inch red border, figured pattern, printed. 2-inch figured stripe across principal end, and an inch stripe across the opposite end; both of same character as the border. | 4 21 | 1 1 | 0 12½ | 0 2 6 | Calcutta. |
| IV. | 128 | Muslin, bleached. Blue flowered pattern. Border marked merely by two slight lines of blue. At each end broad cross stripes and adaptation of body pattern, with pine pattern added.* | 3 0 | 1 0 | 0 6¼ | — | Kathamandoo, Nepal. |
| VIII. | 289 | Santipore Dhotee. Light texture. ¾-inch border, figured in red cotton and Tussah silk, with two inner stripes woven in the plain material. Red stripes across end. | 5 32 | 1 9 | 0 5¼ | 0 5 6 | Santipore, Calcutta. |
| VIII. | 290 | Santipore Dhotee. Light texture. ¾-inch figured border, woven in red and blue thread, with small inner stripe woven in the plain material. 2½-inch figured stripe in yellow, red, and blue thread across one end, and across the other a ⅜-inch blue stripe. | 4 18 | 0 32 | 0 5¼ | 0 5 6 | Santipore, Calcutta. |
| VIII. | 291 | Santipore Dhotee. Light texture. One border orange and blue, and the other crimson and blue. Figured, ¾ inch wide. | 5 20 | 1 10 | 0 6¼ | 0 5 6 | Santipore, Calcutta. |

* It has not been possible to cut the original piece so as to show the pine pattern in every sample.

## III.—KUMMERBUNDS.

The Kummerbund*—literally, waist-band—or sash, as a loom-made article of male attire, has next to be considered.

It is chiefly used by the Mahomedans,—the manner in which the dhotee is worn by the Hindus rendering it less necessary in their case. Both Hindus and Mahomedans, of the richer classes, however, when in full dress almost invariably use it.

When used, as it often is, for effect, it is narrow; sometimes, however, it is of considerable width and bulk. Figures 55 and 57, Pl. VIII., illustrate the manner in which it is worn.

In Northern India these sashes are almost always made of wool and are of different degrees of fineness. Muslin textures, however, are used elsewhere. Ornamentation, when adopted, is confined to the ends, into which coloured threads of various kinds, and occasionally gold, are introduced.

The examples given of this class of manufactures are all woollen. They show the quality of material used, the length of the sash, &c., but afford no remarkable illustrations of pattern; it is, however, thought that there is scope for the advantageous introduction of ornament into the ends of such articles.

| No. of | | Description. | Measurement. | | Weight of piece. | Cost. | Place of Manufacture, or where obtained. |
|---|---|---|---|---|---|---|---|
| Vol. | Sample. | | Length. | Width. | | | |
| | | | yds. ins. | yds. ins. | lbs. oz. | £ s. d. | |
| XVI. | 629 | Waistband of a male Beloochee. Red. Coarse and narrow. Plain. | 5 0 | 0 10 | 1 7½ | — | Beloochistan. |
| XVI. | 630 | Plain, uncoloured. Coarse, but strong texture. | 6 33 | 0 12 | 1 7 | — | Nepal. |
| XVI. | 632 | Plain, uncoloured. - - - - | 5 18 | 0 9½ | 1 0 | — | Thibet. |
| XVI. | 633 | Fair quality, indifferent colour. A red stripe, 1 inch wide, across end. | 3 3 | 0 12 | 2 9 | — | Darjeeling. |
| XVI. | 635 | Plain, coarse material, with, at 9 inches from end, a double line stripe of red. | 5 18 | 0 15 | 2 2 | — | Kangra. |

* Like most Indian terms, which have passed into use as English, this word is spelt in a variety of ways, as Kumerbund, Kamarband, Cummerbund, &c.

# LOOM-MADE ARTICLES OF FEMALE ATTIRE.

## I.—SAREES.

The chief article of female attire in India consists of a long scarf, called a Saree, which both envelopes the body and acts as a covering to the head. It is the common dress of the Hindu women of all ranks, as well as that of a large proportion of Mahomedans. By the Hindus of the northern provinces of India it is occasionally worn along with the petticoat of the Mahomedan. This combination, however, is rare, and, indeed, amongst the poorer classes, especially during the hot weather, *the Saree is the only article of dress employed.*

The mode of wearing the Saree is very much the same all over India, although, of course, the amplitude of its folds, and the quality of the material used, vary with the social position of the women.

As usually worn, one end is passed twice round the waist, the upper border tied in a strong knot, and allowed to fall in graceful folds to the ankle, thus forming a sort of petticoat or skirt—a portion of one leg being only partially concealed by the Hindu. The other end is passed in front across the left arm and shoulder, one edge being brought over the top of the head. It is then allowed to fall behind and over the right shoulder and arm. In Pl. V. and VI. will be found several illustrations of the manner of wearing the Saree. The Brahmin lady, No. 37, Pl. VI., shows its application when it forms almost the complete Hindu clothing; fig. 34, Pl. V., a photograph from an imperfect painting on talc,* shows an instance in which the Saree has been employed to produce the full effect of a petticoat of moderate dimensions. The Mahratta costume of the well-known and celebrated lady—the Begum of Bhopal—as represented to the left in No. 35, Pl. VI. (and in three other groups in the same Plate) is likewise worthy of attention.

The sitting figures in group† 27, Pl. V., represent the mode of adjusting a Saree of less ample dimensions when used by women employed in out-door labour—the end, which falls in front, being passed between the legs, and tucked in behind, forming as it were drawers reaching to the knee. In addition to the petticoat or trowser the Mahomedan women in many parts of Northern India use, instead of the Saree, the *Boorka* or sheet veil, which consists of a covering thrown over the head, with a networked space opposite the eyes, and which is voluminous enough to conceal almost the whole person.

In Burmah the principal article of female dress consists of a square piece of cloth worn over the back and across the breast, one end being secured by thrusting it under the fold which comes over the bosom.

---

* Introduced principally for the purpose of showing the long ornamental end of the Saree, which, however, is represented as having been brought over the right instead of the left shoulder and side of head.

† Reproduced from a photograph (by Johnson) of women employed in the construction of the railway, near Bombay.

With respect to the materials of which the Saree is made, and the character of its texture, a few general remarks may here be made.

As to material, cotton naturally occupies the first place, then mixtures of cotton and silk, and lastly, silk itself. There are no examples given in which wool has been employed, but some of the remarks already made, respecting the introduction of that fibre into fabrics suited for wear in India during the cold season, should be kept in view by the manufacturer, being as applicable to Sarees as to Loongees.

Just as in the case of the Loongees and Dhotees, attention must be paid to the texture of the fabric employed. This requires to be loose and soft, in order to be agreeable to the wearer, and to allow the garment to fall more gracefully into shape.

Indeed, during the hot season, it would be almost impossible to wear a cloth of cotton or silk in the manner the native women of India do, unless it were of open texture and soft and pliable.

With respect to the way in which these long scarfs are embellished by the introduction of borders, &c., we shall find the same variety in the character of the decoration, and the same subordination of ornament to function as in the case of Loongees.

Sarees, made in separate pieces of the proper length, have, almost invariably, ornamental borders of some sort or other; and one end, that exposed to view, has care devoted to its adornment, as in the case of the turban-pieces. The opposite end, being worn next to the body and out of sight, is left nearly plain.

The number of ways in which effect is produced, by the variety of materials and patterns employed to form the borders and ends, will be seen by referring to the descriptions of the groups which follow.

In the note below will be found some terms which have been applied in different parts of India to the Saree or to modifications of it, but the name of Saree is that which is now most commonly employed.*

We now come to the consideration of the special illustrations of this class of loom-made garments.

---

* *Boonnee.* From *Boonna*—to weave. This cloth is made either with a red or black border. The former is worn by Hindu and the latter by Mahomedan women. Dimensions 10 yards by 1 yard.—(Cotton manufacture of Dacca, p. 62.)

*Kilnya.* So called when the piece of cloth is woven so that "two breadths must be stitched together to make one wrapper."—(*Buchanan* in Martin's "Eastern India," Vol. II., p. 93.)

*Dhoti.* In Buchanan's time, in Goruckpore, the wrapper worn by women, when of full size, was called dhoti —a term which in Behar and Bengal is confined to the male dress, where also the appellation *Sari* for the female wrapper was used.—(*Buchanan* in Martin's "Eastern India," Vol. II., p. 93.)

*Chadur, Choddur, Chudder.* Literally a sheet used as a covering by Mahomedan women, but it is also applied to the plain woollen shawls manufactnred at Umritsur and Rampore.

*Sadhie* is a name used for the Saree in the Mahratta country.

*Chundur Kala,* when the Saree is of one colour only, black or red.

*Putta.* A kind of holiday cloth of the Saree class, worn in Dharwar by children at weddings, &c. It is of plain cotton or of silk embroidered according to the station of the wearer.

*Sulleedar.* A silk saree worn by women at festivals in Dharwar.

*Karchori.* A Parsee lady's dress, gold embroidered, of the Saree class.

*Tamieng.* A saree worn by Burmese women.

FEMALE ATTIRE. COTTON, &c.

## 1. Cotton.—Cotton Borders and Ends.

**Of the specimens dealt with in the subjoined table, No. 188, Vol. V. is a good example of an open-textured material, of a common quality, and Nos. 221 and 228, Vol. VI., afford instances in which, although the thread is undyed, its arrangement is made to produce a striped appearance.**

**Nos. 193, 194, 195, Vol. V., are of almost the coarsest kind of fabric made, and show that the special ornamentation even of these is a matter which receives attention.**

| No. of | | Description. | Measurement. | | Weight of piece. | Cost. | Place of Manufacture, or where obtained. |
|---|---|---|---|---|---|---|---|
| Vol. | Sample. | | Length. | Width. | | | |
| | | | yds. ins. | yds. ins. | lbs. oz. | £ s. d. | |
| V. | 188 | Cotton. Open texture. $1\frac{1}{2}$-inch border in red and yellow thread, with slight Kutar pattern on inner edge. At principal end, one $2\frac{1}{4}$-inch and one $\frac{1}{4}$-inch cross stripe in deep red with yellow lines. The opposite end marked only by a $\frac{1}{2}$-inch cross stripe in red thread. Good example of a common texture. | 8 27 | 1 7 | 1 $6\frac{3}{4}$ | 0 3 0 | Ooppaddy. Bought in Madras. |
| V. | 193 | Cotton, coarse, unbleached. Border, a faint red line ($\frac{1}{3}$ inch wide) near edge. The principal end ornamented with a 2-inch crimson cross stripe, two narrower stripes of same colour, and nearer end a $\frac{3}{4}$-inch cross stripe of blue. Opposite end also marked by two cross stripes of crimson, and one of blue. Used by the Burghers. | 3 0 | 1 0 | 1 3 | 0 1 0 | Coimbatore. Bought in Madras. |
| V. | 194 | Cotton, coarse, unbleached. Border, a faint brown stripe near edge. Principal end marked by two narrow cross stripes of reddish brownthreads. A stripe of similar character in opposite end. | 3 0 | 1 0 | 0 13 | 0 1 6 | Bekul in Canara. |
| V. | 195 | Cotton, common material, unbleached. Border, $\frac{1}{6}$-inch chocolate coloured stripe along edge. One $2\frac{1}{2}$ inch and one $\frac{1}{2}$ inch red and yellow stripe across the principal end. At opposite end a narrow stripe of red. | 6 0 | 1 0 | 1 7 | 0 1 9 | Congeveram. Bought in Madras. |
| VI. | 221 | Cotton. Light texture, bleached. 1-inch stripes woven in the material. Border, a $1\frac{1}{4}$-inch stripe of crimson cotton thread. In principal end a $1\frac{1}{4}$-inch cross stripe of crimson thread in the weft. Opposite end marked by a $\frac{1}{2}$-inch cross stripe of blue thread. Borders of different colours; one red, and the other blue. | 4 22 | 1 22 | 0 11 | 0 3 0 | Calcutta. |
| VI. | 227 | Cotton. Light texture. White and yellow stripes ($1\frac{1}{6}$ inch wide) woven in body of garment. $1\frac{1}{2}$-inch border of red cotton, with pattern figured in white thread. In each end a $\frac{1}{4}$-inch cross stripe of crimson thread near the edge. | 4 27 | 1 3 | 0 11 | 0 3 0 | Calcutta. |
| VI. | 228 | Cotton. Light texture. White, with coloured stripes woven in the body of the garment $\frac{1}{4}$ inch wide and $\frac{1}{3}$ inch apart. $1\frac{1}{4}$-inch border, red centre, dark blue and red striped edges. Principal end, for about 17 inches, is of red thread in the weft. At the opposite end a 1-inch faint cross stripe in blue and red thread. | 4 32 | 1 2 | 0 12 | 0 3 0 | Calcutta. |
| VIII. | 287 | Plain white bleached Muslin called Chunderkora. Slight border. | 4 18 | 1 $4\frac{1}{2}$ | 0 6 | 0 2 $7\frac{1}{2}$ | Calcutta. |
| VIII. | 288 | Ditto, ditto, ditto, ditto. | 2 33 | 1 10 | 0 $3\frac{1}{2}$ | 0 2 0 | Calcutta. |

### 2. Cotton (Muslin).—Gold End.

The specimens of Sarees, Nos. 283, 284, 285, Vol. VIII., form a remarkable contrast to the preceding ones. They have no borders, and have been dealt with as a class on account of the special ornamentation of their ends, into each of which a stripe of gold about an inch wide had been inserted.*

They are from Chundeyree, and afford excellent examples of the beautiful fabrics for which that old seat of native manufacture has been so long and so justly celebrated.†

The specimens are unbleached; No. 284 is a plain material; No. 283 is striped; and No. 285 is chequered in the loom. Each has a stripe of gold, about an inch wide, at one end. The lengths and widths of Nos. 283 and 284 are the same, viz., 14 yards and 30½ inches respectively, but 285 is an inch more each way. No. 283 weighs 10¾ ounces, and the other two each 10¼ ounces. The cost of each, in 1854, was the same, viz., 1*l.* 13*s.* 0*d.*

Although silk is occasionally used to form borders and ends to plain cotton materials, no examples occur in the series.

### 3. Cotton (Muslin).—Coloured Cotton Borders; Coloured Cotton and Gold in Ends.

No. 189, Vol. V. A plain and rather coarse muslin. Border (2⅞ inches) of red and yellow cotton stripes, with a narrow line of same, ¼ inch from inner edge. In principal end a 2¼-inch cross stripe of red cotton with ½ inch centre of gold thread. Between this main cross stripe and narrower ones of the same colour, the material is dotted with spots in black thread. Secondary end marked merely by a few threads of red cotton. Length of piece, 8 yards 18 inches; width, 1 yard 9 inches; weight, 1 lb. 4 oz.; cost 6*s.* 9*d.* Woven at Gangam; bought in Madras.

### 4. Cotton.—Silk Borders; Silk and Gold in End.

Example No. 173, Vol. V. A plain, light material; warp of unbleached thread, weft tinged with blue. Border, 1⅓ inch wide, of coloured cotton and crimson and yellow silk. 8½ inches of principal end decorated with 2½-inch cross stripe of gold thread, and several figured stripes of coloured thread and crimson silk. Opposite end marked only by a narrow cross stripe of coloured thread. From Condapore, S. Canara, Madras. Length of piece, 7 yards; width, 1 yard; weight, 1 lb. 3 oz.; cost 10*s.*

### 5. Cotton.—Coloured Thread; Cotton Borders.

In this group there are no special end patterns, the character of the border stripes rendering these, perhaps, as a matter of taste less necessary.

---

* Although grouped with the Sarees these specimens more strictly speaking come under the denomination of piece-goods—it being a by no means uncommon custom to ornament the ends of the finer kinds with the flattened gold and silver wire called *badla*. The wire in such cases is not woven into the fabric, but is put in with the needle —a special class of workmen being employed for the purpose.

† As in the case of Dacca, the manufacture of these prized cloths at Chundeyree has of late been restricted to the fulfilment of occasional orders.

The weavers are described as working in underground workshops, to secure a greater uniformity of moisture in the air, which in the North-Western provinces is usually very dry. The cotton anciently used in the manufacture of the Chundeyree muslins is stated to have been brought from Oomrawuttee, in Berar; and the thread, when of fine quality, was sold for its weight in silver.

We are informed by Captain Meadows Taylor that a similar class of yarn is spun in rooms or cellars carefully closed and with the floors kept constantly watered, at Nandair, Dhunwarum, Narainpett, and other places near Hydrabad in the Deccan.

**No. 226, Vol. VI., is an example of one border—that allowed to come most prominently into sight—being made considerably wider than the other.**

| No. of Vol. | No. of Sample. | Description. | Measurement. Length. | Measurement. Width. | Weight of piece. | Cost. | Place of Manufacture, or where obtained. |
|---|---|---|---|---|---|---|---|
| | | | yds. ins. | yds. ins. | lbs. oz. | £ s. d. | |
| VI. | 222 | Open, gauze-like texture. Blue, with stripes ($\frac{1}{3}$ inch wide, and 1 inch apart) of red, with white edges. Border (1 inch) of red striped with white, yellow, and blue. Has merely a narrow ($\frac{1}{8}$ inch) stripe in principal end. | 3 0 | 0 23 | 0 3 | 0 2 0 | Calcutta. |
| VI. | 223 | Open, gauze-like texture. Blue, with yellow stripes edged with white and red ($\frac{3}{8}$ inch wide, and $\frac{5}{8}$ inch apart). An inch border of red, edged with green at the outer, and with white, blue, and red lines at the inner margins. A few threads of white in both ends. | 2 32 | 0 26 | 0 5½ | 0 2 0 | Calcutta. |
| VI. | 224 | Open, gauze-like texture. Warp of blue and yellow in stripes, $\frac{1}{6}$ inch wide, and $\frac{1}{3}$ inch apart. Weft of crimson. Border, 1¼ inch, stripes of blue, orange, red, and green. Narrow white stripe in each end. | 3 22 | 0 29 | 0 6½ | 0 2 0 | Calcutta. |
| VI. | 225 | Open, gauze-like texture. Red, with $\frac{2}{3}$-inch stripes of green, with $\frac{1}{3}$-inch centre of yellow. Woven the full width. On each side a striped border, 1⅓ inches wide, of dark blue, with pink and white on outer, and orange and white on inner, margin. A $\frac{1}{3}$-inch stripe of yellow across each end. | 3 18 | 0 30 | 0 6 | 0 2 0 | Calcutta. |
| VI. | 226 | Open, gauze-like texture. Dark blue warp, crimson weft. Two borders of different widths. One 11 inches wide with red centre, and blue stripe on outer edge. The other red, but only about 1 inch in width. | 3 18 | 0 29 | 0 6½ | 0 1 9 | Calcutta. |
| VI. | 229 | Open, gauze-like texture. Light green weft and warp. 1-inch border of red, with white lines. Narrow red stripe in principal end. | 2 27 | 0 25 | 0 3 | 0 2 0 | Calcutta. |

## 6. Cotton.—Coloured Thread; Cotton Borders and End.

The examples in this group are described in the following table:—

| No. of Vol. | No. of Sample. | Description. | Measurement. Length. | Measurement. Width. | Weight of piece. | Cost. | Place of Manufacture or where obtained. |
|---|---|---|---|---|---|---|---|
| | | | yds. ins. | yds. ins. | lbs. oz. | £ s. d. | |
| V. | 180 | Cotton, yellow, striped with black lines ½ inch apart. Border (5 inches wide), red, with figured stripes of white in imitation of silver lace. The principal end marked only by double cross lines of black similar to and checking the general pattern stripe. | 8 9 | 1 6 | 2 0 | | Coimbatore, Madras. |
| V. | 181 | Cotton, small blue and green check. Blue thread weft, green thread warp. 2-inch yellow border. Principal end (11 inches) yellow, with narrow cross stripes of blue and green. Opposite end (9½ inches) blue, with $\frac{7}{12}$-inch cross stripe of yellow. The borders of different colours. | 7 9 | 1 4 | 1 8 | 0 5 3 | Pondicherry. Bought in Madras. |

| No. of Vol. | No. of Sample. | Description. | Measurement. Length. | Measurement. Width. | Weight of piece. | Cost. | Place of Manufacture, or where obtained. |
|---|---|---|---|---|---|---|---|
| | | | yds. ins. | yds. ins. | lbs. oz. | £ s. d. | |
| V. | 182 | Cotton, dark chocolate brown. White stripe ($\frac{1}{3}$ inch) in border. One 2-inch and ten narrow cross stripes of white in principal end. One ($\frac{1}{2}$-inch) white stripe in opposite end. | 8 27 | 1 6 | 1 3 | | Arnee. Bought in Madras. |
| V. | 185 | Cotton, yellow, striped with dark blue ($\frac{1}{6}$-inch) lines $\frac{1}{6}$ inch apart. Yellow (3-inch) border, with inch stripe of purple and sundry black lines. Principal end for 15 inches marked by dark blue cross stripes. Strong and durable. Common pattern. | 7 0 | 1 0 | 2 1 | 0 4 3 | Poree Arnee. Bought in Madras. |
| V. | 186 | Cotton, dark blue, striped with yellow. 1-inch yellow border, with blue lines. Principal end, a 4-inch cross stripe of yellow, with $\frac{7}{12}$ inch centre of pinkish red thread. Common material and favourite colour. | 3 18 | 0 27 | 0 10 | 0 1 3 | Congeveram. Bought in Madras. |
| V. | 187 | Cotton, dark blue, with $\frac{1}{8}$-inch stripe of dull red. Border ($2\frac{1}{2}$-inch) formed by yellow and white stripes. The principal end for 13 in. consists of yellow and blue cross stripes. Opposite end marked by a small triple lined cross stripe of yellow near the edge. | 7 0 | 1 0 | 1 10 | 0 2 3 | Bellary. Bought in Madras. |
| V. | 190 | Cotton, white, with dull red stripes $\frac{1}{4}$ inch wide and $\frac{1}{4}$ inch apart. Border ($1\frac{1}{2}$-inch), red thread centre, with yellow edges. Principal end, a check pattern in red and white, with cross stripe ($2\frac{5}{8}$-inch) in deep red and yellow, and nearer end a $\frac{1}{3}$-inch stripe, same colours. Opposite end marked only by a cross line consisting of a few red threads. | 7 28 | 1 4 | 1 3 | 0 4 1 | Arnee. Bought in Madras |
| V. | 191 | Cotton, unbleached, with stripes of reddish tinted threads $\frac{1}{6}$ inch wide and $\frac{1}{6}$ inch apart. Border ($\frac{3}{4}$-inch) chocolate colour, with yellow edge. In principal end a chocolate coloured check, with a $3\frac{3}{4}$-inch cross stripe in same colour, and yellow thread lines. A small chocolate coloured stripe across opposite end. | 5 27 | 1 0 | 1 6 | 0 3 9 | Ventapollam. Bought in Madras. |
| V. | 192 | A rather coarse muslin. A small check formed by lines of a chocolate red colour. Border ($\frac{7}{8}$ inch wide) a red and yellow stripe. Principal end marked by suspension of the chocolate weft line of the pattern, and the introduction of a number of narrow cross stripes and one broad cross stripe of yellow. In opposite end also the check pattern is suspended for about 16 inches, and a single cross stripe of a chocolate red colour woven close to the end. | 9 0 | 1 9 | 2 0 | 0 5 6 | Gangam. Bought in Madras. |
| VI. | 220 | Cotton. Warp and weft red checked, with $\frac{1}{6}$ inch white stripes $\frac{1}{2}$ inch apart in the warp, and $\frac{2}{3}$ inch apart in the weft. 6-inch border of blue, striped at inner edge with yellow. Twelve inches of each end marked by absence of the cross stripes of the check pattern, and occasional substitution of yellow for the red in the weft. | 5 16 | 1 2 | 1 2 | - - - | Gya. |

### 7. COTTON.—COLOURED THREAD; BORDER OF COTTON; SILK IN END.

This group affords the first examples we have as yet seen of Sarees with deep ornamental ends.

It will be observed that the end portion being only required for show, its texture is much closer than that of the body of the garment. By this means the colours employed in the ends are brought out more clearly, while the comfort of the wearer is not interfered with.

**In one case (No. 179, Vol. V.) in order to form the end piece, the original warp threads are entirely discontinued and a new warp is adroitly inserted.**

| No. of | | Description. | Measurement. | | Weight of piece. | Cost. | Place of Manufacture, or where obtained. |
|---|---|---|---|---|---|---|---|
| Vol. | Sample. | | Length. | Width. | | | |
| | | | yds. ins. | yds. ins. | lbs. oz. | £ s. d. | |
| V. | 165 | Reddish chocolate ground, checked with white lines at intervals of half an inch. Border ($3\frac{1}{2}$ inches), figured pattern, woven in coloured cotton thread. At principal end, for 24 inches, a series of yellow silk cross stripes on crimson cotton ground. The opposite end plain chocolate colour, with one narrow cross stripe of yellow. | 7 27 | 1 2 | 1 2 | 0 12 6 | Madras. |
| V. | 166 | Green, checked with orange yellow. Border ($1\frac{3}{8}$ inch wide), yellow, with green and white striped edges. At principal end, for about 19 inches, one 4-inch and several smaller cross stripes of yellow and dark red silk. In the opposite end the check disappears, the warp stripe of yellow only being continued. | 6 18 | 1 0 | 1 6 | 0 5 0 | Sydapet, Madras. |
| V. | 167 | Green, checked with orange yellow, same as last. Border ($1\frac{7}{12}$ inch wide), yellow, edged with blue. Principal end consists of cross stripes in red and white, with 1-inch centre stripe of white silk. Opposite end same as No. 166. | 6 27 | 1 2 | 1 $5\frac{1}{2}$ | 0 4 9 | Madras. |
| V. | 169 | Red, checked with white. Striped borders (2 inches wide) of two different colours. At principal end, several narrow stripes and one $3\frac{1}{2}$ inch cross stripe, all of yellow silk. Opposite end marked by a simple white cross line close to the edge. As in No. 166, the check pattern of the piece is changed near the principal end into a stripe.* | 7 9 | 1 2 | 1 13 | 0 4 6 | Mylapore, bought in Madras. |
| V. | 170 | Crimson, with $\frac{7}{12}$-inch stripes, figured in white thread, running from principal end for about $4\frac{3}{4}$ yards only up the piece. Border (3 inch) of blue, striped with white and yellow warp threads. About 10 inches of principal end ornamented with one wide and a number of narrow cross stripes of yellow silk. Opposite end marked by a simple white cross line near the edge. | 7 27 | 1 2 | 1 7 | 0 12 0 | Cuddalore, bought in Madras. |
| V. | 176 | Dark red, striped with narrow double lines of white $\frac{1}{8}$ of an inch apart. Border ($1\frac{3}{4}$-inch) yellow, faintly striped with green. At 19 inches from principal end, white stripes cease, and the plain dark red ground is ornamented with a series of cross stripes of various breadths in yellow silk. | 7 0 | 1 0 | 0 11 | 0 6 0 | Madras. |
| V. | 177 | Chocolate red, checked by narrow lines of white ($\frac{1}{2}$ inch apart). Border (1-inch) of yellow cotton. Principal end has two cross stripes (one $1\frac{3}{4}$ and one $\frac{3}{4}$ inch) of yellow silk with green cotton. Opposite end marked by a $\frac{1}{2}$-inch stripe of white. | 7 27 | 1 3 | 1 7 | 0 5 0 | Ventapollam, bought in Madras. |
| V. | 178 | Warp, blue, with white stripes. Weft of reddish chocolate. Border ($\frac{3}{8}$ inch wide) of white thread. Principal end (17 inches), consists of cross stripes of dark blue and white cotton, with two 1-inch stripes of white silk, set off with blue and white cotton. Opposite end has merely a double cross line of white. | 7 0 | 0 31 | 0 15 | 0 13 0 | Combaconum, bought in Madras. |

* It will be observed that in some of the specimens it is the small portion of the material attached to the principal end sample which shows the pattern of the body of the piece. In the end which is worn out of sight, the weft colour, which produces the check, is stopped, thus leaving the warp stripes uncrossed.

| No. of Vol. | No. of Sample. | Description. | Measurement. Length. | Measurement. Width. | Weight of piece. | Cost. | Place of Manufacture, or where obtained. |
|---|---|---|---|---|---|---|---|
| | | | yds. ins. | yds. ins. | lbs. oz. | £ s. d. | |
| V. | 179 | Green, with $\frac{1}{12}$-inch stripes, figured in white thread, running up the piece for about $4\frac{3}{4}$ yards only. Border ($3\frac{1}{2}$ inch) in white and orange threads of gold and silver lace pattern, of which the stripes in the body of the piece are probably also an imitation. About 32 inches of the principal end consists of crimson cotton, ornamented with a series of plain and figured cross stripes in yellow silk. To form this end, the green, white, and orange warp threads are discontinued, and a new warp of crimson thread inserted. Opposite end of plain green, marked only by a narrow yellow stripe. | 7 27 | 1 2 | 1 7 | 0 12 0 | Cuddalore, bought in Madras. |
| V. | 183 | Rose red, checked with dark blue. $1\frac{3}{4}$ inch yellow border. In principal end cross stripes of yellow silk. Opposite end marked only by a narrow black and yellow cross stripe close to edge. | 8 0 | 1 4 | 1 8 | 0 5 6 | Sydapet, bought in Madras. |
| V. | 184 | Dark blue. Large check, formed by narrow double-line stripes of yellow, with a flashed white spot in centre of each check. Border ($1\frac{1}{4}$ inch), yellow stripe. At principal end two stripes of deep crimson silk with white cotton. Close to edge a $\frac{3}{8}$-inch stripe of yellow. At opposite end a few stripes of yellow. | 8 0 | 1 3 | 1 12 | 0 3 9 | Ventapollam, bought in Madras. |

## 8. Cotton.—Coloured Thread; Silk Borders; Silk in End.

| No. of Vol. | No. of Sample. | Description. | Measurement. Length. | Measurement. Width. | Weight of piece. | Cost. | Place of Manufacture, or where obtained. |
|---|---|---|---|---|---|---|---|
| | | | yds. ins. | yds. ins. | lbs. oz. | £ s. d. | |
| V. | 171 | Blue, striped with narrow line of white. Border ($2\frac{1}{4}$ inch) of dark crimson silk, with two white stripes in cotton. At principal end three broad cross stripes of dark crimson silk, with two intervening stripes of blue and white cotton. At opposite end a cross stripe ($1\frac{1}{3}$ inch wide) of crimson. | 8 0 | 1 9 | 1 9 | 0 13 0 | Mangalore, bought in Madras. |
| VI. | 213 | Plain chocolate colour. Border ($4\frac{1}{2}$ inches wide) of yellow and crimson silk. Principal end, for 19 inches, of yellow silk, striped with the chocolate cotton of the warp. At the opposite end a $4\frac{1}{4}$-inch cross stripe of yellow silk. | 8 17 | 1 8 | 2 3 | 1 0 0 | Belgaum, Bombay. |
| VI. | 215 | Dark blue. Border ($3\frac{1}{4}$ inch wide) in crimson silk, figured with white, blue, and yellow. Yellow and crimson silk in principal end. Yellow and white cotton cross stripes in opposite end. | 4 16 | 1 3 | 0 11 | 0 4 0 | Surat, Bombay. |
| VI. | 217 | Chocolate, formed by dark crimson weft and blue warp. Border ($5\frac{1}{4}$ inch) of yellow and crimson silk, striped with black and white. Sixteen inches of principal end marked by a weft of yellow silk, with a few narrow cross lines of black. $1\frac{1}{2}$-inch stripe of yellow silk in opposite end. | 8 18 | 1 10 | 2 5 | 0 16 0 | Belgaum, Bombay. |

### 9. Cotton.—Coloured Thread; Silk Borders; Silk and Gold in End.

In Nos. 168, Vol. V., and 216, Vol. VI., gold thread is introduced into the principal end. The silk border of No. 216 affords, like many others from the Dharwar district, an excellent example of quality.

As already stated, it is desirable that in the manufacture of these borders the weft should not be seen through the silk.

No. 168, from Gangam, Madras, a dark red and blue check. Border (5 inch) dark crimson silk, striped with white and yellow and orange silk. Principal end (14 inches) dark crimson silk with four cross stripes of gold thread. Secondary end marked simply by cross stripes of white thread. Length 8 yards, width 1 yard 8 inches, weight 1 lb. 11 oz.; cost 1*l.* 6*s.* 0*d.*

No. 216. Dark blue; border (4¼-inch) of crimson silk with figured stripes of green, white, and yellow silk. Principal end (24 inches) of crimson silk with eight narrow cross stripes of gold thread and white silk. Opposite end, for about 16 inches, of crimson silk, with two 1½-inch cross stripes in white silk.

Length, 8½ yards; width, 1 yard 10 inches; weight, 2 lbs. 2 oz.; cost, 2*l.* 16*s.* 0*d.*

From Belgaum, Bombay.

### 10. Cotton Print.—Printed End.

Under this and the following head (11) are included the examples showing the application of dyeing to the production of end or border patterns.*

No. 367., Vol. X., from Arcot, Madras. Blue ground, with flowered pattern in dark brown, red and white. A cross stripe at one end with flowered design on a chocolate ground. Printed and glazed. Worn by Malay women over the head and shoulders only. Length, 3 yards; width, 1 yard; weight, 12 oz.; price, 1*s.* 6*d.*

No. 371, Vol. X., from Madras, is bleached. Red flowered design enclosing a black sprig of similar pattern. At one end a flowered and scroll pattern printed in red and black. Length, 4½ yards; width, 1 yard; weight, 15 ounces; cost, 4*s.*

* Amongst the piece goods hereafter described we shall find numerous instances of prints which are cut into the requisite lengths to form Sarees, but which are either worn without border and end ornaments, or have these added.

## 11. Cotton Print.—Printed Borders and End.

| Vol. | Sample. | Description. | Measurement. Length. | Measurement. Width. | Weight of piece. | Cost. | Place of Manufacture, or where obtained. |
|---|---|---|---|---|---|---|---|
| | | | yds. ins. | yds. ins. | lbs. oz. | £ s. d. | |
| V. | 196 | Pink ground, with diagonal rows of small red flower within dotted red lines; $1\frac{1}{4}$-inch border in black and red. Principal end (21 inches) ornamented with red and black figured and flowered stripes, among which a deep pine pattern is printed on a plain pink ground. | 8 9 | 1 8 | 1 6 | 0 3 3 | Arcot, bought in Madras. |
| V. | 198 | Coarse. Scarlet ground, with diagonal rows of white spots ($\frac{1}{2}$ inch apart). Of principal end (24 inches) the greater portion is of a bluish black ground, dotted with red and white spots. A flowered pine pattern is also introduced in a 6-inch crimson cross stripe at both ends. | 6 30 | 0 29 | 1 6 | 0 2 $1\frac{1}{2}$ | Cuddapah, bought in Madras |
| V. | 199 | Glazed chintz, flowered pattern, in colours. Border (6 inches) flowered design in colours. Twenty inches of end, chocolate colour, with (12 inch) flowered figures extending from main design towards end of piece. Worn by Malay women for covering shoulders and head. | 2 9 | 1 14 | 0 12 | — | Poonary, bought in Madras. |
| V. | 200 | Glazed chintz. A sexagonal pattern, white and chocolate colour, enclosing a red flower on a light brown ground. Border (6 inches) foliage and flower pattern in colours on a black ground. Twenty inches of end, chocolate colour ground, with (12-inch) flowered figures, extending from main design towards end of piece. Worn by Malay women for covering the shoulders and head. | 2 9 | 1 14 | 0 12 | — | Poonary, bought in Madras. |

## 12. Cotton. Dyed and Printed; Gold Borders and End.

Example No. 197, Vol. V., from Madras. Dark red; diagonal rows of white spots, with red tick in centre. Border of gold thread with Kutar pattern on inner edge. Across principal end, three stripes of gold, of which the widest is an inch. Length, $6\frac{1}{2}$ yards; width, 27 inches; weight, 8 ounces; cost 6*s*.

## 13. Cotton and Silk.—Cotton Borders; Silk Ends.

No. 208, Vol. VI., from Benares, is of crimson cotton with a figure in yellow silk, carried obliquely across the piece. Border $3\frac{1}{4}$ inches wide, with the body pattern repeated in it, but with blue cotton occupying the place of the yellow silk. Principal end (13 inches) of blue cotton with zigzag stripes in yellow silk, and at extreme end a $\frac{1}{3}$-inch stripe of crimson. About 38 inches of opposite end is also blue and of the same pattern, with an inch stripe of red at the end. Length, 4 yds. 28 ins.; width, 34 inches; weight, $8\frac{3}{4}$ ozs.

### 14. Cotton and Silk.—Silk Borders; Silk Ends.

| No. of Vol. | No. of Sample. | Description. | Measurement. Length. | Measurement. Width. | Weight of piece. | Cost. | Place of Manufacture, or where obtained. |
|---|---|---|---|---|---|---|---|
| | | | yds. ins. | yds. ins. | lbs. oz. | £ s. d. | |
| V. | 163 | Check of dark blue cotton and yellow silk. Border (3¼ inch) formed by modification of body pattern. At each end cross stripes of silk, same as that in check. | 7 0 | 1 0 | 1 5 | 0 4 6 | Madras. |
| VI. | 211 | Dark blue cotton striped with lines of fine yellow silk (9 to the inch) border (2 inch) of yellow and crimson silk. Principal end (12½ inches) yellow silk, with two stripes of white silk, each ¾-inch wide. Opposite end marked only by a cross stripe of yellow silk ¾-inch wide. A favourite style of pattern. | 7 32 | 1 5 | 1 13½ | 0 11 0 | Belgaum, Bombay. |
| VI. | 214 | Dark blue cotton, checked by lines of gold-coloured silk (8 to the inch in warp, 6 to the inch in weft.) Border (4½-inch) of crimson with yellow silk at margin. Principal end (18 inches) of rich orange-coloured silk, with two cross stripes of white silk (1 inch wide.) Opposite end marked by a 2-inch cross stripe of yellow silk. | 8 0 | 1 6 | 1 14 | 1 0 0 | Belgaum, Bombay. |
| VI. | 219 | Yellow silk and dark blue cotton stripe. Borders (2⅝-inches wide) of crimson silk, with figured lines in white and yellow silk. The principal end (26 inches) consists entirely of crimson silk, with two 1¼-inch cross stripes in white silk; the blue cotton and yellow silk of the warp being discontinued to make room for the new warp threads of crimson silk. Opposite end marked by a ⅜-inch stripe of crimson across the main pattern. | 7 27 | 1 9 | 2 4 | 1 8 0 | Belgaum, Bombay. |

### 15. Cotton and Silk.—Silk Borders; Silk and Gold in End.

Example No. 172, Vol. V., manufactured at Trichinopoly, but bought in Madras. Dark crimson warp of silk; blue cotton weft; figured with small white flower. Border white silk in imitation of silver lace. At principal end a stripe of gold thread with yellow and red silk stripes at intervals. The secondary end has two stripes of yellow silk. Length of piece, 7¾ yards; width, 1 yd. 5 ins.; weight, 1 lb. 7½ oz.; cost, 1*l.* 1*s.* 0*d.*

### 16. Cotton and Silk.—Gold in Borders and in End.

Example No. 162, Vol. V., made at Tanjore, bought in Madras. Dark crimson; striped with silk of a golden-coloured yellow. Gold border extends for 2 yards from the end, the rest being silk. Principal end (4¼ inches) gold, flowered with coloured silks.

Length, 9 yards; width, 1 yd. 2 ins.; weight, 1 lb. 3 oz.; cost, 1*l.* 5*s.* 0*d.*

### 17. Silk and Cotton, Silk Borders.

In this and the three following groups, the silk predominates over the cotton, so that the fabric has the appearance of being almost entirely silk.

No. 209, Vol. VI., from Benares, warp of crimson and yellow silk in stripes. Weft of dark blue cotton. Striped border of coloured silks.

This fabric and pattern is in common use among the Hindus. The sample has no end ornament as is usual, but one in keeping with the piece itself might be added with advantage.

Length, 9 yards 26 inches; width, 30 inches; weight, 1 lb. 9½ oz.

### 18. Silk and Cotton.—Silk Borders; Silk and Gold in End.

No. 206, Vol. VI., from Nagpore, Berar, is of bright yellow silk, checked with blue and white cotton. Border of crimson silk, with three figured stripes in green, white and yellow silks. Principal end of coloured silk and cotton thread, with two 1½-inch and two ¼-inch stripes of gold thread.

Length of piece, 8 yards 32 inches; width, 1 yard 9½ inches; weight, 1 lb. 7 oz.; cost, 2*l.* 2*s.*

### 19. Silk and Cotton.—Gold in Borders; Gold in End.

No. 207, Vol. VI., from Nagpore, Berar, is a gauze-like material, and the warp consists of yellow and dark crimson silk. Weft, yellow silk and dark crimson coloured cotton.

The borders, crimson silk with gold flowered pattern. In principal end two stripes of gold thread. In opposite end two stripes of white cotton thread.

Length, 9 yards 8 inches; width, 1 yard 9 inches; weight, 1 lb. 3½ oz.; cost, 2*l.* 18*s.*

### 20. Silk.—Silk Borders and End.

This group is represented by No. 174, Vol. V., and No. 210, Vol. VI.

The former comes from Tanjore, Madras, and is of a deep crimson silk checked with white silk. The borders are 7⅔ inches wide, 3 inches being woven in silk in imitation of gold and silver lace, the rest consisting of coloured and figured stripes. The figured stripes at the principal end in this instance extend only to the inner edge of the border which runs through the whole length of the piece. These stripes are green and white, and orange and white alternately, with two rows of small pines in white floss silk. Rather more than a yard of the secondary end consists of coarse yellow silk, with stripes of crimson and white. Length of piece, 8 yards; width, 1 yard 3 inches; weight, 1 lb. 6 oz.; and cost 1*l.* 5*s.*

No. 210, Vol. VI., from Belgaum, in Bombay, is of yellow silk, striped with crimson. The border is of crimson silk, figured with stripes of yellow, white and crimson. One green

FEMALE ATTIRE. MUSLINS, SILK, &c.

line in the border is of cotton. Principal end marked by two 1½-inch cross stripes of white silk.

Length, 7 yards 30 inches; width, 1 yard 6 inches; weight, 1 lb. 15 oz.; cost, 1*l.* 6*s.*

## 21. Silk.—Silk Ends; no Borders.

The examples of this description of garment are included in the following table and all come from Burmah. The patterns and character of the manufacture are peculiar and differ from most of the productions of India proper. The silk used appears to be of fair quality and to be well dyed.

| Vol. | Sample. | Description. | Measurement. Length. | Measurement. Width. | Weight of piece. | Cost. | Place of Manufacture, or where obtained. |
|---|---|---|---|---|---|---|---|
| | | | yds. ins. | yds. ins. | lbs. oz. | £ *s.* *d.* | |
| XIV. | 543 | Silk, with angulated stripes figured in orange, white, yellow, green, and crimson. Woven in plain stripes at centre and ends, the piece being cut in two and sewn together at sides to form garment. | 8 28 | 0 24½ | 1 1¾ | — | Pegu. |
| XIV. | 544 | Silk. Pattern (somewhat similar to, but less elaborate than last-named example) in orange, yellow, white, green, and red, on a dark green ground. About 22 inches of principal end and 11 inches of opposite end, woven in plain stripes of colours same as in body pattern, last example. | 8 28 | 0 25½ | 1 2¼ | — | Pegu. |
| XIV. | 545 | Silk. Pattern, angulated stripes figured in green, yellow, and crimson, on a white ground, very similar in character to the figure of 543, 544. About 20 inches of the principal end, and 15 of opposite end woven in plain coloured stripes. | 8 30 | 0 25 | 1 4 | — | Pegu. |
| XIV. | 547 | Silk. Plain white, green, and crimson stripes. In about 19 inches of end broad cross stripes of white and green 2½ inches wide. | 9 0 | 0 24 | 1 13¼ | — | Pegu. |

## 22. Silk.—Silk Borders; Gold in End.

| Vol. | Sample. | Description. | Measurement. Length. | Measurement. Width. | Weight of piece. | Cost. | Place of Manufacture, or where obtained. |
|---|---|---|---|---|---|---|---|
| | | | yds. ins. | yds. ins. | lbs. oz. | £ *s.* *d.* | |
| V. | 164 | White, figured check towards principal end but plain at opposite one. Border (2¾ inches) of red and yellow silks with "Kutar" pattern in the inner edge. In principal end (23 inches) cross stripes of crimson figured silk with yellow silk and gold thread; terminating with one gold laced stripe 2½ inches wide, and one 2½-inch stripe of crimson figured silk and gold. At opposite end a 1½-inch cross stripe of crimson silk and a double line of same colour nearer end. | 8 18 | 1 12 | 1 15 | 3 10 4 | Berhampore, Gangam, Madras. |

| Vol. | Sample. | Description. | Measurement. Length. | Measurement. Breadth. | Weight of piece. | Cost. | Place of Manufacture, or where obtained. |
|---|---|---|---|---|---|---|---|
| | | | yds. ins. | yds. ins. | lbs. oz. | £ s. d. | |
| V. | 175 | Deep crimson silk. Large check pattern formed by small white silk flashed spots in diagonal rows 1½ inch apart. The borders (2¾ inches) are woven in coloured silks of a gold and silver lace pattern. In the principal end (29 inches) is a series of figured cross stripes in white, green, and yellow silk with two rows of white silk flashed spots of an arrow-headed shape. There are also two stripes of gold on crimson within 4 inches of end. The opposite end is plain deep crimson silk of inferior quality with a single ½-inch cross stripe of yellow. | 8 0 | 1 7 | 1 4 | 1 10 0 | Combaconum, Madras. |
| VI. | 205 | Yellow and green silk check small. Border (6¼ inches) of crimson silk, with yellow, green, and white figured stripes. In principal end (28 inches) the weft stripes of the check are discontinued, and narrow cross stripes of green introduced at intervals of 1½ inches, except in extreme end which consists of a 9-inch stripe of gold thread with flowered edges of coloured silks. Opposite end marked for 5 inches by crimson cross stripes and by modification of check pattern. | 8 29 | 1 12½ | 1 4½ | 3 10 0 | Nagpore, Berar. |
| VI. | 212. | Green, striped with crimson. Border (3 inches) of crimson silk figured with white silk stripes. Principal end (19 inches) plain crimson silk, with two 2⅙-inch cross stripes of gold thread, and, nearer end, a ⅙-inch gold stripe. To form this end, crimson is substituted for the green of the warp as well as for the weft. Opposite end (15 inches) marked by modification of main pattern. | 9 16 | 1 6 | 2 0 | 3 8 0 | Belgaum, Bombay. |

## XXIII.—Silk. Gold Borders; Gold in End.

**No. 161, Vol. V., from Tanjore, Madras, is a gauze material, checked in yellow and crimson. A laced border (5¾ inches wide) of gold thread and coloured silks, extends only seven feet down the piece, the rest of the saree being plain silk.**

**At the principal end there is a broad stripe of gold thread, with four large flowered figures (pine shaped) in coloured silks in it, and there are six smaller but similar figures in an inner stripe.**

**Length,** 8 yards 32 inches ; width, 1 yard 7 inches ; weight, 1 lb. 8¾ oz. ; price 4*l.* 10*s.*

## II. KERCHIEFS FOR HEAD AND SHOULDERS.

Although, as already described, the end of the saree is made to act as a covering for the head, we find in many instances that kerchiefs are specially used for this purpose.

Fig. 28, Pl. V., affords an illustration of the manner in which these are occasionally worn, fastened like a turban with one end falling loose behind. Sometimes they are worn shawl fashion, falling over the shoulders as shown on the female No. 26, Pl. V.

The details given in the table below indicate the character of some of the articles thus employed.

| Vol. | Sample. | Description. | Measurement. Length. | Measurement. Breadth. | Weight of piece. | Cost. | Place of Manufacture, or where obtained. |
|---|---|---|---|---|---|---|---|
| | | | yds. ins. | yds. ins. | lbs. oz. | £ s. d. | |
| X. | 361 | Cotton. Crimson ground, check ½ inch dark blue stripe ½ inch apart. Border on each side formed by modification of pattern. A piece comprises eight kerchiefs. | 0 35 | 0 33 | 0 2½ | 0 0 8 | Coonathoor, Madras. |
| X. | 362 | Cotton. Bright green and crimson Tartan-looking pattern. Fast colours. Eight woven in a piece, similarly to the last example. | 0 30 | 0 28 | 0 3¾ | 0 0 7½ | Coonathoor, Madras. |
| X. | 363 | Cotton. Check pattern. Main check stripe dark brown, with supplemental check of red. Border on each side formed by modification of pattern. Eight woven in a piece. The glaze obtained by rubbing the surface of the fabric with a chank shell. | 1 0 | 1 0 | 0 3⅜ | 0 0 7½ | Venta-pollam, Madras. (363–366) |
| X. | 364 | Cotton. White and black check. Borders formed by modification of pattern. Eight woven in a piece. Like last sample, glazed by means of a chank shell. | 1 0 | 1 0 | 0 3⅜ | 0 0 7½ | |
| X. | 365 | Cotton. Check pattern in red, white, and blue. Borders formed by modification of main pattern. Glazed by rubbing with a chank shell, as in two previous samples. | 1 0 | 1 0 | 0 3½ | 0 0 7½ | |
| X. | 366 | Cotton. Check pattern, white ground with dark blue shaded stripes. Borders formed by modification of main pattern. Glazed by rubbing with a chank shell. | 1 0 | 1 0 | 0 3½ | 0 1 1½ | |
| | | | 1st size. | | | Large size | |
| XII. | 461 | Cotton. Plain with ⅛-inch stripe of red thread in border. Made in two sizes. | 0 27<br>2d size.<br>0 23 | 0 27<br><br>0 23 | — | 0 1 6 | Cundapore, Canara. |
| | | | | | of eight | of eight | |
| XII. | 462 | Cotton. (Plain bleached Calico) with a ¾-inch flowered border printed in red and black. | 0 29 | 0 29 | 1 1 | 0 4 6 | Masulipatum, Madras. |

# PIECE-GOODS.

We have now to consider the varieties of piece-goods employed in the manufacture of made-up articles of dress. The needle is required for the conversion into clothing of a large proportion of the fabrics now to be described; but it must be kept in mind that a proportion by no means insignificant is used for Loongees, Dhotees, and Sarees—that is for the scarf-like garments already described—by being simply cut to the proper lengths, in a few instances ornamental borders and ends being sewed on.*

## MADE-UP GARMENTS.

The articles of attire which we have now to notice are those in which the material has been made to assume various shapes, more in accordance with our European notions of clothing.

We shall in the first instance refer to made-up head-dresses. Commercially speaking, however, these are not important, the quantity of material required for their manufacture being but small. Although the loom-made turban already described forms an important piece of native dress, it does not constitute the only head-dress of the people. On the contrary, among a population comprising innumerable tribes and castes, it may naturally be expected that coverings for the head will be found of every variety of material, form, and ornamentation, —some elegant and some perhaps almost grotesque.

### 1. Made-up Head-dresses.

The skull-cap, made up from various materials, is a common form of head-dress, and is often worn temporarily as a substitute for the more elaborate turban.

Many of the Brahmins in Bhagulpore and also in the South of India, wear a cap of dyed cotton cloth, which sits close to the head and descends with two flaps over the ears; an ugly looking affair, which however, is stated to be the original head-dress of the sacred order.†

Mahomedans sometimes wear the *Taj,* a small conical cap of muslin; and the Brahmins of Sind use the *Arak-chin,* an article of the smoking-cap style, made of white or coloured cotton, and also the *Col,* a cap lined with cotton, with a knob on the top. In the decoration of the skull-cap and smoking-cap forms of head-dress, the Sind Embroiderers produce very effective and tasteful designs, worked in gold, silver, or coloured floss silks, on cloth or velvet; while in Cashmere and Loodianah the shawl pattern and shawl material are often employed. The most gorgeous form of head-dress known in India is probably the bulky *Topee,* formed entirely of gold and silver cloth, and adorned with precious stones. These are made by the Embroiderers of Lucknow, Delhi, and Benares, and are worn only by natives of the highest rank, forming a portion of the *Dress of Honour* which is sometimes presented to persons of distinction by the princes of native courts.

---

* Sewing and embroidering in India is chiefly practised by men, and these in the Northern provinces are mostly Mahomedans, the larger demand on the part of the people of that persuasion for this class of articles having naturally led to their greater expertness as workmen. In the Central and Southern provinces, however, they are nearly exclusively Hindus.

† Buchanan in Martin's "Eastern India." Vol. II. p. 93.

Among the examples of piece goods in this work are classed certain specimens of chintzes, with a peculiar dotted pattern. These are used in making up the mitre-shaped hat of the Parsee, a form of turban frequently recognisable in the busy quarters of London. This peculiar head-dress is made of pasteboard, or other similar stiff and light material, upon which the chintz is stretched and fastened.

The *Sindee Topee* is a cylinder, like an inverted hat, with the brim at the top, and is produced in a variety of colours.

The Moplas of Malabar wear a stiff cap made of twisted silk thread, or of pasteboard, and around this a *Rumal* (or shawl kerchief) is sometimes wound.

Fur caps are also occasionally worn in cold weather, in lieu of the turban or other lighter head-dress—Mahomedan gentlemen using embroidered otter skin (*Sumber-topi*), and Persians the soft black lambskin of Bokhara.

Wool and felt are used in the North and North West. The Guddees, in the Transutlej Division, wear a peculiar conical cap of wool, with long flaps to protect the ears, the front being often decorated with dried flowers, gay feathers, or red seeds threaded like strings of beads. At Simla, the Kunyts wear felt hats and caps, which are sometimes rendered more attractive by the addition of coloured cloth.*

As we have already stated, as a rule, there is no special or made-up head-dress in use among the women of Hindustan,—the end of the Saree or a kerchief being ordinarily employed as a covering for the head. To this, however, there are exceptions, the embroidered skull-cap being occasionally used; whilst in some less civilised parts of the country, as in Kooloo for instance, we find the ladies wearing a small quilted cap of gay chintz, which is adorned with broad chains of berries, beads, and coarse turquoises, and amulets of enamel or china work. This elaborate combination, like the European *bonnet* of the present day, helps to keep in its place the back hair which the owner intertwines with a roll of wool.

### 2. Made-up Body Clothing.

Of articles coming under this head a good general notion will be acquired by examining the illustrations contained in this work.

In Plates I., II., III., IV. the made-up articles shown are (with one exception, No. 24, Pl. IV.), almost entirely of cotton.

In Plate VII. (facing p. 140) coarser woollen fabrics and skins are the materials employed; whilst in Pl. VIII. (facing p. 118) we find garments made of the finer woollen cloths, and of *Kincob*‡ or gold brocade. To the Cashmere shawls which are worn with these brocades, special reference will elsewhere be made.

The standing figure to the left of the centre group No. 4, Pl. I. (facing p. 14), and that to the right, No. 18, Pl. III. (facing p. 22), afford examples of the short Hindu jacket with long, loose sleeves—the material of both is ordinary calico, the second being quilted for use during the cold season.

It will be observed that in the instance in which the front of the jacket is in view the fastening is on the right side. The Hindu fastens his jacket on the right side, while the Mahomedan fastens his on the left, and the two nationalities may almost invariably

* The chief of the Kirghiz tribes at Semipalatinsk, is said to wear a brown conical hat, turned up at the sides, the description indicating a form somewhat like that of the felt *wide-awake* in use in this county.

† As previously stated on the authority of Buchanan (Martin's "Eastern India," Vol. II., p. 699), the needle seems to have been, before the Mahomedan invasion of India, "totally unknown to the Hindus."

‡ *Kinkhaub* is the more correct spelling, but Kincob is the term now commonly used.

be thus known the one from the other, even when the dress, as often happens, is of the same shape and material.*

Fig. 21, Pl. III., shows the ordinary long calico coat now worn by the great majority of well-to-do Hindus. In form this differs but little from the long but somewhat more ample garment which Mahomedans wear.

The standing figure to the left of the group in the centre of Pl. II., and the figures No. 20, Pl. III., and 24, 25, Pl. IV. (facing p. 32), afford additional examples of this article of dress. In the note below will be found the names and descriptions of other garments of the same class either used as upper or as under clothing.†

---

* That in these days, however, there are exceptions to this rule evidence is afforded by the standing figure in the group of Mahomedans—so called in the description which accompanied the original photograph—engaged in the favourite game of chess, in the centre of Pl. II., in which the coat is tied on the right instead of on the left side.

† *Koorta.* This is a loose shirt or under gown worn both by Hindus and Mahomedans. A kind of muslin, called *Kumees* (from the Arabic word *Gumees*, a shirt), manufactured at Dacca, is used for making the finer qualities of this garment. ("Cotton Manufactures of Dacca.")

*Angarkha, Ungurkha, Angrakha, &c.* These names, undoubtedly identical, have been assigned to garments of different characters. Thus one writer states the *Angarkha* to be a sort of shirt worn under the *Jama* and tied in two places on each side of the body; and a close observer of details—Buchanan—says that the *Angrakha* is a short calico vest with sleeves resembling the *Angga* which descends only to the haunches; he states also that the garment, instead of being fastened on both sides, is tied on one side only, viz., on the right by the Hindu, and on the left by the Mahomedan.

Another writer informs us that the *Ungurkha* is a long-skirted gown with long sleeves and closed or covered breasts.

*Minah* and *Angga.* The *Minah* is made of muslin, has sleeves, and is tied across the breast. It descends to below the calf of the leg, and is worn by male Mahomedans in hot weather. The *Angga* is not so long, reaching only to the haunches, and is worn in place of the *Minah.*

*Mirzaee.* An under jacket with long loose sleeves and open cuffs, worn under the *Kuba* by respectable Mahomedans and by upper servants in European employ.

*Kufcha.* An open jacket, differing from the *Mirzaee* in having tight sleeves.

*Kuba.* A long close sort of gown worn by Mahomedans and Hindus. It differs from the *Ungurkha* in being open-breasted, and is worn over the *Mirzaee* or *Koorta.*

*Kaba.* Probably same as the *Kuba.* Described as having very wide sleeves and reaching to the knees. Worn by Mahomedans in place of the *Jama.*

*Jama* or *Jamo.* These names would appear to be given to the outer or dress gown in general wear, in the same manner as the term *Ungurkha* is applied to the under-gown or shirt in its different forms. Buchanan calls the *Jamah* an outer coat of same fashion and material as the *Minah*, but descending to the feet, and states that it forms part of the Mahomedan costume in hot weather. Another writer describes it as having a double-breasted body with loose skirts gathered in close plaits at the waist, and says that it is worn by the higher classes at native courts. In this form it was the ancient court dress of Delhi, where the original Persian (Moghul) pattern was never altered.

*Jaguli.* Mr. Batten, in his report on Kumaon and Gurwhul, describes this as a *Jama* reaching to the knees.

*Chupkan.* A long-skirted gown resembling the *Ungurkha* and the usual dress of respectable male domestics, both Hindu and Mahomedan.

*Duglee, Duglo.* Coats worn by Hindu, Parsee, and Mahomedan males of Western India. The *Duglo* is of cloth.

*Ulba-Joobba.* The Arabian and Persian cloak worn over all other garments. Open in front, and much resembling the English boat-cloak.

*Tubada.* A wide great coat worn by male Hindus.

*Jora.* The Mahomedan dress suit,—comprising,

1. The *Dustar* or *Turban.*
2. The *Nimah.*
3. The *Jamah.*
4. The *Kummerbund.*
5. The *Izar.*

After the jacket or long coat, the article next in importance is the PAEJAMA or TROWSER. It is worn by both sexes, and although its use is as yet greatly confined to the Mahomedan part of the population, the younger members of the Hindu community in the larger towns are beginning to adopt it. In most parts of the country the *Dhotee* is invariably worn under it. As a riding dress the Hindus wear trowsers, but always with the *Dhotee* underneath.

Some Rajput women are said to wear long drawers like the Mahomedans; their use amongst Hindu ladies however, is extremely limited.

The Paejama * is variously made, sometimes wide and free and sometimes tight at the leg and ankle.

The male figures 24 and 25, Pl. IV., and the standing figure to left of the centre group 30 in Pl. V. (facing p. 40) illustrate the first; whilst the figure to the right in same group, and the stalwart devotee, No. 17, Pl. III., show the latter form; the last-named figure also shows a mode of fastening by means of a string tied round the waist.†

Although amongst the female part of the community the use of the trowser is almost entirely confined to those of the Moslem persuasion, we find that the petticoat or skirt, though also of Mahomedan origin, is frequently worn by Hindu women along with the *Saree.*‡

Fig. 26, Pl. V. illustrates what may be termed the simplest form of petticoat. As a rule, it is a garment which is kept within more moderate dimensions than in European countries, but there are instances in which it consumes as many as 60 yards§ of material in the making. It is allowed however to hang in thick dense folds, without any attempt at expansion by mechanical means. The skirt or petticoat shown on the prim-looking dancing girl, No. 31, Pl. V., is of this class.‖

---

* Although this term (*Paejama*), literally leg-clothes, has come to be of pretty general application, strictly speaking it applies only to the loose variety. In the north and east of India the Paejama is for the most part loose. In the central and southern provinces the Paejama is generally tight. By the Mahomedans of Arcot and Southern India generally, a peculiar form of Paejama is used which bulges out at the sides like the European "peg-top" trowsers. *Izar* is in some districts the distinctive name of the kind used by men, and *Turwar* that used to indicate the tight-fitting female trowser, of which the standing figure to right of group 30, in the centre of Pl. V. (facing p. 40), affords an illustration. *Shalwar* and *Gurgi* are two names likewise in use; the former referring to long and the latter to short trowsers or drawers tight at the knee and full above.

† The strings used for this purpose are frequently of a very ornamental character, made of silk net-work like our military sashes, with gold tassels, &c.

‡ Buchanan states (Op. Cit., Vol. II., p. 417) that widows of pure birth are not allowed to use the petticoat, but that those of low caste may.

§ In the India Museum there are two dress-skirts, the one of red and the other of white muslin, which measure respectively 103 and 180 feet in circumference.

‖ *Lahangga*, *Luhinga*, *Ghagra*, and *Peshgeer* are terms used to designate the skirt or petticoat.

*Peshwaz* is the name of a Mahomedan dress reaching to the ankle, and is usually of coloured muslin. The upper portion to the waist is similar to the full dress *Jama*, the lower portion being as much *frilled* as the waistband will carry. The lower part of the skirt is trimmed with bands and flounces of gold lace, and silver and gold tissue; the upper portion being also richly ornamented. This dress is worn by Mahomedan brides, and by Mahomedan ladies on occasions of household festivals; and it forms the invariable costume of Mahomedan dancing women, or of Hindus who dance in the Mahomedan style.

*Peswaj*, however, is given by Buchanan as the name of a gown with sleeves, which reaches to the heels—worn by Mahomedan ladies.

A kind of bodice or close-fitting jacket, of varying dimensions, is now almost universally used by Hindu women. There are, however, one or two districts in which, as before stated, no special needle-made covering for the bosom is worn by *respectable* Hindu women.

The most common form of the bodice worn by Hindu and Mahomedan women, consists of a closely-fitting jacket with short sleeves*, either merely covering the breast or having a back attached to it as well. In the first case the bodice ties behind and the front does not open. In the second, with a back, the ends of the bodice tie in front under the breasts. Another variety of the jacket termed *Koortee* reaches nearly to the waist and sometimes lower, and has very short sleeves. It is worn by Mahomedan women and is frequently used over the former.

Fig. 33, Pl. V., gives a fair idea of the *Cholee* or first variety of bodice, but the sleeves, as there shown, are shorter than is usual among Hindus.

Of the *Koortee* or Mahomedan jacket, with its characteristic short sleeve, no illustration is given.

The figures 34, Pl. V., and those in 35, Pl. VI. (facing p. 50), show the *Cholee* sleeve as most commonly worn by Hindu ladies. As a general rule the sleeve of the Mahomedan cholee reaches less than half-way from the shoulder to the elbow, whereas the Hindu sleeve usually extends just below the elbow.

Our general remarks on the costumes of the people of India may now be considered to be nearly completed—a few observations regarding the application of made-up woollen materials only remaining to be made.

Accordingly, we shall now proceed to describe the *cotton, silk, and other piece goods* employed in the manufacture of the class of garments to which reference has just been made, and in dealing with this part of our subject we shall commence with the finer before proceeding to the coarser materials, though many of the last are, commercially, of most importance.

---

* Called *Kachuree* in some dialects of Western India; the term *Cholee,* although strictly applicable to that which has a back, is the one commonly used.

*Kupissa* or *Kupassa* is the name given to the bodice in Mysore, &c.

Buchanan describes the *Anggiya* as a bodice with very short sleeves, which reaches to the waist, is made of muslin, and is worn under the *Peswaj.* The *Koortee,* by the same authority, is also referred to as having been introduced into Behar from the west.

The *Ungia,* as worn with the petticoat, is closed in front and ties behind. The Cholee, worn with the Saree, on the contrary, is tied in front and closed behind.

Captain Meadows Taylor, to whom we are indebted for some valuable notes under this head of our subject, endorses Buchanan's statement, that before the Mahomedan conquests, the bodice, and other needle-made articles were unknown in India.

## DACCA MUSLINS.

As under this head we shall have occasion to notice the famed and still valued productions of the Dacca loom, we shall here take the opportunity of making some general remarks regarding their *fineness*.

It has long been a subject of interest and doubt whether the finest Dacca muslins have ever been equalled or surpassed by the machine-made muslins of Europe.

An answer has been given to the question by the British manufacturer, who alleges that the hand-spinner of Dacca has produced nothing so fine as some of the examples produced by his machinery. It was asserted, and it has been generally accepted as true, that in the Exhibitions of 1851 and 1862 there were muslins of European make which were finer than anything shown there from India.

Whatever be the state of the case, however, as regards the contest between Dacca and European muslins, *quoad actual* fineness, this at least seems clear—and it is admitted, we believe, by all—that as regards *apparent* fineness India bears the palm. It is said that this is explained by a greater compression of the thread, depending on the peculiar mode of spinning, and by a consequent lessening of its diameter.

We do not think that this fact should be lost sight of. *Apparent* fineness, of course, is not *actual* fineness; but *actual* fineness loses much of its value by seeming coarse. Whether the muslins which disputed with Dacca for the prize were or were not really the finer, it was admitted by our best judges in such matters that they *seemed* not to be so.

In dealing with a vexed question of this kind the first thing to be done is to examine the way in which the relative fineness of the different muslins is practically determined and stated. We cannot show this better than by quoting from a letter which we received from Mr. H. Houldsworth, in February 1864 :—

"It may be useful to repeat here the formula for ascertaining the fineness of yarn when woven. In England it is designated *by the number of hanks in one pound weight of* 7,000 *grs.* A hank is 840 yards, or 30,240 inches. The first step is to count the number of threads of warp and weft in one square inch. This is usually done by the weaver's magnifying glass, which, through an opening of $\frac{1}{2}$ inch, brings the threads in that space distinctly into view. Thus the specimen A B (muslin from Arnee, Madras) counts 40 threads each way in $\frac{1}{2}$ inch, or 80 threads in 1 inch of warp, and 80 of weft, showing that each square inch contains 160 inches of yarn.

$$\text{Thus } \frac{\text{the sq. ins. in the piece} \times 160}{30{,}240} = \text{the hanks in the piece;}$$

and, as the wt. of the piece in grains : the hanks : : 7,000 : No. of the yarn.

Then for A B (the length of which is 15 yds. 18 inches, the width 1 yd. 16 inches, and the weight 6891 grs.),

$$\frac{\overset{\text{Sq. ins. piece.}}{29016} \times \overset{\text{Thds. p. inch.}}{160} \times \overset{\text{inch.}}{7000}}{30240 \times 6891 \text{ grs.}} = \text{No. } 156^{s}.\text{"}$$

Nothing can be more clear or simple than the process here described, but it is, at the same time, very evidently one into which error may easily creep. For instance, if we take two specimens of the same muslin—halving a piece, for example—and if we starch and dress the one half, and leave the other unstarched, by following the manufacturer's method of determining fineness, we shall arrive at the startling conclusion that it is two things at once—that the yarn of which it is *all* made is of *two* distinct qualities. It will be seen that the whole process depends on the determination of the length of yarn in a given weight of cloth; but it is clear that this length will be the same before starching as after, while the weight, on the other hand, will be very different; and this will, of course, affect the estimate of the fineness, and it may do so to a very serious extent.

In the case of the Arnee muslin, which formed the subject of the above calculation, we found the loss in weight, after careful washing, to be 23 per cent., and it would in consequence have the *No.* of its yarn raised from 156 before washing to 203 after washing.

In ascertaining the comparative fineness, therefore, of different woven yarns, this process cannot be safely employed, unless the sizing or starching has been carefully removed from all the specimens examined and compared.

So also it will almost certainly lead to erroneous conclusions if in one muslin the fineness is estimated before, and in another after the yarn is woven. In the first case we find how many hanks or lengths of 840 yards there are in 7,000 grains of yarn, and in the other how many like lengths there are in 7,000 grains of the fabric. But this last will not, or may not, represent 7,000 grains of yarn, but *that weight of a mixture of yarn and size.*

Now it so happens that in assigning those numbers to European muslins which represent their fineness, they have been computed from the yarns before weaving, but the numbers for the Dacca muslins, on the other hand, have always been computed from the fabrics. These last are not nearly so heavily starched as fine European muslins generally are, but still a certain proportion of their weight does consist of size. And this fact has only to be stated to show that the two sets of estimates, when used for purposes of comparison, cannot tell the truth of the matter. If the numbers assigned to Dacca muslins be computed from the examination of the finished fabric, so ought also those for the European—and even then we must take the further and absolutely necessary precaution of having both sets of specimens carefully washed.

Feeling that this dispute as to superiority was really an unsettled thing, we resolved to try to throw some light on it by another mode of inquiry. It was thought this might be done *by a series of determinations of the diameter of the thread, the number of filaments in it, and the diameter of the filaments themselves.* Such measurements could only be ascertained by the aid of the microscope in the hands of persons accustomed to its use, and such assistance was accordingly sought.

Four muslins were selected—two of European and two of Dacca make. Of the European, one was the best exhibited in 1851,* and the other the best exhibited in 1862.† Of those from Dacca, one was the best exhibited in 1862, and the other a still finer one from the India Museum.‡

Each specimen was divided into several portions—and these were given to two skilled observers, who were not told that among the samples sent for examination there were any duplicates. This course was adopted in order to have a thorough test of accuracy in a large comparison of results. Ten sets of measurements for each portion of each specimen were made. In only one case was the discrepancy such as to lead us to conclude that the

---

* Numbered in the Catalogue of the Exhibition as 540s. Of the accuracy of this No., however, there is good reason for doubt.

† Numbered in Catalogue of the Exhibition, 440s. Muslin, manufactured by M. Thivel Michon, of Tavare, from yarn made by H. Houldsworth and Co., of Manchester.

‡ As calculated from the piece these gave 380 and 406 as the Nos. of their yarn.

**observer had made a mistake, probably by an accidental change of sample at one stage of the measurements. The general results bear intrinsic evidence of substantial accuracy—a conclusion which we think a careful examination of the following table will bear out :—**

| Description, &c. | | Diameter of Threads. (Parts of an inch.) | | | Number of Filaments in Thread. | | | Diameter of Filaments in Thread in parts of an inch.† | | |
|---|---|---|---|---|---|---|---|---|---|---|
| | | Minimum. | Maximum. | Mean. | Minimum. | Maximum. | Mean. | Minimum. | Maximum. | Mean. |
| French muslin, manufactured by M. Thibel Michon, of Lavare, from thread of 440's, spun by Thomas Houldsworth & Co. Shown at the International Exhibition of 1862. | 1st sample | ·0020 | ·0040 | ·003000* | 5 | 12 | 8·5* | ·00036 | ·00100 | ·00068* |
| | 2nd ditto | ·0015 | ·003 | ·002200 | 8 | 21 | 12·7 | ·00050 | ·00075 | ·000618 |
| | 3rd ditto | ·00125 | ·003 | ·002025 | 7 | 18 | 11·7 | ·00050 | ·00087 | ·000637 |
| | 4th ditto | ·0015 | ·003 | ·002350 | 10 | 20 | 15·5 | ·00037 | ·00087 | ·000625 |
| | 5th ditto | ·0015 | ·003 | ·002225 | 9 | 26 | 15·8 | ·00050 | ·00087 | ·000687 |
| | **Mean** - | — | — | **·002220** | — | — | **13·8** | — | — | **·0006427** |
| English Muslin, stated to be of 540's yarn. Exhibited in International Exhibition of 1851. | 1st sample | ·0018 | ·0032 | ·0025* | 7 | 14 | 10·5* | ·00030 | ·00084 | ·00057* |
| | 2nd ditto | ·00175 | ·003 | ·00215 | 9 | 23 | 16·7 | ·00050 | ·00075 | ·000575 |
| | 3rd ditto | ·00125 | ·00325 | ·00215 | 7 | 22 | 13·6 | ·00037 | ·00075 | ·000500 |
| | **Mean** - | — | — | **·002167** | — | — | **14·9** | — | — | **·000539** |
| Dacca muslin, *Mulmul Khas* from India Museum. Length, 4 yards.‡ Width, 1 yard. Warp threads per square inch, 100. Weft threads in square inch, 92. Weight of piece, 566·8 grs. Computed No. of yarn in piece, 406's. | 1st sample | ·0014 | ·0032 | ·0023* | 5 | 12 | 8·5* | ·00030 | ·00102 | ·00066* |
| | 2nd ditto | ·001 | ·0025 | ·001625 | 5 | 14 | 9·2 | ·00062 | ·00125 | ·00080 |
| | 3rd ditto | ·00075 | ·002 | ·00135 | 4 | 18 | 8·9 | ·00062 | ·00112 | ·00082 |
| | **Mean** - | — | — | **·001526** | — | — | **9·0** | — | — | **·000803** |
| Dacca muslin, *Mulmul Khas.* Exhibited in Indian section of the International Exhibition of 1862. Length, 10 yds. 12 ins. Width, 1 yard. Warp threads in square inch, 104. Weft threads in square inch, 100. Weight of piece, 1565 grains. Computed No. of yarn in piece, 380's. | 1st sample | ·0015 | ·0035 | ·0025* | 4 | 10 | 7* | ·00038 | ·00098 | ·00068* |
| | 2nd ditto | ·00125 | ·00375 | ·002175 | 5 | 15 | 9 | ·00050 | ·00075 | ·000681 |
| | 3rd ditto | ·00125 | ·00225 | ·001825 | 4 | 12 | 8·1 | ·00062 | ·00087 | ·00095 |
| | 4th ditto | ·001 | ·0025 | ·0017 | 5 | 16 | 8·9 | ·00062 | ·00100 | ·000725 |
| | 5th ditto | .001 | ·0025 | ·001825 | 4 | 17 | 8·8 | ·000375 | ·00100 | ·000725 |
| | **Mean** - | — | — | **·C01896** | — | — | **8·6** | -- | — | **·000719** |

* Those marked thus are the means of the highest and lowest of all the measurements made. The means without the asterisk are calculated from the sum of ten separate measurements. The general means are calculated by using the means marked by the asterisks as one observation, the others being multiplied by ten, and so giving the sum of all the observations from which they are drawn.

† To ascertain this, the size was in each case removed before the separation into filaments was attempted.

‡ This applies to the portion used for experiment; the original length of the piece was 10 yards.

These measurements, so far as they go, lead to the following conclusions :—

1. *That the diameter of the Dacca yarn is less than that of the finest European.* The two finest specimens of the last ever known to have been exhibited, gave ·00222 and ·002167 of an inch, while the two specimens from India gave ·001526 and ·001896 respectively. At first sight this does not appear a great difference, but it is in reality a very appreciable one, and so far as it goes it is distinctly in favour of the Indian fabrics.
2. *That the number of filaments in each thread is considerably smaller in the Dacca than in the European yarns.* The two latter gave 13·8 and 14·9, and the two former 9·0 and 8·6. We were scarcely prepared to find this point of difference so decidedly marked, but no result of the investigation may be more safely accepted as correct.
3. *That the diameter of the ultimate filaments or fibres, of which the cotton of the Dacca yarn consists, is larger than that of the European.* The two last gave ·0006427 inch and ·000539 inch; and the two former ·000803 inch and .000719 inch. Here again the difference is quite decided, and is only in accordance with the results of other investigations into the comparative size of the filaments of Indian and American cotton.

4. *That it appears from the investigation that the superior fineness of Dacca yarn depends chiefly on the fact that it contains a smaller number of filaments.* The mode of spinning—as we shall afterwards find—makes it more compressed, but it is not probable that this greatly affects the result. Even after taking into account the greater thickness of the filaments of the cotton used in Dacca, it is clear, however, that their number, which is so much smaller, must give a finer thread. In other words the eight to nine (8·9 & 9·0) filaments of a diameter of ·000803 and ·000719 as in the best of the two Dacca muslins, must give a thread smaller in size or finer, than the 14 or 15 (13·8 and 14·9) filaments of a diameter of ·0006427 and ·000539 as in the best of the two muslins from Europe.

The measurements of the diameter of the thread were taken from specimens of muslin which were sized, that is in the condition in which they are offered for sale as finished goods. But as it was possible that the sizing might influence these, it was carefully removed from all of them and the measurements repeated.

The results of this part of the investigation are given in the following table:—

| Description. | | Diameter of threads. (Parts of an inch.) | | |
|---|---|---|---|---|
| | | Minimum. | Maximum. | Mean.* |
| French muslin (International Exhibition of 1862). - | 1st sample | ·001 | ·00325 | ·001875 |
| | 2nd ditto | ·00125 | ·00325 | ·001925 |
| | **Mean** | — | — | **·0019** |
| English muslin (International Exhibition of 1851). - | 1st sample | ·001 | ·00275 | ·00180 |
| | 2nd ditto | ·00125 | ·0025 | ·00180 |
| | **Mean** | — | — | **·0018** |
| Dacca muslin (India Museum). - - - - | 1st sample | ·00075 | ·002 | ·00130 |
| | 2nd ditto | ·001 | ·0025 | ·001375 |
| | **Mean** | — | — | **·0013375** |
| Dacca muslin (International Exhibition of 1862). - | 1st sample | ·001 | ·00225 | ·00155 |
| | 2nd ditto | ·001 | ·00225 | ·001575 |
| | **Mean** | — | — | **·0015625** |

* Calculated from ten separate measurements.

This table shows that it was proper to extend and complete the investigation, and that sizing does really affect the diameter of the thread; but it also shows that the Indian maker is still able to claim the palm—*his yarn being finer than anything yet known to have been produced in Europe.**

* In the International Exhibition of 1862, a few yards of muslin, stated to be of No. 700s yarn, spun by Thomas Houldsworth & Co., of Manchester, were shown. Regarding this specimen, Mr. Houldsworth himself remarked that it was too imperfect for any purpose, except to fix the limits of fineness at which cotton yarn can be woven at all. Regarding the specimens of muslin of 440s yarn, exhibited on the same occasion, and a portion from which formed one of the subjects of the investigation here detailed, Mr. Houldsworth states that he considers these a great advance on any muslin exhibited in 1851, chiefly, he adds, "Owing to the introduction "since then of Neilman's combing machine for cotton, by which the quality of fine yarn has been vastly improved, "and made nearly as perfect as the fibre will admit." (Catalogue of the Indian Department of the International Exhibition of 1862, p. 206.) Mr. Houldsworth's further remarks, on this subject, have such an immediate bearing on what has preceded, that we repeat them here. Referring to the muslin (440s) before named, he continues, "A comparison, however, of this muslin with the Dacca piece, as tested by the eye and feel, *would lead "to the opinion that the Indian piece was the finer.* This arises from the difference in the finishing or getting

The condition of the fibre with reference to the amount of twisting which it receives in the process of spinning, constitutes another element of advantage in favour of the Dacca muslins. The subjoined Table* shows the difference between the two in this respect :—

| Description. | | Number of twists in thread per inch. | | |
|---|---|---|---|---|
| | | Minimum. | Maximum. | Mean.* |
| French muslin (International Exhibition, 1862). | 1st sample | 32 | 172 | 73·2 |
| | 2nd ditto | 46 | 166 | 64·4 |
| | **Mean** | — | — | **68·8** |
| English muslin (International Exhibition, 1851). | 1st sample | 26 | 114 | 55·6 |
| | 2nd ditto | 28 | 146 | 57·6 |
| | **Mean** | — | — | **56·6** |
| Dacca muslin (India Museum). | 1st sample | 64 | 260 | 121·8 |
| | 2nd ditto | 46 | 190 | 98·4 |
| | **Mean** | — | — | **110·1** |
| Dacca muslin (International Exhibition, 1862). | 1st sample | 48 | 196 | 82·8 |
| | 2nd ditto | 38 | 144 | 78·6 |
| | **Mean** | — | — | **80·7** |

* Calculated from the sum of ten separate determinations.

In the case of the two first—the European—we find that the number of twists or turns which each inch of the yarn has received in the process of spinning amounts on the average to only 68·8 and 56·6 as compared with 110·1 and 80·7 in the Indian. This is a most important difference, and one which in all probability affords the key to the very superior *durability* of the *hand-made* over the *machine-made* fabric—it being well known that for *wear* these very fine machine-made muslins of Europe are practically useless, whereas the very finest of the hand-made ones from India are proverbially lasting, and bear frequent washing, which the finest English or European muslins do not.†

"up of the two muslins—the French pieces being got up hard and wiry by means of starch, which coats the threads "and makes them appear coarser than they are ; while the Dacca muslin is soft, and appears perfectly free from all "starch or other dressing. It may also be that the India threads, spun by hand, are more condensed in their "substance by the compression of the fingers in the act of spinning than the machine-spun 440s of the Manchester "yarn."

* These calculations were made by Mr. W. T. Suffolk, to whose care and skill I am indebted for the results in the last Table, as well as for the majority of those in the one preceding it. The determination of the number of twists per inch was effected without taking the fabric to pieces, in order to avoid the chance of untwisting. The muslin was placed in a compressorium, gently drawn straight, and then fixed. The twists were counted in a length of half-an-inch, determined by means of a carefully cut aperture, the figures being, of course, doubled to give the twists per inch. Power used a ⅔-yds. binocular = × 60 diameters.

† It might be thought that the greater length of the fibre of the Sea-island cotton, of which these European muslins are made, would neutralize the advantage arising from the superior twisting of the shorter Indian staple ; the difference in favour of the Indian *spinning* is, however, too great for this to hold good. The shorter staple of the Indian cotton may, however, to some extent, account for *machine-made* fabrics of it being less durable than those composed of the longer staple cottons,—although the difference in the length between India cotton and that of the "Middling Orleans," which before the American civil war constituted the bulk of the cotton used in this country, only amounts on the average to $\frac{1}{10}$th of an inch. Another fact must be kept in mind—the filaments of the Indian cotton being thicker than that of the American (Sea Island) are perhaps *individually* stronger ; and, therefore, although called upon to attribute the greater durability of the Dacca muslins to their better spinning, it is possible that the thickness of the ultimate fibre may have something to do with the matter.

*However viewed, therefore, our manufacturers have something still to do. With all our machinery and wondrous appliances, we have hitherto been unable to produce a fabric which for fineness or utility can equal the "woven air" of Dacca—the product of arrangements which appear rude and primitive, but which in reality are admirably adapted for their purpose.*

These arrangements appear to us of such interest that we shall introduce here a short account of the processes of the Dacca manufactures, and for this purpose shall fully avail ourselves of the information contained in an admirable work on the Cotton Manufactures of Dacca,* which we are able to say was written by James Taylor, Esq. This gentleman sent to the Exhibition of 1851 a series of specimens of the Dacca fabrics, with valuable drawings, and other objects, illustrative of the process of manufacture. Soon after the Exhibition, Mr. Taylor wrote the book referred to as the one from which the following extracts are taken. Those who desire a knowledge of the subject more full and minute than the quotations afford, should consult the work itself. In order to make the description as clear as possible, we have had prepared from the drawings in the India Museum, a lithographic representation—opposite—of the chief processes on a larger scale than those which Mr. Taylor used in illustration of his excellent work.

The passages which we have selected and which we here reproduce, are those which describe the processes of *spinning*, *weaving*, *bleaching*, and *dressing*.

### Spinning.

"The cotton in the state of *kāpās* (*i. e.* seeds and wool unseparated) is cleaned and prepared by the women who spin the yarn. Fragments of the leaves, stalks, and capsules of the plant are carefully picked out with the fingers, and the wool adhering to the seeds is then carded with the jaw-bone of the *boalee* fish (*Siluris boalis*), the teeth of which, being small, recurved, and closely set, act as a fine comb in removing the loose and coarser fibres of the cotton, and all extraneous matter, such as minute particles of earthy and vegetable matter, from it. The Hindoo spinner, with that unwearied patience that characterizes her race, sits down to the laborious task of cleaning with this instrument each separate seed of cotton. Having accomplished this, she proceeds to detach the fibres from the seeds. This is done by placing a small quantity of the combed cotton upon a smooth flat board, made of the wood of the Chalta tree (*Dillenia speciosa*), and then rolling an iron pin backwards and forwards upon it with the hands, in such a manner as to separate the fibres without crushing the seeds. The cotton is next teased with a small hand-bow, formed of a piece of bamboo with two elastic slips of the same material inserted into it, and strung with a cord made of catgut, muga silk, or of plantain or rattan fibres, twisted together. The bamboo slips are moveable within the centre piece, and in proportion to the extent they are drawn out, or pushed back, the tension of the cord is increased or diminished. The cotton having been reduced by the operation of bowing to a state of light downy fleece, is spread out and lapped round a thick wooden roller; and, on the removal of the latter instrument, it is pressed between two flat boards. It is next rolled round a piece of lacquered reed of the size of a quill; and, lastly, is enveloped in the smooth and soft skin of the *cuchia* fish, which serves as a cover to preserve it from dust and from being soiled, whilst it is held in the hand, during the process of spinning."

"The finest thread is spun by women generally under thirty years of age. The spinning apparatus, which is usually contained in a small flat work-basket, not unlike the *calathus* of the

* A Descriptive and Historical Account of the Cotton Manufactures of Dacca in Bengal, by a former Resident of Dacca. Publisher, John Mortimer, 1851.

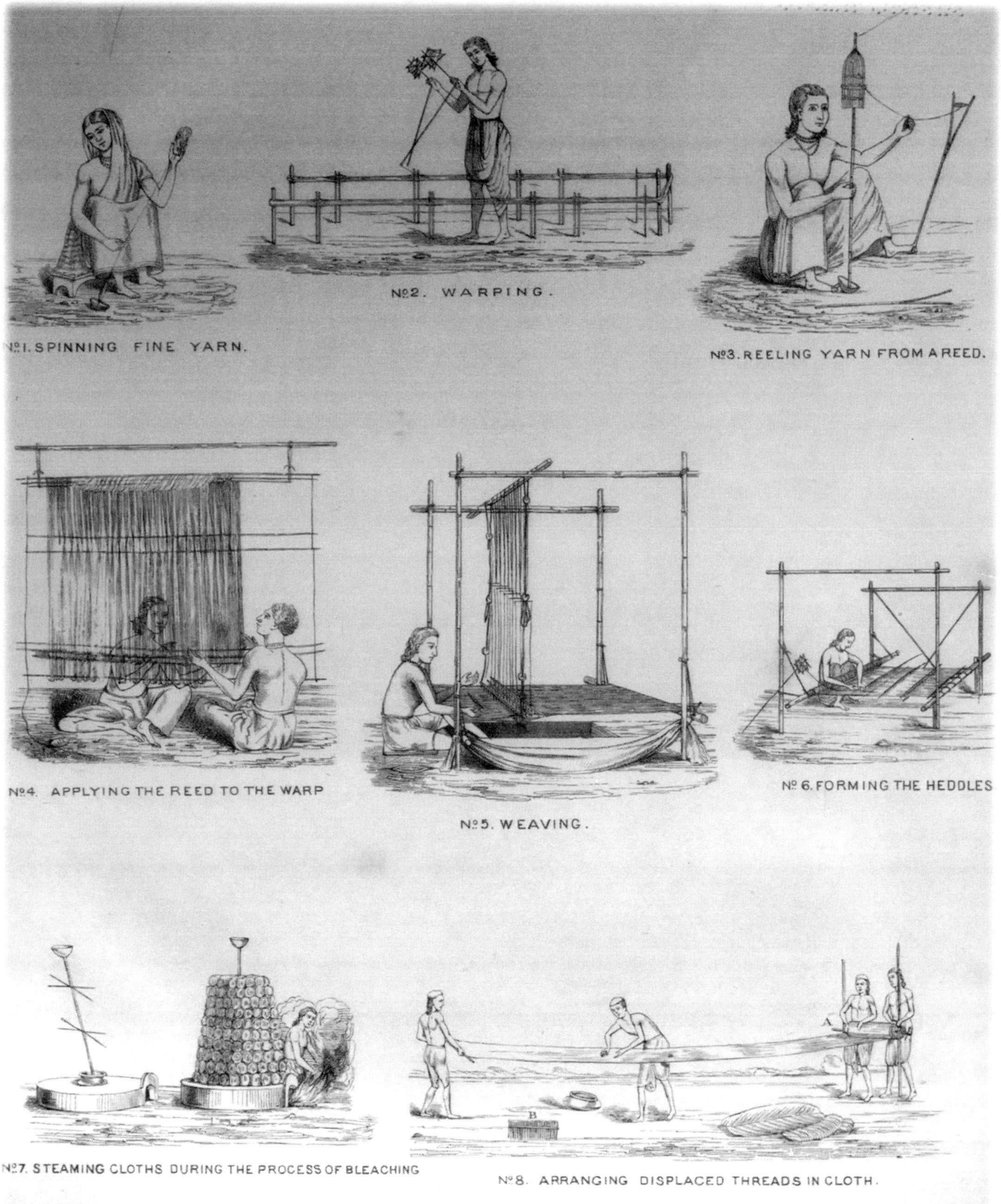


PROCESSES IN THE MANUFACTURE OF DACCA MUSLINS.

ancients, comprises the cylindrical roll of cotton (*pūni*), a delicate iron spindle,* a piece of shell embedded in clay, and a little hollow stone containing chalk-powder, to which the spinner occasionally applies her fingers. The spindle (*tukū'ā*) is not much thicker than a stout needle. It is from ten to fourteen inches in length; and attached to it, near its lower point, is a small ball of unbaked clay, to give it sufficient weight in turning. The spinner (fig. 1, pl. A.) holds it in an inclined position, with its point resting in the hollow of the piece of shell, and turns it between the thumb and forefinger of one hand, while she, at the same time, draws out the single filaments from the roll of cotton held in the other hand, and twists them into yarn upon the spindle. When a certain quantity of the yarn has been spun and collected on this instrument it is wound from it upon a reed. Dryness of the air prevents the filaments of cotton from being sufficiently attenuated or elongated, and is, therefore, unfavourable to the spinning of fine yarn. A certain degree of moisture, combined with a temperature of about 82 degrees, is the condition of the atmosphere best suited to the carrying on of this operation. The Dacca spinners generally work from soon after early dawn to nine or 10 o'clock, A.M., and from three or four in the afternoon till half an hour before sunset. The finest yarn is spun early in the morning before the rising sun dissipates the dew on the grass; or, when this is wanting and the air is unusually dry, it is not unfrequently made over a shallow vessel of water, the evaporation from which imparts the necessary degree of moisture to the filaments of cotton, and enables the spinner to form them into thread.

"The native weavers commonly judge of the fineness of yarn by sight alone. They have no rule or standard for the length of the reels, or instrument by which they can form an estimate of any given weight of thread. The only mode, therefore, of ascertaining the quality of the fine yarn is to weigh the skeins and then measure them on sticks placed in the ground, as in warping—an operation which requires delicate manipulation, and which few except the spinners or weavers themselves can do. Yarn is measured by the *hāth* (cubit), the length of which is stated by the Commercial Resident to be 19¾ inches; and is weighed by the *ruttee*, which is equal to about two grains troy. The standard quality of the yarn used in the manufacture of the muslins formerly sent to the Court of Delhi is said to have been 150 *hāths* in length to one *ruttee* in weight; but was commonly used varied from 140 to 160 *hāths* in length to the above weight—the yarn of 140 *hāths* being employed for the warp, and that of 160 for the weft, of these fabrics. The finest yarn used in the Dacca looms, in the year 1800, did not exceed 140 cubits in length to one *ruttee* in weight. Some, however, is mentioned as having been spun at Sunargong at this time, of the quality of 175 cubits to one *ruttee*. Yarn much finer than this is made at Dacca in the present day. A skein, which a native weaver measured in my presence in 1846, and which was afterwards carefully weighed, proved to be in the proportion of upwards of 250 miles to the pound of cotton. The short fibres of the Dacca cotton, of which the fine thread is made, are not well adapted to spinning by machinery; while, on the other hand, the long, cylindrico-spiral, and more elastic fibres of the American cotton which are best suited to this process, cannot be made into fine yarn with the primitive spindle of the Hindoo. In 1811, a quantity of Sea Island cotton was sent by the Commercial Resident to the different manufacturing stations connected with the Dacca factory for trial, but the spinners were unable to work it into thread, and it was pronounced to be an article unfit for the manufactures of the native looms. The Dacca yarn is said to be softer than mule twist; and I believe it is generally admitted that the fabrics made of it are more durable than muslins manufactured by machinery. The tendency of the fibres to expand from moisture is the criterion by which the native weavers judge of the quality of cotton; and it is mentioned by Mr. Bebb, the Commercial Resident in 1789, as the test which then determined the value of this article as raised in different parts of the district. The cotton which swells the least on bleaching is considered by the weavers as the best, or at least, as the material best suited to the manufacture of fine thread. A common remark among them is, that English yarn swells on bleaching, while Dacca spun thread shrinks and becomes stronger the more frequently it is subjected to that process."

* In some of the eastern districts of Bengal, and in Assam, the spindle is frequently made of a slender piece of bamboo instead of iron.

"A spinner devoting the whole morning to the spindle can make about a half-sicca or tola weight (ninety grains troy) of fine thread in a month. This is considered the maximum quantity. But as spinning is now more a leisure occupation than a professed trade, it is calculated that the average quantity produced in that time, by each of the persons employed in the business, does not much exceed 45 grains weight. Fine thread is weighed either by a small rude balance (*tula*), on the principle of the Roman steel-yard, or in jewellers' scales—the substances used as weights in the latter case being four barleycorns, or a seed of the *Abrus precatorius* (*lāl kūnch*), either of which constitutes a *ruttee*. The price of the finest yarn used in the Dacca looms is eight rupees (16*s.*) per tola weight (180 grains). This is at the rate of about 31*l.* 2*s.* per pound (7,000 grains) avoirdupois."

The steps in the process of weaving "may be described according to the order in which they occur, under the following heads, viz.:—winding and preparing the yarn; warping; applying the reed to the warp; beaming, or applying the warp to the end roll of the loom; preparing the heddles; and lastly, weaving."

## Winding and Preparing the Yarn.

"The yarn when delivered to the weaver is wound on small pieces of reed, or made up in the form of small skeins. The first thing that is done is to steep it in this state in water. It is then reeled in the manner shown in figure 3, Pl. A. A piece of stick is passed through the hollow reed and fixed in the cleft end of a piece of bamboo. The weaver, holding the latter between his toes, draws off the yarn from the reed, which revolves upon the stick through it, and winds it upon the reel, which he holds in the other hand, and whirls round in a small cup of smooth cocoa-nut shell. When the yarn is in the form of a skein, it is put upon a small wheel made of fine splints of bamboo and thread. This is mounted on the end of a stick upon which it is made to revolve, and as the yarn is thus drawn off, it is wound upon the reel."

"The yarn is divided into two portions—viz., a sufficient quantity of the finest of it for the woof (*burna*), and the rest for the warp (*tānā*)."

"The warp thread is steeped for three days in water, which is twice changed daily. On the fourth day it is, after being rinsed, put upon a small wheel, made of splits of reed and thread, and is then reeled—the stick upon which the wheel is mounted being held between the toes, and the reel turned in the manner represented. Skeins of a convenient size having been wound off, are steeped in water, and tightly twisted between two sticks; they are then left upon the sticks and exposed to the sun to dry. They are next untwisted and put into water mixed with fine charcoal-powder, lampblack, or soot scraped from the surface of an earthen cooking vessel. They are kept in this mixture for two days, then rinsed in clear water, wrung out, and hung upon pieces of stick placed in the shade to dry. Each skein having been again reeled, is steeped in water for one night, and is next day opened up and spread over a flat board, upon which it is smoothed with the hand, and rubbed over with a paste or size made of *koie* (paddy or rice, from which the husk has been removed by heated sand), and a small quantity of fine lime mixed with water. Rice, it may be remarked, has formed the basis of the starched used in weaving in India, from remote antiquity. 'Let a weaver,' says Menu, 'who has received ten palas of cotton thread, give them back increased to eleven by the *rice water*, and the like used in weaving, &c., (Menu's 'Institutes,' No. 397.')"

"The skeins after being sized are wound upon large reels, and exposed to the sun—the turns of the thread being widely spread over the surface of the reels in order that they may dry quickly. All the thread is again reeled and sorted preparatory to warping. It is generally divided into three shades of quality—viz., the finest for the right-hand side, the next finest for the left-hand side, and the coarsest for the centre, of the warp. Such is the mode of preparing the yarn for the warp of plain muslins. The yarn for the warp of striped or chequered fabrics, is prepared by twisting a certain number of threads together, namely, two for each stripe of the *doorcea*, and four for that of the *charkanu* muslin, and then sizing and reeling it in the manner above mentioned."

"The yarn for the woof is not prepared till two days previous to the commencement of weaving. A quantity sufficient for one day's work is steeped in water for twenty-four hours. Next day it is rinsed and wound on large reels, and then lightly sized with paste of the same kind as that applied to the warp. From small reels it is wound upon larger ones, and left upon these to dry in the shade. This process of preparing the yarn for the woof is continued daily until the cloth is finished."

## Warping.

"This operation is usually performed in a field or any open spot convenient for the work near the weaver's house. For this purpose, four short bamboo posts are fixed in the ground, at measured distances (varying according to the intended length of the cloth), and several pairs of rods placed between them, the whole forming two parallel rows of rods about four feet apart. The weaver holding a small wheel of warp-yarn in each hand (Fig. 2, pl. A.), passes the latter over one of the posts and then walks along the rows, laying down two threads, and crossing them (by crossing his hands between each pair of rods) until he arrives at the post at the opposite extremity. He retraces his steps from this point, and thus continues to traverse backwards and forwards as many times as there are threads of the warp to be laid down. The small wheels or bobbins on which the warp yarn is wound are made of fine splits of bamboo and thread, and are each attached at a right angle to a short handle, at the end of which there is a *kangch** ring, through which the yarn runs. Two pairs of hand-wheels, one with single, and another with twisted yarn, are used alternately for the warps of striped and chequered muslins."

## Applying the Reed to the Warp.

"The reed is generally applied to the warp after the preceding operation; but sometimes it is not attached until the warp has been fastened to the end roll of the loom. It is made of fine splits of bamboo firmly fixed between ribs of split cane. The finest reed used in the Dacca looms contains only 2,800 dents in a space of 40 inches in length. In order to apply it to the warp, the latter is folded up in the form of a roll or bundle, and suspended from the roof of the weaver's hut, with one end of it unfolded, spread out, and hanging down to within a foot or two from the ground. The reed is then fastened with two slight cords to the bundle and lease rods, and hangs in front of the unfolded portion of the warp. Two workmen seat themselves (Fig. 4, Pl. A), one on each side of the warp. Having cut with a knife a portion of its end loops, the man in front passes an iron wire or sley hook through the first division of the reed to the other workman; and the ends of the two outermost threads being twisted upon it by him, it is drawn back, and the thread thus brought through. In this manner the wire is introduced through all the divisions of the reed in succession, and two threads are drawn through each of them at a time. The ends of the threads are gathered in bunches of five or six, and knotted; and through the loops formed by these knots a small bamboo rod is passed."

* A kind of coarse glass.

### Applying the Warp to the end Roll of the Loom.

"This is done out of doors and generally in the place where the operation of warping is performed. The warp is folded upon the reed in the form of a bundle, and is held by a workman. The end of it is then unfolded, and a thin slip of bamboo having been passed through it, it is received into a longitudinal groove in the end roll (yarn beam), and fastened to it with pieces of string. The end roll rests in two loops of cord attached to two posts, and is turned round with a winch. The warp threads are next arranged. The outermost ones are brought to a distance commensurate with the intended breadth of the cloth, and a portion of the warp being unfolded and put upon the stretch by the person who holds the bundle, two workmen proceed to arrange the threads in its middle. They use a small piece of cane, softened and beaten out at one end into the form of a brush, in order to separate the threads from each other, and then gently tap them with an elastic cane, held in the form of a bow, to bring them into a state of parallelism. The portion of the warp which is thus arranged being carefully wound upon the end roll, another portion is then unrolled and similarly prepared."

### Preparing the Heddles.

"In order to form the heddles, a portion of the warp behind the reed is unfolded and stretched out horizontally in the same manner as it is in the loom. A broad piece of bamboo is then placed edgewise between the threads of the warp, in order that the weaver may have sufficient room to form the loop of the heddles. The reddish coloured twine of which they are made is unwound from a wheel fixed to a post near the weaver, and being passed between the separated threads of the warp to the opposite side, it is fastened to a cane to which is attached an oval piece of wood about eight inches in length. The weaver (fig. 6, Pl. A.) then dips two fingers between the outermost thread of the warp and the one next to it, and brings up a fold or loop of the coloured string which passes upon the inside of the oval piece of wood and is crossed round the cane above. The same process is repeated between every two threads of the warp—the cane and oval piece of wood being gradually moved across the warp as the work proceeds. As two sets of loops are made on each side of the warp, two workmen are generally employed at the same time in forming them. When the loops of one side are finished, the warp is removed from the posts, reversed, and stretched out as before, and then those of the other side are made. By this process the loops of the one side are interlinked with those of the other—the threads of the warp inclosed within them being thereby so placed as either to rise or fall, according as the force applied by the toe of the weaver acts upon the upper or lower loops of the heddles. The canes on which the loops are crossed are fastened by strings to four small bamboo rods—the two upper ones being attached, when placed in the loom, to the slings of the heddles, and the two lower ones to the weights of the treadles."

### The Loom and Operation of Weaving.

"The Indian loom (fig. 5, Pl. A.) is horizontal, and is said by Heeren to resemble that of the ancient Egyptians. At Dacca it is always erected under a roof—either that of the weaver's house, or the cover of a shed built for the purpose. Its lateral standards are four bamboo posts firmly fixed in the ground. They are connected above by side-pieces which support the transverse rods, to which the slings of the lay or batten, and the balances of the heddles, are attached. The warp wound on the end roll (or yarn beam), and having the reed and heddles attached to it, is brought to the loom and fixed to the breast roll (or cloth beam) by a small slip of bamboo, which is passed through the loops of the warp, and received into a longitudinal groove in the beam. Both the end and breast rolls rest either in scooped shoulder-posts, or in strong looped cords attached to the four lateral standards. They are turned round with a winch, and prevented from moving in the opposite direction by a piece of stick, one end of which is inserted into a mortice in the end of the roll, and the other fixed in the ground. The lay or batten consists of two broad flat pieces of wood, grooved on their inner edges for the reception of the reed, which is fixed in its place by iron or wooden pins passed through the ends of the lay. It is suspended from the transverse rod (the counterpart of the cape) above by slings passing through several pieces of sawn shell. By altering the distance between these segments of shell, which is done by lengthening or shortening the intermediate slings, the range of motion of the lay is increased or diminished. The extent of this range of motion regulates, in a great measure, the degree of force which is applied to the weft in weaving; and, as it is necessary to adapt this to the particular texture of the fabric which is to be made, the proper adjustment of this part of the apparatus requires considerable care, and is considered by the weavers as one of the nicest operations connected with the loom. The balances of the heddles, having the slings of the latter attached to their extremities, are equally poised and suspended from the transverse rod above. The treadles are made of pieces of bamboo, and are contained in a pit dug in the ground, of about three feet in length, by two in breadth, and one and a half in depth. The shuttle is made of the light wood of the betel-nut tree (*Areca catechu*), and has spear-shaped iron points. It is from 10 to 14 inches in length, and three quarters of an inch in breadth, and weighs about two ounces. It has a long open space in its centre, in which is longitudinally placed a moveable iron wire, upon which the reed of the weft revolves—the thread passing, as it is thrown off from the latter, through an eye in the side of the shuttle. The temple, or instrument for keeping the cloth on the stretch during the process of weaving, is formed of two rods connected together with cord, and armed at their outer ends with two brass hooks or pins, which are inserted into the edges of the cloth on its under surface."

"The apparatus of the loom being all adjusted, the weaver proceeds to work in the manner shown in the figure. He sits with his right leg bent under him, upon a board or mat placed close to the edge of the pit, and depressing one of the treadles with the great toe of the left foot, and thus forming the shed in the warp above, he passes the shuttle with a slight jerk from one hand to the other, and then strikes home each shot of the weft with the lay. In performing these operations the Hindoo possesses unrivalled skill. Like most of the native artisans of Bengal, the Dacca weaver is of a slender and somewhat delicate form of body. Deficient in physical strength and energy, he is, on the other hand, endowed with fine sensibility of touch, and a nice perception of weight; while he possesses that singular command of muscular action which enables him to use his toes with almost as great effect as his fingers in the exercise of his art. 'The rigid, clumsy fingers of a European,' says Orme, 'would scarcely be able to make a piece of canvass with the instruments which are all that an Indian employs in making a piece of cambric.'* The stretch of the warp in the loom seldom exceeds one yard in length; and the depth of the shed is generally about seven-eighths of an inch. To lessen friction on the threads of the warp during the process of weaving, the shuttle, reed, and lay are all oiled; and to prevent the desiccation of the former in very dry hot weather, a brush made of a tuft of fibres of the *nul* plant (*Arundo karka*) and smeared with mustard oil, is occasionally drawn lightly along their extended surface. When a portion of the cloth, to the extent of 10 or 12 inches, is finished, it is, in order to preserve it from being injured by insects, sprinkled with lime-water, and then rolled upon the cloth-beam, and a portion of the warp unwound from the yarn-beam at the opposite end of the loom. The condition of the atmosphere most favourable to the manufacture

* Fine muslin is meant.

of fine muslins, is that of a temperature of about 82 degrees combined with moisture. The heat and dazzling glare of the sun's rays at mid-day are generally too powerful to admit of the process being carried on at that time, and hence it is a practice among the weavers to work only in the morning and afternoon. The best season for weaving fine muslins is during the months of Assar, Sawan, and Bhadun (from the 13th of May to the 14th of August.) In very dry hot weather it is sometimes necessary, during the operation of weaving, to place beneath the extended yarns of the warp in the loom a few shallow vessels of water, the evaporation from which keeps the threads moist and prevents them from breaking. Doubtless, it is this practice which has given rise to the erroneous notion that Dacca muslins are sometimes woven under water. The time required for the manufacture of a piece of muslin of the usual dimensions (20 yards in length by 1 in breadth) necessarily depends on the quality of the fabric, and the expertness of the weaver employed in making it. In this latter respect there exists great diversity—natural aptitude, hereditary instruction, and constant practice enabling individuals, as they possess these several advantages to a greater or less extent, to attain to different degrees of excellence in the art. In general, the weavers of the different manufacturing stations of the district confine their industry to the weaving of certain kinds of fabrics; but, notwithstanding the degree of tact and manual dexterity suited to their particular work, which they thus acquire from this subdivision of the business, there is yet a considerable difference displayed by the workmen in each department, both in regard to the quantity of work of a certain quality which they are individually capable of producing, and the length of time which they require for doing it. On the subject of the time usually occupied in weaving different fabrics, the Commercial Resident states :—‘ The preparation of the *tānā* or warp thread of a full piece of plain or striped cloth of the Dacca station employs two men, according to the quality of the thread, from 10 to 30 days. The weaving of such cloth employs two persons, one to weave, the other to prepare thread and attend the loom—if of the ordinary or middling plain assortments, from 10 to 15 days—if of the fine, 20—the superfine, 30—the fine superfine, from 40 to 45—and if the cloth be of the fine superfine *dooreas* or *charkana* assortments, 60 days. At other stations, where cloths of higher or less value are made, the time requisite for manufacturing them is proportionally increased or diminished. A half piece of *mulmul khas* or of *Circar Ali* of the finest kind, costing from 70 to 80 rupees, cannot be manufactured in less than five or six months. A whole piece of Narainpore *jehazy* muslin, costing two rupees, can be made in the course of eight days.’ ”

## Bleaching.—Dressing.—Packing.

“ The process of bleaching is carried on in the suburbs of the town of Dacca. Abul Fazul mentions a place called Catarashoonda, in Sunargong, that was celebrated in his time for its water, which gave a peculiar whiteness to the cloths that were washed in it. A similar property is ascribed at the present day to the water found in the vicinity of Dacca, extending from Naraindeah, the place where bleaching is now principally practised, to Tezgong, about four miles distant from it. At the latter station the English, Dutch, and French had extensive bleaching grounds during the time they had factories here, but on the extinction of the foreign trade of the place Tezgong was soon deserted, and is now, to a great extent, overrun with jungle.”

“ The water used in washing cloths at Naraindeah, is taken from wells on the bleaching-ground. In the rainy season, when the rivers are high or full, it percolates through the intervening fine strata of sand, and rises in the wells to within 4 or 5 feet from the surface of the ground ; but in the dry season, when the former are low, it sinks to a depth of about 18 feet, and is frequently thick and muddy and unfit for washing. Cloths are first steeped in large semicircular earthen vessels (*gumlas*), answering the purpose of tubs in this country, and are then beaten, in their wet state, upon a board, the surface of which is generally cut into transverse parallel furrows. This mode of washing has been practised in India from remote antiquity, as appears from an institute of Menu, where it is stated :—' Let a washerman wash the cloths of his employer, little and little, or piece by piece, and not hastily, upon a smooth board of salmali wood.' (Inst. 398.) Fine muslins, however, are not subjected to this rough process, but are merely steeped in water. All sorts of cloths, of whatever texture they may be, are next immersed for some hours in an alkaline ley, composed of soap* and *sajee matee* (impure carbonate of soda). They are then spread over the grass and occasionally sprinkled with water, and when half dried are removed to the boiling-house in order to be steamed. The boiler used for this purpose is an earthen vessel, having a very wide mouth, and of a size capable of containing about 8 or 10 gallons of water. It is placed over a small excavation in the ground, and built up with clay, so as to form a broad flat surface around its neck (fig. 7, Pl. A, facing p. 64), having at one part a slanting opening or passage leading to the excavation below. A hollow bamboo, or reed, fitted with a cup or funnel made of cocoa-nut shell, serves as a tube through which the water is poured into the vessel. The cloths are twisted into the form of loose bundles, and placed upon the broad clay platform, on a level with the neck of the boiler. They are arranged in circular layers, one above the other, around the bamboo tube, which is kept in an upright position by means of the transverse supporters projecting from it, the whole forming a conical pile that rises to a height of 5 or 6 feet above the boiler. The fire is kindled in the excavation below, and as the ebullition of the water proceeds the steam rises through the wide mouth of the vessel, and diffuses itself through the mass of cloths above, swelling by its high temperature the threads of the latter, and allowing the alkali still adhering to them to penetrate more completely into their fibres, and seize on the colouring matter of the cotton.† The operation of steaming is commenced in the evening, and continued all night till the following morning. The cloths are then removed from the boiler, steeped in alkaline ley, and spread over the grass as on the preceding day, and again steamed at night. These alternate processes of *bucking* and *crofting*, as they are technically called, during the day, and of steaming at night, are repeated for 10 or 12 days until the cloths are perfectly bleached. After the last steaming, they are steeped in clear filtered water, acidulated with lime juice in the proportion generally of one large lime to each piece of cloth. Lime juice has long been used in bleaching in all parts of India. Tavernier states that Baroach was celebrated in his time as a bleaching station, on account of its extensive meadows, and the large quantities of lemons raised there; and he further remarks that, ' Throughout the territory of the Great Mogul they make use of the juice of citrons to whiten their calicuts, whereby they make them sometimes so white that they dazzle the sight." Mixed fabrics of cotton and *muga* silk are steeped in water mixed with lime-juice and coarse sugar, which latter article is said to have the effect of brightening the natural colour of the silk. The best season for bleaching is from July to November. At this time the water is clear and pure, and gales, or gusts of wind carrying dust seldom occur to interfere with the drying of the cloths

---

* "Soap appears to have been introduced into India by the Mahomedans, who are still the principal, if not the sole manufacturers of it in Bengal. The Hindoos formerly used, as they still do, a lixivium formed from the ashes of different plants, particularly the plantain tree, in washing clothes. The Indian name of soap—*saboon*—is an Arabic word, and appears to be the origin of *sabun*, which, according to Dr. Clarke, is the name given to soap in the Crimea; and of *savun*, which the same writer also states is applied to it at Genoa.—(*See* Dr. Clarke's "Travels in Russia and on the Don.") The soap manufactured at Dacca is considered the best in Bengal, and was formerly an article of export to different parts of India, Bassora, Jidda, &c. It is composed of the following materials, viz. :—Shell lime, 10 maunds; sajee matee, 16 maunds; common salt, 15 maunds; sesamum oil, 12 maunds; goat's suet, 15 seers."

† "The process of bleaching linen by steam is said to be practised with great success in France. It was brought from the Levant, and was first made known to the public by Chaptal."—(*See* Webster and Parkes's "Encyclopædia of Domestic Economy.")

on the grass. Fine thin fabrics exposed to a strong sun at this season of the year are dried in three-quarters of an hour; cloths of a medium texture, in an hour and and a half; and stout fabrics, in three hours."

"The bleachers are all Hindoos of the caste of *Dhobee* (washermen.) The more wealthy individuals of the class are generally either the proprietors or the renters of the bleach-grounds, and employ a considerable number of washermen, chiefly from Junglebaree, during the bleaching season. The boilers are erected under thatched sheds on the bleaching-field, and there are commonly five or six of them under one roof. Spreading the cloths over the grass or upon bamboo rails was formerly done by a set of workmen called *contadars*, whose business it also was to keep the bleach ground clean, and free of weeds, prickly grass, and whatever tended to injure the cloths. Since the abolition, however, of the Company's factory this has ceased to be a separate business, and is now performed by the other workmen employed on the field. The cost of bleaching depends upon the number of times the cloths are steamed. Including the expense of dressing them, it varies from 30 to 160 rupees (3*l.* to 16*l.*) per 100 pieces."

## Dressing.

"The cloths having been bleached are *dressed* by workmen, who practise the several arts included under that head as distinct trades.

"*Nurdeeahs* arrange the threads of cloths that happen to be displaced during bleaching. They work in the manner shown in fig. 8, Pl. A. The cloth wound upon a roller (*nurd*) is placed between two posts on the bleaching-ground, and is unrolled and carefully examined. The damaged portion of it is then stretched out, and being wetted with water, an instrument like a comb, formed of the spines of the Nagphunee plant (*Cactus indicus*) is drawn lightly along the surface of the displaced threads in order to bring them into their proper places.

"*Rafu-gars* are darners, who repair cloths that have been damaged during bleaching. They join broken threads, remove knots from threads, &c.

"*Rafu-gari* (darning) is a branch of needlework in which Mahomedans display a degree of manual dexterity almost equal to that exhibited by the Hindoos in weaving. An expert *Rafugar* can extract a thread 20 yards long from a piece of the finest muslin of the same dimensions, and replace it with one of the finest quality. This operation, which is called *choonae*, or "picking out a thread," is generally done when a coarse thread is discovered in a web of muslin after bleaching. The *Rafugars* are principally employed in repairing cloths that have been injured during bleaching, in removing weavers' knots from threads, joining broken threads, forming the gold and silver headings on cloths, and sewing the private marks of manufacturers upon cloths before they are sent to be bleached. Most of them are addicted to the use of opium, and generally execute the finest work whilst they are under the influence of this drug. They constitute a distinct class of workmen or Mahomedan guild, and are governed in all matters relating to their business by two elders or chiefs, elected to the office for life, and who preside at their deliberations. They admit none but their descendants in the male line as apprentices into their fraternity. The number of their houses or families at Dacca is estimated at 150.

"*Dagh-dhobees* are washermen who remove spots and stains from muslins. They use the juice of the amroola plant (*Oxalis corniculata*), which is described as yielding an acid like that of sorrel, to take out iron marks; and a composition of ghee, lime, and mineral alkali to efface stains and discolorations, such as are produced by decayed leaves and the plants called Neelbundee and Cuchu.

"*Koondegurs* are workmen who beetle cloths. Muslins are beaten with smooth chank shells

(*Voluta gravis*, Linn.); and cloths of a stout texture with a mallet, upon a block of tamarind wood, rice-water being sprinkled over them during the operation.

"*Istreewallahs* are cloth-ironers. The very fine plain and flowered assortments of fabrics are ironed between sheets of paper. This work is done only by Mahomedans, and appears to have been introduced into India by them.

"The cloths are folded by the *Nurdeeahs*, and then piled up and formed into bales, which are compressed by workmen called *Bustabunds*. This is done by placing them between flat boards, tied together by strong ropes, and tightly twisting the latter with pieces of stick. The ancient mode of packing fine muslins was to inclose them in the hollow joints of bamboo, one of which, forming a tube about 18 inches in length and 1 inch in diameter, was sufficiently large to contain a piece of muslin 22 English yards long and 1 broad. The cylindrical cases of this kind in which the *mulboos khas* muslins were sent to Delhi were lacquered and gilded; and when brought into Dacca from the Government weaving establishments at the *aurungs*, were paraded in great state (as was the case with all articles intended as offerings to the Emperor) through the streets of the town to the residence of the Nawaub prior to their despatch to Court. This mode of presenting muslins to persons of distinction is somewhat similar to that mentioned by Tavernier, who states that Mahomed Ali Beg, on returning to Persia from India, where he had been an ambassador, presented to the King a cocoa-nut shell, about the size of an ostrich egg, studded with pearls; and that on opening it it was found to contain a turban of Indian muslin 60 cubits long."

This concludes our quotation from Mr. Taylor's interesting work. Before proceeding to describe the specimens themselves, we would here offer some observations on the subject of

## SIZING.

Of the cotton goods sent from this country to India a considerable quantity is found to be *mildewed* either on arrival there or soon after. It need scarcely be said that this is a fact of importance, and one which seriously interferes with the success of trade operations.

Efforts have been made to account for it, and the general opinion arrived at is, that it depends on the presence of certain salts in the size used by the British manufacturer. It is not our purpose, however, to enter into any examination of the matter here, and we make these general remarks simply as an introduction to some others regarding the mode of sizing as practised by the native manufacturers of India, in the expectation that what we say may prove suggestive, and in that way, perhaps, of practical utility.

Nothing can be simpler or purer than the size used by the native manufacturer, which may be described as usually consisting of *rice-water*, or, in other words, of starch.

In the case of the Dacca muslins, we know that the rice is treated in a peculiar manner, being parched in hot sand before the removal of its husk, and by that process having its starch probably converted into dextrine. Nothing is added to it except a small quantity of fine lime. It will be observed that it contains neither soaps, nor oleaginous matters, nor other drugs, as is generally the case with the sizing used by the British manufacturer.

No native-made goods are sold by weight, so that there is no inducement to size heavily, and *thus sell starch at the price of manufactured cotton.*

**It is a point of interest, however, and may be one of value, to ascertain what amount of sizing native goods actually contain, and accordingly we submitted a number of samples to examination. The results of this investigation will be found in the following table:—**

| Samples in Fabric Books. Vol. | No. | Description. | Per-centage of weight of fabric which consisted of size. |
|---|---|---|---|
| II. | 78 | COTTON LOONGEE.* | 2·75 |
| „ | 70 | Ditto | 7·67 |
| „ | 59 | Ditto | 9·3 |
| „ | 62 | Ditto | 9·66 |
| „ | 50 | Ditto | 9·72 |
| „ | 80 | Ditto | 12·7 |
| „ | 75 | Ditto | 13·5 |
| „ | 74 | Ditto | 13·52 |
| „ | 52 | Ditto | 15·3 |
| V. | 167 | COTTON SAREE.* | 6·65 |
| „ | 194 | Ditto | 6·94 |
| „ | 170 | Ditto | 9·9 |
| „ | 168 | Ditto | 9·28 |
| „ | 198 | Ditto | 9·56 |
| „ | 197 | Ditto | 10·37 |
| „ | 186 | Ditto | 11·88 |
| „ | 171 | Ditto | 12·89 |
| „ | 187 | Ditto | 13·4 |
| IX. | 331 | MUSLIN, loom-embroidered | 3·8 |
| „ | 330 | Ditto ditto | 4·6 |
| „ | 328 | Ditto Charkhana | 7·8 |
| „ | 325 | Ditto ditto | 7·14 |
| VIII. | 284 | Ditto Chundaree (unbleached) | 9·42 |
| IX. | 322 | Ditto Arnee. Fine quality. | 13·1 |
| „ | 345 | Ditto ditto | 17·71 |
| „ | 329 | Ditto Charkhana | 18·46 |
| „ | 347 | Ditto ditto | 20·9 |
| — | — | Ditto Arnee. Superfine quality. | 23·78 |
| XII. | 464 | CALICO. *Watered Isree.* | 2·19 |
| „ | 468 | Ditto, coarse | 2·99 |
| „ | 471 | Ditto *Dungary cloth.* | 7·02 |
| „ | 463 | Ditto, fine, from Rajahmundry | 9·2 |
| „ | 473 | Ditto *Dungaree* | 13·8 |

* Size determined in portion cut from centre of piece, *i.e.*, excluding borders and ends.

It will be seen from the foregoing table that the quantity of size used by the native manufacturer varies considerably, and that not in one class of goods only but in all classes. Some of the Loongees and Sarees gave as much as 12 to 15 per cent. of their weight as starch, while others yielded only 3 to 6 per cent. The details tabulated above are the results of a series of careful observations, and to persons interested in the subject will probably prove worthy of study.

Our plan leads us now to the detailed account of the various piece goods, specimens of which are contained in the 18 volumes to which this work forms a key, and, undoubtedly, the first in point of interest are the muslins.

## MUSLINS.

These are of various qualities, and go under different designations. We shall arrange them in groups, and begin with

### 1. Muslins.—Fine; Plain; White.

A large proportion of these, and certainly the most famous of them, are manufactured at Dacca, and thus it happens that we are in the habit of speaking of all the very fine muslins of India as Dacca muslins. But we shall see from the table which follows, that other places in India produce fabrics of extreme delicacy and beauty, though the Dacca weaver has unquestionably the first place, having never as yet been beaten either in India or out of it. No one will examine them, and marvel that they should have received such poetic names as "The Evening Dew, "The Running Water," and "The Woven Air."*

"The common dimensions of a piece of Dacca muslin," says Mr. Taylor,† "are 20 yards in length by one in breadth. The number of threads in the warp is reckoned by the number of dents in the reed used in weaving the fabric; but as two threads pass through each division of this instrument, the actual number is twice that expressed by the weavers. There are more threads in the warp than in the woof—the latter being to the former, in a piece of muslin weighing 20 tolas or siccas (3500 grs.), in the proportion of 9 to 11. One end of the warp is generally fringed, four or five threads being twisted together and knotted; and in this respect it may be remarked the Dacca muslins resemble the mummy-cloths of Egypt, both ends of which have frequently fringed borders, not unlike those of a shawl. The value of a piece of plain muslin is estimated by its length, and the number of threads in the warp, compared with its weight. The greater the length and number of threads, and the less the weight of the piece, the higher is its price. It is seldom, however, that a web of the finest muslin consists wholly of the finest thread which it is possible to spin. It is often difficult to procure a sufficient quantity of this article for the loom; and hence it is a common practice among the weavers to manufacture a piece of what is called the finest muslin of thread of three or more degrees or shades of quality. The very fine muslins of Dacca have always been made to order, and chiefly for persons of rank and wealth in India; and though the demand for them of late years has been extremely limited, compared with what it was in the time of the Mogul court, it has yet proved sufficient to preserve the art of making them from falling into disuse."

The finest of the Dacca muslins go under the name of *Mulmul Khas*, or King's Muslin, and this is the one which has been used in the comparison we have instituted between the finest Indian and the finest European fabrics. It is generally made in half pieces, each measuring 10 yards by 1, and there are usually 1000 to 1800 threads in the warp. As stated in the Table p. 61, the weight of a piece 1 yard wide and 4 yards long was found to be 566 grains, and the weight of another piece, of the same width, but 10 yards 12 inches long, was found to be 1565 grains. The prices of these were at the rate of 1*l.* per yard.

The *Abrawan*, or *Running Water*, is considered the second quality, and a specimen of it will be found in Vol. VII., No. 241.

The specimen in question was cut from a piece which measured 20 yards by one, and weighed 7½ ounces. The price paid for the piece was 6*l.* 4*s.*, or about 6*s.* 2*d.* per yard.

---

* Though a specimen of the finest quality is not given in the Books, yet there are several examples which are certain to excite admiration.

† "Dacca Cotton Manufactures," pp. 42 and 58.

"The Hindoos," says Mr. Bolts, "amuse us with two stories, as instances of the fineness of this muslin. One, that the Emperor Aurungzebe was angry with his daughter for showing her skin through her clothes; whereupon the young princess remonstrated in her justification, that she had seven *jamahs* or suits on; and another, that in the Nabob Allaverdy Khawn's time, a weaver was chastised and turned out of the city of Dacca for his neglect in not preventing his cow from eating up a piece of *Abrooan*, which he had spread and carelessly left on the grass."*

That which is commonly regarded as third in quality is the *Shabnam*, or *Evening Dew*, of which a good specimen will be found in Vol. VII., No. 243. When spread on the ground they say it can scarcely be distinguished from dew on the grass, and hence its fanciful name. The facts regarding this muslin are as follows:—A piece, 19 yards and 14 inches long and 34 inches wide, weighed 6½ ounces. The price paid for it was 64*s.*, or about 3*s.* 3½*d.* per yard.

The *Circar Ali* comes next, and of it also a good specimen is given—No. 242, Vol. VII. It is said to have been formerly manufactured for the Nawaubs of the province. A whole piece of this measured 20 yards, and was 1 yard in width. The weight of this piece was 6¾ ounces, but in this case the price has not been given.

After the *Circar Ali*, in respect of fineness, comes the *Tunzeb*, so far at least as concerns the specimens given in the books; but the *Jungle Khassa* and *Nyansook* are also muslins of considerable beauty. The weight and price of these will be found in the Table.

Other muslins from the Dacca looms are known by the following names:—*Buddun Khas, Kumees, Jhuna* (much worn by dancing women), *Rang, Alaballee*, and *Turudam* (a muslin once imported into this country under the name of *Tarendam*).

The other examples given in the table are the productions of other parts of India. Of these the most celebrated and the best known, after those of Dacca, are the muslins of *Arnee* in Madras. Nos. 322, Vol. IX., and 459, Vol. XII., are beautiful specimens. The piece from which the former was cut measured 15 yards and 18 inches in length, and 52 inches in width, weighed 13 ounces; and cost no less than 12*l.* 5*s.*, or about 15*s.* 9¾*d.* per yard.†

| No. of | | Description. | Measurement. | | | | Weight of piece. | | Cost. | | | Place of Manufacture, or where obtained. |
|---|---|---|---|---|---|---|---|---|---|---|---|---|
| | | | Length. | | Width. | | | | | | | |
| Vol. | Sample. | | yds. | ins. | yds. | ins. | lbs. | oz. | £ | s. | d. | |
| VII. | 241 | *Abrawan*, or *Running Water* - | 20 | 0 | 1 | 0 | 0 | 7½ | 6 | 4 | 0 | Dacca. |
| VII. | 242 | *Circar Ali.* Fine quality - - | 20 | 0 | 1 | 0 | 0 | 6¾ | — | | | ,, |
| VII. | 243 | *Shubnam*, or *Evening Dew* - - | 19 | 14 | 0 | 34 | 0 | 6½ | 3 | 4 | 0 | ,, |
| VII. | 244 | *Tunzeb.* Fine quality - - | 21 | 5 | 1 | 0 | 0 | 12¼ | 5 | 0 | 0 | ,, |
| VII. | 245 | *Nyansook.* Good quality, used for neckerchiefs, &c. | 19 | 18 | 1 | 7 | 1 | 2¼ | 4 | 0 | 0 | ,, |
| VII. | 246 | *Jungle Kharssā.* Good quality - | 21 | 6 | 1 | 5 | 1 | 9¼ | 5 | 2 | 0 | ,, |
| VIII. | 286 | - - - - - - - | 15 | 30 | 1 | 2 | 1 | 2¾ | 0 | 4 | 3 | Shahabad, Patna. |
| IX. | 321 | *Sullah.* Fine quality - - - | 13 | 0 | 1 | 0 | 0 | 9 | 4 | 4 | 0 | Cuddapah, Madras. |
| IX. | 322 | *Sullah.* Superfine quality - - | 15 | 18 | 1 | 16 | 0 | 13 | 12 | 5 | 0 | Arnee, Madras. |
| XII. | 459 | *Chunderkana.* Second quality, for handkerchiefs. | 8 | 0 | 1 | 2 | 0 | 12 | 0 | 18 | 0 | ,, |
| XII. | 460 | Similar to Dacca muslin in softness of texture. | 12 | 0 | 1 | 3 | 0 | 11½ | 0 | 12 | 0 | Hyderabad, Deccan. Bought in Madras. |

* Bolts' "Considerations on the Affairs of India," page 206. From "Cotton Manufactures of Dacca," pp. 44, 45.

† This, however, is probably one of those instances in which the "Committee" had paid an unnaturally high price to the native manufacturers.

## 2. Muslins.—Dooreea, or Striped; White.

The Dooreea, or Striped Muslin, is stated to derive its name from each thread in the stripes being composed of two threads twisted together.

No. 249, Vol. VII., is from Dacca. The length of the piece from which it was cut was 10 yards, the width 1 yard, and it weighed 13¾ oz. Its cost was 1*l.* 4*s.*, or about 2*s.* 4¾*d.* per yard.

The five other examples given in the books and referred to in the Table, are from as many different places, and four of them are admirable examples of their kind.

| No. of Vol. | No. of Sample. | Description. | Measurement. Length. | Measurement. Width. | Weight of piece. | Cost. | Place of Manufacture, or where obtained. |
|---|---|---|---|---|---|---|---|
| | | | yds. ins. | yds. ins. | lbs. oz. | £ *s.* *d.* | |
| VII. | 247 | Bleached. Striped in the loom (eight stripes to the inch). | 13 14 | 0 28 | 0 10½ | — | Gwalior. |
| VII. | 248 | Bleached. Striped in the loom (triple stripes ⅓ inch wide and ⅙ inch apart.) | 10 6 | 1 0 | 0 12½ | — | Radnagore. |
| VII. | 249 | Bleached. Very fine. Striped in the loom. Stripes very fine, 14 to the inch. | 10 0 | 1 0 | 0 13¾ | 1 4 0 | Dacca. |
| VIII. | 281 | Coarse, unbleached. Small ⅛-inch warp stripes, ⅙ inch apart. A piece comprises four lengths of 3 yds. 22 ins. There is a fag between each piece. | 14 18 | 0 30½ | 2 2 | 0 3 6 | Nagpore, Berar. |
| IX. | 323 | *Dorreea Sullah*, bleached. Stripe ⅝ inch wide, and ⅝ in. apart, formed by six narrow lines in the warp, | 10 18 | 0 27 | 0 15 | 0 6 0 | Hyderabad, Deccan. Bought in Madras. |
| IX. | 324 | Good quality, bleached. 1$\frac{1}{12}$-inch stripe, formed by 12 thread lines in the warp. | 14 0 | 1 4 | 1 4 | 0 15 0 | Arnee, Madras. |

### 3. Muslins.—Charkana, or Chequered; White.

The Charkana, or chequered muslins, is, as regards manufacture, very similar to the Dooreea. They differ in the breadth of the stripes, their closeness to each other, and the size of the squares.

These muslins, according to Taylor, are thought to have been "included among the Indian cloths called *diakrossia* in the 'Periplus of the Erythrian Sea'—a term which is rendered *striped* by Apollonius."

Nos. 250 and 251, Vol. VII., from Dacca, and Nos. 327 and 329, Vol. IX., from Arnee, Madras, are admirable examples of their kind. The subjoined table affords the requisite particulars regarding this class of muslins.

| No. of | | Description. | Measurement. | | Weight of piece. | Cost. | Place of Manufacture, or where obtained. |
|---|---|---|---|---|---|---|---|
| Vol. | Sample. | | Length. | Width. | | | |
| | | | yds. ins. | yds. ins. | lbs. oz. | £ s. d. | |
| VII. | 250 | Good quality. Check. A fine lined stripe $\frac{1}{3}$ inch wide, and $\frac{1}{3}$ inch apart in weft and warp. | 9 26 | 0 35½ | 0 15 | 1 0 0 | Dacca. |
| VII. | 251 | Check. A $\frac{3}{4}$-inch lined stripe, $2\frac{1}{8}$ in. apart, in weft and warp. | 9 29 | 1 0 | 0 10½ | 1 0 0 | " |
| VIII. | 282 | Coarse, unbleached. Small check of eight lines to an inch. A piece comprises four lengths of 3 yds. 22½ inches each, woven with a fag between. | 14 18 | 0 24½ | 2 0¾ | 0 3 6 | Nagpore, Berar. |
| IX. | 325 | *Charkana Sullah.* Small check - | 7 0 | 0 33 | 1 4 | 0 5 10 | Arnee, Madras. |
| IX. | 326 | *Charkana Sullah.* Ditto - | 7 0 | 0 34 | 1 1 | 0 5 10 | " |
| IX. | 327 | *Charkana Sullah.* Fine quality. Check. Double line at $\frac{1}{3}$ inch distances. | 10 0 | 1 4 | 0 9 | 1 4 6 | " |
| IX. | 328 | *Charkana Sullah.* Coarse. Check. Double line at $\frac{1}{6}$ inch distances. | 13 0 | 1 2 | 1 14 | 0 8 0 | Nellore, Madras. |
| IX. | 329 | *Charkana Sullah.* Finest quality. Check. $\frac{1}{4}$-inch cross stripe $1\frac{1}{3}$ inch apart. | 15 18 | 1 4 | 1 2 | 4 11 0 | Arnee, Madras. |

## 4. Muslins.—Jamdanee or Figured.

The Jamdanee or loom-figured muslins, from the exquisite delicacy of manipulation which many of them display, may be considered the *chef-d'œuvre* of the Indian weaver. From their complicated designs they have always constituted the most expensive productions of the Dacca loom. Those manufactured for the Emperor Aurungzebe are stated to have cost 31*l.*; whilst some manufactured in 1776 reached the extravagant price of 56*l.* per piece.

The manufacture of the finer Jamdanee muslin was long retained as a monopoly in the hands of Government—the weavers, as stated by Raynal, being forbidden, under pecuniary and corporeal penalties, to sell to any person a piece exceeding the value of 72 livres, or about three guineas. The native and the European merchants were obliged to purchase these muslins through brokers specially appointed by Government. These agents paid a considerable sum annually for the privilege they enjoyed, and in return they charged a per-centage on all the sales made by them.

The following is Taylor's account of the mode of weaving this class of Muslins:—

"In manufacturing figured (*jamdanee*) fabrics, two weavers sit at the loom. They "place the pattern, drawn upon paper, below the warp, and range along the track of the "woof a number of cut threads equal to the flowers or parts of the design intended to "be made; and then, with two small fine-pointed bamboo sticks, they draw each of these "threads between as many threads of the warp as may be equal to the width of the "figure which is to be formed. When all the threads have been brought between the "warp they are drawn close by a stroke of the lay. The shuttle is then passed by one "of the weavers through the shed, and the weft having been driven home, it is returned "by the other weaver. The weavers resume their work with their pointed bamboo sticks, "and repeat the operations with the lay and shuttle in the manner above described, observing "each time to pass the flower threads between a greater or less number of the threads of "the warp, in proportion to the size of the design to be formed."

| No. of | | Description. | Measurement. | | Weight of piece. | Cost. | Place of Manufacture, or where obtained. |
|---|---|---|---|---|---|---|---|
| Vol. | Sample. | | Length. | Width. | | | |
| | | | yds. ins. | yds. ins. | lbs. oz. | £ s. d. | |
| VII. | 253 | Figured pattern, in 1 inch squares closely arranged in diagonal order. | 11 20 | 1 0 | 0 13$\frac{3}{4}$ | 3 18 0 | Dacca. |
| VII. | 254 | Figured diamond shaped pattern intersected by diagonal lines. | 10 0 | 0 31 | 0 11 | 3 18 0 | " |
| VII. | 259 | Vertical stripes, 1$\frac{1}{6}$ inch wide. Flowered diamond pattern with open margins. In space between stripes, flowered diamond-shape spots, at intervals of 1$\frac{3}{4}$ ins., pass in a diagonal direction through the whole piece. | 9 14 usually 10 yds. | 0 33 | 0 11$\frac{1}{5}$ | 3 18 0 | " |

## 5. Muslins.—Woven with Coloured Thread; Striped, Checked, and Figured.

| No. of Vol. | No. of Sample. | | Description. | Measurement. Length. yds. ins. | Measurement. Width. yds. ins. | Weight of piece. lbs. oz. | Cost. £ s. d. | Place of Manufacture, or where obtained. |
|---|---|---|---|---|---|---|---|---|
| IX. | 330 | Striped. | Fine quality. A double stripe, green cotton figure. Angulated. | 15 0 | 0 32 | 1 0 | 1 8 0 | Chicacole, Madras. |
| IX. | 337 | Striped. | Medium quality. A $\frac{5}{8}$ inch stripe formed by 8 pink lines in warp. | 7 0 | 0 32 | 0 9 | 0 3 0 | Arnee, Madras. |
| IX. | 343 | Striped. | Stripes of black thread alternately $\frac{5}{12}$ inch and $\frac{1}{6}$ inch in width. | 13 0 | 1 2 | 1 $4\frac{1}{4}$ | 0 11 0 | Nellore, Madras. |
| IX. | 332 | Checked. | Check formed by $\frac{1}{4}$-inch stripes, $1\frac{1}{2}$ inch apart, alternately pink and green. | 15 0 | 0 39 | 1 $0\frac{1}{2}$ | 0 6 $1\frac{1}{2}$ | Arnee, Madras. |
| IX. | 333 | Checked. | Check formed by $\frac{5}{6}$-inch stripes, 2 ins. apart, alternately pink and green in warp and weft. | 10 0 | 0 32 | 0 $12\frac{1}{2}$ | 0 10 0 | ,, ,, |
| IX. | 334 | Checked. | Check formed by $\frac{2}{3}$-inch pink stripes, $2\frac{3}{4}$ ins. apart. | 15 0 | 1 2 | 1 $3\frac{1}{2}$ | 0 15 0 | ,, ,, |
| IX. | 335 | Checked. | Check formed by a $\frac{1}{2}$-inch stripe of 4 pink lines $1\frac{1}{3}$ inch apart. | 7 0 | 0 30 | 1 0 | 0 4 0 | Chicacole, Madras. |
| IX. | 336 | Checked. | Check formed by $\frac{1}{4}$-inch blue stripes, $1\frac{1}{3}$ ins. apart. | 7 0 | 0 32 | 1 0 | 0 4 0 | ,, |
| IX. | 338 | Checked. | Check formed by narrow red lines, $\frac{1}{6}$-inch apart. | 7 18 | 1 1 | 0 10 | 0 3 0 | Arnee, Madras. |
| IX. | 339 | Checked. | Check formed by narrow red stripes, $\frac{3}{8}$-inch apart. | 7 0 | 0 32 | 0 15 | 0 4 0 | Chicacole, Madras. |
| IX. | 340 | Checked. | Similar to the last, except that the colour is green. | 7 0 | 0 32 | 0 $15\frac{1}{2}$ | 0 4 0 | ,, |
| IX. | 341 | Checked. | Check formed by narrow dark blue stripes, $\frac{3}{4}$ inch apart. | 15 0 | 1 2 | 1 5 | 0 15 0 | Arnee, Madras. |
| IX. | 342 | Checked. | Similar to 341, but in red. - - | 15 0 | 0 30 | 1 3 | 0 6 0 | Chicacole, Madras. |
| VIII. | 308 | Figured. | Pattern, an outline check of blue, every other row of squares being dotted with spots alternately red and blue. | 7 25 | 0 29 | 1 $0\frac{1}{2}$ | — | Benares. |
| VIII. | 309 | Figured. | A small dark blue figure, with crimson centre in diagonal order, and at $\frac{1}{2}$-inch distances. | 8 0 | 1 1 | 1 $1\frac{1}{2}$ | — | Benares. |
| IX. | 331 | Figured. | Figure. Green and crimson flower in diagonal order, at 2 inch distances. | 16 0 | 0 31 | 1 3 | 0 14 0 | Chicacole, Madras. |

## 6. Muslins.—Printed.

| No. of Vol. | No. of Sample. | Description. | Measurement. Length. | Measurement. Width. | Weight of Piece. | Cost. | Place of Manufacture, or where obtained. |
|---|---|---|---|---|---|---|---|
| | | | yds. ins. | yds. ins. | lbs. oz. | £ s. d. | |
| IX. | 344 | Black ground, square red spots, with yellow centres, alternating with triple spots of white. | 4 9 | 1 0 | 0 7 | 0 4 0 | Trichinopoly, Madras. |
| IX. | 345 | Crimson ground, 2-inch squares formed by cross diagonal rows of square green spots, with central dotted circular figure. | 4 18 | 1 0 | 0 7 | 0 4 0 | Ditto. |
| IX. | 346 | Black ground, squares formed by white spots, each square enclosing four square red spots, with yellow centre. | 4 18 | 1 0 | 0 7½ | 0 4 0 | Ditto. |
| IX. | 347 | Crimson ground, irregular squares of yellow spots, each square enclosing four green spots and a circular centre of yellow spots. | 4 18 | 1 0 | 0 6½ | 0 4 0 | Madras. |
| IX. | 348 | Black ground, 1½ inch square, formed by diagonal rows of alternately square spots (red), and triple spot (yellow), with a circular centre figure of white spots. | 4 18 | 1 0 | 0 7½ | 0 5 0 | Ditto. |
| IX. | 349 | Crimson ground, angulated cross stripes of white spots, with square green spots in similar order intervening. | 4 27 | 0 38 | 0 6 | 0 4 0 | Ditto. |
| IX. | 350 | Crimson ground, curved scroll and straight lines of white spots, interspersed with square green spots, with yellow centres. | 4 18 | 1 2 | 0 6½ | 0 4 0 | Cuddapah, Madras. |

## 7. Muslins.—Gold and Silver Printed.

For a description of the process by which this kind of ornamentation is effected, see p. 19. It will be observed that in two of the examples referred to in the table the paint-brush has been employed in order to produce effect.

| No. of Vol. | No. of Sample. | Description. | Measurement. Length. | Measurement. Width. | Weight of Piece. | Cost. | Place of Manufacture, or where obtained. |
|---|---|---|---|---|---|---|---|
| | | | yds. ins. | yds. ins. | lbs. oz. | £ s. d. | |
| VII. | 271 | Plain white muslin, flower printed in gold in diagonal order, at 1½-inch distances. | 9 27 | 1 25 | 1 0 | — | Jeypore, Rajpootana. |
| VII. | 272 | Dyed muslin. Dotted diagonal lines in silver, forming squares, each enclosing a spot of silver, the centre of each spot being dotted (by hand) with a small scarlet spot, *ticked* with black. | 0 33 | 1 5 | 0 3 | 0 4 6 | Hyderabad, Deccan. |
| VII. | 273 | Piece incomplete. Dyed muslin. A star pattern in silver, in diagonal order at 1¼-inch distances, encircled by dotted wreath-shaped pattern. In centre of each flower a dark green and black spot, painted by hand. Border* (1½ in.) a scroll flower pattern, with "Kutar" pattern in inner edge, printed in silver, and striped by hand with green and black. | 0 33 | 1 7 | 0 3 | 0 4 6 | Hyderabad, Deccan. |

* Only some of the examples in the books show this.

## CALICOES, &c.

We have now to speak of the Calicoes and other cotton fabrics, which at one time occupied such an important place in the list of exports from India to this and other European countries.* It is not our purpose to enter here into the question of the value of the trade in textiles now existing between India and other parts of the world, but the facts shown in the following Table are so suggestive that we have been induced to include it in the present work.

As contrasted with the value of the cotton goods imported into India, the value of those exported from it to other countries is comparatively small. It is interesting to observe, however, that during the 15 years comprehended in the Table, the total value of the exports of cotton manufactures from India, so far from declining, has actually increased. It will be observed that the value of the calicoes and yarns she sends to Great Britain varies considerably from year to year, and has, on the whole, diminished. This diminution during the two years 1863-4 and 1864-5 has, however, been much more than balanced by increased exports to China, Arabia, Persia, and other parts.

TABLE showing the VALUE of COTTON GOODS (including TWIST and YARN) exported from India and each Presidency to all parts of the World from 1850–51 to 1864–5.

| Years. | Whence Exported. | Countries to which Exported. | | | | | | | Value of Total Exported to all parts. |
|---|---|---|---|---|---|---|---|---|---|
| | | United Kingdom. | France. | Other parts of Europe. | America. | China. | Arabian and Persian Gulfs. | Other parts. | |
| | | Value. | Value. | Value. | Value. | Value. | Value. | Value. | |
| | | £ | £ | £ | £ | £ | £ | £ | |
| 1850–51 | Bengal | 917 | 4 | — | 942 | 1,289 | 17,364 | 93,403 | 113,919 |
| | Madras | 46,054 | 246 | — | 54 | 12 | 3,261 | 125,106 | 174,733 |
| | Bombay | 1,830 | — | — | — | 1,442 | 267,992 | 77,735 | 348,999 |
| | ALL INDIA | 48,801 | 250 | — | 996 | 2,743 | 288,617 | 296,244 | 637,651 |
| 1851–52 | Bengal | 794 | — | — | 861 | 929 | 11,908 | 103,046 | 117,538 |
| | Madras | 70,163 | — | — | — | 2 | 3,087 | 132,562 | 205,814 |
| | Bombay | 11 | — | — | 1 | 774 | 305,862 | 118,493 | 425,141 |
| | ALL INDIA | 70,968 | — | — | 862 | 1,705 | 320,857 | 354,101 | 748,493 |
| 1852–53 | Bengal | 461 | — | 40 | 1,572 | 8,310 | 13,990 | 99,948 | 124,321 |
| | Madras | 136,095 | 113 | — | 1 | 56 | 1,521 | 123,981 | 261,767 |
| | Bombay | 66 | 112 | — | — | 1,749 | 411,663 | 130,379 | 543,969 |
| | ALL INDIA | 136,622 | 225 | 40 | 1,573 | 10,115 | 427,174 | 354,308 | 930,057 |
| 1853–54 | Bengal | 4,681 | 35 | — | 2,775 | 474 | 16,246 | 16,125 | 40,336 |
| | Madras | 102,607 | — | — | 1 | — | 2,077 | 105,262 | 209,946 |
| | Bombay | 818 | — | — | — | 353 | 363,460 | 154,226 | 518,857 |
| | ALL INDIA | 108,106 | 35 | — | 2,776 | 827 | 381,783 | 275,613 | 769,139 |
| 1854–55 | Bengal | 15,018 | — | — | 270 | 758 | 20,125 | 16,722 | 52,893 |
| | Madras | 68,050 | — | — | — | — | 700 | 114,405 | 183,155 |
| | Bombay | 512 | — | — | — | 3,592 | 392,965 | 183,986 | 581,055 |
| | ALL INDIA | 83,580 | — | — | 270 | 4,350 | 413,790 | 315,113 | 817,103 |
| 1855–56 | Bengal | 1,440 | 814 | 423 | 89 | 1,006 | 11,288 | 16,124 | 31,184 |
| | Madras | 35,410 | 39 | — | 253 | — | 648 | 97,532 | 133,882 |
| | Bombay | 288 | — | — | — | 553 | 431,386 | 181,944 | 614,171 |
| | ALL INDIA | 37,138 | 853 | 423 | 342 | 1,559 | 443,322 | 295,600 | 779,237 |
| 1856–57 | Bengal | 5,352 | 224 | 185 | 104 | 328 | 33,117 | 13,226 | 52,536 |
| | Madras | 39,952 | 42 | — | 40 | 2 | 1,086 | 84,599 | 125,721 |
| | Bombay | 30 | — | — | — | 878 | 493,443 | 208,216 | 702,567 |
| | ALL INDIA | 45,334 | 266 | 185 | 144 | 1,208 | 527,646 | 306,041 | 880,824 |
| 1857–58 | Bengal | 1,504 | 10 | 350 | 345 | 29,210 | 24,939 | 25,315 | 81,673 |
| | Madras | 33,515 | 98 | — | — | — | 1,246 | 94,197 | 129,056 |
| | Bombay | 78 | — | — | — | 2,425 | 428,534 | 167,417 | 598,454 |
| | ALL INDIA | 35,097 | 108 | 350 | 345 | 31,635 | 454,719 | 286,929 | 809,183 |

* Muslins were also exported to a considerable extent.

TABLE showing the VALUE of COTTON GOODS, &c. exported from India from 1850–51 to 1864–65—*continued.*

| Years. | Whence Exported. | Countries to which Exported. | | | | | | | Value of Total Exported to all parts. |
|---|---|---|---|---|---|---|---|---|---|
| | | United Kingdom. | France. | Other parts of Europe. | America. | China. | Arabian and Persian Gulfs. | Other parts. | |
| | | Value. | Value. | Value. | Value. | Value. | Value. | Value. | |
| | | £ | £ | £ | £ | £ | £ | £ | |
| 1858-59 | Bengal | 3,686 | 238 | — | 339 | 229 | 15,677 | 13,651 | 33,820 |
| | Madras | 22,594 | 78 | — | — | — | 987 | 89,460 | 113,119 |
| | Bombay | 17 | — | — | — | 1,198 | 504,836 | 160,614 | 666,665 |
| | ALL INDIA | 26,297 | 316 | — | 339 | 1,427 | 521,500 | 263,725 | 813,604 |
| 1859–60 | Bengal | 1,510 | 167 | 35 | 518 | 4,816 | 10,128 | 9,112 | 26,286 |
| | Madras | 27,284 | 41 | 11 | 1 | — | 801 | 83,609 | 111,747 |
| | Bombay | 310 | — | — | — | 7,558 | 387,813 | 229,872 | 625,553 |
| | ALL INDIA | 29,104 | 208 | 46 | 519 | 12,374 | 398,742 | 322,593 | 763,586 |
| 1860–61 | Bengal | 293 | 5 | — | 246 | 1,185 | 3,885 | 16,762 | 22,376 |
| | Madras | 39,617 | 822 | — | — | 5 | 224 | 82,419 | 123,087 |
| | Bombay | 17 | — | — | — | 9,944 | 433,095 | 190,596 | 633,652 |
| | ALL INDIA | 39,927 | 827 | — | 246 | 11,134 | 437,204 | 289,777 | 779,115 |
| 1861–62 | Bengal | 740 | 156 | — | — | 779 | 8,476 | 10,259 | 20,410 |
| | Madras | 52,070 | 1,162 | — | — | 12 | 1,080 | 91,471 | 145,795 |
| | Bombay | 435 | — | — | — | 6,560 | 359,583 | 213,019 | 579,597 |
| | ALL INDIA | 53,245 | 1,318 | — | — | 7,351 | 369,139 | 314,749 | 745,802 |
| 1862–63 | Bengal | 678 | 33 | — | 179 | 1,345 | 4,935 | 16,708 | 23,878 |
| | Madras | 51,193 | 1,496 | — | — | — | 259 | 79,687 | 132,635 |
| | Bombay | — | — | — | — | 454 | 331,781 | 296,356 | 628,591 |
| | ALL INDIA | 51,871 | 1,529 | — | 179 | 1,799 | 336,975 | 392,751 | 785,104 |
| 1863–64 | Bengal | 904 | 958 | — | 14 | 6,469 | 13,934 | 97,297 | 119,576 |
| | Madras | 23,070 | 802 | — | — | — | 16 | 103,300 | 127,188 |
| | Bombay | 513 | — | — | — | 25,158 | 582,910 | 307,768 | 916,349 |
| | ALL INDIA | 24,487 | 1,760 | — | 14 | 31,627 | 596,860 | 508,365 | 1,163,113 |
| 1864–65 | Bengal | 3,769 | 71 | — | 153 | 5,773 | 2,118 | 66,992 | 78,876 |
| | Madras | 5,573 | 315 | — | — | — | 218 | 90,713 | 96,819 |
| | Bombay | 259 | — | — | — | 29,558 | 542,522 | 295,558 | 867,897 |
| | ALL INDIA | 9,601 | 386 | — | 153 | 35,331 | 544,858 | 453,263 | 1,043,592 |

## CALICOES.—BLEACHED AND UNBLEACHED.

The next Table will be found to give the necessary details connected with the calicoes and other plain cotton fabrics, of which examples are given in the books. The first group in the Table will be found to refer to the common unbleached fabrics which, under names varying in different localities, constitute a large proportion of the clothing of the poor. They are also used for packing goods, and as a covering for the dead, for which last purpose a large quantity is employed both by Hindoos and Mahomedans. These fabrics in Bengal pass under the names of *Garrha* and *Guzee*. In Western and Southern India they are known under the more general term of *Khadi*,* which includes a greater variety in quality of material. The manufacture in India of the commoner of these fabrics is not likely to be affected by competition with European fabrics, for the native-made thread of which they consist can be sold at a less price than any similar yarn as yet exported from this country.

* *Dungaree* is the common Bombay designation.

The second group in the Table includes bleached goods. The first example given, No. 463, Vol. XII., is perhaps as beautiful a specimen of calico as it is possible to produce.*

In this division, likewise, will be found some specimens like the ordinary *Punjum cloths*, which during the last century occupied such a prominent place in the exports from Madras. The usual lengths of such cloths were 36 cubits, or 18 yards, and they varied in width from 38 to 44 inches, 14 lbs. being the common weight. Pieces of half the above-named length were exported under the name of *Salempores.*

| No. of Vol. | No. of Sample. | | Description. | Measurement. Length. | Measurement. Width. | Weight of Piece. | Cost. | Place of Manufacture, or where obtained. |
|---|---|---|---|---|---|---|---|---|
| | | | | yds. ins. | yds. ins. | lbs. oz. | £ s. d. | |
| VIII. | 305 | Unbleached. | Coarse gauze-like fabric, used for Sarees, &c. (piece incomplete). | 2 12 | 1 1 | 0 6¼ | — | Benares. |
| VIII. | 302 | Unbleached. | Coarse (piece incomplete) - - | 2 11½ | 0 28 | 0 8½ | — | Ditto. |
| VIII. | 303 | Unbleached. | Gurrah cloth (ditto) - - | 9 19 | 0 21 | 1 5¾ | — | Ditto. |
| VIII. | 304 | Unbleached. | Coarse - - - - - | 2 14 | 1 0 | 0 12 | — | Ditto. |
| VIII. | 306 | Unbleached. | Gurrah cloth, coarse - - | 2 12 | 0 27 | 0 3¾ | — | Ditto. |
| XII. | 470 | Unbleached. | Punjum cloth - - - | 35 0 | 1 0 | — | 0 9 6 | Vizagapatam, Madras. |
| XII. | 463 | Bleached. | Fine quality, made to order - | 33 0 | 1 0 | 4 14 | 9 0 0 | Rajamundry, Madras. |
| XII. | 464 | Bleached. | Watered Isree, longcloth, good quality | 11 24 | 1 0 | 2 4 | 1 6 0 | Nellore, Madras. |
| XII. | 465 | Bleached. | Isree, plain, longcloth, medium quality | 6 18 | 0 31 | 1 12 | 0 4 0 | Vizagapatam, Madras. |
| XII. | 466 | Bleached. | Punjum cloth (22's), coarse quality - | 10 9 | 1 4 | 2 5 | 0 7 0 | Nellore, Madras. |
| XII. | 467 | Bleached. | Ditto (20's), (ditto) - | 18 18 | 1 2 | 4 14 | 0 18 0 | Vizagapatam, |
| VIII. | 297 | Bleached. | Gurrah cloth, 1st quality - - | 12 18 | 0 28 | 2 12 | 0 4 0 | Agra, N.W. Provinces. |
| VIII. | 299 | Bleached. | Ditto ditto - - | 16 18 | 0 31 | 3 12 | 0 3 0 | Patna. |
| VIII. | 300 | Bleached. | Ditto - - - - | 12 0 | 0 34 | 3 0 | 0 4 0 | Agra. |
| VIII. | 301 | Bleached. | Dhootee cloth - - - | 4 12 | 1 0 | 1 4 | — | Bhurtpore. |
| VIII. | 298 | Miscellaneous. | Guzzy cloth, 2d quality - - | 17 18 | 0 18 | 1 13 | 0 2 0 | Agra. |
| IV. | 142 | Miscellaneous. | Bleached cotton material. An imitation of English moleskin. | 9 20 | 0 26 | 5 5 | 0 12 10½ | Loodiana, Punjab. |
| XII. | 469 | Miscellaneous. | Unbleached figured dimity for sheeting, called soojney. | 3 0 | 1 17 | 1 14 | 0 6 3 | Madras. |
| XII. | 468 | Miscellaneous. | Canvas bleached (kind of *Duck*) - | 12 0 | 0 30 | 5 0 | 0 7 0 | Nellore, Madras. |

* An attempt was made to determine the length of the filaments or staple of which this and other specimens are made. The discrepancies in the results obtained led to the rejection of the great majority of the measurements. In the present instance it would appear that the mean length of the staple would not exceed six-tenths of an inch.

## CANVAS.—COTTON.

The next group is one which will be regarded with interest. It embraces specimens of the fabrics used in the construction of the tents,* which for months of every year constitute the home of a considerable portion of the European community in India. It also embraces specimens of the canvas employed for the sails of the numerous vessels which ply between the different Eastern ports. The strength, lightness, and other good qualities of the cotton sailcloth manufactured in India recommend it to more attention than it has hitherto received in this country. The quantity of cotton annually consumed in India in the manufacture of sail and tent cloth is very large.

| No. of Vol. | No. of Sample. | | Description. | Measurement. Length. | Measurement. Width. | Weight of Piece. | Cost. | Place of Manufacture, or where obtained. |
|---|---|---|---|---|---|---|---|---|
| | | | | yds. ins. | yds. ins. | lbs. oz. | £ s. d. | |
| XII. | 471*a* | Tentcloth. | Canvas of large Indian tent, exhibited in 1851. | — | — | — | — | Jubbulpore. |
| XII. | 471 | Tentcloth. | *Dungaree*, for tents (piece incomplete) | — | 0 15½ | — | — | Salem, Madras. |
| XII. | 474 | Tentcloth. | *Dungaree*. Quality occasionally used for tents. | 11 0 | 0 23 | 2 6 | 0 2 0 | |
| VIII. | 307 | Sailcloth. | Thick and stout, 1st quality, bleached. Orange, green, and red stripes at about a yard from end of piece. | 5 0 | 0 22½ | 4 12¼ | 0 2 6 | Cutch, Bombay. |
| XII. | 472 | Sailcloth. | Country canvas - - - | 19 0 | 0 23 | 10 11 | 0 9 6 | Rajahmundry, Madras. |
| XII. | 473 | Sailcloth. | *Dungaree*, unbleached - - | 16 0 | 0 23 | 6 10 | 0 6 0 | Salem, Madras. |

## COLOURED COTTON GOODS.

We come now to the coloured cotton piece goods in which the yarn itself has been first dyed. In the arrangement of this group we have as far as possible paid attention to the function which the articles are intended to fulfil. For instance, in the Table which follows, the fabrics designed for trouserings will be found, whilst in the next are inserted those used for skirts or petticoats.

It must not, however, be supposed that some of the examples so classified may not be equally suitable for both purposes or for more purposes than one; indeed, we know that they very often are so employed—what is used for skirts by the women being frequently employed as trousering by men.

### 1. Cotton.—Woven with Coloured Thread; chiefly used for Trousers.

In the first division in the following Table we have included specimens showing a material and pattern called *Sousee*, which is chiefly employed for trousering, and which very frequently, as we afterwards shall have occasion to show, is composed of a mixture

* Kathee and Salembaree are names given to the fabrics of which tents are made.

of cotton and silk. The patterns of these *Sousee*-cloths are very similar, although the product of places very distant from each other.

The second group in the Table comprehends a class of goods of a considerably stouter description, and affords examples of the thick, warm stuffs which we have already stated to be so acceptable at certain periods of the year in India.*.

| No. of Vol. | No. of Sample. | | Description. | Measurement. Length. yds. ins. | Measurement. Width. yds. ins. | Weight of Piece. lbs. oz. | Cost. £ | s. | d. | Place of Manufacture, or where obtained. |
|---|---|---|---|---|---|---|---|---|---|---|
| II. | 70 | 1. Cotton Sousee. | Green ground, brown stripes (4 to the inch), speckled with white, made by Lubbays, and extensively used. | 8 9 | 1 0 | 1 9 | 0 | 7 | 6 | Mylapore, or St. Thomas's, Madras. |
| II. | 74 | | Coarse. Stripes of blue thread, dotted with white on a chocolate coloured ground. Worn by the Lubbays. | 6 18 | 1 0 | 1 11 | 0 | 2 | 7½ | Kurnool, Madras. |
| IV. | 132 | | Blue, narrow ⅛ inch figured stripes, alternately white and crimson, and dark blue and yellow. | 2 32 | 0 18 | 0 6½ | 0 | 3 | 0 | Shikarpore. |
| IV. | 133 | | Black, ⅙ inch plain red stripes, ¼ inch apart. | 2 35 | 0 17 | 0 4 | 0 | 2 | 3 | Surat, Bombay. |
| IV. | 135 | | Blue. White and crimson stripe, ⅙ inch wide, 1¼ inch apart. | 2 30 | 0 18 | 0 4 | 0 | 2 | 0 | Shikarpore, Sinde. |
| IV. | 136 | | Blue weft, blue and crimson warp, with very narrow stripes of white and blue, 14 to the inch. | 7 31 | 0 21 | 0 14 | 0 | 2 | 0 | Surat, Bombay. |
| IV. | 137 | | Red, striped, with very narrow white lines, ⅓ inch apart. | 7 0 | 0 22 | 0 14 | 0 | 2 | 0 | Surat, Bombay. |
| IV. | 138 | | Red warp, blue weft, ⅓ inch stripes, ⅕ inch apart, of pale blue. | 15 29 | 0 20 | 1 5 | 0 | 5 | 0 | Surat, Bombay. |
| IV. | 139 | | Yellow, ⅙ inch stripes, white and black, ¼ inch apart. | 2 34 | 0 18 | 0 5½ | 0 | 2 | 0 | Shikarpore, Sind. |
| IV. | 140 | | Pale blue, with ⅙ inch stripes of white, ⅔ inch apart, with intervening lines in dark blue, yellow, and crimson. | 3 3 | 0 18 | 0 5¼ | 0 | 2 | 0 | Surat, Bombay. |
| XI. | 418 | | Small, ⅛ inch, dark blue stripe (warp) on a ground of white thread in the warp, and blue in the weft. | 10 0 | 0 20 | 2 2 | 0 | 3 | 0 | Palamcottah. |
| XII. | 453 | | Blue ground, with narrow stripes of yellow. | 6 0 | 0 29 | 0 15 | 0 | 2 | 4½ | Coonatoor, Madras. |
| IX. | 357 | | Red warp, blue weft - - - | 6 9 | 0 25 | 0 10¼ | 0 | 3 | 0 | Coonatoor, Madras. |
| XII. | 450 | | Red warp, blue weft, used for *trouserings and petticoats* by Mahomedans. | 6 0 | 0 26 | 0 10 | 0 | 3 | 0 | Syempettah, Madras. |
| IV. | 143 | 2. Cotton for Pantaloons. | Black and white striped pattern, ⅙ inch black stripe, ⅓ inch apart. | 3 0 | 0 28 | 1 5 | 0 | 1 | 6 | Loodiana, Punjab. |
| IV. | 144 | | Black and white striped pattern, blue threads running through stripe, ⅙ inch black stripe, ⅜ inch apart. | 2 24 | 0 25 | 1 3½ | 0 | 1 | 6 | Ditto. |
| IV. | 145 | | Dark blue, angulated striped pattern | 3 0 | 0 25 | 1 8 | 0 | 1 | 6 | Ditto. |
| IV. | 146 | | Grey check - - - | 7 0 | 0 27 | 1 10½ | 0 | 5 | 0 | Ditto. |
| IV. | 147 | | Dark grey, black and blue cross stripes ¾ inch apart. | 3 0 | 0 26 | 1 2 | 0 | 1 | 6 | Ditto. |
| IV. | 148 | | Black corded material with a dark blue weft. | 3 2 | 0 27 | 1 7½ | 0 | 3 | 0 | Ditto. |
| IV. | 149 | | Small dark blue, check or plaid pattern. | 3 0 | 0 25 | 0 11½ | 0 | 2 | 0 | Ditto. |
| IV. | 150 | | Black ground, with check of dark blue, ⅙ inch lines, ⅓ inch apart. | 6 4 | 0 25 | 1 5½ | 0 | 5 | 0 | Ditto. |
| XII. | 455 | | Stout twill, a figured pattern in dark red, blue, and white. | 5 11 | 0 25 | 1 10 | 0 | 4 | 1½ | Cuddalore. |
| XII. | 456 | | Stout twill, figured pattern, blue and white. | 5 12 | 0 22 | 1 10 | 0 | 2 | 6 | Ditto. |

* Some of the specimens shown here and elsewhere have been manufactured by the native weaver to suit *European* wants in India.

## 2. Cotton.—Woven with Coloured Thread; chiefly for Skirts.

Of the two groups contained in this Table, the first comes from Nepal and the second from Pegu. Both are interesting as showing characteristics in manufacture of places widely separated. Of the peculiar skirt materials employed by the women of Pegu, other examples will be found under the head of silk piece goods.

| No. of Vol. | No. of Sample. | | Description. | Measurement. Length. | Measurement. Width. | Weight of piece. | Cost. | Place of Manufacture, or where obtained. |
|---|---|---|---|---|---|---|---|---|
| | | | | yds. ins. | yds. ins. | lbs. oz. | £ s. d. | |
| VI. | 236 | 1 | Dark blue, with stripes of yellow, brown, and white. Coarse. | 5 11 | 0 29 | — | — | Kathamandoo, Nepal. |
| VI. | 237 | 1 | Brown stripes, dotted alternately with yellow and white spotted figure, which is, however, omitted in the last 9 inches of the piece. | 6 0 | 0 30 | 2 9 | — | Kathamandoo, Nepal. |
| VI. | 238 | 1 | Dark blue, with a $\frac{1}{4}$-inch stripe (blue and white chequered pattern), $\frac{1}{3}$ inch apart. | 5 0 | 0 31 | 1 9 | — | Kathamandoo, Nepal. |
| VI. | 239 | 1 | Blue, with, in some portion of piece, crimson thread in the weft. Stripes $\frac{1}{3}$ inch wide and $\frac{1}{4}$ inch apart, dark blue, with flashed white spots at intervals, and edges of red and yellow. | 4 25 | 0 28 | 1 11 | — | Kathamand Nepal. |
| VI. | 240 | 1 | Plain, chocolate colour. $\frac{1}{4}$-inch stripes $\frac{1}{4}$ inch apart, alternately blue and yellow and blue and white. | 5 0 | 0 28 | 1 10 | — | Kathamandoo, Nepal. |
| VI. | 230 | 2 | Blue warp and red weft throughout, with triple rows of cross stripes in yellow (weft threads) to 14 inches from the upper part of the skirt piece, which is white cotton, in the weft. The piece is the $\frac{1}{2}$ length, the other portion being similar to the sample. Worn by Burmese women. | 2 16 | 0 23 | 0 $6\frac{1}{2}$ | — | Pegu. |
| VI. | 231 | 2 | Blue warp, pink weft throughout, with triple rows of green stripes (weft thread) in the lower part of the skirt, and closer stripes of green divided by 3 blue stripes nearer the upper part, 13 inches of which is of the plain material. The sample shows one-half the whole length of the piece, the other half being similar to the pattern. Worn by Burmese women | 2 12 | 0 $23\frac{1}{2}$ | 0 $6\frac{1}{4}$ | — | Pegu. |
| VI. | 232 | 2 | Blue warp, white weft throughout, with triple rows of yellow stripes (weft) in the lower part of the skirt, and closer stripes of yellow divided by 3 dark blue cross stripes nearer the upper part, 13 inches of which is of the plain material. The sample shows one-half the whole length of the piece, the other half being similar to pattern. Worn by Burmese women. | 2 8 | 0 22 | 0 $6\frac{1}{4}$ | — | Pegu. |

| No. of Vol. | No. of Sample. | Description. | Measurement. Length. | Measurement. Width. | Weight of Piece. | Cost. | Place of Manufacture, or where obtained. |
|---|---|---|---|---|---|---|---|
| | | | yds. ins. | yds. ins. | lbs. oz. | £ s. d. | |
| VI. | 233 | The lower part of skirt piece has quadruple rows of dark blue cross stripes, on a green ground of blue (warp) and yellow (weft), with a group of narrower stripes near the upper part, which, for 13 ins., is of blue (warp) and pink (weft). Sample shows one-half the full length of piece, the other half being similar to pattern. Worn by Burmese women. | 2 8 | 0 24 | 0 6¼ | — | Pegu. |

### 3. Cotton.—Woven with Coloured Thread; Checks and Tartan Patterns.

In the following Table will be found various checks and tartans, many of which are admirable imitations of well-known patterns in this country. They are chiefly used for skirts, petticoats, &c. Some of the *shepherd tartans* are also used for making up into trousers.

| No. of Vol. | No. of Sample. | Description. | Measurement. Length. | Measurement. Width. | Weight of piece. | Cost. | Place of Manufacture, or where obtained. |
|---|---|---|---|---|---|---|---|
| | | | yds. ins. | yds. ins. | lbs. oz. | £ s. d. | |
| VIII. | 313 | Stripes, ⅓-inch, alternately yellow and blue in the warp, and green, crimson, and blue in the weft. | 6 18 | 0 23 | 1 5½ | 0 3 0 | Broach, Bombay. |
| VIII. | 314 | Large tartan pattern - - - - | 12 0 | 0 22½ | 2 11¼ | 0 6 0 | Broach, Bombay. |
| VIII. | 316 | Large tartan pattern. Blue, white, black, and pink twill. | 8 15 | 0 25 | 1 12 | 0 6 0 | Loodiana, Punjab. |
| VIII. | 317 | Small check of yellow ¼-inch stripe in weft and warp, alternately with ¼ inch of unbleached cotton, | 5 26 | 0 25 | 0 12½ | 0 3 0 | Loodiana, Punjab. |
| VIII. | 318 | Large blue check on a plain ground, intersected by quadruple lines of pink in weft and warp. | 8 33 | 0 26 | 1 1 | 0 3 0 | Loodiana, Punjab. |
| IX. | 359 | Tartan pattern - - - - | 6 0 | 0 21 | 0 14 | 0 4 0 | Pulicat, Madras. |
| IX. | 360 | Tartan pattern - - - - | 6 0 | 0 22 | 0 14 | 0 4 0 | Mylapore, Madras. |
| XI. | 401 | Tartan pattern - - - - | 6 0 | 0 21 | 0 13 | 0 3 10½ | Ditto. |
| XI. | 402 | Tartan pattern - - - - | 5 27 | 0 21 | 0 13 | 0 3 0 | Coonatoor, Madras. |
| XI. | 403 | Small black and white check on a red ground. | 11 21 | 0 22 | 1 3 | 0 5 6 | Tanjore, Madras. |

| No. of | | Description. | Measurement. | | Weight of Piece. | Cost. | | | Place of Manufacture, or where obtained. |
|---|---|---|---|---|---|---|---|---|---|
| Vol. | Sample. | | Length. | Width. | | | | | |
| | | | yds. ins. | yds. ins. | lbs. oz. | £ | s. | d. | |
| XI. | 404 | **Small dark green check on a ground of a lighter green shade.** | 6 0 | 0 31 | 0 12 | 0 | 5 | 0 | Cuddalore, Madras. |
| XI. | 405 | **Small dark blue check on a dark crimson ground.** | 6 0 | 0 31 | 0 14 | 0 | 4 | 6 | Cuddalore, Madras. |
| XI. | 406 | An open check of blue, with a red line in centre of main stripes, on an uncoloured ground. | 5 20 | 0 26 | 0 11 | 0 | 2 | 0 | Pulicat, Madras. |
| XI. | 407 | Check, ⅓-inch stripes of blue in weft and warp, ¼ inch apart, with crimson line margins, on a green ground. | 5 23 | 0 22 | 0 14 | 0 | 4 | 0 | Mylapore, Madras. |
| XI. | 408 | Uncoloured ground. An open check of ¼-inch stripes of light green, ⅝-inch apart, with 4 intervening lines in the same colour. | 6 13 | 0 25 | 0 12 6 drs. | 0 | 2 | 6 | Coonatoor, Madras. |
| XI. | 409 | A light green check, ¼-inch stripes one way, ⅙-inch the other, on an uncoloured ground. | 6 8 | 0 25 | 0 12½ | 0 | 2 | 6 | Coonatoor, Madras. |
| XI. | 410 | An open check of green stripes, 1 inch apart, with double lined check of scarlet thread intervening, on an uncoloured ground. | 7 6 | 0 26 | 0 12 | 0 | 2 | 6 | Coonatoor, Madras. |
| XI. | 411 | An open check of red stripes with blue margins, and subordinate check of two blue lines intervening, on an uncoloured ground. | 6 30 | 0 26 | 0 11 | 0 | 2 | 6 | Coonatoor, Madras. |
| XI. | 412 | An open check of alternate blue and crimson stripes on an uncoloured ground. | 6 0 | 0 28 | 0 14 | 0 | 3 | 0 | Pulicat, Madras. |
| XI. | 413 | **Check. A ⅔-inch stripe of green and scarlet in weft and warp, with a slender green line intervening, on an uncoloured ground.** | 6 26 | 0 26 | 0 15 | 0 | 4 | 6 | Teroomaly, Madras. |
| XI. | 414 | Check, a blue and red stripe, ⅔-inch in warp, rather narrower in the weft, and ½ inch apart, with a fine white line in centre of each stripe, on an uncoloured ground. | 7 0 | 0 26 | 0 15 | 0 | 3 | 9 | Coonatoor, Madras. |
| XI. | 41 | **Tartan pattern** - - - - | 6 9 | 0 18 | 1 0 | 0 | 3 | 6 | Masulipatam, Madras. |
| XI. | 416 | Small blue and white check - - | 10 27 | 0 20 | 1 10 | 0 | 3 | 6 | Cuddalore, Madras. |
| XI. | 417 | Ditto ditto - - | 6 0 | 0 27 | 1 10 | 0 | 6 | 0 | Ditto. |
| XII. | 454 | Small black and white check - - | 8 0 | 0 32 | 2 5 | 0 | 5 | 3 | Masulipatam, Madras. |

## PRINTED COTTON GOODS.

The next group of cotton fabrics which we have to consider consists of those in which printing is employed. It naturally sub-divides itself into two, first those in which the pattern is printed on a white ground, and second those in which it is printed on a coloured ground. Fabrics of this character are used chiefly for women's skirts or petticoats, but they are also used for Sarees—a portion of the piece, of a proper length, being cut off, and borders and ends being occasionally added. In addition to these uses they are also pretty largely employed to make counterpanes, linings for tents, &c.

Among the specimens in the books there are some good and some bad,—that is as regards the character and execution of the printing. They exhibit, however, in a very satisfactory manner, the style of pattern which pleases the Indian taste and which proves saleable. One characteristic of this style is that the pattern is small. *Large, staring, gaudy* patterns are evidently not popular. The native taste condemns and rejects them. Indeed it is clear that the principles of art are more likely to be violated when the pattern is large than when it is small.

As regards *execution*, it will be found that Native work is not equal to European. Our machinery and appliances are more perfect, and our printing is consequently better. But while this is true, as the rule, there are marked exceptions; and among the specimens in the Books will be found some which are as beautiful and as well finished as anything the British manufacturer can produce.

The native dyer and printer has attained great skill in fixing his colours, and this point is one which deserves serious consideration. It must always be remembered that the body-clothing of the Hindu is frequently washed, and by a process which is extremely rough. It is essential, therefore, that the colours should be thoroughly fast. A failure in this entirely destroys the value of the fabric, and hence many of the prints sent from this country have fallen into disrepute,—our manufacturers not having fully recognized the necessity of sending no printed goods to India but those in which all the colours are fast.

Dyed and printed cotton fabrics are produced in many parts of India, or perhaps more properly speaking here and there over the whole country. Masulipatam, Arnee, and Sydapet, in the Madras Presidency, are famous for their *Chetee* or Chintzes.* Those of Masulipatam are known under the name of *kalam-kouree* (which literally means "firm colour") and exhibit great variety in style and quality.

As already indicated these printed goods have been divided into two groups—those in which the printing is on a white, and those in which it is on a coloured ground. These are given in the three following tables. The second of the Tables contains one specimen (Vol. VIII. 320), which is simply dyed and not printed. The third contains nothing but Palempores or bed-covers, some of which are admirable illustrations of Indian printing (151, 152, 153, 154, and 155, Vol. IV.), while others (156 and 157, Vol. IV.) can scarcely be praised.

---

* This word (from Chhint, Hind:—variegated), as well as Calico, is of Indian origin, and in that fact we have another indication of the position which India once occupied as an exporter of Cotton manufactures.

## TABLE 1. COTTON.—PRINTED ; WHITE GROUND.

| No. of Vol. | No. of Sample. | Description. | Measurement Length. | Measurement Width. | Weight of piece. | Cost. | Place of manufacture, or where obtained. |
|---|---|---|---|---|---|---|---|
| | | | yds. ins. | yds. ins. | lbs. ozs. | £ s. d. | |
| VIII. | 310 | Pattern, ½-inch diagonal stripes of flowers, of two different patterns, ⅝-inch apart: in intervening space, sprigs of flowers at ¾-inch distances, also in diagonal order. Colours, red, green, and black. | 5 28½ | 1 1 | 1 4¾ | — | Futtygurh, N.W.P. |
| VIII. | 311 | Pattern, a ⅔-inch circular flower and foliage in close diagonal order. Colours, green and red. | 5 30½ | 1 1½ | 1 4½ | — | Futtygurh. |
| VIII. | 312 | A well filled inch check pattern of small foliage and flowers in green, red, and black. | 5 31½ | 1 11½ | 1 5½ | — | Futtygurh. |
| X. | 368 | Small, close, figured pattern in red, on a white ground. | 3 24 | 1 5 | 0 15½ | 0 2 0 | Masulipatam, Madras. |
| X. | 369 | Rather coarse texture. Neat pattern, in red and black, of flowers arranged in diagonal rows. | 5 26 | 1 1 | 1 5 | 0 3 9 | Masulipatam, Madras. |
| X. | 370 | Good pattern and material. Pattern, a small neat bouquet, in red, blue, and black, in diagonal order, on a white ground of bleached cotton. | 3 27 | 1 2 | — | 0 8 0 | Masulipatam, Madras. |
| X. | 376 | Pattern, a small red circle, in diagonal rows at ⅓-inch distances. On this piece is a slight border of three printed red lines. | 3 18 | 1 6 | 0 14 | 0 2 1½ | Ponnary, Madras. |
| X. | 377 | Pattern, a red flower with black stalk, arranged, diagonally, in rows, on a white ground dotted throughout with small black spots. | 3 18 | 1 8 | 0 14 | 0 2 0 | Arcot, Madras. |
| X. | 378 | Pattern, a small red foliage and flower figure running throughout the piece. | 3 18 | 1 8 | 0 14 | 0 2 0 | Ditto. |
| X. | 379 | Pattern (imperfectly printed), a small dotted figure in red. | 3 18 | 1 2 | 0 12 | 0 2 0 | Ditto. |
| X. | 381 | Pattern, flowered figure in red and black, intersected by cross diagonal lines and curves of the same character. | 3 18 | 1 5 | 1 0 | 0 2 0 | Ditto. |
| X. | 382 | Pattern, a large red flower, with black stems and foliage, in diagonal rows. | 3 18 | 1 0 | 0 12 | 0 2 0 | Ditto. |
| X. | 383 | Pattern, a red stripe edged and figured with black, and on the intervening white space or stripe, a small red flower with black foliage running throughout. | 9 18 | 1 0 | 2 12 | 0 4 1½ | Ponnary, Madras. |
| X. | 388 | Pattern (good), a small flower in dark blue and red, arranged in diagonal rows. | 6 0 | 1 0 | 1 5 | 0 4 6 | Masulipatam, Madras. |

### TABLE 1. COTTON.—PRINTED, &c.—*cont.*

| No. of Vol. | No. of Sample. | Description. | Measurement. Length. | Measurement. Width. | Weight of Piece. | Cost. | Place of Manufacture, or where obtained. |
|---|---|---|---|---|---|---|---|
| | | | yds. ins. | yds. ins. | lbs. oz. | £ s. d. | |
| X. | 387 | Pattern, a small flower sprig in black and brown, arranged in diagonal rows. | 5 0 | 1 0 | 0 15 | 0 2 0 | Sydapat, Madras. |
| X. | 390 | Coarse cotton. Pattern, a flowered pine, of good design, 3½ ins. in length and in close order. Colours, yellow, red, and black. | 5 27 | 1 0 | 1 12 | 0 3 1½ | Ditto. |
| X. | 391 | Coarse cotton. Pattern, a large flowered pine, 6½ ins. long, in black and brown, on a plain ground. | 6 0 | 1 0 | 1 12 | 0 3 1½ | Ditto. |
| X. | 398 | White ground. Print. A large flower and foliage pattern, in black and dark. | 5 0 | 1 4 | 0 9 | 0 2 7½ | Arcot, Madras. |
| X. | 399 | Print. A large leaf and scroll pattern in green and black. | 5 0 | 1 4 | 1 3 | 0 2 1½ | Ditto. |
| X. | 400 | Print. Well designed scroll and foliage pattern, in black and green on a white ground. | 5 0 | 1 4 | 1 7 | 0 2 7½ | Ditto. |

### TABLE 2. COTTON.—PRINTED; COLOURED GROUND.

| No. of Vol. | No. of Sample. | Description. | Measurement. Length. | Measurement. Width. | Weight of piece. | Cost. | Place of manufacture, or where obtained. |
|---|---|---|---|---|---|---|---|
| | | | yds. ins. | yds. ins. | lbs. ozs. | £ s. d. | |
| VIII. | 315 | *Peshgeer.* A material of English thread, woven and printed in India. Used for petticoats of poorer classes. A deep crimson cotton, surface coloured, with flowered pattern in black with white spots, in diagonal order. | 5 0 | 0 32 | 1 2½ | 0 4 0 | Shikarpore, Sind. |
| VIII. | 319 | Yellow cotton, surface coloured. Print, a small rose in red and green, in diagonal order. | 5 26 | 1 1½ | 1 5½ | — | Futtygurh, N.W.P. |
| X. | 372 | A large pine pattern in black and white, printed on a deep red or scarlet (surface coloured) ground. Used for petticoats. | 7 18 | 1 0 | 1 12 | 0 3 1½ | Bellary, Madras. |
| X. | 373 | Red ground. Pattern, a figured stripe in black and white alternately with a small scrolled pattern of foliage and flowers. | 4 0 | 1 6 | 1 1 | 0 2 7½ | Ponnary, Madras. |
| X. | 374 | Coarse Fabric. Red ground. Pattern, a flower in white, black, and badly printed green, and arranged in diagonal rows. | 7 0 | 0 30 | 1 7 | 0 2 0 | Arcot, Madras. |

## Table 2. Cotton.—Printed, &c.—*cont.*

| No. of | | Description. | Measurement. | | Weight of Piece. | Cost. | Place of Manufacture, or where obtained. |
|---|---|---|---|---|---|---|---|
| Vol. | Sample. | | Length. | Width. | | | |
| | | | yds. ins. | yds. ins. | lbs. oz. | £ s. d. | |
| X. | 375 | Coarse fabric. Red ground, with 1-inch figured stripes in black and white, ¾ inch apart. In intervening spaces, rows of small pines in black and white, with patches of green apparently added by hand. | 9 0 | 1 0 | 2 10 | 0 4 1½ | Ponnary, Madras. |
| X. | 380 | Imperfectly printed. Black ground, with a small white star-shaped flower in the centre of a circle, formed by a small flowered pattern in red and white. | 4 18 | 1 4 | 1 3 | 0 3 1½ | Ponnary, Madras. |
| X. | 384 | A chocolate red ground. Pattern, small white dots forming zigzag stripes, running across the piece. | 6 18 | 1 7 | 1 12 | 0 3 10½ | Ponnary, Madras. |
| X. | 385 | Dark brown ground. Pattern, a small "creeper" - like figure in white throughout, with a red flower at intervals, and in diagonal rows. | 7 0 | 0 19 | 1 9 | 0 3 3 | Bellary, Madras. |
| X. | 386 | Deep red ground. Pattern, small ¾-inch squares, formed by black and white dotted lines ; in centre of each square a small star-shaped figure, also in black and white. | 4 0 | 1 6 | 1 1 | 0 2 7½ | Ponnary, Madras. |
| X. | 389 | Deep red ground. Pattern, a small white pine in the centre of a square formed by faint diagonal lines of white spots. | 5 18 | 1 6 | 1 8 | 0 3 4½ | Ditto. |
| X. | 392 | Deep red ground. ⅓-inch stripes of dark red, not quite close together, to give the effect of a narrow white stripe on a red ground. Badly printed. | 7 0 | 0 29 | 1 9 | 0 2 0 | Arcot, Madras. |
| X. | 393 | Black ground. Pattern, rows of small white spots in diagonal order. A pattern and colour much used by the Parsees. | 9 0 | 1 2 | 2 8 | 0 4 1½ | Ponnary, Madras. |
| X. | 394 | Red ground. Pattern, horizontal stripes of white spots, somewhat similar to the "flashed" stripe in a pattern produced in silk in Benares and Hyderabad. | 7 0 | 0 31 | 1 12 | 0 2 3 | Ponnary, Madras. |
| X. | 395 | Coarse. A dark purple ground. Pattern, horizontal zigzag stripe in white. Similar to patterns in silks from Benares and Hyderabad. | 9 0 | 1 0 | 2 10 | 0 4 1½ | Ponnary, Madras. |
| X. | 396 | Black ground, with the small horizontal zigzag stripes which form a feature in some of the Mushroos from Hyderabad, &c. | 7 9 | 0 32 | 1 10 | 0 2 3 | Arcot, Madras. |
| X. | 397 | Called *Gud-ka-cheet*. A blue ground with flower or pine, in black, brown and white, printed in diagonal rows. Used for petticoats by Malays of the poorer classes. | 4 18 | 0 31 | — | 0 2 0 | Agra. |
| VIII. | 320 | Coarse cotton, dyed with indigo. - | 8 6 | 0 34 | 3 1½ | 0 3 6 | Beejapore. |

## TABLE 3. COTTON.—PRINTED; PALEMPORES, OR BED-COVERS.

| No. of Vol. | No. of Sample. | Description. | Measurement. Length. | Measurement. Width. | Weight of Piece. | Cost. | Place of Manufacture, or where obtained. |
|---|---|---|---|---|---|---|---|
| | | | yds. ins. | yds. ins. | lbs. oz. | £ s. d. | |
| IV. | 151 | Flowered pine pattern on green ground, with 3½ inch border. | 3 13 | 1 24 | 1 3¼ | — | Futtygurh, Bengal. |
| IV. | 152 | Flowered stripes, alternately pink, white, and green, with flowered border. | 3 12 | 1 21 | 1 0¼ | — | Ditto. |
| IV. | 153 | White ground, centre small flowered pattern, 3½ inch border. | 3 12 | 1 26 | 0 15½ | — | Ditto. |
| IV. | 154 | Green ground, yellow circular spots, with flowered centres. | 6 0 | 1 7 | 1 1½ | — | Ditto. |
| IV. | 155 | Red ground, flowered circular pattern, with special borders. | 3 9 | 1 24 | 1 1 | — | Ditto. |
| IV. | 156 | White ground, with large flowered pattern in centre, special borders and ends. Poor example. | 4 21 | 1 18 | 1 4 | 0 4 0 | Shikarpore, Sinde. |
| IV. | 157 | Large-flowered pattern. Better print than No. 156, but not nearly so good as the Futtygurh specimens. Special pattern in end. | 5 0 | 1 18 | 1 15 | 0 6 0 | Ditto. |
| IV. | 160 | Yellow ground, small flowers in crimson and dark green, arranged in oblique stripes. | 3 8 | 1 22 | 1 8 | 0 2 6 | Hazara, Punjab. |
| XII. | 475 | Glazed chintz; centre pattern a large flowered design in colours on a white ground, with a deep 11-inch border of elaborately designed stripes of pines, flowers, and foliage in white and red coloured ground. Four woven in one piece. | 1 12 | 1 12 | Of four. 1 7 | 0 3 6 | Masulipatam, Madras. |
| XII. | 476 | Unglazed chintz, large flowered pattern, centre in red, green, &c., with 4¼ inch border. A deep (20 inch) end, with special stripes of similar design, enclosing a row of flowered pines in colours. Printed on uncoloured cotton. Two pieces sewn together, form complete "Palampore," or bed cover. | 2 9 | 1 23 | 0 13 | 0 1 5 | Paumodee, Madras. |
| XII. | 477 | Unglazed chintz, pattern a large figure 4 inches in diameter, printed in black within a square formed by brown foliage pattern. At the end, a row of 6-inch figures of armed Sepoys, printed in black, and enclosed by two scrolls of foliage and flowers of good design, and printed in brown. | 2 0 | 1 0 | 0 8 | 0 1 3 | Masulipatam, Madras. |
| XII. | 478 | Unglazed chintz, large radiated circular figure, 3 inches in diameter, in brown, within a square formed by another figure printed in black; 10¾ inch border, formed by foliage and flowers, with figures of birds printed in black, and enclosed by two scrolls of foliage and flowers printed in brown. | 2 14 | 1 14 | 0 13 | 0 2 0 | Masulipatam, Madras. |

## COTTON.—MISCELLANEOUS.

A number of articles have been brought together under this heading, which it was difficult otherwise to group. As they had special functions, it was thought that it might serve a useful purpose to keep them together, using function rather than quality or pattern as the basis of the grouping.

They are all cotton fabrics, but some are white and others coloured.

Not a few of them, such as the Table Napkins, Doyley's, and Pocket-handkerchiefs, are manufactured to suit European wants, and these illustrate the imitative power of the native manufacturer. One of the bed-covers—*ruzzai*—(433) is a specimen of Indian quilting. A considerable quantity of raw cotton is used for this purpose, as quilting is often resorted to in the northern districts in order to produce garments which will give a proper protection against the cold.

Tapes form a considerable article of native manufacture, being extensively used in the making of bedsteads. The purpose to which they are applied shows that they must be strong. A width of two to three inches is common.

| No. of Vol. | No. of Sample. | | Description. | Measurement. Length. | Measurement. Width. | Weight of piece. | Cost. | Place of Manufacture, or where obtained. |
|---|---|---|---|---|---|---|---|---|
| | | | | yds. ins. | yds. ins. | lbs. oz. | £ s. d. | |
| XII. | 457 | Pocket Handkerchiefs. | Cotton (muslin), deep border, (3¾ inches), plain stripes, woven in material. | 0 20 | 0 20 | — | 0 4 6 per dozen. | Nellore, Madras. |
| XII. | 458 | Pocket Handkerchiefs. | Cotton (muslin), deep borders (3½ inches), plain stripes, woven in material. | 0 20 | 0 20 | — | 0 8 0 per dozen. | Ditto. |
| XI. | 419 | Table Napkins. | Damask pattern, unbleached - | 0 21 | 0 21 | — | 0 7 0 per dozen. | Madras. |
| XI. | 420 | Table Napkins. | Ditto, ditto - - | 0 19 | 0 19 | — | 0 8 0 per dozen. | Cuddalore, Madras. |
| XI. | 421 | Table Napkins. | Diaper, small pattern, ditto - | 0 22 | 0 22 | — | 0 8 6 per dozen. | Ditto. |
| XI. | 424 | Table Napkins. | Damask pattern, ditto - - | 0 30 | 0 29 | — | 0 13 0 per dozen. | Masulipatam, Madras. |
| XI. | 428 | Table Napkins. | Ditto, ditto - - | 0 23 | 0 23 | — | 0 3 0 per dozen. | Broach, Bombay. |
| XI. | 426 | Table Napkins. | Plain diaper, bleached - - | 0 17 | 0 17 | — | 0 2 3 per dozen. | Masulipatam, Madras. |
| XI. | 422 | Towels. | Huckaback, unbleached - - | 0 35 | 0 35 | — | 0 13 0 per dozen. | Cuddalore, Madras. |
| XI. | 429 | Towels. | Ditto, ditto - - | 0 33 | 0 33 | — | 0 2 3 per dozen. | Broach, Bombay. |
| XI. | 425 | Towels. | Diaper pattern, ditto - - | 0 36 | 0 31 | — | 0 8 0 per dozen. | Chingleput, Madras. |
| XI. | 427 | Towels. | Khadee cloth, ditto - - - | 0 32 | 0 31 | — | 0 4 0 per dozen. | Salem, Madras. |
| XI. | 423 | Towels. | Stout plain material, bleached Khadee cloth. | 0 33 | 0 22 | — | 0 4 0 per dozen. | Cuddalore, Madras. |
| XI. | 430 | Towels. | Bleached small diaper pattern. A 3-inch border, with a flower and foliage scroll pattern, printed in red on plain woven fabric. *Made to order.* | 0 27 | 0 25 | — | 0 3 0 per dozen. | From Goa, sent from Madras. |

TABLE. COTTON.—MISCELLANEOUS, &c.—*cont.*

| No. of Vol. | No. of Sample. | | Description. | Measurement. Length. | Measurement. Width. | Weight of Piece. | Cost. | Place of Manufacture, or where obtained. |
|---|---|---|---|---|---|---|---|---|
| | | | | yds. ins. | yds. ins. | lbs. oz. | £ s. d. | |
| XI. | 431 | DOYLEYS. | A green stripe, checked by a faint blue stripe on a crimson ground. | 0 13 | 0 13 | — | 0 9 0 per dozen. | Madras. |
| XI. | 432 | DOYLEYS. | Crimson and blue check - - | 0 13 | 0 13 | — | 0 8 3 per dozen. | Cuddalore, Madras. |
| IV. | 158 | PALEMPORES,* OR BED-COVERS. | Bleached diaper pattern, diaper pattern woven in pink thread, and cross stripes at ends. | 4 32 | 1 18 | 1 15 | 0 15 0 | Hoshyarpore, Punjab. |
| IV. | 159 | PALEMPORES,* OR BED-COVERS. | Bleached. Border, blue stripe, 7 inch blue stripe across each end. | 4 7 | 1 13 | 2 8 | — | Loodiana, Punjab. |
| XI. | 433 | PALEMPORES,* OR BED-COVERS. | Cotton, quilted with the needle - | 2 6 | 1 10 | 2 4 | — | Hyderabad, Deccan. |
| XII. | 479 | PALEMPORES,* OR BED-COVERS. | *Soojney.* Counterpane. A large diaper kind of pattern, produced by weaving the design in bleached thread in an unbleached ground. End marked by a modification of the diaper pattern, $1\frac{3}{4}$ inch of extremity quite plain, with a small fringe. | 2 9 | 1 4 | 2 0 | 0 4 6 | Kurnool, Madras. |
| XII. | 480 | PALEMPORES,* OR BED-COVERS. | *Soojney.* A large diaper pattern similar to last, but in bleached cotton on a dark red ground. End marked by a modification of this design, and a small portion of end of plain uncoloured material. Slight fringe at extremity. | 2 9 | 1 4 | 2 0 | 0 4 6 | Kurnool, Madras. |

* Called also Pulungposh.

# SILK.

We have now to illustrate the silk, or silk and cotton piece goods which form an extensive article of manufacture in many parts of India, chiefly for home consumption, but partly also for export, as will be seen by reference to the following Table A., which shows the quantities and value of the silk goods exported from India and from each Presidency to all parts of the world from 1850–51 to 1864–65.

In the Tables which follow the examples in the Books, these manufactures have been grouped under four heads :—

(1.) In the first one are included the plain, striped, and checked fabrics, which consist of silk and cotton, and are employed for Trowserings, and occasionally also for Skirts and Cholees.

(2.) In the second group we have an important class of fabrics, also consisting of silk and cotton, and commonly known under the name of Mushroo, which is a satin with a cotton back. It is a favourite material, and is used in a variety of ways by the well-to-do classes for dress purposes, covering cushions, &c. Some idea of the variety and beauty of the patterns produced in this material will be gathered from an inspection of the specimens in the Books.*

(3.) In the third Table are included the specimens in which silk alone is the textile material employed. These, like the others, are used for making up trowsers and other articles of attire, and also for linings. It will be observed that in the description of the different patterns, some are noted as being favourites with the Hindu, and others with the Mahomedan portion of the community.†

(4.) In the fourth Table we have a few examples of *printing* on silk as used for the production of a class of goods in vogue amongst the Parsees and employed by them for Sarees, Trowserings, &c. No. 549, Vol. XIV., showing a dark spot in the centre of a white line, illustrates the material and pattern used for making the peculiar mitre-shaped Turban worn by the Parsees. The spots, however, on the fabrics most commonly employed are smaller than those in the specimen referred to. The white margin round the dark central spot is produced by hitching up, and tying a thread around small portions of the cloth, which on transference to the dye-trough is not affected by the

---

* All Mushroo's wash well, especially the finer kinds. As this manufacture is principally used for Cholees, petticoats, and for trousers of both sexes, washing becomes indispensable, and the dyes used are in all cases fast, not fading with time, or becoming streaky or cloudy after being wetted. In any imitation of these fabrics, the best dyes would be necessary, and such careful weaving as would enable the gloss to be preserved in the washing as in the Mushroo fabrics, otherwise they would be of no value. English or French satins are more beautiful both in colour and texture ; but it is needless to say they will not wash, and therefore would not supply the place of "Mushroos."

† Stated on the authority of the Lahore Central Committee, which forwarded to the International Exhibition of 1862 a valuable collection of the patterns prevailing in the Punjab.

colour employed. In many specimens the *ties* are very fine and close to each other, and, consequently, involve the expenditure of much time and trouble in their production.

The rapidity with which the successive little portions of silk are hitched up and ligatured by an experienced hand is, however, very remarkable.

This pattern is extremely difficult to imitate exactly, and, as it is one of those results in which a certain charm arises from the absence of the perfect regularity usually effected by machine operations, it is probable that it will still continue to be produced in the laborious and comparatively expensive manner just described.*

The only other example of a silk material to which we would refer is that presented by No. 555, Vol. XIV., a red silk gauze, from Bhagulpore, stated to be used for mosquito curtains.

The original length of the piece was 11 yards, the width 31 inches, the weight 5¾ ounces, and the price 1*l.* 12*s.* 0*d.*, a sum, probably, very considerably beyond its real value. Although the only example of a mosquito curtain material here given is of silk, it has to be mentioned that this is a very rare application, light cotton gauze or net being the article usually employed. The greater portion of the *nets* exported from this country are employed in the manufacture of mosquito curtains, which are extensively used in India both by Europeans and well-to-do natives.

The foregoing concludes the only remarks which we have considered it necessary to make regarding the fabrics manufactured from true silk, the produce of the *Bombyx mori*.

---

* That it is *possible*, however, to produce by machinery at least some classes of this kind of goods, was shown by the "Batiks" manufactured in Holland and shown by Previnaire et Cie., of Haarlem, in the Exhibition of 1862.

(A.) TABLE showing the QUANTITIES (as far as can be ascertained) and the VALUE of SILK GOODS (exclusive of Chussums) Exported from India and each Presidency to all parts of the World from 1850–51 to 1864–65.

| Years. | Whence Exported. | COUNTRIES TO WHICH EXPORTED. United Kingdom. | | France. | | Other parts of Europe. | | America. | | China. | | Arabian and Persian Gulfs. | | Aden and Suez. | | Straits Settlements. | | Other parts. | | Total Exported to all parts. | |
|---|---|---|---|---|---|---|---|---|---|---|---|---|---|---|---|---|---|---|---|---|---|
| | | Quantity. | Value. | Quantity. | Value. | Quantity. | Value. | Quantity. | Value. | Quantity. | Value. | Quantity. | Value. | Quantity. | Value. | Quantity. | Value. | Quantity. | Value. | Quantity. | Value. |
| | | Pieces. | £ | Pieces. | £ | Pieces. | £ | Pieces. | £ | Pieces. | £ | Pieces. | £ | Pieces. | £ | Pieces. | £ | Pieces. | £ | Pieces. | £ |
| 1850-51 | Bengal | 559,892 | 309,419 | 1,957 | 1,259 | 1,032 | 720 | 7,543 | 4,330 | 559 | 730 | 908 | 275 | — | — | 23,154 | 12,955 | 4,559 | 2,974 | 590,604 | 332,657 |
| | Madras | 21 | 55 | — | — | — | — | — | — | — | — | 7 | 11 | — | — | 3,781 | 1,805 | 34 | 38 | 3,843 | 1,909 |
| | Bombay | 571 | 1,737 | — | — | — | — | — | — | 983 | 304 | 19,337 | 11,138 | 855 | 517 | 6,237 | 4,267 | 2,594 | 2,694 | 30,577 | 20,657 |
| | **ALL INDIA** | **560,484** | **311,211** | **1,957** | **1,259** | **1,032** | **720** | **7,543** | **4,330** | **1,542** | **1,034** | **20,252** | **11,424** | **855** | **517** | **33,172** | **19,027** | **7,187** | **5,706** | **634,024** | **355,223** |
| 1851-52 | Bengal | 408,256 | 224,406 | 405 | 266 | 294 | 182 | 2,089 | 1,058 | 76 | 42 | 259 | 75 | — | — | 1,006 | 417 | 27,230 | 13,288 | 439,615 | 239,734 |
| | Madras | 36 | 96 | — | — | — | — | — | — | — | — | — | — | — | — | 129 | 68 | 472 | 228 | 637 | 392 |
| | Bombay | 12 | 33 | — | — | 4 | 4 | 15 | 6 | 9,050 | 955 | 10,498 | 7,867 | 935 | 834 | 15,185 | 7,661 | 3,256 | 2,739 | 38,955 | 20,099 |
| | **ALL INDIA** | **408,304** | **224,535** | **405** | **266** | **298** | **186** | **2,104** | **1,064** | **9,126** | **997** | **10,757** | **7,942** | **935** | **834** | **16,320** | **8,146** | **30,958** | **16,255** | **479,207** | **260,225** |
| 1852-53 | Bengal | 502,960 | 267,803 | 423 | 230 | 1,879 | 1,010 | 2,608 | 1,455 | — | 276 | 2,407 | 897 | — | — | — | 777 | — | 14,725 | — | 287,173 |
| | Madras | 25 | 51 | — | — | — | — | — | — | — | — | 203 | 67 | — | — | 67 | 42 | 5,977 | 621 | 6,272 | 781 |
| | Bombay | — | 2 | — | — | — | — | — | — | — | 211 | — | 15,892 | — | 1,723 | 11,460 | 7,035 | — | 2,378 | — | 27,241 |
| | **ALL INDIA** | **502,985** | **267,856** | **423** | **230** | **1,879** | **1,010** | **2,608** | **1,455** | — | **487** | — | **16,856** | — | **1,723** | — | **7,854** | — | **17,724** | — | **315,195** |
| 1853-54 | Bengal | 522,883 | 276,747 | 2,128 | 1,068 | 1,004 | 502 | 12 577 | 7,431 | 262 | 215 | 429 | 105 | 9,113 | 4,802 | 2,055 | 997 | 19,312 | 9,804 | 569,763 | 301,671 |
| | Madras | 17 | 29 | — | — | — | — | — | — | — | — | — | — | — | — | 79 | 42 | 1,602 | 790 | 1,788 | 861 |
| | Bombay | — | 53 | — | — | — | — | — | — | — | 150 | — | 5,140 | — | 1,382 | — | 4,322 | — | 2,743 | — | 13,799 |
| | **ALL INDIA** | — | **276,829** | **2,128** | **1,068** | **1,004** | **502** | **12,577** | **7,431** | — | **365** | — | **5,254** | — | **6,184** | — | **5,361** | — | **13,337** | — | **316,331** |
| 1854-55 | Bengal | 443,187 | 230,214 | — | 923 | 6 | 3 | 5,244 | 3,470 | — | 30 | 1,461 | 436 | 11,830 | 6,022 | 1,890 | 578 | 16,273 | 6,901 | 479,891 | 248,577 |
| | Madras | 26 | 51 | — | — | — | — | — | — | — | — | — | — | — | — | 1,349 | 863 | 846 | 720 | 2,221 | 1,634 |
| | Bombay | 4 | 19 | — | — | — | — | — | — | 1,277 | 172 | 19,061 | 6,874 | 5,135 | 2,936 | 4,372 | 1,788 | 2,009 | 1,453 | 31,858 | 13,242 |
| | **ALL INDIA** | **443,217** | **230,284** | — | **923** | **6** | **3** | **5,244** | **3,470** | — | **202** | **20,522** | **7,310** | **16,965** | **8,958** | **7,611** | **3,229** | **19,128** | **9,074** | **513,970** | **263,453** |
| 1855-56 | Bengal | 569,104 | 317,183 | 297 | 211 | 606 | 318 | 3,339 | 1,940 | 36 | 23 | 5,572 | 1,334 | 3,773 | 2,589 | 1,215 | 377 | 2,027 | 1,033 | 585,969 | 325,008 |
| | Madras | 45 | 243 | — | — | — | — | — | — | — | — | — | — | — | — | 2,428 | 1,327 | 1,205 | 880 | 3,678 | 2,450 |
| | Bombay | 140 | 128 | — | 10 | — | — | — | — | 79 | 172 | 8,604 | 6,227 | 6,684 | 4,434 | 9,207 | 1,349 | 2,322 | 1,257 | 27,036 | 13,577 |
| | **ALL INDIA** | **569,289** | **317,554** | **297** | **221** | **606** | **318** | **3,339** | **1,940** | **115** | **195** | **14,176** | **7,561** | **10,457** | **7,023** | **12,850** | **3,053** | **5,554** | **3,170** | **616,683** | **341,035** |
| 1856-57 | Bengal | 437,860 | 241,230 | 3,108 | 1,618 | 153 | 109 | 2,187 | 1,243 | — | 71 | 3,928 | 959 | 3,587 | 2,016 | — | 620 | — | 853 | 452,431 | 248,719 |
| | Madras | 40 | 119 | — | — | — | — | — | — | — | — | — | — | — | — | 749 | 482 | 856 | 685 | 1,645 | 1,286 |
| | Bombay | — | 54 | — | — | — | — | — | — | 2,158 | 624 | — | 14,300 | — | 9,320 | 13,668 | 4,560 | — | 2,587 | — | 31,445 |
| | **ALL INDIA** | — | **241,403** | **3,108** | **1,618** | **153** | **109** | **2,187** | **1,243** | — | **695** | — | **15,259** | — | **11,336** | — | **5,662** | — | **4,125** | — | **281,450** |
| 1857-58 | Bengal | 154,510 | 92,682 | — | 570 | 455 | 250 | — | 354 | 14 | 7 | 219 | 120 | 3,526 | 3,183 | — | 4,081 | — | 2,014 | — | 103,261 |
| | Madras | 15 | 10 | — | — | — | — | — | — | — | — | 9 | 3 | — | — | 44 | 26 | 2,051 | 948 | 2,119 | 987 |
| | Bombay | — | — | — | — | — | — | — | — | 33,720 | 1,368 | — | 27,130 | — | 16,742 | 19,078 | 5,146 | — | 3,590 | — | 53,976 |
| | **ALL INDIA** | **154,525** | **92,692** | — | **570** | **455** | **250** | — | **354** | **33,734** | **1,375** | — | **27,253** | — | **19,925** | — | **9,253** | — | **6,552** | — | **158,224** |

TABLE (A.) SHOWING QUANTITIES OF SILK, &c.—*continued.*

| Years. | Whence Exported. | United Kingdom. | | France. | | Other parts of Europe. | | America. | | China. | | Arabian and Persian Gulfs. | | Aden and Suez. | | Straits Settlements. | | Other parts. | | Total Exported to all parts. | |
|---|---|---|---|---|---|---|---|---|---|---|---|---|---|---|---|---|---|---|---|---|---|
| | | Quantity. | Value. | Quantity. | Value. | Quantity. | Value. | Quantity. | Value. | Quantity. | Value. | Quantity. | Value. | Quantity. | Value. | Quantity. | Value. | Quantity. | Value. | Quantity. | Value. |
| | | Pieces. | £ | Pieces. | £ | Pieces. | £ | Pieces. | £ | Pieces. | £ | Pieces. | £ | Pieces. | £ | Pieces. | £ | Pieces. | £ | Pieces. | £ |
| 1858-59 | Bengal | — | 157,374 | — | 759 | — | 211 | — | 234 | — | 219 | — | 480 | — | 1,399 | — | 322 | — | 1,958 | — | 162,956 |
| | Madras | 181 | 221 | — | — | — | — | — | — | — | — | — | — | — | — | 998 | 621 | 1,754 | 1,295 | 2,933 | 2,187 |
| | Bombay | 2,800 | 843 | 35 | 72 | — | — | — | 1,588 | — | 1,275 | — | 20,154 | — | 6,821 | — | 2,649 | — | 14,613 | — | 48,015 |
| | ALL INDIA | — | **158,438** | — | **831** | — | **211** | — | **1,822** | — | **1,494** | — | **20,634** | — | **8,220** | — | **3,592** | — | **17,866** | — | **213,108** |
| 1859-60 | Bengal | 275,880 | 146,212 | 786 | 449 | 447 | 242 | 686 | 995 | 23 | 12 | 61 | 31 | 2,629 | 1,459 | 1,266 | 896 | 4,442 | 2,409 | 286,220 | 152,795 |
| | Madras | — | 6 | — | — | — | — | 1 | 1 | — | — | — | — | — | — | 2,604 | 1,058 | 1,915 | 1,396 | 4,519 | 2,461 |
| | Bombay | — | 120 | — | — | — | — | — | — | — | 1,071 | — | 18,748 | — | 8,098 | — | 4,299 | — | 3,917 | — | 36,253 |
| | ALL INDIA | — | **146,338** | **786** | **449** | **447** | **242** | **687** | **996** | — | **1,083** | — | **18,779** | — | **9,557** | — | **6,253** | — | **7,812** | — | **191,509** |
| 1860-61 | Bengal | 167,262 | 96,493 | 1,513 | 916 | — | 14 | 823 | 1,322 | 25 | 30 | 261 | 121 | 832 | 430 | — | 1,616 | — | 901 | 171,847 | 101,843 |
| | Madras | 27 | 27 | — | — | — | — | — | — | — | — | — | — | — | — | 115 | 53 | 2,098 | 1,609 | 2,240 | 1,689 |
| | Bombay | 367 | 237 | 2 | 3 | — | — | — | — | 7,219 | 789 | 13,350 | 8,547 | 6,056 | 3,598 | 9,085 | 4,390 | 1,376 | 1,691 | 37,455 | 19,255 |
| | ALL INDIA | **167,656** | **96,757** | **1,515** | **919** | — | **14** | **823** | **1,322** | **7,244** | **819** | **13,611** | **8,668** | **6,888** | **4,028** | — | **6,059** | — | **4,201** | **211,542** | **122,787** |
| 1861-62 | Bengal | — | 129,828 | — | 652 | — | 50 | — | 57 | — | 102 | — | 1,087 | — | 1,814 | — | 3,192 | — | 1,588 | — | 138,370 |
| | Madras | — | 81 | — | — | — | — | — | — | — | — | — | — | — | — | — | 220 | — | 984 | — | 1,235 |
| | Bombay | — | 195 | — | — | — | — | — | — | — | 581 | — | 10,258 | — | 14,420 | — | 1,932 | — | 1,815 | — | 29,201 |
| | ALL INDIA | — | **130,104** | — | **652** | — | **50** | — | **57** | — | **683** | — | **11,345** | — | **16,234** | — | **5,344** | — | **4,337** | — | **168,806** |
| 1862-63 | Bengal | — | 118,628 | — | 2,664 | — | 111 | — | 24 | — | 168 | — | 977 | — | 1,457 | — | 1,141 | — | 4,806 | — | 129,976 |
| | Madras | — | 61 | — | — | — | — | — | — | — | — | — | — | — | — | — | 1,152 | — | 1,758 | — | 2,971 |
| | Bombay | — | 9 | — | — | — | — | — | — | — | 1,486 | — | 12,692 | — | 12,218 | — | 650 | — | 4,344 | — | 31,419 |
| | ALL INDIA | — | **118,718** | — | **2,664** | — | **111** | — | **24** | — | **1,654** | — | **13,669** | — | **13,675** | — | **2,943** | — | **10,908** | — | **164,366** |
| 1863-64 | Bengal | — | 70,918 | — | 669 | — | — | — | 149 | — | 161 | — | 434 | — | 1,314 | — | 2,352 | — | 4,511 | — | 80,508 |
| | Madras | — | 7 | — | — | — | — | — | — | — | — | — | — | — | — | — | 1,761 | — | 2,526 | — | 4,294 |
| | Bombay | — | 56 | — | 2 | — | — | — | — | — | 1,268 | — | 13,096 | — | 10,442 | — | 1,713 | — | 3,728 | — | 30,305 |
| | ALL INDIA | — | **70,981** | — | **671** | — | — | — | **149** | — | **1,429** | — | **13,530** | — | **11,756** | — | **5,826** | — | **10,765** | — | **115,107** |
| 1864-65 | Bengal | 108,130 | 62,979 | 3,278 | 2,401 | — | — | 25 | 47 | 144 | 47 | 7,695 | 3,391 | 16,609 | 6,492 | 754 | 433 | 5,552 | 3,767 | 142,187 | 79,557 |
| | Madras | 30 | 39 | — | — | — | — | — | — | — | — | — | — | — | — | 883 | 863 | 4,244 | 3,534 | 5,157 | 4,436 |
| | Bombay | — | 1,148 | — | 55 | — | — | — | — | — | 1,674 | — | 8,022 | — | 7,671 | — | 149 | — | 3,886 | — | 22,605 |
| | ALL INDIA | — | **64,166** | — | **2,456** | — | — | 25 | 47 | — | **1,721** | — | **11,413** | — | **14,163** | — | **1,445** | — | 11,187 | — | **106,598** |

## 1. Silk and Cotton.—Plain, Striped, and Checked.

| No of Vol. | No of Sample. | | Description. | Measurement. Length. | Measurement. Width. | Weight of Piece. | Cost. | Place of manufacture, or where obtained. |
|---|---|---|---|---|---|---|---|---|
| | | | | yds. ins. | yds. ins. | lbs. oz. | £ s. d. | |
| XII. | 447 | | Shot, pink silk warp and blue cotton weft. For petticoats. | 11 15 | 0 23 | 0 $14\frac{1}{2}$ | 0 10 0 | Tanjore, Madras. |
| IV. | 134 | Striped; for Trowserings, &c. | White, with narrow lines of pale green silk, 10 to the inch. $\frac{3}{4}$ inch border, a plain red silk stripe. For trowserings. | 9 18 | 0 21 | 1 2 | 0 10 0 | Lahore. |
| IV. | 141 | Striped; for Trowserings, &c. | Green cotton, with small $1\frac{1}{12}$-inch yellow stripe dotted with white thread and crimson silk, $\frac{1}{8}$ inch apart. Border ($\frac{5}{8}$ inch) of deep crimson silk. For trowserings. | 5 22 | 0 21 | 0 12 | 0 4 0 | Rutul Mudpore, Punjab. |
| IX. | 355 | Striped; for Trowserings, &c. | Green cotton, with $\frac{1}{3}$-inch stripes of crimson and white silk in the warp $\frac{1}{4}$ inch apart. | 11 27 | 0 22 | 1 10 | 0 8 6 | Tanjore, Madras. |
| XII. | 444 | Striped; for Trowserings, &c. | Crimson cotton, with green cotton and figured yellow silk stripes. A piece comprises six of this measurement, woven with a "fag" between. For cholees. | 0 24 | 0 19 | 0 $1\frac{1}{2}$ | 0 1 9 per cholee piece. | Trichinopoly, Madras. |
| XII. | 446 | Striped; for Trowserings, &c. | Gauze, blue cotton weft, and red silk warp, with flashed cross stripes of white, 2 inches apart. For petticoats. | 7 0 | 0 23 | 0 13 | 0 14 0 | Trichinopoly Madras. |
| XII. | 448 | Striped; for Trowserings, &c. | Dark blue cotton weft, and a silk warp. Pattern, black ground with flashed spots, yellow and white, and $1\frac{1}{3}$ inch figured stripes of crimson, yellow, and white silks, $\frac{5}{8}$ inch apart. Used for trowserings by Mahomedans of both sexes. Soosee, for trowserings. | 7 0 | 0 33 | 0 14 | 0 8 0 | Trichinopoly, Madras. |
| XII. | 449 | Striped; for Trowserings, &c. | Dark blue cotton weft, and crimson silk warp. Pattern, flashed spotted stripes in white across piece 1 inch apart. Soosee, for trowserings and dress skirts. | 8 0 | 1 0 | 0 15 | 0 8 0 | Syempettah, Madras. |
| XII. | 451 | Striped; for Trowserings, &c. | Dark blue cotton weft, and crimson silk warp. Pattern, a fine line warp stripe in white silk. Soosee, for trowserings and petticoats. | 7 0 | 0 33 | 0 12 | 0 8 0 | Trichinopoly, Madras. |
| XII. | 452 | Striped; for Trowserings, &c. | Dark blue cotton weft, narrow stripes in warp, of red and yellow silk. Soosee, for trowserings. | 11 0 | 0 27 | 1 9 | 0 8 0 | Trichinopoly, Madras. |
| IX. | 352 | Checked. | Crimson silk and black and white cotton check. | 11 27 | 0 22 | 1 0 | 0 7 0 | Tanjore, Madras. |
| IX. | 353 | Checked. | White cotton, with green and crimson silk check. | 11 27 | 0 22 | 1 0 | 0 7 6 | Ditto. |
| IX. | 356 | Checked. | Rose colour silk, with small dark blue cotton check. | 12 0 | 0 22 | 1 0 | 0 9 6 | Ditto. |
| IX. | 358 | Checked. | Light texture, dark blue cotton, with check of crimson silk. | 11 27 | 0 22 | 1 0 | 0 9 0 | Ditto. |
| XIV. | 542 | Checked. | Yellow silk in warp, all cotton weft. Pattern, a small faint red check. | 10 18 | 0 28 | 1 $6\frac{1}{4}$ | — | Agra, N.W.P. |

## 2. Silk and Cotton.—Mushroo or Satin; Plain, Striped, and Figured.

| No. of | | Description. | Measurement. | | Weight of Piece. | Cost. | Place of manufacture, or where obtained. |
|---|---|---|---|---|---|---|---|
| Vol. | Sample. | | Length. | Width. | | | |
| | | | yds. ins. | yds. ins. | lbs. oz. | £ s. d. | |
| XIII. | 500 | Plain rose pink colour - - - - | 5 31 | 0 31 | 1 2 | 1 18 0 | Hyderabad, Deccan. |
| XIII. | 507 | Plain dark green - - - - | 5 37 | 0 30½ | 1 2½ | 1 16 0 | Hyderabad, Deccan. |
| XIII. | 510 | Plain crimson - - - - | 6 0 | 0 32 | 1 4 | 1 16 0 | Hyderabad, Deccan. |
| XIII. | 514 | Ditto, lighter shade than last example - | 4 22 | 0 31 | 0 10½ | 1 18 0 | Hyderabad, Deccan, bought in Madras. |
| XIII. | 515 | Plain white - - - - | 4 16 | 0 32½ | 0 15 | 1 9 0 | Hyderabad, Deccan. |
| XIII. | 486 | Crimson, with a loom embroidered flower (2 inches in length) in green and yellow silks. | 5 19 | 0 32 | 1 10½ | 2 0 0 | Hyderabad, Deccan, bought in Madras. |
| XIII. | 487 | Deep purple, flowered with crimson, white, green, and yellow. | 5 0 | 0 30½ | 1 7 | 2 0 0 | Hyderabad, Deccan, bought in Madras. |
| XIII. | 492 | Deep crimson, with figured white silk stripes. | 4 24 | 0 29 | 0 11 | 0 11 6 | Tanjore, Madras. |
| XIII. | 493 | Yellow, and deep crimson stripes, with spots of white. | 6 15 | 1 0 | 1 10½ | 0 16 0 | Tanjore, Madras. |
| XIII. | 494 | A bronze coloured ground, with figured green stripes. | 6 30 | 1 0 | 1 2 | 1 16 0 | Hyderabad, Deccan, bought in Madras. |
| XIII. | 495 | Deep purple ground, striped with a narrow line of yellow, dotted with crimson. Across the piece are zigzag stripes of white silk, tinged with crimson. | 6 9 | 0 33 | 1 7 | 0 16 0 | Tanjore, Madras. |
| XIII. | 496 | Stripes of plain crimson, yellow, and green (the last named with a central line of red), divided by figured and flowered stripes in crimson, yellow, and white silks. | 5 0 | 1 0 | 1 10 | 0 17 0 | Trichinopoly, Madras. |
| XIII. | 497 | Dark green ground, with cross stripes of flashed spots in white. | 6 0 | 0 31 | 1 4½ | 1 7 0 | Hyderabad, |
| XIII. | 498 | Figured stripes, separated alternately by plain green, blue, and yellow stripes, with central line of crimson and red, and a plain crimson stripe, with yellow central line. | 5 0 | 1 0 | 1 5 | 0 17 0 | Trichinopoly, Madras. |

TABLE 2.—*continued.*

| No. of | | Description. | Measurement. | | Weight of piece. | Cost. | Place of Manufacture, or where obtained. |
|---|---|---|---|---|---|---|---|
| Vol. | Sample. | | Length. | Width. | | | |
| | | | yds. ins. | yds. ins. | lbs. oz. | £ s. d. | |
| XIII. | 499 | Yellow, with figured stripes. Same pattern as No. 494. | 5 32 | 0 30½ | 1 4 | 1 18 0 | Hyderabad, Deccan. |
| XIII. | 501 | Crimson, with small zigzag cross stripes in white silk. | 6 0 | 0 32 | 1 3½ | 1 16 0 | Hyderabad, Deccan, bought in Madras. |
| XIII. | 502 | A deep purple, with a shaded stripe in the warp. | 3 20 | 0 34 | 0 13 | 0 11 0 | Trichinopoly, Madras. |
| XIII. | 503 | Crimson, with small zigzag cross stripes in white silk. | 6 9 | 0 33 | 1 9 | 0 17 0 | Trichinopoly, Madras. |
| XIII. | 504 | Crimson, with cross stripes of flashed spots in yellow silk. | 5 31 | 0 26 | 1 2 | 1 18 0 | Hyderabad, Deccan. |
| XIII. | 505 | Figured stripes in orange, yellow, and crimson; the intervening spaces alternately green, purple, and crimson, through which (but intersected by the figured stripe) run zigzag cross stripes of yellow on the green, and white on the purple and crimson ground colour. | 6 41 | 0 34½ | 1 11½ | 1 0 0 | Tanjore, Madras. |
| XIII. | 506 | Purple, with a zigzag cross stripe of white like 501 and 503, but tinged with crimson. | 4 27 | 0 35 | 1 6 | 0 17 0 | Trichinopoly, Madras. |
| XIII. | 508 | Dark crimson, with narrow white lines in warp, 1 inch apart. | 5 0 | 1 0 | 1 5 | 0 17 0 | Trichinopoly, Madras. |
| XIII. | 509 | Orange, with narrow stripes of white, with dark crimson edges. | 6 15 | 1 0 | 2 7 | 0 18 0 | Tanjore, Madras. |
| XIII. | 511 | Bright yellow, with narrow figured stripes in crimson, yellow, white, and purple silks; the intervening spaces dotted with rows of flashed spots, alternately crimson and green, arranged to run in diagonal order throughout piece. | 5 27 | 0 27 | 1 6 | 1 16 0 | Hyderabad. |
| XIII. | 512 | Rose pink, with figured stripes, of pattern similar to 494 and 499. | 5 33 | 0 30 | 1 1 | 1 15 0 | Hyderabad, Deccan, bought in Madras. |
| XIII. | 513 | Plain amber colour, with stripes figured with flashed spots of an arrow-head shape, in green, crimson, and yellow silk. | 6 14 | 1 0 | 1 6 | 0 14 0 | Trichinopoly, Madras. |

## 3. Silk.—Plain, Striped, Checked, and Figured.

| No. of Vol. | No. of Sample. | | Description. | Measurement. Length. | Measurement. Width. | Weight of piece. | Cost. | Place of Manufacture, or where obtained. |
|---|---|---|---|---|---|---|---|---|
| | | | | yds. ins. | yds. ins. | lbs. oz. | £ s. d. | |
| XIV. | 521 | Plain. | Red. Stout fabric. Extensively used in the Punjab for making up, and also for lining garments. Favourite old Mahomedan colour. | 17 15 | 0 21½ | 2 9¾ | 3 0 0 | Lahore. |
| XIV. | 522 | Plain. | Shot. Blue warp, crimson weft. Favourite Hindu colour. | 13 9 | 0 21½ | 1 8½ | 1 16 0 | Lahore. |
| XIV. | 523 | Plain. | Light green. Favourite Mahomedan colour. | 15 31 | 0 20½ | 2 1 | 3 0 0 | Lahore. |
| XIV. | 524 | Plain. | Shot. Crimson warp, blue weft. Favourite Hindu colour. | 24 0 | 0 20½ | 2 8¼ | 3 9 0 | Lahore. |
| XIV. | 532 | Plain. | Rose-coloured. "Golabee Durreeace." | 6 11 | 0 13 | 0 4 | 0 10 6 | Agra, N.W.P. |
| XIV. | 540 | Plain. | Pink. "Yeolah." Thin texture - | 11 0 | 1 5 | 1 3 | 5 7 3 | Ahmednugger, Bombay. |
| XIV. | 541 | Plain. | Bright yellow - - - | 39 18 | 0 11½ | 1 0¼ | 1 9 8½ | Agra. |
| IV. | 131 | Striped. | Yellow, with ¾-inch stripes of deep crimson. In 2-inch space between each, eight narrow black and white stripes. Used for trowserings. | 6 17 | 0 28 | 0 12 | 0 18 10½ | Deyra Ishmael Khan. |
| IX. | 354 | Striped. | Deep crimson, striped with dark blue fine lines, 15 to the inch. Used for trowserings. | 9 0 | 0 30 | 0 10 | 0 18 0 | Tanjore, Madras. |
| XIII. | 516 | Striped. | Red ground, with figured zigzag stripes. For trowserings. | 9 4 | 0 37 | 0 14 | 1 10 0 | Trichinopoly, Madras. |
| XIII. | 517 | Striped. | Red ground, with flowered stripes in white and yellow. In centre of intervening spaces a double line of yellow with a centre tinged by an underthread of blue. For trowserings. | 8 27 | 0 35 | 1 2 | 2 2 0 | Trichinopoly, Madras. |
| XIII. | 518 | Striped. | Green, with flashed spots faintly marked in yellow running in rows across piece. Used for trowserings, &c. | 11 0 | 0 33 | 0 14½ | 2 0 0 | Trichinopoly, Madras. |
| XIII. | 519 | Striped. | Stripes of orange, yellow, red, and green crosswise through the piece, and, intersected by the orange and yellow stripe, a series of flashed spots in white and yellow. For trowserings. | 9 0 | 0 34 | 0 12 | 0 17 0 | Trichinopoly, Madras. |
| XIII. | 520 | Striped. | Amber-coloured, with faint longitudinal lines of white, ¼ inch apart. For trowserings. | 9 6 | 0 34 | 0 11½ | 0 19 0 | Tanjore, Madras. |
| XIV. | 525 | Striped. | Deep crimson, with narrow warp lines of green, ⅜ inch apart. Old Mahomedan pattern. | 17 33 | 0 21½ | 2 7 | 3 0 0 | Lahore. |
| XIV. | 526 | Striped. | Yellow, with narrow warp lines of red, ⅜ inch apart. Old Hindu pattern. | 15 0 | 0 22 | 2 3 | 4 6 0 | Lahore. |
| XIV. | 527 | Striped. | Deep crimson, with narrow warp lines of white, ⅜ inch apart. Favourite Hindu pattern. | 18 0 | 0 21½ | 2 8 | 3 6 0 | Lahore. |
| XIV. | 528 | Striped. | Green, with narrow warp lines of red, ⅜ inch apart. Old Hindu pattern. | 16 15 | 0 21 | 2 2¼ | 3 0 0 | Lahore. |

TABLE 3.—*continued.*

| No. of Vol. | No. of Sample. | | Description. | Measurement. Length. | Measurement. Width. | Weight of piece. | Cost. | Place of Manufacture, or where obtained. |
|---|---|---|---|---|---|---|---|---|
| | | | | yds. ins. | yds. ins. | lbs. oz. | £ s. d. | |
| XIV. | 529 | | Plum-coloured, with narrow warp lines of yellow, $\frac{3}{8}$ inch apart. Old Hindu pattern. | 15 26 | 0 $21\frac{1}{2}$ | 2 5 | 2 16 0 | Lahore. |
| XIV. | 530 | | Shot. Pink weft. Light blue warp, with narrow lines of red, $\frac{3}{8}$ inch apart. Old Mahomedan pattern. | 16 18 | 0 21 | 1 $13\frac{1}{4}$ | 2 6 0 | Lahore. |
| XIV. | 531 | | Shot. Crimson weft. Blue warp, with narrow lines of yellow, $\frac{5}{16}$ of an inch apart. Old Hindu pattern. | 8 0 | 0 19 | 0 $10\frac{3}{4}$ | 1 2 6 | Deyra Ishmael Khan. |
| XIV. | 537 | | White ground, with $\frac{1}{6}$-inch stripes of yellow and red, alternately with a $\frac{1}{16}$-inch stripe of purple, $\frac{1}{16}$ inch apart. | 5 18 | 0 $31\frac{1}{2}$ | 0 $11\frac{1}{2}$ | — | Bhawulpore, Punjab. |
| XIV. | 538 | | *Elaiche.* A rose-crimson ground with narrow warp lines of white, $\frac{1}{8}$ inch apart. Old Hindu pattern. | 19 11 | 0 19 | 1 5 | 1 14 0 | Agra. |
| XIV. | 539 | | *Durreeaee.* Yellow ground, with cross stripe of red and green alternately with a double line stripe of a reddish-brown colour. | 14 14 | 0 11 | 0 $6\frac{1}{4}$ | 0 10 6 | Agra. |
| XIV. | 546 | | Green, pink, yellow, and crimson stripes. A peculiar pattern, with a flashed angulated figure throughout. | 8 26 | 0 $27\frac{1}{2}$ | 1 $1\frac{1}{4}$ | — | Pegu. |
| IX. | 351 | CHECKED. | Tartan pattern - - - | 9 0 | 0 22 | 0 15 | 1 2 0 | Tanjore, Madras. |
| XIV. | 533 | CHECKED. | *Sungee Charkhanah.* Check pattern. The various coloured stripes crossed by small angulated lines also of different tints. | 4 33 | 0 27 | 0 $7\frac{3}{4}$ | 1 10 0 | Benares. |
| XIV. | 535 | CHECKED. | White silk, with faint lavender-colour stripes in the warp checked by 1-inch stripes of a dark purple colour in the weft. | 15 0 | 1 0 | 1 $10\frac{1}{2}$ | — | Bhagulpore. |
| XIV. | 536 | CHECKED. | White silk, with open check formed by a broad and a narrow stripe of purple. | 15 0 | 1 0 | 1 10 | — | Berhampore. |
| XIII. | 485 | FIGURED. | Silk brocade. Green ground, with closely studded pattern of a small star-shaped flower in white silk, with central spot in crimson silk. | 5 14 | 0 31 | 1 8 | — | Hyderabad, Deccan. Bought in Madras. |
| XIV. | 534 | FIGURED. | Pink ground, with stripes ($\frac{1}{2}$ inch wide and $\frac{3}{8}$ inch apart), figured with a circular flower pattern in crimson silk, and margins formed by a yellow and black dotted line. | 5 32 | 0 $28\frac{1}{2}$ | 0 $15\frac{1}{2}$ | — | Bhawulpore, Punjab. |

## 4. Silk.—Printed.

| No. of Vol. | No. of Sample. | Description. | Measurement. Length. | Measurement. Width. | Weight of Piece. | Cost. | Place of Manufacture, or where obtained. |
|---|---|---|---|---|---|---|---|
| | | | yds. ins. | yds. ins. | lbs. oz. | £ s. d. | |
| XIV. | 548 | *Lahe meenia.* Blue. Pattern, a circular flower in light green, arranged diagonally, and interspersed with small round spot of same colour. Border, 12 inches wide, scroll, with "Kutar" inner edge; all in circular red spots. | 1 11 | 1 21 | 0 5¼ | 0 6 0 | Surat, Bombay. |
| XIV. | 549 | "Black Lahe," black ground. Pattern, square dark red spots, with inner circle of white and central dot of black, arranged in irregular diagonal order. Border, 2¼ inches wide, of crimson silk, pattern marked in white spots, with dotted centre. Whole surface glazed subsequent to printing. | 1 10 | 0 29 | 0 1¾ | 0 6 0 | Surat, Bombay. |
| XIV. | 550 | Crimson silk. Pattern (arranged in diagonal rows) a white spot, with crimson central dot; larger design than the foregoing. Border, 3¼ inches wide, black, with figured pattern formed by white spots with dotted centre, interspersed with red spots, with inner circle of white and central speck of black. | 0 31½ | 0 30 | 0 2 | 0 3 0 | Surat, Bombay. |
| XIV. | 551 | Deep purple ground. Pattern, a check formed by cross diagonal rows (¾ inch apart) of dark red circular spots, in each square of the check four similar spots. Border, 2 inches wide, a dotted scroll pattern, with "Kutar" inner edge. | 0 32 | 0 31 | 0 2 | 0 5 3 | Surat, Bombay. |

## WILD SILKS.

In the Table which follows are included the examples given in the Books of Textiles made from what, in contradistinction to the foregoing, or cultivated variety, may be called Wild Silks. Of these the *Tussur*, *Eria*, and *Moonga* are the most common, and fabrics made of some of them—and particularly of the Moonga—have probably been known in the East from time immemorial.

Although Tussur is the variety of *wild silk* best known in this country, the Moonga, from its superiority in point of gloss and other qualities, is that most commonly employed, especially for the manufacture of mixed fabrics, and for some kinds of embroidery.

No. 294, Vol. VIII., is an example of a fabric consisting of cotton striped with Moonga silk.

Mixed fabrics of this description are stated by Taylor to form the fourth class of the Textile manufactures of Dacca, the cotton yarn used in their manufacture ranging from $30^s$ to $80^s$.

The Silk—*Muga* or *Moonga*—is imported into Dacca from Sylhet and Assam. It is prepared for the loom by being first steeped in water mixed with powdered turmeric, and afterwards in lime juice. It is next rinsed, dried, and sized with paste made of parched rice and water, without an admixture of lime, and then reeled and warped in the same manner as cotton thread. The cloths of this class are of considerable variety both as regards texture and pattern. Some consist chiefly of cotton, with only a silk border or a silk flower or figure, in each corner; others are striped, chequered, or figured with silk throughout the body of the cloth. The different varieties may amount to thirty in number, but the principal ones are the *Kutawroomee*, *Nowbutee*, *Azeezoola*, and *Luchuck*.

These cloths are made exclusively for the markets of Arabia. Some, indeed, are occasionally shipped to Rangoon, Penang, and places to the eastward, but the far greater portion of them is exported to Jidda, whence they are sent into the interior of the country. A considerable quantity of them is sold at the annual fair held at Meena, in the vicinity of Mecca. They are made into turbans, gowns, vests, &c. by the Arabs. They were formerly transported from Jidda to Egypt, and were at one time the principal articles of export from Dacca to Bassora, whence they were sent to various parts of Mesopotamia and to Constantinople.

Of the Eria, two examples of fabrics from which (Nos. 559 and 560, Vol. XIV.) are given, little need here be said. Although possessed of great durability, the Eria, like the Tussur, is defective in the gloss which gives such beauty to true silk.

| No. of | | Description. | Measurement. | | Weight of Piece. | Cost. | Place of Manufacture, or where obtained. |
|---|---|---|---|---|---|---|---|
| Vol. | Sample. | | Length. | Width. | | | |
| | | | yds. ins. | yds. ins. | lbs. oz. | £ s. d. | |
| XIV. | 556 | Tussur silk, *plain* - - - - | 10 18 | 1 1 | 1 15¼ | 0 15 10½ | Warungul, Deccan. |
| XIV. | 557 | Tussur silk, *dyed*. Grey warp and blue weft. A twilled material. | 11 0 | 0 26 | 1 7½ | 0 13 0 | Bhagulpore, |
| XIV. | 558 | Tussur silk, a large *coloured* check or plaid on a blue ground, woven in coloured Tussur thread. | 9 18 | 0 25½ | 1 4 | 0 13 0 | Bhagulpore. |
| XIV. | 559 | Eria silk, "Dooklee," a coarse material in *uncoloured* thread. | 4 0 | 0 34 | 1 6 | 0 4 0 | Cachar. |
| XIV. | 560 | Eria silk "Endi," a coarse material of dyed Eria silk, dyed chocolate red. | 3 2 | 1 4 | 1 4 | — | Darjeeling. |
| VIII. | 294 | Cotton, with ⅜ inch stripes of Moonga silk in the warp, ¼ inch apart. | 4 16 | 1 0 | 0 8 | — | Dacca. |

The following description, by Buchanan, of the preparation of Tussur (or, as he renders it, Tasar) thread and its manufacture in Bhagulpore, although given with a certain reservation as to the accuracy of some of the details, will be read with interest.

It has to be premised, however, that the description here given refers to a period long anterior to the present.

"Of the weavers who work in Tasar silk, a few weave cloth entirely of that material, but the quantity is so trifling that I shall take no further notice of it, and confine myself to detail the accounts of the mixed cloth called Bhagulpuri, because almost the whole of it is woven in the vicinity of that town; for out of 3,275 looms, stated to be in the district, 3,000 of these were said to be in the Kotwali division. The women of the weavers mostly wind the thread, although the men sometimes assist. These people are so timid, that no great reliance can be placed on what they say; but I shall mention what was stated by two men that came to me at Mungger from Bhagulpoor.

"A woman takes five pans of cocoons (405), and puts them in a large earthen pot with 600 sicca weight of water, a small mat being placed in the bottom to prevent the cocoons from being burned. A small quantity of potash, tied in a bit of cloth, is put into the pot, along with the cocoons, which are boiled about an European hour. They are then cooled, the water is changed, and they are again boiled. The water is poured off, and the cocoons are put into another pot, where they stand three days in the sun covered with a cloth to exclude insects. On the fourth day they are again boiled, with 200 sicca weight of water, for rather less than an hour, and then poured into a basket, where they are allowed to cool, after which they are washed in cold water, and placed to dry on a layer of cow-dung ashes, where they remain spread, and covered with a cloth, for six hours. The woman then picks out such cocoons as are not quite ready for winding, and exposes them for a day or two to the sun, which completes the operation. The outer filaments of the cocoon are then picked off, and form a substance called Jhuri, of which the potters make brushes used for applying a pigment to their vessels. The fibres from 4 to 5 cocoons are then wound off on a miserable conical reel which is twirled round by one hand, while the thread is twisted on the thigh, the cocoons adjusted, and the broken fibres joined by the other. The cocoons while winding are not placed in water. This thread is called Lak, and after the Lak has been removed, there remains another inferior kind of filament, called also Jhuri, which is wound off, and is purchased by those who knit strings. Even the cocoons, that have been burst by the moth, are wound off; but owing to the frequent joinings give a weaker silk. When the Tasar is neither very high nor very low, that is, when 405 cocoons cost a rupee at Bhagulpoor, a woman boils and winds this number in 10 days.

"The kinds of cloths, most usually made, are as follows:—

"1st. Duriyas, the warp consists of three parts of cotton, and two parts of Tasar of different colours. The woof is all cotton of one colour, so that the cloth is striped lengthways, and is dyed entirely by the weavers in the thread. The pieces are most usually from 20 to 22 cubits long by $1\frac{1}{2}$ broad, and on an average sell at 42 annas. The cotton thread costs 22 annas, the Tasar $10\frac{1}{2}$ annas. A man can weave monthly $7\frac{1}{2}$ pieces.

"2nd. Namunahs are pieces from 20 to 22 cubits long and $1\frac{3}{4}$ broad; the most common price is 44 annas. The warp contains about 35 parts of cotton thread, and 21 of Tasar, disposed in stripes of a different pattern from those of the Duriya. The woof is all cotton. The cotton costs 21 annas, the Tasar 14 annas. The dying done by the weaver, the drugs costing 1 anna. The loom makes seven pieces a month.

"3rd. Chaharkhanahs. The pieces are about 18 cubits long and $\frac{7}{8}$ of a cubit wide. The average value is $2\frac{1}{2}$ rs. Each loom weaves $6\frac{1}{2}$ pieces in the month. The warp requires 10 parts of cotton, and 15 parts of Tasar; the woof 10 parts of cotton and 18 parts of Tasar, so that the pieces are checkered. The cotton thread is worth 6 annas, the Tasar 1r. 6as. The dyeing costs 4 annas.

"4th. Baftahs are pieces of an uniform colour, dyed after being woven. The pieces are of the same size with the Namunahs. All the warp is Tasar, the woof is cotton. The former costs 18 annas, the latter 20 annas; the dyeing and washing cost from 3 to 6 rs. for 20 pieces, or on an average 3 annas. The common price of the pieces is about 3rs. (from $2\frac{1}{2}$ to 5rs.) In the month a loom weaves $6\frac{1}{2}$ pieces. The foregoing kinds are mostly made for exportation; the following is mostly made for country use:—

"5th. Khariasri are pieces 12 cubits long and 2 cubits broad. They differ in size and fineness from the Duriyas. The Tasar costs 6 annas, the cotton $7\frac{1}{2}$ annas; the pieces on an average worth $1\frac{13}{16}$rs. and a man weaves eight pieces a month. The weaver dyes this kind.*

---

* Buchanan in "Martin's Eastern India," Vol. II. pp. 271–4.

## LOOM-EMBROIDERY.—GOLD AND SILVER.

In the subjoined Table are included the specimens in which gold and silver thread are employed in the decoration of piece goods.

The first group shows certain specimens in which the ornamentation is confined to the introduction of a gold border, which is used as a finish to the Cholee sleeve, &c.

In the second division, the piece—also for making up into Cholees—is striped with gold and silver throughout.

The third group shows examples of gold figured Mushroos.

In the fourth and last division, we come to the still more highly ornamental fabric to which the term Kincob* is applied.

Of the variety and beauty of the patterns produced in India by these combinations in the loom of silk, gold, and silver, only a faint idea can be obtained from the specimens given in the books.

Those who may desire to acquire fuller information, may do so by consulting the Collection at the India Museum.

The European manufacturer who may have attempted the introduction of metal into his fabrics, will all the more readily comprehend and admire the results obtained by the Indian weaver. The gold or silver thread used in the manufacture of the articles now under notice, is made by twisting the flattened wire, called *Badla*, around silk thread. The workmen who manufacture the gold and silver thread are called *Batwaiya* or *Kalabatu—Nakad* being the name applied to those who wind and twist the silk to make it fit for the operations of the former, whilst the weaver of the cloth itself is called *Tashbaf*.

The following description, by Captain Meadows Taylor, of the process by which gold and silver thread, called *Kullabutoon*, is manufactured in India will be read with interest.

" For gold thread, a piece of silver about the length and thickness of a man's forefinger is gilded at least three times heavily with the purest gold, all alloy being previously most carefully discharged from the silver. This piece of gilt silver is beaten out to the size of a stout wire, and is then drawn through successive holes in a steel plate until the wire is literally 'as fine as a hair.' The gilding is not disturbed by this process, and the wire finally appears as if of fine gold. It is then flattened in an extremely delicate and skilful manner. The workman, seated before a small and highly polished steel anvil, about two inches broad, with a steel plate in which there are two or three holes, set opposite to him and perpendicular to the anvil, and draws through these holes as many wires—two, or three as it may be—by a motion of the finger and thumb of his left hand, striking them rapidly but firmly with a steel hammer, the face of which is also polished like that of the anvil. This flattens the wire perfectly; and such is the skill of

* The name of this material is rendered in a variety of ways—Kincob, Kuncob, Kincaub, Kumkhwab, Keemkab, and lastly, Kinkhap. The fourth—kumkhwab—is the most correct rendering of the original Persian word; although Kincob, as being best known, is that which we have chosen.

manipulation, that no portion of the wires escapes the blow of the hammer, the action of drawing the wire, rapid as it is, being adjusted to the length which will be covered by the face of the hammer in its descent. No system of rollers or other machinery, could probably ensure the same effect, whether of extreme thinness of the flattened wire, or its softness and ductility.

"The method of winding the wire upon silk thread is also peculiar, and is effected as follows:

"The silk is very slightly twisted, and is rolled upon a winder. The end is then passed over a polished steel hook, fixed to a beam in the ceiling of the workshop, and to it is suspended a spindle with a long thin bamboo shank, slightly weighted to keep it steady, which nearly touches the floor. The workman gives the shank of the spindle a sharp turn upon his thigh, which sets it spinning with great rapidity. The gold wire, which has been wound on a reel as it passes behind the maker, is then applied to the bottom of the silk thread near the spindle and twists itself upwards, being guided by the workman as high as he can conveniently reach, or nearly his own height, upon the thread: but it is impossible to describe in exact terms, the curiously dexterous and rapid process of this manipulation. The spindle is then stopped; the thread now covered with wire is wound upon the spindle and fastened in a notch of the shank, when the silk thread is drawn down and the spindle is again set spinning with the same result as before. Certain lengths of the gold thread—'*kullabutoon*'—are made into skeins, and so sold or used by weavers.

"On examination of '*kullabutoon*,' the extreme thinnesss and flexibility of the flattened wire and its delicacy and beauty will at once be apparent, in comparison with attempts at a similar result, which are observable in Irish poplins or other brocades of Europe, which are made by rolling machinery. It is remarkable also, that the Indian brocades, gold and silver alike, never tarnish, but retain their lustre and colour even though washed. This is the result of the absolute purity both of the silver and gold employed, a point which, in Europe, is probably very little considered. There is no doubt that in India '*kullabutoon*' with considerable alloy in the wire, is also made and used; but never enters into the higher classes of manufactures."*

* A proof of the superiority of the Indian, over the European gold and silver wire as usually manufactured, was afforded at the late Dublin Exhibition; during the progress of which, the chief exhibitors of the Irish Poplins in which gold and silver thread was used, had to change their specimens on account of their becoming tarnished: whereas the metal embroidered fabrics from India, shown on the same occasion, retained their colour and lustre throughout.

## GOLD AND SILVER LOOM-EMBROIDERIES.

| No. of | | Description. | Measurement. | | Weight of piece. | Cost. | Place of Manufacture, or where obtained. |
|---|---|---|---|---|---|---|---|
| Vol. | Sample. | | Length. | Width. | | | |
| | | **SILK.—STRIPED AND CHECKED.—GOLD BORDERS ONLY.** | yds. ins. | yds. ins. | lbs. oz. | £ s. d. | |
| VI. | 201 | Blue silk, with $\frac{1}{8}$-inch stripes of darker blue, $\frac{1}{4}$ inch apart, this stripe being flowered at $\frac{1}{4}$-inch distances with white silk spots. Border, $2\frac{1}{2}$ inches wide, of rich gold lace pattern in crimson silk, with green silk lines. For cholees. | 4 27 | 1 $1\frac{1}{2}$ | 1 1 | 2 16 0 | Sattara, Deccan. |
| VI. | 202 | Green silk, with $\frac{1}{3}$-inch stripes of crimson, with black and white line. Border ($2\frac{1}{2}$ inches wide) of rich gold lace pattern in crimson silk, with green silk lines. For cholees. | 4 0 | 0 $35\frac{1}{2}$ | 0 11 | 2 16 0 | Sattara, Deccan. |
| VI. | 203 | Green silk. In the warp, narrow ($\frac{1}{8}$-inch) stripes of white with a crimson centre line, $\frac{1}{4}$ inch apart, checked by a similar but faint stripe in the weft. 3-inch border of rich flowered gold lace pattern in crimson silk, with green silk marginal lines. For cholees. | 4 23 | 1 1 | 1 0 | 4 0 0 | Sattara, Deccan. |
| VI. | 204 | Crimson silk. Narrow dotted white and black stripes ($\frac{1}{6}$ inch apart) in the warp, checked by similar lines in the weft, but in white only $\frac{1}{4}$ inch apart. 3-inch border of gold flowered lace pattern in crimson silk, with green silk marginal lines. For cholees. | 4 21 | 1 0 | 0 $14\frac{1}{2}$ | 4 0 0 | Sattara, Deccan. |
| | | **SILK.—STRIPED WITH GOLD OR SILVER.** | | | | | |
| XII. | 441 | Deep crimson silk, with ($\frac{1}{4}$ inch apart) small stripes of green silk into which two threads of gold are introduced in the warp. Six of these for six cholees, woven with a fag between, constitute one piece. | 0 17 | 0 29 | 0 $1\frac{1}{2}$ | 0 1 9 | Tanjore, Madras. |
| XII. | 442 | Pattern, small crimson silk stripes ($\frac{1}{3}$ inch apart), into which two silver threads are introduced. The ground is of blue silk warp and red silk weft, with a dotted angular figure in the blue silk of the warp. A piece comprises six of this measurement, woven with a connecting fag. | 0 17 | 0 29 | 0 $1\frac{1}{2}$ | 0 1 9 | Tanjore, Madras. |
| XII. | 443 | Pattern, small crimson silk stripes, $\frac{1}{2}$ inch apart, into which two silver threads are introduced. The ground of green silk warp and crimson weft, woven with a small green dotted figure. Six of these form a piece. | 0 17 | 0 29 | 0 $1\frac{1}{2}$ | 0 1 9 | Tanjore, Madras. |

| No. of Vol. | No. of Sample. | Group | Description. | Measurement. Length. | Measurement. Width. | Weight of piece. | Cost. | Place of Manufacture, or where obtained. |
|---|---|---|---|---|---|---|---|---|
| | | | | yds. ins. | yds. ins. | lbs. oz. | £ s. d. | |
| XIII. | 488 | Mushroo.—Gold Figured. | Green ground, deep crimson stripe, $2\frac{1}{8}$ inches wide, with lace pattern edges in yellow silks, and scroll and flower pattern centre in gold thread. In the intervening spaces a $1\frac{3}{4}$-inch flower in yellow silk and gold thread alternating with a small circular flower in gold thread. | 4 18 | 0 35 | 1 12 | 2 2 0 | Trichinopoly, Madras. |
| XIII. | 489 | Mushroo.—Gold Figured. | Deep purple ground, and figured stripe ($\frac{3}{8}$ inch wide) in yellow and crimson silk. In the intervening space a flower sprig in gold thread alternating with two small circular flowers, also in gold thread. | 4 27 | 0 24 | 0 14 | 2 4 0 | Trichinopoly, Madras. |
| XIII. | 490 | Mushroo.—Gold Figured. | Green ground, with small $\frac{1}{8}$-inch stripes of gold thread and crimson silk. | 6 0 | 0 28 | 1 5 | — | Hyderabad, Deccan. |
| XIII. | 491 | Mushroo.—Gold Figured. | Deep purple ground, striped with lines of white silk. In the intervening spaces a series of $\frac{1}{2}$-inch circular spots in gold thread, arranged in diagonal order across piece. | 4 18 | 0 24 | 0 14 | 2 4 0 | Tanjore, Madras. |
| VII. | 275 | Silk.—Gold Figured (Kincob). | Lavender-coloured silk gauze, with $\frac{3}{4}$-inch flowered stripes ($1\frac{1}{2}$ inch apart) in diagonal order. The flower in the stripe repeated between the stripes in three rows, closely woven in similar diagonal order, viz., left to right. The whole of the pattern in gold thread. | 4 20 | 0 34 | 2 $4\frac{1}{2}$ | — | Benares, N.W.P. |
| XIII. | 481 | Silk.—Gold Figured (Kincob). | Deep crimson silk (satin), with rows of flower sprigs in gold thread, intersected by a double row of smaller circular flowers, also in gold thread. Made up into all kinds of garments for both sexes of the richer classes. | 5 0 | 0 26 | 0 11 | 2 16 0 | Trichinopoly, Madras. |
| XIII. | 482 | Silk.—Gold Figured (Kincob). | Deep purple silk, with longitudinal figured stripes in crimson silk and gold thread. In the intervening spaces a row of small pines in gold thread alternating with a small figured spot in silver. | 5 9 | 0 34 | 0 15 | 1 11 0 | Tanjore, Madras. |
| XIII. | 483 | Silk.—Gold Figured (Kincob). | Deep crimson silk (satin). A richly figured pattern in gold thread, enclosing a flowered design, of which the upper portion is in gold thread and the lower part or base of the figure is in bright green and yellow floss silks. | 4 27 | 0 24 | 0 14 | 3 0 0 | Trichinopoly, Madras. |
| XIII. | 484 | Silk.—Gold Figured (Kincob). | Deep purple silk. A flowered pine-shaped figure in gold thread, in rows 4 inches apart, with two rows of a circular ($\frac{1}{2}$-inch) flower, and three rows of smaller spots, all worked in gold thread in the intervening spaces. Used for dress skirts. | 5 0 | 0 27 | 0 11 | 2 10 0 | Trichinopoly, Madras. |

## GOLD AND SILVER TISSUES.

In these Tissues the flattened wire—called *Taash*—instead of being twisted round silk thread, is itself used—the warp or the weft, as the case may be, being of very fine silk thread, so as to interfere as little as possible with the continuity of the surface presented by the metal. It is thus that the *cloths of gold and silver*, of which we hear in Eastern countries, are made. These are employed in India by the rich as sashes, for mantles to throw round their children's shoulders, for marriage garments, &c. An examination of the examples given in the books and described in the Table below will afford a good idea of this class of fabrics.

| No. of Vol. | No. of Sample. | | Description. | Measurement. Length. | Measurement. Width. | Weight of Piece. | Cost. | Place of Manufacture, or whence procured. |
|---|---|---|---|---|---|---|---|---|
| | | | | yds. ins. | yds. ins. | lbs. oz. | £ s. d. | |
| VII. | 261 | Gold.—Plain, Striped, and Figured. | Fine crimson silk weft, warp of flattened gold wire. (No. 270 illustrates the use of this kind of cloth as a basis for hand embroidery.) | 2 31 | 0 24 | 0 5 | about. 1 16 0 | Hyderabad, Deccan. |
| VII. | 263 | | Fine crimson silk weft, warp of gold, and striped with crimson silk cord. | 2 33 | 0 26½ | 0 5¾ | — | Hyderabad, Deccan. |
| VII. | 265 | | Fine crimson silk weft, warp of gold striped with green silk cord. | 2 0 | 0 25 | 0 4 | about. 1 16 0 | Hyderabad, Deccan. |
| VII. | 268 | | Warp of crimson silk, weft of gold (figured). | 1 9 | 0 28 | 0 5¼ | — | Moorshedabad, Bengal. |
| VII. | 262 | Silver.—Plain, Striped, and Figured. | Fine white silk weft, warp of flattened silver wire. | 2 32 | 0 23½ | 0 5¼ | — | Hyderabad, Deccan. |
| VII. | 264 | | Fine white silk weft, warp of silver - | 1 0 | 0 22½ | 0 1¾ | — | Hyderabad, Deccan. |
| VII. | 267 | | Warp of white silk, weft of silver - | 1 4 | 0 33½ | 0 4¼ | — | Moorshedabad, Bengal. |
| VII. | 266 | | Fine white silk weft, warp of silver, striped with crimson silk cord. | 2 33 | 0 24 | 0 5¼ | — | Hyderabad, Deccan. |
| VII. | 269 | | Warp of white silk, weft of silver, square figured pattern. | 1 8 | 0 31 | 0 5¼ | — | Moorshedabad, Bengal. |

In addition to these tissues, gold and silver lace is made in some quantity at Benares, Aurungabad, Boorhampore, Moorshedabad, Patna, Surat, and other places. It is of two kinds. That called *Kenari* is from one to three inches in width, whilst the *Gota* is only from $\frac{1}{8}$ to $\frac{7}{8}$ of an inch in breadth.

The gold and silver wire is usually of a superior quality. Occasionally, however, an inferior article of gilt or silvered copper wire is employed. Of the importance of using only the very best materials in the manufacture of articles likely to be subjected to the operation of washing, we have already spoken.

In the India Museum Collection is a loom-embroidered fabric from Thibet, to which some allusion may here be made. It has been received under the name of *Tachu*, and its ornamentation has been effected by using a weft of gilt paper, which has been cut into very narrow strips for the purpose.

## HAND-EMBROIDERY.

We have now to speak of Hand or Needle Embroidery, a kind of work in which the Native shows admirable skill, and one which, in all probability, is destined yet to occupy a somewhat important place amongst the list of manufactured articles exported from India to this and to other European countries.

A few examples of this sort of embroidery have been inserted in the books, and are classed in the two following Tables, but, just as in the case of the fabrics last considered, these are not calculated to afford an adequate notion of the immense number of ways in which not merely the professional embroiderer, but many of the native ladies of Hindustan, produce patterns of exquisite taste and skill.

Every kind of fabric, from the coarsest muslin to the richest cashmere cloth, is thus decorated; and though Dacca and Delhi are the places best known for their embroideries, there are numerous other places in India in which the workers are equally skilful.

Dacca, however, has for a very long time been celebrated for its *Zar-do-zi* or embroidery.

"From Dacca," says the Abbé de Guyon, writing in 1774, "come the best and finest Indian embroideries in gold, silver, or silk, and those embroidered neckcloths and fine muslins which are seen in France."

The art is considered to have been first introduced into Bengal from the banks of the Euphrates. On this subject, Taylor remarks that, "In the ninth century the merchants of Bussora carried on a direct trade with Eastern India and China. Many Mahomedans settled at this time in the principal ports of these countries, and, doubtless, they introduced from the West such arts, and, among others, that of embroidery, as were required to prepare the goods suited to the markets of Arabia. This conjecture," he adds, "regarding the origin of embroidery in Bengal, is, in addition to the fact of this art being only practised by Mahomedans, further strengthened by the tradition at Dacca that the needles formerly used there were procured from Bussora; and likewise by the circumstance of Bussora and Jidda having been, from time immemorial, the great marts for the embroidered goods of Bengal."*

The following is the description given by Taylor of the embroidery frame, the manner of working, &c.:—

"The cloth is stretched out in a horizontal bamboo frame of rude construction, raised about a couple of feet from the ground, and the figures intended to be worked or embroidered are drawn upon it by designers, who are generally Hindoo painters (*nuqash*) On woollen cloths the outlines are traced with chalk, and on muslin with pencil, and the body of the design copied from coloured drawings. The embroiderers, seated upon the floor around the frame, ply the needle, which, it may be remarked, they do not draw *towards*, but, on the contrary, push *from* them, as is the case with all native sewers in India. In place of scissors they commonly use a piece of glass or Chinaware to cut the threads. The *zar-doz*, or embroiderers, constitute a distinct society or Mahomedan guild of artisans."

---

* Taylor's "Cotton Manufactures of Dacca," p. 102.

**The examples given in the Books, and grouped in the subjoined Tables 1 and 2, embrace representatives from three of the four principal varieties into which Indian hand embroideries may be divided.**

## 1. Hand Embroidery.—Cotton and Silk.

| No. of Vol. | No. of Sample. | | Description. | Measurement. Length. | Measurement. Width. | Weight of Piece. | Cost. | Place of Manufacture, or where obtained. |
|---|---|---|---|---|---|---|---|---|
| | | | | yds. ins. | yds. ins. | lbs. ozs. | £ s. d. | |
| VII. | 252 | With Cotton—Chikan. | *Phool Kary.* A striped muslin embroidered with sprigs of flowers. | 13 13 | 0 28 | 0 $14\frac{1}{4}$ | — | Gwalior. |
| VII. | 255 | | Diagonal stripes of flowers in white cotton, with intervening smaller sprigs. | 10 0 | 0 34 | 1 $0\frac{3}{4}$ | 4 0 0 | Dacca. |
| VII. | 256 | | Plain muslin embroidered with large flower sprig. | 10 0 | 0 35 | 0 $13\frac{1}{4}$ | 3 18 0 | Ditto. |
| VII. | 257 | | Vine leaf and grape pattern, with intervening double rows of flower sprigs. | 10 0 | 1 0 | 1 5 | 4 0 0 | Ditto. |
| VII. | 258 | | Flower sprigs in diagonal order, - | 10 0 | 1 0 | 0 $9\frac{1}{2}$ | 3 18 0 | Ditto. |
| VII. | 260 | | *Bootee.* Plain muslin with needle-worked spots in crimson. | 10 0 | 1 0 | 0 $13\frac{1}{4}$ | 1 10 0 | Ditto. |
| VIII. | 293 | With Moonga Silk, &c. (Kashida.) | Embroidered with Moonga silk. Pattern, a check formed by cross lines of small leaf pattern, $\frac{1}{2}$-inch apart and in diagonal order. | 4 24 | 1 $1\frac{1}{2}$ | 0 $12\frac{3}{4}$ | — | Ditto. |
| VIII. | 292 | | **Piece of Moonga silk and cotton, in alternate stripes. Cotton stripes embroidered with foliage pattern in Moonga silk.** | 4 9 | 0 $33\frac{1}{2}$ | 0 $10\frac{3}{4}$ | — | Ditto. |
| VIII. | 295 | | Cotton and Moonga silk check, embroidered with circular and star-shaped flowers in Moonga silk. | 4 17 | 0 33 | 0 $13\frac{1}{4}$ | — | Ditto. |
| VIII. | 296 | | Cotton and Moonga silk in alternate stripes. The cotton stripes embroidered with blue, red, and yellow flowers. | 4 $12\frac{1}{2}$ | 0 $33\frac{1}{2}$ | 0 $11\frac{1}{4}$ | — | Ditto. |
| VI. | 234 | | Red twill cotton material, with narrow black cross stripes: $2\frac{1}{2}$-inch border embroidered with coloured silks. The full piece is cut across at centre and joined at sides to form a dress-skirt. | 1 29 | 0 26 | 1 1 | — | Sylhet. |
| VI. | 235 | | Light blue cotton with cross stripes of dark blue: $2\frac{1}{2}$-in. border, embroidered with coloured silk and cotton. The full piece is cut across the centre and joined at sides to form a dress-skirt. | 1 29 | 0 25 | 1 1 | — | Ditto. |

## 2. Hand-Embroidery.—Gold, Silver, Tinsel, and Beetle Wings.

| No. of | | Description. | Measurement. | | Weight of Piece. | Cost. | Place of Manufacture, or whence obtained. |
|---|---|---|---|---|---|---|---|
| Vol. | Sample. | | Length. | Width. | | | |
| | | | yds. ins. | yds. ins. | lbs. oz. | £ s. d. | |
| VII. | 274 | White muslin, with gold flowers | 1 4 | 1 0 | 0 3 | — | Madras. |
| VII. | 276 | Red muslin, scroll and foliage pattern, worked in flattened gold wire, with flower sprigs in gold and beetle wing. | 9 22 | 1 3 | 1 11½ | — | Madras. |
| VII. | 277 | White muslin, thickly embroidered with gold and tinsel. | 1 29 | 1 13 | 0 12 | — | Madras. |
| VII. | 278 | White muslin, embroidered with gold and tinsel. | 2 2 | 1 8 | 0 6½ | — | Madras. |
| VII. | 279 | White muslin, embroidered with gold and tinsel. | 3 7 | 1 12 | 0 8¼ | 7 10 0 | Madras. |
| VII. | 280 | White muslin, embroidered with gold and tinsel. | 3 3 | 1 8 | 0 9½ | — | Madras. |
| XII. | 445 | Green silk gauze, embroidered with gold flowers. An inch wide border of gold lace, with figured edges of crimson silk. For cholees. | 0 22 | 1 7 | — | 0 13 0 | Hyderabad, Deccan, bought in Madras. |
| XIV. | 552 | Silk gauze, crimson weft, blue warp; embroidered with gold flowers. | 8 0 | 1 0 | 0 6½ | 0 19 0 | Trichinopoly, Madras. |
| XIV. | 553 | Green silk gauze, embroidered with gold flowers. | 8 0 | 0 34 | 0 6½ | 0 19 0 | Trichinopoly, Madras. |
| XIV. | 554 | Crimson silk gauze, embroidered with gold flowers. | 8 0 | 1 0 | 0 5¼ | 0 19 0 | Trichinopoly, Madras. |
| VII. | 270 | Gold cloth, embroidered with gold thread, beetle wing, and silver tinsel. | 2 22 | 0 20 | 0 6¼ | — | Madras. |

In the first part of Table 1 we have specimens of cotton embroidery on muslin, known under the name of *Chikan work*, termed also *Chikan-Kari* or *Chikan dozee.* It includes a great variety of figured or flowered work on muslin for gowns, scarfs, &c. It also comprises a variety of net-work, which is formed by breaking down the texture of the cloth with the needle, and converting it into open meshes. According to Taylor, Mahomedan dresses are frequently ornamented in this manner; and he adds that there are about thirty varieties of this kind of work, of which the *Tarter* and *Sumoonderlah* are considered the principal. It is said that the business of Chikan-Kari embroidery affords employment to a considerable number of men and women in the town of Dacca.

In the second division of the first table we have a class of embroideries which, although of a comparatively coarse description, occupy a position of some importance, on account of the extent to which they are still exported to Arabia. These consist of fabrics of Moonga silk, or of Moonga silk and cotton, embroidered either with cotton or Moonga silk, but generally the latter.

The following is Taylor's description of this class of goods:—

"Some of these cloths are embroidered in the cotton portion of the warp with the needle, and are then called *Kashida.* They vary in size from one and a quarter to six yards in length, and from one to one and a quarter yards in breadth. Their price ranges from 2 to 20 rupees (4*s.* to 40*s.*) per piece.

"Cloth printers (*chipigurs*) are employed to stamp the figures for embroidering on the *khasida* cloths. The stamps which they use for this purpose are small blocks of the wood of the *khutul* tree, having the figures carved in relief. The dye is a red earth, which is brought from Bombay, and is apparently what is called "Indian earth" imported into that place from the Persian Gulf. It is mixed with gum mucilage when applied to the cloth, and is easily effaced by washing.

"This kind of embroidery forms the leisure occupation of the majority of the females of poor Mahomedan families in the town. The cloths having the figures stamped upon them are distributed among the embroiderers of this class, and are worked by them when not engaged in their domestic duties. The merchants who carry on this business employ male and female agents to distribute the cloths and silk and cotton thread among the embroiderers, and through them they make occasional advances of wages to the latter, as the work proceeds. The amount earned by each embroiderer is a small pittance, not exceeding on an average ten or twelve shillings in the year. These cloths are prepared solely for the markets of Bussora and Jidda, but chiefly for the latter, to which a considerable quantity of them is exported annually."

In the next, or third division (Table 2) are included the examples in which gold, silver, tinsel, and beetle (*Sternocera orientalis*) wings are employed in the decoration of muslin, silk and gold cloth.

Of the beautiful (silk on cloth) embroidery of Sind, and the still better known embroideries in silk and gold on scarfs and shawls of Cashmere cloth, for which Delhi and other places in the north of India are famous, no examples are given in the Books. To form an opinion of the beauty and extent of these the India Museum Collection must be consulted.*

The following is a statement of the kinds of silk and of gold wire employed in needle embroidery at Dacca. The silk is of two sorts, first common, formerly exported under the name of Dacca silk; and, second, floss silk.

Of the gold and silver thread and wire, the varieties are:—

1. *Goolabatoon*, for embroidering muslins.
2. *Goshoo*, for embroidering caps.
3. *Sulmah*, for embroidering caps, slippers, Hookah snakes, &c.
4. *Boolun*, for the manufacture of gold lace and brocade.

---

## LACE.

Of the ornamental net-work, wrought of threads of silk, flax, cotton, or of gold or silver interwoven, to which the term *lace* is usually applied, no examples have been given in the Books. The making of lace of this kind is of only recent introduction, and hitherto has been confined to Nagercoil and a few other places in Southern India. Some of the specimens shown at the Exhibition of 1851 and of 1862† attracted attention, and the subject is alluded to here chiefly on account of lace being one of the hand-fabrics which India may yet supply to this and other countries.

---

* Some of the shop-windows in London frequently display beautiful examples of the class of articles here alluded to.

† Regarding the specimens of lace made under Mrs. Caldwell's directions at the Edaiyangudi Missionary School in Tinnevelly, to which a certificate of Honourable Mention was awarded in 1862, the Jury remarks, "White and black lace from Tinnevelly, showing considerable aptitude for this class of manufacture, and that with perseverance great progress would likely be made."

Some good specimens of India-made lace are to be seen in the India Museum Collection.

## WOOL.

We have now to place before the reader such information as we possess regarding fabrics made of wool.

In treating of these we shall reverse the order hitherto adopted, and speak first of the more elaborate productions of the native loom, particularly of those known as Cashmere shawls, leaving the commoner fabrics for after consideration.

### CASHMERE SHAWLS.

Some of the ways in which the Cashmere shawl is worn by Native gentlemen will be seen in Pl. VIII.*—opposite—the persons of the three first figures being adorned with this costly production.

The importance of the Cashmere shawl manufacture as an article of export, will be gathered from the subjoined Table, which shows the value of the Cashmere shawls exported from India to various countries during the past fifteen years.

---

* This *Plate*, on account of our having after its execution chosen, under the head of Woollen-goods, to deal first with Cashmere Shawls, is made to precede instead of follow Pl. VII.

MALE ATTIRE. CASHMERE SHAWLS. CHOGAS, &c.

TABLE showing the QUANTITIES (as far as can be ascertained) and the VALUE of CASHMERE SHAWLS EXPORTED from INDIA and each PRESIDENCY to all PARTS of the WORLD from 1850-51 to 1864-65.

| Years. | Whence Exported. | Countries to which Exported. | | | | | | | | | | | | | | | | Total Exported to all Parts. | |
|---|---|---|---|---|---|---|---|---|---|---|---|---|---|---|---|---|---|---|---|
| | | United Kingdom. | | France. | | Other Parts of Europe. | | America. | | China. | | Arabian and Persian Gulfs. | | Suez. | | Other Parts. | | | |
| | | Quantity. | Value. | Quantity. | Value. | Quantity. | Value. | Quantity. | Value. | Quantity. | Value. | Quantity. | Value. | Quantity. | Value. | Quantity. | Value. | Quantity. | Value. |
| | | Pieces. | £ | Pieces. | £ | Pieces. | £ | Pieces. | £ | Pieces. | £ | Pieces. | £ | Pieces. | £ | Pieces. | £ | Pieces. | £ |
| 1850-51 | Bengal | 1,258 | 15,939 | 3 | 9 | — | — | 168 | 1,316 | — | — | 3 | 14 | — | — | 26 | 221 | 1,458 | 17,499 |
| | Madras | 42 | 238 | — | — | — | — | — | — | — | — | 1 | 7 | — | — | — | — | 43 | 245 |
| | Bombay | 8,675 | 118,561 | — | — | — | — | — | — | 2 | 105 | 1,330 | 16,760 | 1,830 | 18,022 | 67 | 517 | 11,904 | 153,965 |
| | **ALL INDIA** | **99,75** | **134,738** | **3** | **9** | — | — | **168** | **1,316** | **2** | **105** | **1,334** | **16,781** | **1,830** | **18,022** | **93** | **738** | **13,405** | **171,709** |
| 1851-52 | Bengal | 359 | 4,758 | — | — | — | — | 119 | 1,017 | — | — | — | — | — | — | 19 | 154 | 497 | 5,929 |
| | Madras | — | — | — | — | — | — | — | — | — | — | — | — | — | — | — | — | — | — |
| | Bombay | 7,137 | 109,090 | 1 | 35 | 185 | 3,582 | — | — | 2 | 18 | 1,684 | 21,079 | 972 | 5,725 | 116 | 812 | 10,097 | 140,341 |
| | **ALL INDIA** | **7,496** | **113,848** | **1** | **35** | **185** | **3,582** | **119** | **1,017** | **2** | **18** | **1684** | **21,079** | **972** | **5,725** | **135** | **966** | **10,594** | **146,270** |
| 1852-53 | Bengal | 1,048 | 13,606 | 1 | 57 | — | — | 249 | 601 | — | — | — | — | — | — | 2 | 43 | 1,300 | 14,307 |
| | Madras | 12 | 307 | — | — | — | — | — | — | — | — | — | — | — | — | 1 | 30 | 13 | 337 |
| | Bombay | 10,151 | 165,498 | — | — | 197 | 2,906 | — | — | 14 | 445 | 1,554 | 21,954 | 1,365 | 9,446 | 117 | 766 | 13,398 | 201,015 |
| | **ALL INDIA** | **11,211** | **179,411** | **1** | **57** | **197** | **2,906** | **249** | **601** | **14** | **445** | **1,554** | **21,954** | **1,365** | **9,446** | **120** | **839** | **14,711** | **215,659** |
| 1853-54 | Bengal | — | 5,039 | — | 3,512 | — | 30 | — | 2,732 | — | — | — | — | — | 10,377 | — | 420 | — | 22,110 |
| | Madras | — | 236 | — | — | — | — | — | — | — | — | — | — | — | — | — | — | — | 236 |
| | Bombay | 8,000 | 122,659 | 2 | 100 | — | — | — | — | 15 | 188 | 912 | 11,777 | 1,229 | 11,110 | 469 | 1,973 | 10,627 | 147,807 |
| | **ALL INDIA** | — | **127,934** | — | **3,612** | — | **30** | — | **2,732** | **15** | **188** | **912** | **11,777** | — | **21,487** | — | **2,393** | — | **170,153** |
| 1854-55 | Bengal | — | 14,730 | — | 4,368 | — | 70 | — | 7,923 | — | 50 | — | — | — | 12,652 | — | 631 | — | 40,424 |
| | Madras | — | 348 | — | — | — | — | — | — | — | — | — | — | — | — | — | — | — | 348 |
| | Bombay | 6,941 | 134,567 | 39 | 1,141 | — | — | — | — | 7 | 124 | 536 | 17,020 | 447 | 3,081 | 1,258 | 185 | 8,228 | 157,118 |
| | **ALL INDIA** | — | **149,645** | — | **5,509** | — | **70** | — | **7,923** | — | **174** | **536** | **17,020** | — | **15,733** | — | **816** | — | **197,890** |
| 1855-56 | Bengal | — | 14,322 | — | 16,018 | — | 10 | 9 | 2,021 | — | 77 | — | — | — | 18,749 | — | 152 | — | 51,349 |
| | Madras | — | 716 | — | — | — | — | — | — | — | — | — | — | — | — | — | 26 | — | 742 |
| | Bombay | 5,745 | 137,129 | 54 | 1,355 | — | — | — | 37 | 15 | 469 | 578 | 5,619 | 1,783 | 12,159 | 57 | 420 | 8,241 | 157,188 |
| | **ALL INDIA** | — | **152,167** | — | **17,373** | — | **10** | — | **2,058** | — | **546** | **578** | **5,619** | — | **30,908** | — | **598** | — | **209,279** |
| 1856-57 | Bengal | — | 10,793 | — | 59,69 | — | 495 | — | 4,239 | — | 185 | — | 2 | — | 11,851 | — | 339 | — | 33,873 |
| | Madras | 21 | 139 | — | — | — | — | — | — | — | — | — | — | — | — | — | — | 21 | 139 |
| | Bombay | 11,479 | 216,975 | 41 | 1,338 | — | — | — | — | 4 | 68 | 850 | 9,228 | 4,041 | 28,342 | 266 | 677 | 16,681 | 256,628 |
| | **ALL INDIA** | — | **227,907** | — | **7,307** | — | **495** | — | **4,239** | — | **253** | — | **9,230** | — | **40,193** | — | **1,016** | — | **290,640** |
| 1857-58 | Bengal | — | 2,246 | — | 6,219 | — | — | — | 2,640 | — | 321 | — | — | — | 392 | — | 39 | — | 11,857 |
| | Madras | 25 | 245 | — | — | — | — | — | — | — | — | — | — | — | — | — | — | 25 | 245 |
| | Bombay | 6,788 | 169,038 | 384 | 18,796 | — | — | — | — | 27 | 149 | 1,102 | 6,407 | 1,957 | 19,173 | 554 | 1,953 | 10,812 | 215,516 |
| | **ALL INDIA** | — | **171,529** | — | **25,015** | — | — | — | **2,640** | — | **470** | **1,102** | **6,407** | — | **19,565** | — | **1,992** | — | **227,618** |

TABLE showing the QUANTITIES and the VALUE of KASHMERE SHAWLS EXPORTED from INDIA, &c.—*continued.*

| Years. | Whence Exported. | Countries whither Exported. | | | | | | | | | | | | | | | | Total Exported to all Parts. | |
|---|---|---|---|---|---|---|---|---|---|---|---|---|---|---|---|---|---|---|---|
| | | United Kingdom. | | France. | | Other Parts of Europe. | | America. | | China. | | Arabian and Persian Gulfs. | | Suez. | | Other Parts. | | | |
| | | Quantity. | Value. | Quantity. | Value. | Quantity. | Value. | Quantity. | Value. | Quantity. | Value. | Quantity. | Value. | Quantity. | Value. | Quantity. | Value. | Quantity. | Value. |
| | | Pieces. | £ | Pieces. | £ | Pieces. | £ | Pieces. | £ | Pieces. | £ | Pieces. | £ | Pieces. | £ | Pieces. | £ | Pieces. | £ |
| 1858–59 | Bengal | — | 7,785 | — | 12,576 | — | 280 | — | 1,306 | — | 8 | — | — | — | 884 | — | 135 | — | 22,974 |
| | Madras | 43 | 255 | — | — | — | — | — | — | — | — | — | — | — | — | 2 | 5 | 45 | 260 |
| | Bombay | 10,265 | 220,772 | 1,145 | 40,325 | — | — | — | — | 4 | 115 | 2,529 | 17,808 | 944 | 7,180 | 177 | 593 | 15,064 | 286,793 |
| | **ALL INDIA** | — | **228,812** | — | **52,901** | — | **280** | — | **1,306** | — | **123** | **2,529** | **17,808** | — | **8,064** | — | **733** | — | **310,027** |
| 1859–60 | Bengal | — | 18,534 | — | 12,513 | — | 80 | — | 1,501 | — | 500 | — | — | — | 1,972 | — | 1,672 | — | 36,772 |
| | Madras | 63 | 526 | 1 | 4 | — | — | — | — | — | — | — | — | — | — | 4 | 13 | 68 | 543 |
| | Bombay | 8,339 | 182,038 | 245 | 4,296 | 9 | 230 | — | — | 4 | 155 | 1,749 | 22,984 | 963 | 4,858 | 186 | 952 | 11,495 | 215,513 |
| | **ALL INDIA** | — | **201,098** | — | **16,813** | — | **310** | — | **1 501** | — | **655** | **1,749** | **22,984** | — | **6,830** | — | **2,637** | — | **252,828** |
| 1860–61 | Bengal | — | 23,520 | — | 10,748 | — | 60 | — | 2,731 | — | 652 | — | — | — | 1,542 | — | 180 | — | 39,433 |
| | Madras | 28 | 300 | — | — | — | — | — | — | — | — | — | — | — | — | — | — | 28 | 300 |
| | Bombay | 13,598 | 266,944 | 1,133 | 19,144 | — | — | — | — | 14 | 437 | 1,984 | 16,505 | 451 | 7,665 | 109 | 665 | 17,289 | 311,360 |
| | **ALL INDIA** | — | **290,764** | — | **29,892** | — | **60** | — | **2 731** | — | **1,089** | **1,984** | **16,505** | — | **9,207** | — | **845** | — | **351,093** |
| 1861–62 | Bengal | — | 27,893 | — | 8,570 | — | 102 | — | 85 | — | 44 | — | 25 | — | 1,851 | — | 336 | — | 38,906 |
| | Madras | 14 | 147 | — | — | — | — | — | — | — | — | — | — | — | — | 10 | 98 | 24 | 245 |
| | Bombay | 14,511 | 383,301 | 488 | 7,528 | — | — | 9 | 180 | 4 | 218 | 2,523 | 24,040 | 129 | 4,857 | 90 | 166 | 17,754 | 420,290 |
| | **ALL INDIA** | — | **411,341** | — | **16,098** | — | **102** | — | **265** | — | **262** | — | **24,065** | — | **6,708** | — | **600** | — | **459,441** |
| 1862–63 | Bengal | 1,181 | 56,004 | 100 | 4,704 | 3 | 21 | 221 | 1,447 | 4 | 118 | — | — | 19 | 890 | 169 | 809 | 1,697 | 63,993 |
| | Madras | 15 | 110 | 3 | 8 | — | — | — | — | — | — | — | — | — | — | 1 | 4 | 19 | 122 |
| | Bombay | 134,34 | 207,193 | 1 | 60 | — | — | — | — | 3 | 125 | 1,649 | 22,728 | 1,355 | 8,764 | 51 | 172 | 16,493 | 239,042 |
| | **ALL INDIA** | **14,630** | **263,307** | **104** | **4,772** | **3** | **21** | **221** | **1,447** | **7** | **243** | **1,649** | **22,728** | **1,374** | **9,654** | **221** | **985** | **18,209** | **303,157** |
| 1863–64 | Bengal | 1,056 | 33,244 | 573 | 21,082 | 1 | 5 | 1 | 12 | 3 | 66 | 22 | 106 | 27 | 583 | 504 | 14,916 | 2,187 | 70,014 |
| | Madras | 5 | 51 | — | — | — | — | — | — | — | — | — | — | — | — | 5 | 33 | 10 | 84 |
| | Bombay | 9,289 | 161,804 | 147 | 7,550 | — | — | 5 | 15 | 3 | 125 | 882 | 14,562 | 2,613 | 20,398 | 138 | 839 | 13,077 | 205,293 |
| | **ALL INDIA** | **10,350** | **195,099** | **720** | **286,32** | **1** | **5** | **6** | **27** | **6** | **191** | **904** | **14,668** | **2,640** | **20,981** | **647** | **15,788** | **15,274** | **275,391** |
| 1864–65 | Bengal | — | 20,553 | — | 68,032 | — | — | — | 3,148 | — | 248 | — | 192 | — | 821 | — | 157 | — | 93,151 |
| | Madras | 42 | 531 | — | — | — | — | — | — | — | — | — | — | — | — | 5 | 51 | 47 | 582 |
| | Bombay | 7,723 | 121,832 | 387 | 9,550 | | — | — | — | 8 | 416 | 1,590 | 12,338 | 2,458 | 16,495 | 76 | 134 | 12,242 | 160,765 |
| | **ALL INDIA** | — | **142,916** | — | **77,582** | — | — | — | **3,148** | — | **664** | — | **12,530** | — | **17,316** | — | **342** | — | **254,498** |

It has to be noted that, although the name of *Cashmere* attaches to all the shawls of the description under notice, a very considerable proportion of them are now manufactured within our own territory. The following extract from the Report of the Lahore Central Committee for the last International Exhibition (1862) affording, as it does, the latest information on the subject, is here inserted; and this, although involving some repetition of details, will be followed by an extract from the Report of the Sub-Committee appointed in connexion with the Exhibition of 1851, and also by Moorcroft's still more elaborate, but much less recent, account of the manufacture as practised in Cashmere at the period of his travels through Ladak and Cashmere between the years 1819 and 1825.

Referring to shawls, the manufacture of the Punjab, the Lahore Committee (1862) state:—

"This is now by far the most important manufacture in the Punjaub; but thirty years ago it was almost entirely confined to Kashmere. At the period alluded to, a terrible famine visited Kashmere; and, in consequence, numbers of the shawl-weavers emigrated to the Punjaub, and settled in Umritsur, Nurpur, Dinangar, Tilaknath, Jelalpur, and Loodianah, in all of which places the manufacture continues to flourish. The best shawls of Punjaub manufacture are manufactured at Umritsur, which is also an emporium of the shawl trade. But none of the shawls made in the Punjaub can compete with the best shawls made in Kashmere itself; first, because the Punjaub manufacturers are unable to obtain the finest species of wool; and secondly, by reason of the inferiority of the dyeing, the excellence of which in Kashmere is attributed to some chemical peculiarity in the water there. On receipt of the raw pashum or shawl wool, the first operation is that of cleaning it; this is done generally by women; the best kind is cleaned with lime and water, but ordinarily the wool is cleaned by being shaken up with flour. The next operation is that of separating the hair from the pushum; this is a tedious operation, and the value of the cloth subsequently manufactured varies with the amount of care bestowed upon it. The wool thus cleaned and sorted is spun into thread with the common 'churka' or native spinning-machine. This is also an operation requiring great care. White pashumeea thread of the finest quality will sometimes cost as much as 2*l.* 10*s.* a lb. The thread is next dyed, and is then ready for the loom. The shawls are divided into two great classes—1. Woven shawls, called *Teliwalah;* 2. Worked shawls.

"Shawls of the former class are woven into separate pieces, which are, when required, sewn together with such precision that the sewing is imperceptible. These are the most highly prized of the two. In worked shawls, the pattern is worked with the needle upon a piece of plain pashumeea or shawl cloth.

"A woven shawl made at Kashmere of the best materials, and weighing 7 lbs., will cost in Kashmere as much as 300*l.*; of this amount the cost of the material, including thread, is 30*l.*, the wages of labour 100*l.*, miscellaneous expenses 50*l.*, duty 70*l.*

"Besides shawls, various other articles of dress, such as chogas, or outer robes, ladies' opera-cloaks, smoking-caps, gloves, &c., are made of pashumeea.

"Latterly great complaints have been made by European firms of the adulteration of the texture of Kashmere shawls; and there is no doubt that such adulteration is practised, especially by mixing up Kirmanee wool with real pashum. In order to provide some guarantee against this, it has been proposed that a guild or company of respectable traders should be formed, who should be empowered to affix on all genuine shawls a trade mark, which should be a guarantee to the public that the material of the shawl is genuine pashum, especially as the Indian Penal Code provides a punishment for those who counterfeit or falsify trade marks, or knowingly sell goods marked with false or counterfeit trade-marks.

"At Delhi shawls are made up of pushumeea, worked with silk and embroidered with gold lace. A very delicate shawl is made of the wool of a sheep found in the neighbourhood of Ladak and Kulu; the best wool is procurable in a village near Rampur, on the Sutlej; hence the fabric is called 'Rampur chudder.' Other woollen manufactures in the Punjaub are Peshawur chogas, made of the wool of the Dumba sheep, and of camel's hair, and chogas made of Patti, or the hair of the Cabul goat."

Of the raw woollen substances used in the Punjaub for the manufacture of shawls, and for some of the fabrics which will afterwards be referred to, the Committee give the following description:—

"1. *Pushum*, or shawl wool, properly so called, being a downy substance, found next the skin and below the thick hair of the Thibetan goat. It is of three colours: white, drab, and dark lavender (Tusha).

"The best kind is produced in the semi-Chinese Provinces of Turfan Kichar, and exported *viâ* Yarkand to Kashmere. All the finest shawls are made of this wool, but as the Maharajah of Kashmere keeps a strict monopoly of the article, the Punjab shawl-weavers cannot procure it, and have to be content with an inferior kind of Pashum produced at Chathan and exported *viâ* Leh to Umritsur, Nurpur, Loodianah, Jelapur, and other shawl-weaving towns of the Punjab. The price of white pashum in Kashmere is for uncleaned, 3*s.* to 4*s.* per lb.; ditto, cleaned, 6*s.* to 7*s.* per lb. Of Tusha ditto, uncleaned, 2*s.* to 3*s.* per lb.; cleaned, from 5*s.* to 7*s.*

"2. *The fleece of the Dumba sheep of Cabul and Peshawur.*—This is sometimes called *Kabuli Pashum*. It is used in the manufacture of the finer sorts of chogas, an outer robe or cloak with sleeves, worn by Affghans and other Mahomedans of the Western frontier.

"3. *Wahab Shahi*, or *Kirmani Wool*.—The wool of a sheep found in Kirman, a tract of country in the south of Persia, by the Persian Gulf. It is used for the manufacture of a spurious kind of shawl-cloth, and for adulterating the texture of Kashmere shawls.

"4. *The hair of a goat common in Kabul and Peshawur*, called *Pat*, from which a texture called *Pattu* is made.

"5. *The woolly hair of the camel.*—From this a coarser kind of choga is made.

"6. *The wool of the country sheep of the Plains.*—Regarding the production of wool in the Himalayan or Sub-Himalayan portion of the Punjab, the last year's Revenue Report states that 'there can be no doubt that the valleys of the Sutlej, Ravee, Chandrabaga (or Chenab), Namisukh, and other tributaries of the Indus, supply grazing grounds not to be surpassed in richness and suitableness in any part of the world. The population inhabiting them are chiefly pastoral; but owing to sloth and ignorance, the wool they produce is but small in quantity, full of dirt and ill-cared for in every way.' The government of the Punjab have made efforts to improve the breed by the importation of Merino rams, but hitherto with little success. However, a truss of Merino wool produced at Huzara, a hill district to the north-west of the Punjab, and sent to England in 1860, was there valued at 1*s.* 6*d.* per lb."

The following is an extract from the Report on Cashmere shawls by the Committee for the Exhibition of 1851, to which reference has already been made.*

---

* Extracted from the Official Illustrated Catalogue of the Exhibition of 1851. Members of the Committee, Dr. H. Falconer, Joseph Agaberg, and Jorykissen Mookerjee.

"The principal articles of pushmina, or shawl-wool, manufacture may be classified under the following heads:—

I. DOSHALLA, or long shawls, 3½ by 1½ guz.

II. KUSSABA, or square shawls, 1½ or 2½ guz. square.

III. JAMEWARS, or striped shawl pieces, 3¾ by 1½ guz.

IV. ULWAN, or plain white shawl cloth.

V. Miscellaneous, such as carpets, canopies, saddle-cloths, and various articles of dress, stockings, gloves, turbans, &c.

## I. DOSHALLAS, OR LONG SHAWLS.

"*Doshallas*, or long shawls, invariably manufactured and sold in pairs, are the most esteemed production of the looms of Cashmere. They vary greatly according to the richness of the patterns, all of which are distinctly named, and according to the colours of which the dyers profess to make upwards of fifty tints, but the Sub-Committee will confine themselves to the leading colours, viz., black, white, crimsons, purple, blue, green, and yellow.

"Of the finest *doshallas*, the principal varieties in pattern depend upon the amount of decoration of *mitton*, or centre piece, the *pulla*, or border pieces, being always richly flowered. The following are the leading kinds:—

1. *Khale mitton*, or plain field shawls;
2. *Poor mitton*, or full flowered field;
3. *Chand-dar, chantahi-dar, alifda koonj boothadar;*

according to ornament, being a moon or circle in the centre, four half-moons, green sprigs on a plain ground, a group of flowers at the corners, or any combination of these.

"The Sub-Committee would restrict their consideration of the colours to eight kinds, viz., 1. White, *sada* or *safaed*. 2. Black, *mooshkee*. 3. Crimson, *goolanar*. 4. Scarlet, *kermisi*. 5. Purple, *ooda*. 6. Blue, *ferozee*. 7. Green, *zingare*. 8. Yellow, *zurd*.

"Fine long shawls with plain fields of handsome patterns (*khalli mitton*) are procurable at about 1,200 rupees per pair, and full flowered (*poor mitton*) at about 1,500 rupees. Taking the average of these 1,350 rupees, as representing the price of the third class, including *chand-dar, chantahi-dar*, &c., and as the average price of the whole; and supposing a pair of each of the above eight colours were ordered of the three several classes of pattern we should have twenty-four pairs of shawls, at 1,350 rupees, making 32,400 rupees in all.

## II. KUSSABAS, OR SQUARE SHAWLS.

"*Kussabas*, or square shawls, called also *Roomals*, are of two classes, viz., *Kanee Roomal*, or loom-manufactured, and *Umlee Roomal*, or needle-embroidered shawls. In form they are more suited to the taste of the Europeans than the long shawls, and are made and sold singly. They run through the same range of colour and pattern as the long shawls. The needle-worked kinds are much cheaper than the loom-manufactured, and the embroidery is far superior in pattern and execution to the scarfs and shawls embroidered at Delhi. Assuming eight colours and three patterns of each of the *Kanee Roomal*, at an average of 400, 300, and 500 rupees each, twenty-four square shawls would cost 9,600 rupees, and the same number of needle-worked of *Umlee Roomals*, at an average of 225, 150, to 300 rupees, would cost 5,400 rupees.

### III. Jamewars.

" *Jamewars* form the third great class: they are handsome striped loom-wrought fabrics of rich patterns, of which the French striped coloured muslins are printed imitations. They are manufactured of an infinity of patterns, but the principal kinds are the *Rega-bootha*, or small flowered; the *Kirkha-bootha*, or large flowered; and the *Jhaldar*, or netted patterns. The most elaborately worked cost as much as 2,000 rupees each.

### IV. Ulwan.

" *Ulwan*, or plain shawl wool-cloth, is woven like plain muslin, without flower or ornament, and is made in pieces of various lengths. It forms the centre portion or *mitton* of shawls, and is used for turbans and cummurbunds. It is well adapted for ladies' dresses. Eight pieces of twenty yards each of the different colours above-named, at six rupees per yard, would cost 960 rupees.

Another fabric is made which may be included under the same head as *Ulwan*, called *Muleedah-pushmina*, being intended to imitate European broad-cloths. It is formed of *Ulwan* manipulated in a peculiar manner in water, so as by rubbing to teaze out the wool of the thread and raise it into a nap. A piece of twenty yards, at six rupees, would cost 120 rupees.

" A coarser fabric of the same class is manufactured in the Hill State, to the north-west of Simla, called *Puttoo-peshmina*, which possesses great softness and warmth—in many respects rivalling fine broadcloth."

The following is Moorcroft's * account of the shawl manufacture in Kashmir:

" The first task of the spinner is to separate the different materials of which the fleece consists, usually in about the following proportions:

| | |
|---|---|
| Coarse hair - - - | $1\frac{1}{2}$ seers† |
| Seconds or *Phiri* - - | $\frac{3}{8}$ ,, |
| Dust and foreign substances | $2\frac{1}{8}$ ,, |
| Fine wool - - - | 2 ,, |
| | 6 ,, or 1 tarak. |

" Much attention is requisite to free the wool from the hair, and the process is a tedious one.

" The next step is cleaning and separating the wool. A quantity of husked rice is steeped in clean cold water, for a day and a night, or longer, until it becomes soft, when it is ground, or bruised upon a stone slab, to fine flour. Thin layers of this and of the picked wool are laid alternately, and squeezed with the hand until they are completely intermixed. A little water may occasionally be sprinkled over the heap, if the weather is hot and dry, else it is not necessary. Soap is never used, as it makes the wool harsh; and its employment in Hindustan being communicated to the Kashmirians, induced them to boast that in this matter, at least, they were more knowing than the Europeans. After being thus treated for about an hour, the flour is shaken out, the wool opened and torn to pieces, chiefly by the nails, and made into somewhat square, thin, elastic pads called *Tumbu*. In this process the *Phiri*, or seconds wool, is extricated. Though too coarse

* Moorcroft's Travels in Kashmir, &c., pp. 168 to 194. Vol. II. Murray: London, 1841.

† The ordinary Indian seer is a little over 2 lbs., and *may be* that to which Moorcroft here alludes.

for fine shawls it is used in the manufacture of those of inferior quality, and of a strong shawl cloth called "*Patu.*" The *tumbu* is then worked out into a thin, flat roving, about half a yard long, which is called a *Málá*. The málá is folded up to the size of the tumbu, and deposited in a deep pot of red earthenware, called a *Taskas*, to be out of the way of dust or accident, till required for the spinning wheel.

"The wheel is constructed on the same principle as that used in Hindustan, but varying in neatness of form and finish, according to its price; the rudest, the *Takhtidar*, or *Pachimdar*, costs a half rupee; the *Katzker*, which is the most serviceable, three or four rupees; and *Pakhchedar*, which is used by those who spin for amusement only, costs from six to 16 rupees. The iron spindle is enclosed in a cylindrical tube of straw or reed grass, and runs through two elastic twists of grass; and instead of one line of radii, or spokes, supporting a continued circular wooden rim, there are two circular parallel walls of flat spokes in contact at their edges, leaving between them, at their outer circumference, an empty space. A hair cord, fastened to the loose end of one of the spokes, is carried across the space or trough to the end of the next spoke but one on the opposite side, and having been passed round, it returns to a spoke on the side from which it began. By a continuation of this process a rim is formed of a surface of hair cord, over which runs a small band that is said to be seldom cut by the friction to which it is exposed. The principle kept in view by this arrangement of spindle and rim, is to produce a continuance of soft elastic movements without jerk or stiffness, to prevent the yarn breaking on the occurrence of any slight interruption in drawing it out.

"Women begin to work at daybreak, continue with little interruption the whole day, if not taken off by other domestic affairs; and extend their labour until very late in the night, spinning by moonlight, when available, and when they cannot afford to purchase oil for a lamp. The fine wool is commonly spun into about 700 gaz,* each gaz consisting of 16 girahs, about equal to nails. This yarn is doubled and formed into twist, which is cut into 200 lengths, each length of 3½ gaz, this measure being suited to the length of the warp for a shawl. From the *phiri*, or seconds wool, about 100 gaz of yarn are also produced.

"The yarn of the fine wool is sold sometimes by measure and sometimes by weight. A hundred lengths of yarn of fine wool doubled, and each 3½ gaz, bring ordinarily seven tangas, or about seven pence. But if the same kind of yarn be sold without being doubled or twisted, the price is regulated by weight—a pal bringing from 12 annas to one rupee four annas, according to the demands of the market. The yarn from *phiri*, or seconds wool, is sold only by measure, but the gaz employed consists of no more than 12 girahs, or nails, that is, of four girah less than the gaz in ordinary use. 100 yards of *phiri* twist, and each of two short gaz, or of 24 girah, sell for one and a half tanga†, three pice, or about three half-pence. Although calculations upon this matter can be little more than approximations, yet 3*d.* or 3½*d.* per day, or from 3 rupees to 3 rupees 8 annas, or from 6*s.* to 7*s.* a month, may be taken as the general earnings of an industrious and expert spinner in Kashmir: out of which, however, must be subtracted the price of the wool, leaving only 1 rupee 8 annas (or about 3*s.*) for her labour.

"If shawl wool be furnished to a spinner to clean and to spin, 8 annas are paid for spinning one pal, or 3⅓ rupees weight of yarn of the requisite quality for shawls. Sheep's wool,

---

* The Gaz or Guz is about 1 yard. The Girah is given as 2¼ inches.

† Thirty-two tangas or annas equal two rupees.

spun by contract, is paid for by the pao, or $\frac{1}{4}$ seer, at the rate of from 2 tangas, or 4 pice, to 12 annas per pao, according to the fineness of the yarn; and the spinning of this quantity into yarn suited for shawls will occupy a woman for eight days. There are several varieties of thread, distinguished by different degrees of fineness. From one pal of clean, fine, shawl wool a spinner will draw from 100 to 1,000 threads of $3\frac{1}{2}$ gaz each. There is not such a difference between the price of coarse and of fine yarn as might be expected, owing to the greater expenditure on the former of a material that is dear, and on the latter, of labour that is cheap. Shawl wool is sometimes spun by men with a loose spindle like that used in Ladakh. These men are called *Trakhans*, and the yarn thus spun is the finest; but very little of it is now made. Girls begin to spin at the age of 10, and 100,000 females are employed in this occupation in Kashmir. About one-tenth of this number are supposed to spin for the purpose of obtaining shawls for themselves, or for other members of their families, and nine-tenths to earn a livelihood.

"The *Puimangù* keeps a shop for the purchase of yarn, but also sends people to collect it from the houses of the spinners, who give notice of their approach by ringing a bell. The yarn is sold to the weavers at a profit of from one pice to a tanga in the rupee. As a large stamp duty is levied on shawl goods when finished, the exportation of the yarn is forbidden, and the prohibition is enforced by heavy fines and imprisonment. Much of it is, nevertheless, exported to those places in the Punjab where the expatriated weavers have settled.

"Having ascertained the kind of pattern most likely to suit the market, the weaver applies to persons whose business it is to apportion the yarn according to the colours required; and when this is settled, he takes it to another, whose function it is to divide the yarn into skeins accordingly, and each skein is delivered to the *Rangrez*, or dyer. When the body of the cloth is to be left plain, the *phiri*, or seconds yarn, is alone given to be dyed. This is generally about the thickness of common cotton sewing thread, is loosely twisted, of a coarser quality than the yarn used for the cloth, and is prepared for employment in flowers, or other ornaments, from its standing higher, and being, as it were, embossed upon the ground.

"The dyer prepares the yarn by steeping in cold water. He professes to be able to give it 64 tints, most of which are permanent. Each has a separate denomination; as for instance, the crimson is termed *Gulanar* (pomegranate flower); the best kind is derived from cochineal imported from Hindustan; inferior tints are from *Lac* and *Kirmis* (*Chermes*), distinguished as *Kirmisi, Kirmdana*, and *Kirmisi* lac, or cochineal, and lac chermes; logwood is used for other red dyes; blues and greens are dyed with indigo, or colouring matter extracted by boiling from European broad cloth. Logwood is imported from Mooltan, and indigo from India. Carthamus and saffron, growing in the province, furnish means of various tints of orange, yellow, &c. The occupation of a dyer is invariably hereditary. The whiter and finer the fibre of the wool, and the finer the yarn into which it is made, the more capable it is said to be of receiving a brilliant dye; and this is one reason why the fine white wool of the goat is preferred to that of sheep.

"The *Nakatu* adjusts the yarn for the warp and for the weft. That intended for the former is double, and is cut into lengths of $3\frac{1}{2}$ gaz, anything short of that measure being considered fraudulent. The number of these lengths varies from 2,000 to 3,000, according to the closeness, or openness of texture proposed, and the fineness or coarseness of the yarn.

"The weft is made of yarn which is single, but a little thicker than the double yarn or twist of the warp. The weight of the weft is estimated at half more than that of the warp. The *Nakatu* receives the yarn in hanks, but returns it in balls: he can prepare in one day the warp and weft for two shawls.

"The *Pennakamguru*, or warp dresser, takes from the weaver the yarn which has been cut and reeled and stretching the lengths by means of sticks into a band, of which the threads are slightly separate, dresses the whole by dipping it into thick boiled rice water. After this the skein is slightly squeezed, and again stretched into a band, which is brushed and suffered to dry; by this process each length becomes stiffened and set apart from the rest.

"Silk is generally used for the warp on the border of the shawl, and has the advantage of showing the darker colours of the dyed wool more prominently than a warp of yarn as well as hardening and strengthening, and giving more body to the edge of the cloth. When the border is very narrow it is woven with the body of the shawl; but when broader, it is worked on a different loom, and afterwards sewn on the edge of the Shawl by the *Rafugar*, or fine drawer, with such nicety, that the union can scarcely be detected. The silk is twisted for the border warp by the *Tabgar*. The warp differs in breadth, the narrowest consisting of 20, and the broadest of 100 threads. From the *Tabgar* the silk is handed to the *Alakaband*, who reels it and cuts it into the proper lengths. The operation of drawing, or of passing the yarns of the warp through the heddles, is performed precisely in the same way as in Europe, and the warp is then taken by the *Shal-baf*, or weaver, to the loom. The weavers are all males, commencing to learn the art at the age of 10 years. In all transactions there are two parties, the master, or *Ustád*, and the scholar, or *Shahgird*, the former being the capitalist, the latter the mechanic. Work is executed under four different conditions: first, for wages, when it almost always happens that a system of advances has occurred, by which the workman is so deeply indebted to his employer that he may, in some sort, be considered as his bondslave. Secondly, upon contract, of which the common term is, that one pice is paid for every hundred needles carrying coloured yarn that shall have been each once passed round as many yarns of the warp. Third, a sort of partnership, in which the *Ustád* finds all the materials, and the workmen give their labour. When a shawl is sold, the outlay of the *Ustád* is deducted from the price, and the remainder is divided into five shares, of which one goes to the master, and the other four to the workmen. The fourth mode is an equal division of the proceeds; in which case the master not only finds the materials, but feeds the workmen. Three men are employed upon an embroidered shawl of an ordinary pattern for three months, but a very rich pair will occupy a shop for 18 months.

"The loom differs not in principle from that of Europe, but is of inferior workmanship. An *Ustád* has from three to 300 in his establishment, and they are generally crowded together in long, low apartments. When the warp is fixed in the loom, the *Nakash*, or pattern drawer, and the *Tarah-guru* and *Talim-guru*, or persons who determine the proportion of yarn of different colours to be employed, are again consulted. The first brings the drawing of the pattern in black and white. The *Tarah-guru*, having well considered it, points out the disposition of the colours, beginning at the foot of the pattern, and calling out the colour, the number of threads to which it is to extend, that by which it is to be followed, and so on in succession, until the whole pattern has been described. From his dictation the *Talim-guru* writes down the particulars in a kind of character or shorthand, and delivers a copy of the document to the weavers.

"The workmen prepare the *tujis,* or needles, by arming each with coloured yarn of about four grains weight. These needles, without eyes, are made of light smooth wood and have both their sharp ends slightly charred, to prevent their becoming rough or jagged through working. Under the superintendence of the *Tarah-guru,* the weavers knot the yarn of the *tuji* to the warp. The face, or right side of the cloth, is placed next to the ground, the work being carried on at the back or reverse, on which hang the needles in a row, and differing in number from 400 to 1,500, according to the lightness or heaviness of the embroidery. As soon as the *Ustád* is satisfied that the work of one line or woof is completed, the comb is brought down upon it with a vigour and repetition, apparently very disproportionate to the delicacy of the materials.

"The cloth of shawls is generally of two kinds, one plain, or of two threads, one twilled, or of four threads. The former was, in past times, wrought to a great degree of fineness, but it has been, of late, less in demand. The various twilled cloths are usually from five to 12 girahs, or nails, wide. Shawls are twilled, and are commonly about 24 nails broad, and differ in their extent of field. Two persons are employed in weaving a cloth of this breadth. One throws the shuttle from the edge as far as he can across the warp, which is usually about half way. It is there seized by the second weaver, who throws it onwards to the opposite edge, and then returns it to his companion, who, in his turn, introducing his fingers into the warp, forwards the shuttle to the edge whence it started, and then recommences the operation. The cloth thus made is frequently irregular, the threads of some parts of the woof being driven up tightly, and in others left open, from which results a succession of bands, sufficiently distinguishable whilst without colour, but still more obvious when dyed. The open texture is, in a degree, remediable by the introduction of fresh threads; but there is no sufficient cure for that which has been much compacted. One might be led to suspect that there existed some radical defectiveness in the principle of this mode of weaving not readily mastered, were not pieces of cloth found occasionally of an almost perfect regularity of texture. But the greatest irregularity is discoverable in those shawls which have the deepest and heaviest borders, and a further examination compels me to retract an observation somewhere made of the artist being so much engrossed by attention to the work of the pattern as to neglect the structure of the field. The edge of the warp in the loom is filled with the heavy thread of the *phiri,* or seconds yarn, charged also with colour, so that in a few lines the front of the worked part advances beyond that of the plain part or field, and an endeavour to equalize this betrays the weaver into a work which proves fruitless; and, in general, the heavier the embroidery on the border, and, of course, the higher the price of the shawl, the less regular is the structure of the cloth. Such indeed, in some instances, is the degradation of the cloth in the field, as to induce some foreign merchants to cause it to be removed, and another piece to be engrafted within the edge of the border. But in this case there is no other remedy than in a judicious selection of a sheet of the same breadth and fineness; for, although two breadths of the narrow cloth might fit the vacant space, yet these must be joined by the *rafugar* in the middle; and, although this can be so done that the band differs not in thickness from the rest of the cloth, yet the joint is discernible when held between the eye and the light, from the threads in the joined breadth not being continuous in the same line; whereas any irregularity of this nature is drowned in the edge of the border. The best practice to ensure a good field seems to consist in weaving the border, in every case, separately, and inserting the field by the *Rafugar.*

"When finished, the shawls are submitted to the *Purusgar*, or cleaner, whose business it is to free the shawl from discoloured hairs or yarn and from ends or knots: he either pulls them out severally with a pair of tweezers, or shaves the reverse face of the cloth with a sharp knife; any defects arising from either operation are immediately repaired by the *rafugar*. At this stage of the manufacture the shawls are sent to the Collector of the Stamp Duties, by whom an *ad valorem* duty of 26 per cent. is levied, and each piece is then stamped and registered. The goods are now handed over to the *Wafarosh*, or person who has advanced money on them to the manufacturer, and to the *Mohkim*, or broker, and these two settle the price and effect the sale to the merchant; the former charges interest on his advances, the latter a commission, varying from 2 to 5 per cent. The purchaser takes the goods unwashed, and often in pieces, and the fine-drawer and washerman have still to do their part.

"When partly washed, the *Dhobi*—or washerman—brings the shawls to the merchant, that they may be examined for any holes or imperfections; should such occur, they are remedied at the expense of the seller; if there are none, the washing is completed. This is done with clear cold water, using soap very cautiously to white parts alone, and never to embroidery. Coloured shawls are dried in the shade; white ones are bleached in the open air, and their colour is improved by exposure to fumes of sulphur. After being washed, the shawls are stretched in a manner which answers, in some degree, to calendering. A wooden cylinder in two parts is employed for this purpose, round which the shawl, folded so as not to be quite so broad as the cylinder is long, is carefully wrapped, being occasionally damped to make it fold tighter; the end is sewn down, two wedges are then gradually driven between the two parts of the cylinder at the open extremities, so as to force them asunder, and the surrounding folds of the shawl are thus stretched to as great an extent as is consistent with its texture. The piece remains in this state for two days, when it is removed to be packed. The packages are of various dimensions, but they are formed on one principle: the shawls are separated by sheets of smooth, glazed, and coloured paper, and they are placed between two smooth planks of wood, with exterior transverse bars, which, projecting beyond the planks, offer a purchase for cords to tie them together: the whole is then placed in a press, or under heavy weights, for some days, when the planks are withdrawn, and the bale is sewed up in strong cloth: over this a cover of tús, or of birch bark, is laid, and an envelope of wax cloth is added, and the whole is sewed up as smoothly and lightly as possible in a raw hide, which, contracting in drying, gives to the contents of the package a remarkable degree of compactness and protection.

"An immense variety of articles of shawl stuff are manufactured in Kashmir, besides the shawls themselves. Of them, also, there are two chief varieties, those made in the manner described, and the worked shawl (*doshali amli*), in which the whole of the embroidery is worked on the cloth, with needles having eyes, and with a particular kind of woollen thread, instead of the silk employed in the usual embroidered work. In the *amli* shawl, the pattern which is in every case delineated, but which at the loom is read off in certain technical terms from a book, is covered with transparent paper, upon which the outlines of the composition are slightly traced with a charcoal twig, and the traced lines are permanently defined by being pricked through with a small needle. The cloth intended to receive the pattern is rubbed strongly upon a smooth plank, with a piece of highly polished agate or cornelian, until it is perfectly even and regular. The pricked pattern is then stretched upon the cloth, and some fine coloured powder, charcoal or chalk, is passed slightly over the paper, which, penetrating through the holes, transfers the outline to the cloth underneath. This is next more accurately delineated with some coloured powder, rendered tenacious by mucilage of gum arabic, which, when the work is completed, is readily detached in dust by the hand.

"The use of patterns by the chain stitch embroiderer, and the carpet weaver of Kashmir, is more restricted to a confined number of forms, by being transferred from a wooden block to the cloth, in regard to the former, and to paper in respect to the latter.

"The following are the chief articles of this manufacture, with their usual prices.

"Shawls in pairs form the principal article of this manufacture, and have different names, according to their nature and quality, as plain white, coloured, embroidered in the loom, or by the hand with the needle, viz. :—

*Patu Pashmini*, sometimes made of Asal-tús, but more frequently of the coarse kinds of shawl wool, is in length 4 gaz and in breadth 1½ gaz. This is thick, and used as a blanket or for outer clothing. Price from five to six rupees per gaz.

*Shala Phiri*, as its name denotes, is made of phiri, or seconds wool. Its length is from 3½ to 4 gaz; breadth, 1½ gaz. Price from 20 to 30 rupees per piece.

*Halwan*, or plain white cloth, of fine shawl wool, without flower, border, or other ornament, differs in length, but is 12 girahs in breadth, and is used for turbans and for dyeing. Price from 3 to 6 rupees per gaz.

*Jowhar Shala Sadu*, or shawl with a narrow edging of coloured yarn, is from 3½ to 3¾ gaz in length and 1½ in breadth. Price from 50 to 60 rupees per piece.

"As all the following shawls are of the same dimensions, viz., 3½ gaz in length, and 1½ gaz in breadth, it is unnecessary to affix the measures to their several names.

*Shala Hashiadar*, edged by a single border. Price from 60 to 70 rupees.

*Shala Dohashiadar*, has a double border. Price from 40 to 70 rupees.

*Shala Chahar Hashiadar* has four borders. Price from 60 to 70 rupees.

*Hashiadar Khosar, or Khalil Khani*, has two borders and two tanga, sometimes with, at others without a flower in the corners. 40 to 50 rupees.

*Hashiadar Kingridar*. This has a border of the usual form with another withinside, or nearer to the middle, resembling the crest of the wall of Asiatic forts, furnished with narrow niches or embrasures for wall pieces, or matchlocks, whence its name. 100 to 150 rupees.

*Dhourdar* has an ornament running all round the shawl, between the border and the field. 200 to 2,200 rupees per pair.

*Mathandar*, has flowers or decorations in the middle of the field. 300 to 1,800 rupees per pair.

*Chand'dar* has a circular ornament or moon in the centre of the field. 500 to 1,500 rupees per pair.

*Choutahidar* has four half-moons. 300 to 1,500 rupees per pair.

*Kunjbuthadar* has a group of flowers at each corner. 200 to 900 rupees per pair.

*Alifdar* has green sprigs, without any other colour, on a white ground or field. 120 to 1,150 rupees per pair.

*Kaddar* has large groups of flowers, somewhat in the form of the cone of a pine, with the ends or points straight, or curved downwards.

*Dokaddar* has two heights of such groups, and

*Sekaddar* has three rows, and so on to five and upwards; in the latter case, however, the cones are somewhat small. 100 to 800 rupees per pair.

"The ornaments of shawls are distinguished by different names, as *Pala*, *Hashia*, *Zanjir*, *Dhour*, &c., and these are divided into different parts. By the term *Pala*, is meant the whole of the embroidery at the two ends, or, as they are technically called, the heads of the shawl.

The *Hashia*, or border, is disposed commonly one at each side in the whole length, and if double or triple, gives particular denomination to the shawl.

The *Zanjir*, or chain, runs above and also below the principal mass of the Pala, and, as it were, confines it.

The *Dhour*, or running ornament, is situated to the inside in regard to the *Hashia* and the *Zanjir*, enveloping immediately the whole of the field.

The *Kunjbutha* is a corner ornament, or clustering of flowers.

The *Mattan* is the decorated part of the field or ground.

*Butha* is the generic term for flowers, but is specifically applied when used alone to the large cone-like ornament which forms the most prominent feature of the Pala. Sometimes there is only one line of these ornaments, extending from the lowest *Zanjir* to the upper one. When there is a double row, one above the other, the *Butha* is called *Dokad*, *Sehkad*, up to five, after which it takes the name of *Tukaddar*.

Each *Butha* consists of three parts ; viz., the *Pai* or foot or pediment of leaves generally ; the *Shikam*, or belly, and the *Sir*, or head. The head is either erect, straight, curved, or inclined. If the *Butha* slope generally it is named *Butha-kaj*. The *Thal*, or net, is the work which separates the different *Buthas*, but sometimes the interstice is without ornament.

*Jamawar* signifies, literally, a gown piece. The length of this cloth is $3\frac{3}{4}$ gaz, and the breadth $1\frac{1}{2}$ gaz. This article branches into many varieties, as *Khirkhabutha*, large compound flowers, consisting of groups of smaller ones. This is used by the Persians and Afghans.

| | Rupees per piece. |
|---|---|
| *Rezabutha* (small flowers thickly set) | 200 to 700 |
| *Thaldar* (network) | 500 to 1,700 |
| *Islimi* | 250 to 400 |
| *Mehramat* | 150 to 300 |
| *Khatherast* | 150 to 750 |
| *Marpech* | 200 to 350 |
| *Kalmkar* | 300 to 1,000 |
| *Zakhe Angur* | 300 to 500 |
| *Chaporast* | 300 to 7,000 |
| *Dogul, Seh-gul, Chahar-gul, &c.* | 500 to 1,000 |
| *Barghe Bed* | 250 to 400 |
| *Gulisant* | 200 to 900 |
| *Duazdeh Khat* | 700 to 1,500 |
| *Duazdeh rang* | 800 to 1,400 |
| *Gule parwane* | 300 to 450 |
| *Kaddhar* | 300 to 2,000 |
| *Kayhamu, Sabzkar, Safed* | 120 to 130 |

" These are made by the shawl weaver alone, and go largely into Hindustan, where they are dyed, the small green flowers being previously tied up in hard small knots, so as to be protected from the action of the dye, and are, of course, when untied, each surrounded by a small white field. Small eyes of spots of yellow, red, and of other colours, are supposed to harmonize with the green flowers and the new ground, and these are added by embroiderers of *Chikkandoz*.

*Kasabeh* or *Rumal*, women's veils, square shawls. These are from one-and-a-half to two-and-a-half gaz square, and are called

| | |
|---|---|
| *Khathdar* | 300 to 500 rupees. |
| *Mehramat* | 150 to 300 ,, |

*Islimi*, with the 13 other patterns of the Jamawars ; and in addition there are—

| | |
|---|---|
| *Chaharbagh* | 300 to 350 rupees. |
| *Hashia* | 100 to 175 ,, |
| *Chand* | 50 to 200 ,, |
| *Shash Mantahi* | 250 to 200 ,, |
| *Feringi*, exported chiefly to Russia | 100 to 500 ,, |
| *Chantahi* | 150 to 400 ,, |
| *Tara Armeni*, exported chiefly to Armenia and Persia | 100 to 250 ,, |
| *Tara Rumi*, exported chiefly to Turkey | 120 to 300 ,, |
| *Sada* for domestic use | 12 to 15 ,, |

*Shamlas*, or girdles for the waist, worn by the Asiatics, are 8 gaz in length, and 1½ gaz broad, of various colors and patterns, and vary from 50 to 2,000 rupees a piece, according to the richness of the work.

*Doshala* or shawls, which contain three palas instead of two, go only to Thibet, and sell for 100 to 150 rupees.

*Goshpech* or *Patka*, or turbans, are in length from 8 to 10 gaz, breadth 1 gaz, and of all colours. One variety has two *palas*, two *zanjirs*, and two *hashias*. 150 to 800 rupees.

*Mandila*, another variety, sometimes has a *zanjir*, and sometimes is without this ornament. This latter is from 8 to 10 gaz in length, and about 12 giras broad. 45 to 70 rupees.

*Khalin Pashmina*, shawl carpets. This is sold at 20 to 40 rupees the square gaz of only three-quarters, and is made of any size in a single piece.

*Nakash.* Trousers. Some are with, others without, seams. The former are made of two pieces, which are sewn together by the *rafugar*, the latter by the *jarab saz*, or stocking maker. 200 to 500 rupees per pair.

*Chaharkhana*, netted cloth. Length indefinite; breadth, 1½ gaz; used by women. 5 to 10 rupees per gaz.

*Gulbadan.* Length indefinite, breadth from 14 girahs to one gaz. 5 to 6 rupees per gaz.

*Lungi*, girdles. Length 3½ gaz; breadth, 1½ gaz. These differ from *Shamlas* by being in narrow check, and bordered by lines of different colours. 50 to 70 rupees.

*Takhin*, caps, 8 annas to 4 rupees.

*Jarab*, short stockings. *Guldar* and *Mehramat*, flowered and striped. 1 to 5 rupees.

*Moze Pashmina*, long stockings. 5 to 25 rupees.

*Sakkab Posh*, canopies. 300 to 1,500 rupees.

*Darparda*, curtains for doors and windows. Same price as Jamawar, by measure.

*Kajjari Asp*, saddle cloths, by measure.

*Kajjari Fil*, elephant's housing, by measure.

*Balaposh* or *Palang Posh*, quilt or coverlet. 300 to 1,000 rupees.

*Galaband*, cravat. 12 to 300 rupees.

*Pistanband*, neckerchief. 5 to 15 rupees.

*Langota*, waist-belts. 15 to 30 rupees.

*Postin*, cloths left long in the nap to line pelisses. 500 to 1,000 rupees.

*Paipech*, leggings. Length, 2 gaz; breadth, 1 gira, of all colors. From 2 to 10 rupees.

*Yezar*, or *Izarband*, waist-strings. 1 to 15 rupees.

*Takhia*, pillow bier. Same price as Jamawar.

*Khalita*, bags or purses. 8 annas to 2 rupees.

*Kubbur Posh*, shrouds or covers for tombstones. Same price as Jamawar.

*Takposh*, covers or hangings in front of recesses or cupboards; and

*Khwanposh*, dish covers or napkins, of various qualities and patterns. From 30 to 500 rupees a piece."

The following remarks on the shawl-wool of the domestic goat of Ladakh, and on that of the wool of the Wild Goat, including a notice of the manner in which the shawl-wool is picked from the fleece are also from Moorcroft:—

"One of the most important articles of the trade of Ladakh is shawl-wool, of which it forms in some degree the source, but in a still greater the entrepôt between the countries whence the wool is chiefly supplied, Rodokh and Chan-than, and that in which it is consumed, Kashmir. The wool is that of a domestic goat, and consists of the under fleece or that next the skin beneath the outer coat of hair; the breed is the same in Ladakh as in Lassa, Great Tibet and Chinese Turkistan, but the wool is not so fine as in the breeds of the districts on its eastern and northern frontier. The fleece is cut once a year, and the wool, coarsely picked either in the place from whence it comes or at Lé, is sold by the importer to the merchants at that city, by whom it is sent on to Kashmir. The Raja and Khalun deal extensively in this trade, but it is also shared by merchants both from Kashmir and Turan. About 800 loads are annually exported to

Kashmir, to which country, by ancient custom and engagements, the export is exclusively confined, and all attempts to convey it to other countries are punished by confiscation. In like manner it is considered in Rodokh and Chan-than as illegal to allow a trade in shawl-wool except through Ladakh, and in the latter country considerable impediments are opposed to the traffic in wool from Yarkand, although it is of superior quality and cheapness. The hair of the goat after it is separated from the wool is made into ropes, blankets, and bags for home use, and as wrappers for bales of merchandise.

" Besides the fleece of the domesticated goat, that of the wild goat, under the denomination of *Asali Tus*, is exported in smaller quantities to Kashmir. It is of a light brown colour and exceeding fineness, and is worked into shawls, a kind of soft cloth called *Tusi*, and linings for shawl-wool stockings ; very few shawls, however, are made from this materal.

" In general the pickers of shawl-wool are paid by the hair, but in this case the hair is considered unfit for making into ropes, &c. Shawls made of this material would be much softer, lighter, and warmer than those of ordinary fabric. When, without being picked, the Asali Tus is worked into Tusi it forms a warm, soft cloth of a drab or gray colour which is much worn in the hills. This article must be always high priced from the difficulty of procuring the animal that produces it, the wild goat rarely venturing within gun-shot during the day, and being obtained only by snares at night, when they come down from the mountains to browse in the valleys."*

" On my way to Digar I had an opportunity of witnessing the manner in which the shawl-wool was extracted from the fleece. After the hair of the goat had been cut short with a knife in the direction of its growth, or from the head towards the tail, a sort of comb was passed in the reversed direction, and brought away the finer wool almost unmixed with the coarse hair. The comb consisted of seven pegs of willow tied side by side and secured by cross bars ; the pegs were cut away at the points to the thickness of quills and were made slightly to diverge from each other. The operation was roughly performed, and brought away scales of the cuticle along with the wool. The wool, however, was at this season easily detached, for it is a curious provision of nature that with the setting in of warmer weather the delicate woolly clothing nearest the skin of the mountain animals being no longer needed, becomes loosened in its attachment, and is removed, if not by man, by the animals themselves. I noticed the yaks at the end of April very busy rubbing themselves with their horns and bringing off the finer hairs in considerable quantities. In sheep and dogs the wool rose to the end of the hair, and either fell off or was got rid of by the animals rolling on the ground or rubbing themselves against trees, &c., and I was told that the wild goats and sheep relieve themselves in the same manner of a vesture indispensable to their comfort in winter, but unnecessary and inconvenient in the heat of summer."†

---

* Moorcroft's "Travels in Kashmir," &c., vol. I., p. 346. † Op. cit., vol. I., p. 410.

## CASHMERE CLOTH AND WOOL FOR SHAWLS, &c.

In the following Table are inserted the particulars regarding the specimens of Cashmere cloths and of the portions of the Shawls which are shown in the books.

| No. of Vol. | No. of Sample. | | Description. | Measurement. Length. | Measurement. Width. | Weight of Piece. | Cost. | Place of Manufacture, or where obtained. |
|---|---|---|---|---|---|---|---|---|
| | | | | yds. ins. | yds. ins. | lbs. oz. | £ s. d. | |
| XVIII. | 667 | Plain Cloths. | Bright crimson, fine quality | 7 0 | 1 10 | 2 4 | 3 0 0 | Loodiana, Punjab. |
| XVIII. | 668 | | Black, first quality. Chiefly used for Chogas. | 4 10 | 0 19 | 0 12 | — | Cashmere. |
| XVIII. | 669 | | White, fine quality | 7 0 | 1 19 | 2 12 | 4 0 0 | Loodiana, Punjab. |
| XVIII. | 670 | | Magenta, first quality | 5 0 | 0 28 | 1 1¼ | 2 15 0 | Cashmere. |
| XVIII. | 671 | | Black, second quality | 5 0 | 0 26 | 1 0 | — | Cashmere. |
| XVIII. | 672 | | Grey, second quality | 5 8 | 0 26 | 0 14½ | 3 0 0 | Cashmere. |
| XVIII. | 673 | | Green, fine texture | 6 20 | 1 6 | 0 15 | 3 10 0 | Cashmere. |
| XVIII. | 674 | | Purple, fine texture | 5 0 | 0 26 | 0 14 | — | Cashmere. |
| XVIII. | 675 | | Crimson, second quality | 5 10 | 0 25 | 0 15 | — | Cashmere. |
| XVIII. | 678 | | Crimson, coarse shawl cloth, inferior in quality. | 6 21 | 0 27 | 1 7 | — | Lahore. |
| XVIII. | 664 | Shawls. | Jamewar, striped and figured, fine quality. | 3 14 | 1 19 | 2 8 | 7 0 0 | Kangra. |
| XVIII. | 665 | | Red ground, pine pattern throughout | 3 9 | 1 15 | 2 2 | — | Cashmere. |
| XVIII. | 666 | | Green ground, pine and flowered pattern. | 3 0 | 1 6 | 2 7 | — | Cashmere. |

No attempt could, of course, be made to illustrate, in this way, the patterns of the Shawls. The three examples (Nos. 664, 665, and 666, Vol. xviii) have merely been inserted to show the material in its worked, or loom-embroidered condition.

The ten specimens of the cloth are, however, calculated to give a good idea of the beauty of the dye, and the delicious softness of the fabric which forms, so to speak, the base of the Cashmere Shawl—the comfort of which in wear, however, perhaps is diminished by the quantity and weight of the material with which it is so profusely but charmingly decorated.

In the preceding description of the wool employed in the manufacture of the true Cashmere shawl, it will be observed that considerable importance is attached to the fact that it should, in all cases, consist of the down called *pushum*, which is found upon goats pastured in Ladak and other elevated regions to the north of the Himalayas. There are no doubt very excellent reasons for this distinction; but on this point we would remark that whatever these may be, the preference given to the Goat Wool cannot be ascribed merely to its superior fineness. These *downs* act as a protection from the intense cold, and it is probable that all the hair-bearing animals in these regions possess them to some extent. The Yâk and Camel, and even the Shepherd's Dog,* we know to do so, and the down of the two former is often found to be quite as fine as that of the Shawl-Goat itself. Again the beautifully fine sheep's wool of which the Rampore Chuddar is said to be manufactured, frequently equals, in softness, that from the goat: it would appear, however, not to admit, equally with the latter, of the attachment of dyes, and it is probably in this respect that the chief difference is to be found.

---

* Vigne, "Travels in Kashmir," vol. II. p. 124.

**On the subject of the sources of the different wools employed in the manufacture of various fabrics found in Northern India, considerable obscurity prevails. The group to which we have next to allude affords an illustration of this.**

## PUTTOO; CAMEL'S HAIR CLOTH, &c.

The material called *Puttoo*, of which the examples given in the books are embraced in the next Table, is usually considered to be manufactured from the inferior qualities of shawl-wool, and such may often be the case; but the fine down of other animals as, for instance, the camel, is, we believe, capable of making a fabric equally good in respect of *softness*. Two *boná fide* examples of Camel Hair Cloth are given in the end of the Table, and the latter of the two (No. 686) is found to contain a wool or down quite as fine as that in some of the true shawl-cloth fabrics.

The Puttoo is generally employed by the natives for making up into long coats called Chogas, of the form of which the figures 55, 56, and 57 at bottom of Pl. VIII., afford illustrations.

The Choga is ornamented in a variety of ways, generally by means of silk braiding.

Those made of the fine Cashmere cloth are often gold embroidered (See two sitting figures to left in group 54, Pl. VIII., facing p. 118).

Plate IX.—opposite next page—gives a very good illustration of ornamental braiding of the back, collar, and sleeves of a Choga of Cashmere cloth of the Puttoo variety, in which the material has been thickened, and a *pile* raised by some mechanical process.

This is a class of work in which the Native excels, and it is probable that were shapes suited to European taste supplied, he would find a steady market in the West for articles made of the fine woollen cloths which he has at command.

| No. of | | Description. | Measurement. | | Weight of piece. | Cost. | Place of Manufacture, or where obtained. |
|---|---|---|---|---|---|---|---|
| Vol. | Sample. | | Length. | Width. | | | |
| | | | yds. ins. | yds. ins. | lbs. oz. | £ s. d. | |
| XVII. | 648 | "Foorook" or "Puttoo." Dark chocolate brown. Superior quality. Thick material. | 11 0 | 0 15 | 9 11 | 0 12 0 | Lassa. Obtained from Kangra. |
| XVII. | 649 | "Puttoo." Thick, uncoloured material - | 6 29 | 0 12 | 3 7 | 0 18 0 | Lassa. Obtained from Kangra. |
| XVIII. | 680 | "Puttoo" Kid cloth. Wrapper; fine quality. Plain white. Sewn together, two pieces form the complete cloak or covering. | 4 29 | 0 31½ | 4 1 | 3 4 0 | Lahore. |
| XVIII. | 681 | "Puttoo." Kid cloth. Dark grey. Fine quality. | 3 24 | 1 10 | 2 9 | 1 3 3 | Lahore. |
| XVIII. | 682 | "Puttoo." Kid cloth. Plain - - | 9 22 | 0 27 | 3 15 | — | Thibet. |
| XVIII. | 683 | "Toosee," or "Tose" Cloth. Grey mixture. | 12 27 | 0 13 | 2 15 | 3 0 0 | Baltistan. Obtained at Kangra. |
| XVIII. | 684 | Plain dark grey. Used as a wrapper. Narrow line of green silk in selvage. | 2 18 | 1 20 | 1 12 | — | Lahore. |
| XVIII. | 692 | Plain, coarse brown woollen, uncoloured. Inferior quality. Two pieces sewn together form a garment. | 4 18 | 2 12 | 3 7½ | 1 6 0 | Lahore. |
| XVIII. | 685 | "Burruch." Camel's hair cloth. Used for "Chogas," or dressing gowns, &c. | — | — | — | — | Hyderabad, Scind. |
| XVIII. | 686 | "Burruch" or Camel's Hair Cloth. Much worn by Europeans as well as natives. | 8 13 | 0 13 | 1 14 | 0 9 0 | Meshed. |

## SULUNG OR KERSEYMERE-LIKE CLOTHS.

In the next Table we have grouped certain fabrics which, unlike the Puttoo, are of a rather harsh description, like our Kerseymere cloths. These are occasionally used for Chogas, although not in such favour for that purpose as the soft, pleasant, Puttoo.

It would seem, however, that both are produced from the wool or hair of the same animals. This arises partly from the process of manufacture, and partly from the quality of the hair which varies according to the age as well as the part of the animal from which it is taken.

Although, therefore, these Kerseymere-like cloths are probably chiefly produced from the hair of the Shawl Goat, we are of opinion that just as the down of the Camel and Yak may be used for the manufacture of the finest Puttoo, so may the less fine hair of the same animals be employed to make the class of goods of which we are now speaking.*

| No. of | | Description. | Measurement. | | Weight of piece. | Cost. | Place of Manufacture, or where obtained. |
|---|---|---|---|---|---|---|---|
| Vol. | Sample. | | Length. | Width. | | | |
| | | | yds. ins. | yds. ins. | lbs. oz. | £ s. d. | |
| XVI. | 624 | "Kooroon"† or "Sulung" cloth. Light grey colour, plain. Fine quality. | 20 0 | 0 16½ | 3 2 | * about 0 2 3 per yard. | Sulung, between Lassa and China. |
| XVI. | 625 | "Kooroon" or Sulung cloth. Reddish chocolate colour. Fine quality. | 20 0 | 0 16½ | 3 2 | * about 0 2 3 per yard. | Ditto. |
| XVI. | 626 | "Kooroon" or "Sulung" cloth. Light drab colour. Fine quality. | 20 0 | 0 17 | 3 2 | * about 0 2 3 per yard. | Ditto. |
| XVI. | 627 | "Kooroon" or "Sulung" cloth. Dark brown colour. Fine quality. | 20 0 | 0 16½ | 3 2 | * about 0 2 3 per yard. | Ditto. |
| XVIII. | 679 | Kerseymere material. Plain purple. Used for cloaks or Chogas. | — | — | — | — | Cabool. |
| XVIII. | 693 | Kerseymere material; plain uncoloured, white. Good quality. Used for making Loée or wrap. | 6 28 | 1 23 | 4 6 | — | Bickaneer. |
| XVI. | 631 | Woollen. Plain, uncoloured. The two widths sewn together form one garment piece. Rather softer than 693, but rough. | 7 18 | 1 22 | 7 0 | 0 18 6 | Dharwar. Sent from Madras. |

* This price was the cost per yard in Cashmere.

† These Kooroon cloths—called also Sulung—are stated to be made at a place called "Sulung, between Lassa and China," the exact locality of which, however, we have been unable to determine.—Thousands of pieces of these cloths are said to be used in Turkistan.—Some colours are not fast; others are permanent.

Camel hair is very extensively used in Russia for the manufacture of various thick, coarse fabrics, and is becoming known in the Bradford and Leicester trade for working up in a variety of ways. That imported into this country is from the Levant, but the fine soft down which is the produce of higher and colder latitudes is still comparatively unknown.

* An attempt made to distinguish, by means of the microscope, the hair employed in the manufacture of the different fabrics referred to in this and the two following tables, has not been productive of results sufficiently distinctive to permit of their being made use of for the purpose of detecting the "adulterations" alluded to in the Punjab Report. The subject is one, however, to which we shall probably take occasion to recur.

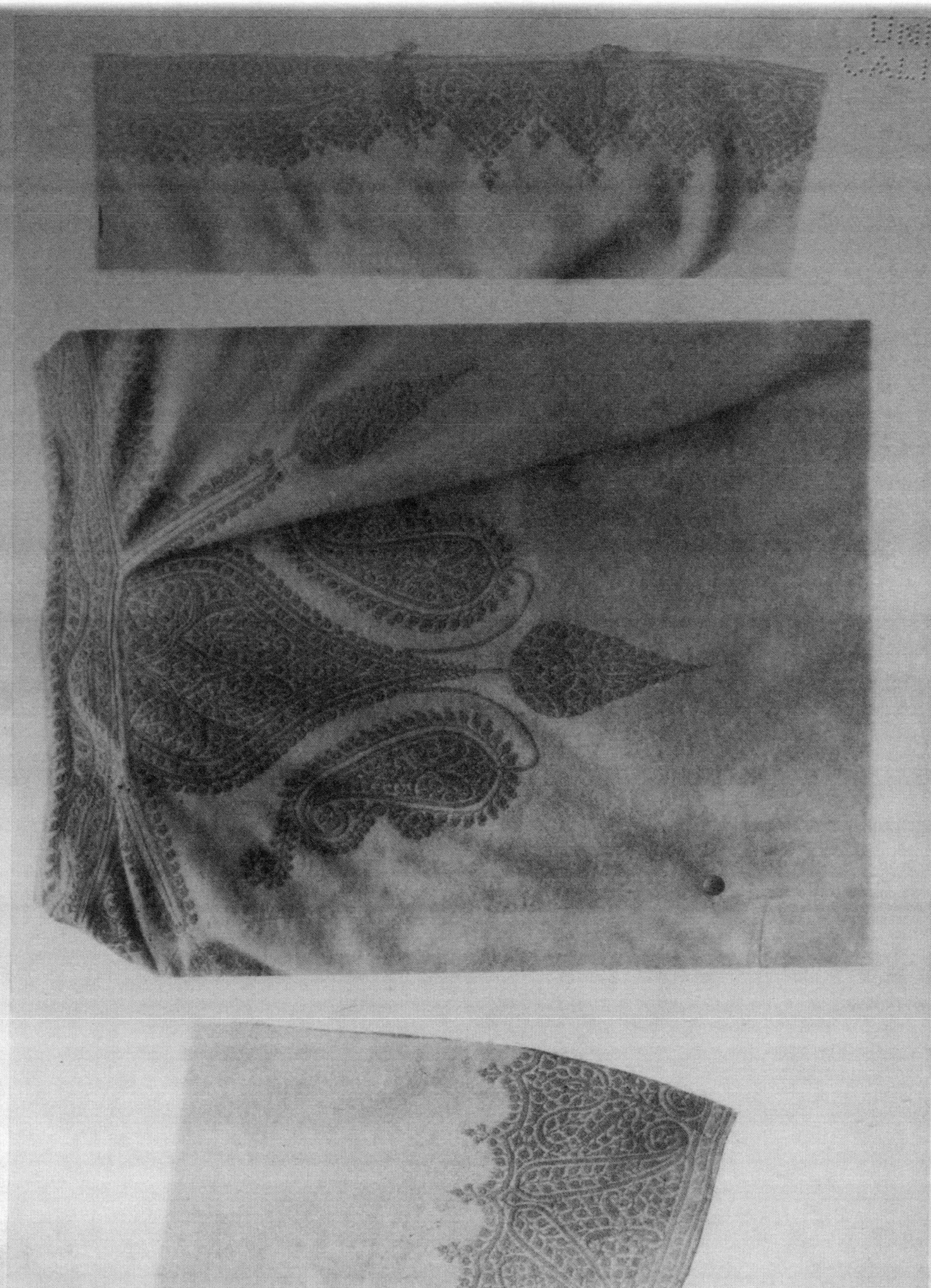

The following remarks,* by Captain T. Hutton, on the wool of the Bactrian Camel will be read with interest :

" The animal is so thickly clothed during winter with this wool, and its quality appears to me so much superior to most of those specimens of wools obtained in Armenia and Koordistan by Captain Conolly, that I should expect the article, if imported, to form a valuable commodity in the European markets. The wool of this animal is as yet but little used, a small quantity only being exported from Bokhara to Cabul, and I believe to Umritsur in the Punjab. The great bulk of it is said to be sent at present to Russia, and manufactured into a kind of broadcloth, called *Salatiska*, which is worn by soldiers."

Referring to certain specimens of the hair or wool of the Camel accompanying his note, Captain Hutton continues :

" No. 1 is a sample of the wool taken from the sides and back of a full-grown male Bactrian camel, in the winter clothing. It is so thickly disposed, that the skin of the animal can with difficulty be discerned beneath it, even when the wool is turned back for that purpose. In the spring, as the temperature grows milder, the whole of this wool detaches itself from the skin, being pushed off in masses and flakes by the hair which springs up beneath it, and which forms the summer clothing of the animal. It is at this season pulled or cut off, and after being cleaned, is either manufactured into woollens of different texture for home consumption, or exported in a raw state to Russia ; a small quantity also finds its way to Cabul and the Punjab. It is produced abundantly both in Bokhara and Balk, and the Steppes of Tartary. This wool is called " *koork*," or down. It appears to be little inferior in fineness to that procured from some breeds of Shawl Goats, while it possesses a decided advantage over them all, in being both of a much longer fibre, and far more easily freed from the hair.

" No. 2 is a specimen of coarse thread spun from this wool by the hand, *i.e.*, without the aid of the wheel ; the wool is gathered into a mass, a small portion twisted into a thread by the fingers, and then attached to a cross stick with a weight ; or to a stone which is kept twirling round, while small portions of the wool are continually added. The threads thus made are coarse, and liable to break from being too loosely twisted. This method is, however, very generally practised, more especially in these districts ; the same also prevails in most parts of the Himalaya, and is in use even in the provinces of India in the spinning of cotton threads for common purposes.

" Woollens made from threads thus twisted are far more difficult to weave than those manufactured from threads spun by the hand-wheel, as the looseness of the twist often causes them to catch and break as the shuttle passes to and fro.

" No. 3 is a sample of the wool and hair taken from the fore-arm.

" No. 4 is taken from the under part of the neck and throat.

" The hairs in these samples are so long, that the trouble of cleaning the wool, would, I should imagine, be much lessened, and probably the hair itself might prove an useful article for making pencils and other brushes. These wools are all taken from an animal which wintered at Candahar, so that the probability is that the staple was not so long as it would have been had the camel remained in the more northern districts. There is also another thing to be observed, which is, that the beast was not worked during the winter season, and consequently the wool was uninjured by the friction of a load. It is both shorter and coarser

* Journal of the Asiatic Society of Bengal ;—1842 ; Vol. IX., p. 1185.

when the animal has been laden. No doubt, too, there may be as much difference between the wools of different camels as between sheep; but the samples sent may be deemed upon the whole a fair selection, considering the limited range of my observation on the subject.

"No. 5 is a sample of wool taken from the humps of a male Bactrian camel that had been much worked during winter.

"No. 6 is from the sides of the same animal.

"No. 7 from the neck and forearm.

"These are natural ringlets or bunches. The colour of these wools is generally that of the specimens sent, but the long hair of the neck and forearm sometimes has a reddish or ferruginous tinge.

"That which I have termed 'hair,' appears to be not very much, if at all, inferior to some of the coarser wools of Europe, while it possesses a decided advantage in being more than double the length of any sheep wool.

"In addition to the above I enclose a sample of a woollen cloth made from the soft wool procurable from the young dromedary.

"This is called '*Buruk Shootur-i.*' It is made by the Huzareehs of the Cabul neighbourhood. It is manufactured in pieces of 15 to 18 inches wide, by 6 to 8 yards long, and the price varies with the size from 8 to 30 rupees per piece. There are other woollens, which are called '*kart*' and '*oormuk.*'

"*Oormuk* forms part of the dress of the Turcoman people. It comes also from Bokhara. This is chiefly purchased by the wealthy, and sells from fifty to one hundred rupees per piece.

"*Kart* is somewhat similar to this. It comes from Bokhara and Turkistan, and is made from the wool of the yearling dromedary."

Of the hair of the Yak, to which reference has been made, the chief manufacture, *in point of bulk*, is a cloth used for making the black tents which constitute the only habitation of the people of Ladakh and other districts in the centre of Asia. The same material is also employed in making the bags which are used in the conveyance of goods of all kinds.

## CUMBLEES, OR BLANKETS, &c.

In the subjoined Table are included the particulars connected with the examples of the fabrics made of sheep's wool, or of mixtures of sheep's wool with camel and horse-hair.

In grouping these, reference has been had to the quality of the different examples.

Most of these fabrics are from wool produced either in the south, or in the plains of India, and they accordingly exhibit characteristics of the harsh hairy covering which suffices for the protection of the animal in these warm latitudes.

| No. of | | | Description. | Measurement. | | Weight of piece. | Cost. | Place of Manufacture, or where obtained. |
|---|---|---|---|---|---|---|---|---|
| Vol. | Sample. | | | Length. | Width. | | | |
| | | | | yds. ins. | yds. ins. | lbs. oz. | £ s. d. | |
| XVII. | 651 | Thick Blanketing Material, Soft Texture. | Coarse. Across end, three roughly marked stripes in red and brown, 3½ inches apart. | 7 18 | 0 12 | 3 8 | — | Thibet. |
| XVII. | 653 | | Coarse; plain, uncoloured - | 7 9 | 0 14 | 5 10 | | Ditto. |
| XVII. | 658 | | Coarse; plain, uncoloured - | 2 25 | 1 26 | 5 0 | — | Oodeypore. |
| XVII. | 663 | | Coarse; plain, uncoloured - | 3 16 | 2 9 | 9 14 | — | Jeypore. |
| XVII. | 659 | | Large coloured check, English pattern. | 4 0 | 2 21 | 15 15 | 1 0 0 | Delhi. |
| XVI. | 634 | Thick Material, Harsh Texture. | Thick, coarse, uncoloured, used for trowserings. | — | — | — | — | Kangra. |
| XVII. | 650 | | Thick, coarse, uncoloured. Used for coats and cloaks by the peasants of Kohat. | — | — | — | * | Kohat. |
| XVII. | 654 | | Thick, coarse, uncoloured; dark brown sheep's wool. Fringed ends. | 2 27 | 1 2 | 2 10 | 0 1 0 | Bangalore. Sent from Madras. |
| XVI. | 638 | Thinner Material; Harsh, Close Texture. | Plain, uncoloured; strong and rough. | 7 0 | 2 3 | 7 15 | 0 11 3 | Sattara. |
| XVI. | 639 | | Plain, dark chocolate colour. Used for making shawls for the Lamas or priests. | 14 0 | 0 9 | 2 0 | — | Thibet. |
| XVI. | 640 | | Black and white check pattern - | 5 5 | 1 29 | 5 2 | 0 18 0 | Delhi. |
| XVI. | 641 | | Plain black, strong. Ends fringed. | 3 14 | 1 13 | 2 15 | 0 6 0 | Beejapoor. |
| XVI. | 643 | | Plain black. Fringed ends - | 7 22 | 2 6 | 8 8 | — | Beckaneer, N.W. India. |
| XVII. | 645 | | Plain black. Fringed ends - | 3 6 | 1 8 | 3 4 | 0 10 0 | Bellary. Sent from Madras. |
| XVII. | 655 | Wool and Hair. | Wool mixed with camels' hair. Very stout and thick, similar to No. 654 in texture. | 2 20 | 1 18 | 5 0 | 0 1 6 | Bangalore. Obtained in Madras. |
| XVII. | 657 | | Wool and horsehair. Black, with a chequered stripe. Coarse and harsh texture. Used for rugs. | 18 14 | 0 10 | 10 13 | — | Kangra. |

* Sufficient material for trowsers for about 2*s.* 6*d.*

## WOOLLENS.—STRIPED.

The three specimens (Nos. 646, 647, and 656) included in the next Table afford examples of patterns in vogue at Sikkim, as well as in Nepal and Thibet.

The group (44) at top of Plate VII.,* facing next page, shows the manner in which the fabric is made up for wear in Sikkim—the similarity to the Scotch kilt is very obvious. Figures 46 and 47 in the same Plate illustrate the way in which the *Cumblee* is worn in the cold weather for the protection of the head and shoulders. Fig. 48 shows a scanty woollen garment in the made-up form, and No. 43, with standing figure in group 49, illustrate the wearing of a large wrapper and thick hooded cloak of felt, a material in common use in many parts of High Asia, to which reference has now to be made.

* This Plate, on account of our having, after its execution, chosen to deal first with the Cashmere Shawls, is made to follow, instead of precede, Pl. VIII.

| No. of Vol. | No. of Sample. | Description. | Measurement. Length. | Measurement. Width. | Weight of Piece. | Cost. | Place of Manufacture, or where obtained. |
|---|---|---|---|---|---|---|---|
| | | | yds. ins. | yds. ins. | lbs. oz. | £ s. d. | |
| XVII. | 646 | Woollen. Green, with cross stripes in blue, crimson, white, &c. Colours good. Pattern similar to Darjeeling productions. | — | — | — | — | Sikim. Obtained from Thibet. |
| XVII. | 647 | Woollen. Very strong. Green, with 1¼ inch cross stripes in crimson, yellow, blue, and white, ¾ inch apart. Good colours. Worn by both sexes. Darjeeling figure. | 19 0 | 0 9½ | 6 14 | — | Thibet. |
| XVII. | 656 | Woollen. Coarse quality. Black, with ⅜ inch crimson, yellow, and white stripes. Made and used by the Hill tribes. Sewn together to form any desired width. | 2 9 | 0 15 | 2 0 | — | Kathmandoo. |

## FELTS.

Nos. 660, 661, and 662 in the books, the particulars of which are included in the next and last Table in this division, are three specimens of Felt; the first being from Ladak, and the other two from Jeypore and Rajpootana.

These felts are used for blankets and cloaks, and for making into leggings, &c.

Coloured wool is often used with great effect in the production of patterns upon the surface of the material.

The following is the description of the manufacture of felts, or *Namads*, given by Major H. B. Lumsden in his "Mission to Kandahar, 1860."

"The mode of manufacture is apparently very simple, and the beauty and accuracy of the patterns in the finer kinds is astonishing. A large mat, called *chappar*, formed of the stems of the Guinea grass, bound together with thin cords and crushed, is the principal instrument used in their production, and for the finer kinds a large knife is used for mowing down the surface to an equal level and developing the clearness of the pattern. The *Un*, which is the best sort of felt, consists entirely of sheep's wool, is usually a mixture of wool with goat's and camel's hair picked and cleaned.* This is spread out evenly on the '*chappar*' which is then rolled up with firm pressure with the feet (the Peshwaries employ the back of the forearm in this process) unrolled and re-rolled from the opposite end. This process of rolling backwards and forwards, which occupies a considerable time, owing to the slow and continued to-and-fro action that accompanies the rolling and unrolling and revolving is continued for four or five hours, by which time the fibres have become firmly and intimately interwoven.† The felt is now taken up, washed

* He tells us in another part of the work that great attention has to be paid to having the wool thoroughly carded and cleaned first.

† In order to assist the felting-process we believe that hot water is employed in connexion with the operation here described.

MALE ATTIRE. WOOLLENS AND SKINS.

with soap and water, dried, and again stretched on the *chappar*, when coloured patches of wool are arranged according to pattern on its surface, and the whole is then again submitted to the rolling process for four or five hours, after which the felt is completed and fit for use. The finer kinds are trimmed with a mowing-knife, which greatly improves the appearance and brings out the distinctness of the colours. These felts are commonly used as carpets, cushions, bedding, horse-clothing, &c., and by nomades as a warm lining for their hair tents. They vary in price from one to two rupees to fifty or sixty rupees per piece, according to pattern, size, and quality."

| No. of | | Description. | Measurement. | | Weight of Piece. | Cost. | Place of Manufacture, or whence procured. |
|---|---|---|---|---|---|---|---|
| Vol. | Sample. | | Length. | Width. | | | |
| | | | yds. ins. | yds. ins. | lbs. oz. | £ s. d. | |
| XVII. | 660 | Felted material. Plain uncoloured body. End for 6½ inches ornamented with coloured silks in diamond pattern, formed by the needle. Used for leggings, &c. | 0 31 | 0 18 | 0 9 | 0 1 0 | Ladak. |
| XVII. | 661 | Felted material, for cloak to cover the head and body. Large circular figure in coloured wool pressed into the surface of the piece.* | 1 21 | 2 21 | 3 13 | — | Jeypore, Rajpootana. |
| XVII. | 662 | Felted material. Large circular figure formed by fragments of bright coloured cloth pressed into the surface of the felt.* | 3 0 | 1 20 | 4 8 | — | Ditto. |

* Not shown in all the samples.

This concludes our remarks on woollen fabrics used as articles of body clothing. But the wool *on* the skin is also occasionally employed for that purpose. Figures 45 and 50, Pl. VII., facing p. 140—opposite—afford illustrations of sheep's skin used for this purpose in Sind and elsewhere in North-western India.

# CARPETS AND RUGS.

The class of manufactures to which we have now to refer are of interest not merely as frequently affording examples of taste of the highest order, but likewise on account of the probable commercial importance of some of them to India at a future period.

In India, as in all other countries where it is the custom of the inhabitants to sit on the floor or ground, rugs or carpets, varying in size from less than a yard to many feet square, are in common use amongst all classes, except, perhaps, the very poorest.

The manufacture is, therefore, one of very considerable extent; but although the common kinds are made in almost every district throughout the country, the production of those of a superior description is confined to a comparatively small number of places. Amongst these some, such as Ellore and Masulipatam (in Madras), Warungul (near Hydrabad in the Deccan), Benares, Mirzapore, and Goruckpore, have long been favourably known, and appear calculated to retain their position, whilst in other localities the attempt to imitate European patterns is producing a degradation in the character of the productions which, if persisted in, will prove fatal to the trade.

In place of the beauty and truthfulness of the native design, some of the carpets and rugs lately imported into this country are simply hideous—pale colours in contrast with raw yellows and blues—common European chintz patterns intermixed with the distorted remains of fine native designs.

| No. of Vol. | No. of Sample. | | Description. | Measurement. Length. | Measurement. Width. | Weight of Piece. | Cost. | Place of Manufacture, or whence procured. |
|---|---|---|---|---|---|---|---|---|
| | | | | yds. ins. | yds. ins. | lbs. oz. | £ s. d. | |
| XI. | 435 | Cotton Suttringees. | *Suttringee*, Rug, blue stripes | 1 32 | 0 32 | 2 4 | 0 3 0 | Mangalore, Madras. |
| XI. | 436 | Cotton Suttringees. | *Suttringee*, Rug, blue stripes | 5 13 | 2 20 | 15 3 | 0 2 0 | Mangalore, Madras. |
| XI. | 437 | Cotton Suttringees. | *Suttringee*, Rug, blue and white. This is an example of the Sepoy regulation rug. | 2 14 | 1 4 | 2 5 | 0 2 0 | Palamcottah, Madras. |
| XI. | 438 | Cotton Suttringees. | *Suttringee*, blue and white | 2 16 | 1 6½ | 2 14 | 0 2 0 | Palamcottah, Madras. |
| XI. | 439 | Cotton Suttringees. | *Suttringee*, figured stripes in blue and red. | 2 30 | 1 24 | 8 11 | — | Agra, N.W.P. |
| XI. | 440 | Cotton Suttringees. | *Suttringee*, figured stripes in blue, red, and white. | 2 30 | 1 19 | 8 13 | — | Agra, N.W.P. |
| XVIII. | 699 | Cotton Suttringees. | *Suttringee*, coloured stripes | 2 30 | 1 24 | — | — | Agra, N.W.P. |
| XI. | 434 | | Sleeping rug, with looped pile,* of bleached cotton. The rug from which the samples have been cut was formed by two pieces sewn together. | 2 8 | 1 24 | 6 2 | — | Upper Assam. |
| XVIII. | 698 | | Cotton Carpet; short pile | 3 12 | 1 24 | — | — | Wurrungul, Deccan. |
| XVIII. | 695 | Woollen. | Deep pile | — | — | — | — | Ellore, Madras. |
| XVIII. | 696 | Woollen. | Short pile | 2 16 | 1 18 | — | — | Wurrungul, Deccan. |
| XVIII. | 697 | Woollen. | Short close pile | — | — | — | — | Bokhara. |
| XVIII. | 700 | | Silk, short pile | 2 20 | 1 18 | — | — | Wurrungul, Deccan. |

* There is also a woollen fabric called Pureepuz the pile of which is formed of loops.

These errors are not those into which the native artist will fall, *if left to himself.*

They are, in the majority of instances, forced upon him by his European employer, who, believing in the rose and daffodil patterns of his youth, has yet to acquire the power of appreciating the higher and more refined art of the people amongst whom, for a time, his lot has been cast.*

The carpets and rugs manufactured in India are of five kinds. The first is made entirely of cotton, and is of a close, stiff texture, and smooth surface. The ordinary name for these is *Suttringee*, and they may be said to be made here and there over the whole country, their use being almost universal. Several examples of the material of which these are made are given in the Books and referred to in the Table. They are extremely durable. No great variety is attempted in the patterns, which are usually modifications of blue and white stripes, with, occasionally, as in No. 440, the introduction of a figure.

In the second kind, the warp, like the last, is of cotton, but the woof is of wool. These are striped and woven in the same way as the ordinary Suttringee, which is by far the most common variety.

The Loom employed in weaving both these is horizontal, without either treadles or reed, and the warp is stretched out the whole length and breadth of the piece intended to be wrought. The woof is not thrown across with a shuttle, but is passed through by several workmen, who bring the threads together with wooden combs in place of a reed. The narrowest piece requires two men, and eight or ten are employed when the breadth is great.

The third kind is made of cotton, like the first, but instead of presenting the plain surface of the two last, a short thick-set pile of cotton is worked into it. This pile the workmen introduce with great dexterity, and, after a time, produce the pattern, which is frequently very handsome as well as intricate, without even looking at it.

The warp is placed vertically, and the various colours employed to form the pattern hang down from bobbins between the warp and the workmen. The woof is passed by the hand, and then driven home by the comb.

No. 698, Vol. XVIII, the last of the series, affords a specimen of the kind of carpet here alluded to, while the chromo-lithograph on Pl. X.—facing next page—attempts to exhibit the pattern and colouring of a very beautiful carpet, manufactured at Warungul, near Hyderabad, Deccan, and now in the India Museum.

In the fourth group we place carpets and rugs in which the pile is of wool. Three examples of these are given in the books with the object of showing the fabric, it being, of course, beyond our power to exhibit the pattern in this way.

These three examples have, moreover, been selected for us by Mr. Vincent Robinson for the purpose of showing the kind of material most suited for this market, the pattern according to his recommendation being left to the best native skill in Textiles of this sort that can be found on the spot.

---

* A striking instance of this was afforded by a large carpet made in one of our Indian gaols of Berlin wool, and sent to the International Exhibition of 1862. The pattern consisted of big roses and other flowers, grotesquely distorted, and was, we believe, considered quite a *chef d'œuvre* by the gentleman who directed and superintended its execution. At the termination of the Exhibition it sold for less than the original cost of the wool.

No. 695, Vol. XVIII., is an example of a pile which is too long, or, as it is called, deep, to be recommended.

No. 696, from Warungul, a place which in point of quality of texture and of beauty of pattern has furnished some of the best examples of this class of goods ever sent to this country from India, is that which is considered suitable for imitation, and that which probably could be practically obtained; although No. 697, from Bokhara, is the example nearest to perfection in the way of a carpet texture of the kind in question.

In the fifth and last division we place silk carpets, or those in which the pile is of that expensive material.

No. 700, the last example given in the Books, affords a specimen of this beautiful, but for all ordinary purposes, too costly production.

These silk carpets, however, frequently display a richness and beauty which it would be difficult, if not impossible, to obtain from the use of any other textile substance, and may possibly come into occasional use in the houses of the rich in this and other European countries. In India they are often used by the great on State occasions.

In Plate XI.—following Pl. X. opposite—are given four illustrations of carpets and rugs in the India Museum Collection, which we have considered it expedient to present simply in outline, it being extremely difficult by any method short of the most careful hand-work to do justice to the colouring.

The foregoing concludes our remarks on the Textile Manufactures of India proper.

No 1.

No 2.

No 3.

No 4.

W.GRIGGS.PHO & LITH.

CARPETS & RUGS.

W. Griggs, Photo & Chromo Lith | India Museum, London

COTTON CARPET

# FABRICS FROM CENTRAL ASIA AND RUSSIA.

In Vol. XV. of the series of sample books we have included a number (67) of specimens of fabrics which are stated to have been manufactured in various parts of what is usually known as Central Asia, and also in Russia.

These are of very considerable interest as affording a key to some of the kinds of Textile materials suited to the wants and tastes of the vast population inhabiting the countries to the north and northwest of the Himalayas; and these along with many other productions are, probably, capable of being supplied from the *Indian side* by the exercise of British and Native enterprise.

The specimens alluded to were originally purchased in the Shikarpore Bazaar, in Upper Sind, and forwarded to Sir Henry Willock, when chairman of the Court of Directors of the East India Company.

The samples, so far as we have been able to ascertain, were unaccompanied by any special memorandum giving the particulars of the collection, so that we are unable to say to whom we are indebted for the selection of the specimens.

The information furnished with the labels attached to the samples, giving the place of manufacture, the name of the material, and the price at which it was bought in Shikarpore has been transferred to the subjoined Table in which the various examples have been grouped geographically and in the following order, viz., from *Bokhara*, *Meshed*, *Herat*, *Yezd*, *Balk*, *Kokan*, and lastly *Russia*.

Although the information as given would imply that the samples were, in each case, manufactured at the place mentioned, the statement must be taken with a certain amount of reservation, as we believe that at least some of them are from China, while a few others not inserted under the head of Russia are probably from that country.*

* The cotton twilled material called Naukrr, also Naka, in white, and also in blue, green, &c., is a favourite throughout all parts of Turkistan. Regarding this class of goods, Mookhtar Shah, of Cashmere, who, in 1852, sent to Major George Macgregor, Deputy Commissioner of Lahore, certain samples brought by merchants from Turkistan, writes, "Of the Naka cloths from Russia, and all parts of Turkistan, and through the country of Khorassan, thousands of camel-loads are annually brought into Bokhara, and from thence they are taken to other countries.

"They are named in the Turkish language, but it is unknown by what name they are called in Russia, but in Khorassan and Cashmere they are called by the Turkish names. They are universally used, and are of various colours. * * * Ten or fifteen thousand pieces are brought to Cabool alone. They are made up at Bokhara in dresses called Chogha.

"All the middling classes and the poor make use of them. Each piece makes not less than three Choghas. The merchants make their purchases at Bokhara, and carry them to other countries, pricing their goods according to the distance they have to travel."

The Book containing the samples, and the Report from which the above is an extract is in our possession. A few of the examples differ from those referred to in the Tables, and may, together with the information attached to them, prove of use for reference.

| Vol. | No. | Description. | Measurement. | | Weight of Piece. | Cost. |
|---|---|---|---|---|---|---|
| | | | Length. | Width. | | |
| | | FROM BOKHARA. | yds. ins. | yds. ins. | lbs. oz. | £ s. d. |
| XV. | 561 | *Uddrussa.* Silk and cotton. Cotton weft. Striped, with coloured silk in the warp. Dark and light green, crimson, pink, and blue. Watered surface. | 7 0 | 0 11½ | — | 0 8 0 |
| XV. | 562 | Silk. Light texture. Weft of blue, warp of crimson. A 2-inches wide border with 1 inch yellow centre, with edges of blue, white, and crimson lines. Principal end consists of a broad cross stripe of gold-coloured yellow silk with central and marginal lines in purple and crimson. | — | 0 25 | — | — |
| XV. | 563 | Known as *Uddrussa* in Bokhara, and *Elacha* in Sind. Twilled material. Cotton weft, coloured silks in warp. Large irregular pattern in crimson, yellow, white, and green, with watered surface. Used for linings for coats. | 7 9 | 0 12 | — | 0 11 0 |
| XV. | 564 | Called *Uddrussa* in Bokhara, and *Elacha* in Sind. Silk and cotton. Twilled material. Cotton weft. Coloured silks in warp. Large pattern, blue, white, crimson, yellow, and green on a black ground. Surface watered. "Much prized and sought after." | 3 16 | 0 19½ | — | 0 13 0 |
| XV. | 565 | *Ulukh.* Silk and cotton. Cotton weft, coloured silks in warp. Peculiar pattern in flashed colours, viz. white, crimson, yellow, green, and purple on a blue ground. Watered surface. | 3 6 | 0 20½ | — | 0 10 0 |
| XV. | 566 | *Goolbuddan.* Silk, for trowserings. Purple, with narrow stripe of white and crimson. | 0 32 | 0 29 | — | 0 2 10 |
| XV. | 567 | Silk. Light texture. A flashed pattern in yellow, white, purple, green, &c. on a crimson ground. Border (2 inches wide), with 1 inch yellow centre stripe, with purple, crimson, and white lined edges. Principal end (6½ inches) of crimson silk, with a broad weft stripe of yellow. | — | 0 26 | — | — |
| XV. | 568 | *Bakisum* and *Elacha.* Silk and cotton striped. Weft of cotton, warp of silks in crimson, light blue, green, and yellow stripes of various widths. Twilled material, with watered surface. Obtainable at most of the marts of North Western India. | 5 0 | 0 12½ | — | 0 12 0 |
| XV. | 569 | *Kootnee.* A glazed cotton chintz. Stripes of various colours and widths. In pretty general use. | 3 18 | 0 21½ | — | 0 8 0 |
| XV. | 570 | Glazed cotton. Stripes of various widths and colours, principally crimson, green, and yellow. | — | 0 11 | — | — |
| XV. | 571 A. B. | *Khoodbauf.* A. Silk. Light texture. Small pattern of angulated stripes in white silk on a figured green ground. B. Similar material and pattern, the figured ground being brown instead of green. | 1 0 | 0 29 | — | 0 4 6 |
| XV. | 572 A. | Cotton or chintz. Glazed. Stripes of a chequered pattern in green, yellow, and red, with plain central stripe of green in a yellow ground; and a flashed red figure in rows between the stripes. | — | 0 20 | — | — |
| | 572 B. | Ditto. Glazed. Red ground, with an inch stripe consisting of a small figured centre enclosed within blue stripes. | | | | |
| XV. | 573 | *Nauker.* Cotton. Plain green twilled material - - | — | 0 14 | — | — |
| XV. | 574 | *Goolbuddan.* Striped silk in various colours, blue, green, yellow, purple, &c. Border a green stripe with white and crimson line edges. | 0 32 | 0 25 | — | 0 3 11 |
| XV. | 575 | *Kunawey.* Plain yellow silk - - - - - | 0 30 | 0 27½ | — | 0 2 7½ |
| XV. | 576 | Ditto. Shot silk. Crimson warp. Yellow weft - | 0 30 | 0 27½ | — | 0 2 7½ |
| XV. | 577 | Ditto. Shot silk. Light blue weft. Crimson warp - | 0 30 | 0 27½ | — | 0 2 7½ |
| XV. | 578 | Ditto. Plain green silk - - - - - | 0 30 | 0 27½ | — | 0 2 7½ |
| XV. | 579 | Ditto. Shot silk. Pink warp. White weft - - | 0 30 | 0 27½ | — | 0 2 7½ |
| XV. | 580 | Ditto. Shot silk. Green warp. Crimson weft - | 0 30 | 0 27½ | — | 0 2 7½ |
| XV. | 581 | Ditto. Shot silk. Light blue warp. Yellow weft - | 0 30 | 0 27½ | — | 0 2 7½ |
| XV. | 582 | Ditto. Shot silk. Dark blue warp. Crimson weft - | 0 30 | 0 27½ | — | 0 2 7½ |

| Vol. | No. | Description. | Measurement. Length. | Measurement. Width. | Weight of Piece. | Cost. |
|---|---|---|---|---|---|---|
| | | **FROM MESHED.** | yds. ins. | yds. ins. | lbs. oz. | £ *s.* *d.* |
| XV. | 583 | ***Boolbool Chrshum.*** Silk gauze. Small figure. Crimson weft, yellow warp. | — | 0 28 | — | — |
| XV. | 584 | ***Boolbool Chrshum.*** Silk gauze. White, with small diamond-shaped figure. | — | 0 21 | — | — |
| XV. | 585 | ***Boolbool Chrshum.*** Silk. Dark crimson weft. Green warp. Green diamond-shaped figure, similar to that of No. 584. | — | 0 16 | — | 0 5 6 per yard |
| XV. | 586 | ***Boolbool Chrshum.*** Silk. Pink warp. White weft, forming diamond pattern similar to last example. | — | 0 24 | — | 0 5 6 per yard |
| XV. | 587 | Flowered silk damask. Crimson ground, with blue flower | — | 0 16 | — | — |
| XV. | 588 | Silk. Figured stripes (small damask pattern) in blue, green, orange, yellow, white, &c. | — | 0 20 | — | — |
| XV. | 589 | Flowered silk damask. Pink warp, flowered in weft with yellow silk. | — | 0 18 | — | — |
| XV. | 590 | Flowered yellow silk damask. Shaded figure - - | — | 0 18 | — | — |
| XV. | 591 | Flowered crimson silk damask. Shaded figure - - | — | 0 18 | — | — |
| XV. | 592 | Silk, with figured stripes. Bright yellow ground with stripes of crimson flowers, enclosed within faint lines of blue. | — | 0 24 | — | — |
| XV. | 593 | Silk. Same pattern as last sample, but on a white ground | — | 0 24 | — | — |
| | | **FROM HERAT.** | | | | |
| XV. | 594 | *Ubra* or *Shalwal.* Figured silk cloth. Pine and flower pattern in colours on green ground (Shawl pattern). Used for *Chogas* and other garments. | — | 0 25½ | — | 0 10 0 per yard |
| XV. | 595 | Ditto, ditto, ditto. Pattern; flower and foliage scrolls on a dark blue ground. | — | 0 25½ | — | 0 10 0 per yard |
| XV. | 596 | Ditto, ditto, ditto. Scroll and flower striped pattern; prevailing ground colour crimson. | — | 0 25½ | — | 0 10 0 per yard |
| XV. | 597 | Ditto, ditto, ditto. Angulated stripes of pine and flower pattern in colours; prevailing ground colours green and crimson. | — | 0 25½ | — | 0 10 0 per yard |
| XV. | 598 | Ditto, ditto, ditto. A flowered pine pattern in colours on crimson ground. | — | 0 25½ | — | 0 10 0 per yard |
| XV. | 599 | *Atlas.* Satin surface, plain. Crimson silk warp, and red cotton weft. | — | 0 29 | — | — |
| XV. | 600 | *Atlas.* Satin surface, plain. Black silk warp, and black cotton weft. | — | 0 17½ | — | — |
| XV. | 602 | *Atlas.* Satin surface, plain. Yellow silk warp, and yellow cotton weft. | — | 0 28 | — | — |
| XV. | 601 | Naukrr. Brown cotton cloth - - - - | — | 0 17 | — | — |
| | | **FROM YEZD.** | | | | |
| XV. | 603 | *Goolbuddan.* Silk piece goods, used for trowserings. A small speckled yellow and blue stripe in a crimson ground. | — | 0 18 | — | — |
| | | **FROM BALK.** | | | | |
| XV. | 604 | Silk brocade. Bright yellow satin surface, with small flowered crimson stripes in diagonal order. | — | 0 29 | — | about 0 4 0 per yard |
| XV. | 605 | Silk brocade. Yellow silk warp. Crimson weft. Satin surface. | — | 0 29½ | — | about 0 4 0 per yard |
| XV. | 606 | *Boodul.* Figured silk: a brilliant amber colour - - | — | from 0 9 to 0 17 | — | about 0 2 0 per yard |
| XV. | 607 | *Boodul.* Silk. Rich crimson, figure somewhat similar to last example. | — | from 0 9 to 0 17 | — | about 0 2 0 per yard |
| XV. | 608 | *Boodul.* Flimsy silk. Deep blue, with small rectangular spots. | — | 0 17 | — | about 0 2 0 per yard |

| No. of | | Description. | Measurement. | | Weight of Piece. | Cost. |
|---|---|---|---|---|---|---|
| Vol. | Sample. | | Length. | Width. | | |
| | | | yds. ins. | yds. ins. | lbs. oz. | £. s. d. |
| XV. | 609 | *Boodul.* Silk. Blue, damask pattern - - - | — | 0 19 | — | — |
| XV. | 610 | Silk. Large pattern in flashed colours, purple, yellow, white, crimson, &c. Similar in pattern to the Uddrussa of Bokhara, and Elacha of Sind. | 6 0 | 0 25 | — | 0 13 0 |
| | | **FROM KOKAN.** | | | | |
| XV. | 611 | Silk and cotton. A silk gauze with a little cotton. Striped pattern. | — | 0 28 | — | — |
| XV. | 612 | Silk gauze. Crimson, striped pattern - - - | — | 0 28 | — | — |
| XV. | 613 | *Dasija.* Silk gauze, yellow, with faint stripes of an angulated pattern in white silk. | 0 30 | 0 26 | — | 0 1 1½ |
| XV. | 614 | *Dasija.* Silk gauze, striped similarly to last example - | 0 30 | 0 26 | — | 0 1 1½ |
| | | **FROM RUSSIA; OBTAINED IN BOKHARA.** | | | | |
| XV. | 615 | *Saujoo Gool Goshen.* Blue figured silk, large flowered damask pattern. | — | 0 30 | — | — |
| XV. | 616 | Satin damask. Large figure in yellow overrunning broad stripes of purple, crimson, and green. | 0 31 | 0 20 | — | 0 7 0 |
| XV. | 617 | Satin damask. Large figure in yellow overrunning broad stripes of light blue, crimson, and green. | 0 31 | 0 20 | — | 0 7 0 |
| XV. | 618 | Satin damask. Broad stripes of crimson and green, with a large figure in yellow, alternating with narrow figured stripes of various patterns and colours. | 0 31 | 0 20 | — | 0 7 0 |
| XV. | 619 | Satin damask. Broad stripes of green and crimson, with figured designs in yellow silk. | 0 31 | 0 20 | — | 0 7 0 |
| XV. | 620 | Satin damask. Broad stripes of purple, orange, green, crimson, and light blue, with large flowered figure in yellow running throughout. | 0 31 | 0 20 | — | 0 7 0 |
| XV. | 621 | Satin damask. Broad stripes of light blue, green, and crimson, alternating with large figured and flowered patterns in yellow silk. | 0 31 | 0 20 | — | 0 7 0 |
| XV. | 622 | Woollen. Printed in bright colours. Pattern, figured stripes. | — | 0 33 | — | — |
| XV. | 623 | *Naukrr.* Cotton. A kind of twilled material, light blue and white stripes. Stated to have been manufactured at Ooroos. | — | 0 13 | — | — |

# APPENDIX.

## Memorandum on the Distribution in Britain and India of the Collections of Specimens of the Textile Manufactures of India.

(See Note to *Introduction*, p. 9.)

1. The Collections in question consist of twenty sets of eighteen volumes. Each set contains seven hundred *working samples* of cotton, silk, and woollen textiles of native manufacture, obtained from various places in India. The corresponding specimens in the different sets bear the same number, and all are accompanied by details respecting the length, breadth, and weight, &c., of the *pieces* of which they originally formed a part.

2. This collection of samples affords a guide to a large class of manufactures suited to the Indian market which has as yet received but little attention in this country; and it illustrates the principles which must be observed in the attempt to introduce designs which will please the tastes of a people whose appreciation of art, as applied to Textile decoration, is of a high order.

3. With reference to the disposal of the work, the following remarks are submitted:— The original intention was that the whole of the twenty sets should be distributed in this country. Further consideration, however, points to the expediency of placing a certain number of them in India: 1st, because this course will facilitate those trade operations between the two countries which it is the object of the work to promote and encourage; and 2ndly, because it is possible that the collection may be of direct use to the Indian manufacturer. Whatever opinions may be entertained regarding the expediency of fostering the mill-system in India, there can be no doubt as to the *right* which the Indian manufacturer has to participate in a measure like the present, so that he may at least be placed on an equal footing with the manufacturers of this country.

4. It seems to be clearly for the advantage of India that every facility should be given to the introduction, from this country, of such manufactures as can be supplied to the people there more cheaply than by hand labour on the spot. The *many* will thus be benefited, and the hardship which may possibly fall upon the *few* will not be serious or long felt, since their labour will soon be diverted into new and, in all probability, more profitable channels.

5. The chief advantage, however, which is likely to attend the distribution in India of a certain number of the sets of Textile specimens will, it is believed, arise from the opportunity which will thereby be afforded to the agent in India of directing the attention of his correspondent here to the articles suited to the requirements of his constituents. It will facilitate the giving of orders in a manner which will constitute a safer trade operation than if the manufacturer were of his own accord to imitate certain examples, and then send the goods to India *on speculation*. For instance, the agent in India may call his Home Correspondent's attention to a certain number in a certain volume, and ask him to send out something as like it as possible, or with such alterations as he may see fit to suggest.

6. So also by the aid of this collection an agent in this country may easily order *from India* such goods as he may think would suit this market. Still further, the collection will show the manufacturer or merchant in one part of India the classes of goods produced elsewhere in India, and in the way just described give him facilities for making purchases.

7. Another advantage likely to accrue from the work in question and other similar efforts to impart a practical knowledge of our Indian manufactures, is that we shall be able to determine what productions can and what cannot be made most cheaply by machinery. This is a point which it is important to decide. It will probably be found that many of the more elaborate India patterns will have still to be produced by hand.

8. It is, therefore, recommended that of the twenty sets of volumes, thirteen remain in this country and that seven be sent to India.

9. In deciding what places in this country should be chosen, those seats of commerce more immediately interested in Textile Manufactures naturally come first, and after these come such places as possess Industrial Museums or other institutions calculated to afford the necessary protection, facilities of access, &c.

10. The proposed distribution, as will be observed from the following list, will still leave some important places unsupplied. These are, however, in almost every instance situated near to one or other of the selected localities, and as the conditions attached to the gift should secure free access to the work to all persons practically interested, the disadvantage here alluded to will not prove serious.

11. The places referred to are Belfast; Bradford*; Dublin; Edinburgh*; Glasgow; Halifax*; Huddersfield*; Liverpool; Macclesfield*; Manchester; Preston*; and Salford*—making, with the one retained in this Department for permanent reference, thirteen in all.

---

* The places marked with an asterisk are those for presentation to which sanction has already been obtained through the application of their authorities.

12. In India I have to recommend that a set be placed in each of the following places, viz.: Calcutta, Madras, Bombay, Kurrachee, the North-western Provinces, the Punjab, and lastly in Berar.

13. With respect to the three last-named divisions either Allahabad, Mirzapore, or Agra in the North-western Provinces, Umritsur or Lahore in the Punjab, and Oomrawutte or Nagpore in Berar, will probably be found the most suitable, but it may be left to the respective Governments of the divisions in question to decide on the exact locality.

14. Regarding the conditions on which the gift should be presented,—the first should be that due provision be made for its permanent protection, and that freedom of access be afforded to all properly recommended and practically interested persons.

15. The sets should be assigned in trust to the chief commercial authorities in the selected places, for the use not only of those connected with the district in which they are deposited, but of non-residents also, who can show a practical interest in Textile manufactures. The proposed plan of sending seven of the sets to India, diminishes the number of commercial centres in this country which will receive a copy, and it therefore becomes the more necessary that those which do get one should be required to make it easy of access to agents, merchants, and manufacturers who reside in those which do not.

16. This should apply also to the foreign manufacturer or agent who may wish to consult the collection. The interests of India require that nothing should be done to prevent her from receiving the benefits which may arise from competition between different sources of supply, or to interfere with the extension to other countries of the knowledge of the manufactures and products she is prepared to sell.

17. It is admitted to be for the mutual advantage of India and of this kingdom that the most intimate commercial relations should exist between *them*. Nothing will conduce to this more certainly than a full and correct knowledge of what India can produce and what her people want. The means of acquiring this knowledge these volumes furnish, so far at least as Textile Manufactures are concerned. The twenty sets may be regarded as twenty Industrial or Trade Museums, placed here and there in the two countries, and it is but a reasonable expectation that they will be extensively studied and consulted by the manufacturers of both. The result of this will assuredly be an increased interchange of commodities. The British manufacturer will learn what goods are likely to prove saleable in India, and what he can produce more cheaply than the native can; while the British merchant may find among some of the delicate fabrics of India, or of those which are elaborately decorated, articles which it will be profitable to import, because they can be made more cheaply in the East. In addition to this, in consequence of each set being as much as possible an exact counterpart of all the others, these Museums will facilitate trade operations in the way already described, and will enable merchants to give, and manufacturers to execute, *orders* more readily and more accurately than they otherwise could.

18. In conclusion, I have now to suggest that the authorities in the selected districts should, previously to the actual presentation of the work, undertake as follows :—

1st. To provide for the permanent protection of the work by placing it in the charge of a proper and responsible person, or persons, in a suitable building.

2nd. To afford the requisite facilities for consulting the work ; subject, however, to the condition that under no circumstances shall any of the volumes be removed for purposes of exhibition or reference.

3rd. That access to the work be given to any person bearing an order to that effect signed by the President, Vice-President, or Secretary of the Society of Arts ; the Presidents, Vice-Presidents, or Secretaries of the Chambers of Commerce ; the Chairman or Secretary of the Association of Chambers of Commerce ; the President, Vice-President,or Secretary of the Cotton Supply Association ; the Chairman, Vice-Chairman, or Secretary of the Cotton Brokers Association ; the Chairman, Vice-Chairman, or Secretary of the Liverpool East India and China Association ; by the Presidents, Vice-Presidents, Chairmen, Vice-Chairmen, or Secretaries of such other Associations for the promotion of Commerce as now exist, or may hereafter be formed ; and by the Reporter on the Products of India.

(Signed) J. FORBES WATSON,
Reporter on the Products of India to the
Secretary of State for India in Council.

INDIA MUSEUM, *July* 1866.

NOTE.—The foregoing conditions having been agreed to by the Chambers of Commerce of Belfast, Bradford, Glasgow, Halifax, Liverpool, and Manchester ; by the Industrial Museum of Scotland in Edinburgh ; by the Industrial Museum of Ireland in Dublin ; by the Huddersfield Mechanics' Institution ; by the Towns of Macclesfield and Preston ; and by the Borough of Salford for the Royal Peel Park Museum,—a Set of the Volumes in question has been presented to each of these places, making, in addition to the India Museum, attached to the Department of the Reporter on the Products of India, thirteen places in this country where the Work can be consulted by persons practically interested in the matter. With respect to the seven Sets for India : These, under the instructions of the Secretary of State for India in Council, have been forwarded for deposition in Calcutta, Madras, Bombay, and Kurrachee, and in such places in the North-Western Provinces, in the Punjab, and in Berar, as the respective Governments of the Divisions in question may decide upon. As soon as the exact localities have been determined by the authorities in India, intimation thereof will be made both in this country and in India.

# LIST OF SAMPLES IN WORK SHOWING THE TEXTILE MANUFACTURES OF INDIA.

## Vol. 1.—TURBANS.

| No. | Description.* Name and Use. | Material. | Quality, &c. | Length. yds. ins. | Width. yds. ins. | Weight. lbs. ozs. | Price.† £ s. d. | Whence procured, Place of Manufacture, &c. |
|---|---|---|---|---|---|---|---|---|
| 1 | Turban - - - | Cotton - - | Bleached. Common material - - | 15 0 | 0 12 | 0 6 | - - - | Calcutta. |
| 2 | Ditto - - | Ditto - - | Ditto. ditto - - | 23 0 | 0 12 | 0 12 | - - - | Bhurtpore, 34 miles from Agra. |
| 3 | Ditto - - - | Ditto - - | Ditto - - - - - - | 6 18 | 1 0 | 0 15 | - - - | Lahore, Punjab. |
| 4 | Ditto - - | Ditto - - | - - - - - - | 8 18 | 1 0 | - - | - - - | Ditto |
| 5 | Ditto - - - | Ditto - | Bleached. Thin texture - - | 16 0 | 1 3 | 0 14 | - - | Kangra, Punjab. |
| 6 | Ditto - - - | Ditto - - | Ditto. Fine texture - - | 20 0 | 0 11 | 0 8 | - - - | Cashmere. |
| 7 | Ditto - - - | Ditto - - | Ditto. Plain ends - - - | 24 0 | 0 12 | 0 8¾ | - - - | Gya, 280 miles north-west from Calcutta. |
| 8 | Ditto - - - | Ditto - - | Ditto - - - | 23 18 | 0 13 | 1 2 | - - - | Sind. |
| 9 | Ditto - | Ditto - - | Unbleached. Coarse thick material - | 3 18 | 0 9 | 0 11 | - - - | Arracan. |
| 10 | Ditto - - | Ditto - - | Made in India of English thread - | 22 0 | 0 13½ | 0 9 | - - - | Benares. |
| 11 | Ditto - - - | Ditto - - | Of Indian thread; made same time as No. 10. | 22 0 | 0 13½ | 0 12 | - - - | Ditto. |
| 12 | Ditto - - - | Ditto - - | Bleached. Fine light texture - - | 17 0 | 0 12 | 0 7 | - - - | Hoshiarpore, Punjab. |
| 13 | Ditto - - - | Ditto - - | Fine - - - - | 33 0 | 0 10 | 0 9 | - - - | Hyderabad, Deccan. |
| 14 | Ditto - - - | Ditto - - | Ditto - - - - - - | 20 0 | 0 9 | 0 9 | - - - | Ditto. |
| 15 | Ditto - - - | Ditto - - | Unbleached - - - | 29 0 | 0 12½ | 0 7½ | - - - | Chunderee. |
| 16 | Ditto - - - | Ditto - - | Gauze. Good texture - - - | 21 0 | 0 9 | 0 6 | 0 4 8 | Madras. |
| 17 | Ditto - - - | Ditto - - | Unbleached - - - - | 21 0 | 0 10½ | 0 10 | - - - | Hyderabad, Deccan. |
| 18 | Ditto - - | Ditto - - | Ditto - - - - | 33 0 | 0 13 | 0 9 | - - - | Ditto. |
| 19 | Ditto - - - | Ditto - - | Dyed. Two gold stripes extend down centre of principal end for four yards. | 19 18 | 0 13 | - - | - - - | Oodeypore, Rajpootana. |
| 20 | Ditto - - | Ditto - - | Colours laid on - - - - | 14 0 | 0 10 | 0 7 | - - - | Bhurtpore, 34 miles west of Agra. |
| 21 | Ditto - - - | Ditto - | Scarlet. Printed gold centre - - | 14 18 | 0 7 | 0 7 | - - | Ditto. |
| 22 | Ditto - - - | Ditto - - | Red dye. Gold stripes in centre and sides throughout whole length. Gold spots on 4½ yards of principal end. | 13 0 | 0 17 | 0 12 | - - - | Hoshiarpore, Punjab. |
| 23 | Ditto - - - | Ditto - - | - - - - - - | 18 18 | 0 9 | 0 4 | - - - | Jeypoor, Rajpootana. (Nos. 23–29) |
| 24 | Ditto - - - | Ditto - - | Fine texture - - - - | 17 18 | 0 9 | 0 3½ | - - - | |
| 25 | Ditto - - - | Ditto - - | Ditto - - - - | 18 18 | 0 8½ | 0 4 | - - - | |
| 26 | Ditto - - - | Ditto - - | Ditto - - - - | 18 18 | 0 9 | 0 4 | - - - | |
| 27 | Ditto - - - | Ditto - - | Ditto - - - - | 24 0 | 0 11 | 0 8 | - - - | |
| 28 | Ditto - - - | Ditto - - | Ditto - - - - | 17 0 | 0 9 | 0 3¾ | - - - | |
| 29 | Ditto - - - | Ditto - - | Ditto - - - - | 21 0 | 0 10 | 0 5½ | - - - | |
| 30 | Ditto - - - | Ditto - - | Coarse - - - - | 15 0 | 0 9 | 0 9½ | - - - | Sydapet, Madras. |
| 31 | Ditto - - - | Ditto - - | Common material and pattern - - | 12 0 | 0 11 | 1 0 | 0 2 7½ | Pomady, Bought in Bazaar, Madras. |
| 32 | Ditto - - - | Ditto - - | Ditto - - - - | 16 18 | 0 9 | 0 15¾ | 0 3 0 | Pomady, Madras. |
| 33 | Ditto - - - | Ditto - - | Ditto - - - - | 23 0 | 0 12 | 0 · 13 | 0 10 0 | Madura, Madras. |
| 34 | Ditto - - - | Ditto - - | - - - - - - | 16 18 | 0 10 | 0 15½ | 0 3 1½ | Madras. |
| 35 | Ditto - - - | Ditto - - | Square head covering. Gold thread borders. | 2 24 | 2 24 | 0 12 | 0 13 0 | Madura, Madras. |
| 36 | Ditto - - - | Cotton, with gold thread. | The dye used is said to be remarkable for its excellence. The gold thread stripes extend 12 yards down centre of principal end, and 4½ yards of opposite end. 10 yards are entirely plain. | 26 18 | 0 15 | 1 3½ | 4 0 0 | Ditto. |
| 37 | Ditto - - - | Ditto - - | Gold stripes down principal end for 6 yards, the remainder plain. | 23 0 | 0 12 | 0 13 | 2 0 0 | Ditto. |
| 38 | Ditto - - | Silk and Cotton - | - - - - | 20 18 | 0 10 | 0 8¾ | 0 11 0 | Berhampore, Gangam, Madras. |
| 39 | Ditto - - | Ditto - - | Cotton, with crimson silk ends. Head covering, nearly square. Gold border on each side. | 3 18 | 1 9 | 1 11 | 2 15 3 | Coimbatore, Madras. |
| 40 | Ditto - - - | Cotton - - | Deep gold borders. Head covering, nearly square. | 1 22 | 1 16 | 0 6½ | - - - | Bhurtpore, near Agra. |

* The description given in this and the following Tables is that which originally accompanied the samples, and it is in some instances imperfect. For correct classification and details see text.

† The prices given in this and the following Tables represent the cost of the articles in 1854. For farther remarks on this head see *foot-note*, p. 17.

VOL. 2.

## GARMENTS FOR MEN.

| No. | Description. | | | Length. | Width. | Weight. | Price. | Whence procured, Place of Manufacture, &c. |
|---|---|---|---|---|---|---|---|---|
| | Name and Use. | Material. | Quality, &c. | | | | | |
| | | | | yds. ins. | yds. ins. | lbs. ozs. | £ s. d. | |
| 41 | Man's garment - - | Cotton - - - - | Gold flowered border and end. Favourite texture. | 8 21 | 1 19 | 1 0 | 3 12 0 | Madura. Bought in Madras. |
| 42 | Ditto - - - | Ditto - - - | Fine light texture. Two pieces woven, as usual, in one length, with a "fag" between to permit of their being readily separated. | Long piece, 5 27; Short piece, 3 4 | 1 13 | 1 3 | 1 10 0 | Woopparaddy, Madras. |
| 43 | Ditto - - - | Muslin - - - | - - - - - - | 2 0 | 2 0 | 0 6 | 0 11 0 | Arnee, Madras. |
| 44 | Ditto - - - | Cotton - - - | Silk in principal ends and borders. Two pieces woven in one length, with a "fag" between to permit of their being readily separated. | Long piece, 5 9; Short piece, 3 9 | 1 9 | 1 8 | 0 8 0 | Salem, Madras. |
| 45 | Ditto - - - | Ditto - - - | Common texture. Two pieces woven in one length, with "fag" between to permit of their being readily separated. | Long piece, 5 18; Short piece, 3 4 | 1 10 | 1 9 | 0 3 0 | Gangam, Madras. |
| 46 | Ditto - - - | Ditto - - - | Two pieces woven in one length, with "fag" between to permit of their being readily separated. | Long piece, 5 20; Short piece, 2 27 | 1 2 | 1 4 | 0 2 6 | Gangam. Bought in Madras. |
| 47 | Ditto - - - | Ditto - - - | Gauze texture. Ditto - ditto - | Long piece, 5 4; Short piece, 2 27 | 1 6 | 0 14 | 0 2 3 | Nagang. Bought in Madras. |
| 48 | Boy's garment - - | Ditto - - - | Borders of different colours, silk in end | 1 34 | 0 27 | 0 $2\frac{9}{16}$ | 0 1 4 | Congeveram, Madras. Bought in Madras. |
| 49 | Man's garment - - | Ditto - - - | Two pieces woven in one length, with "fag" between to permit of their being readily separated. | Long piece, 3 0; Short piece, 2 27 | 1 18 | 1 11 | 0 8 6 | Woozzoor, Madras. |
| 50 | Ditto - - - | Ditto - - - | Ditto - - - - - | Long piece, 3 9; Short piece, 2 18 | - - | 1 6 | 0 3 9 | Nellore, Madras. |
| 51 | Ditto - - - | Muslin - - - | - - - - - - | 3 0 | 1 9 | 1 3 | 0 10 6 | Arnee, Madras. |
| 52 | Ditto - - - | Cotton - - - | Coarse muslin - - - - | 7 27 | 1 9 | 0 13½ | 0 3 0 | Nagang. Bought in Madras. |
| 53 | Ditto - - - | Ditto - - - | Good texture. Two pieces woven in one length, with "fag" between to permit of their being readily separated. | Long piece, 5 9; Short piece, 3 0 | 1 9 | 1 11 | 0 8 0 | Salem, Madras. |
| 54 | Ditto - - - | Ditto - - - | Two pieces woven in one length, with "fag" between to permit of their being readily separated. | Long piece, 4 18; Short piece, 2 27 | 1 6 | 1 2½ | 0 2 1½ | Congeveram. Bought in Madras. |
| 55 | Ditto - - - | Ditto - - - | Ditto - - - - - | Long piece, 4 27; Short piece, 2 27 | 1 4 | 1 6 | 0 5 6 | Ditto. |
| 56 | Ditto - - - | Ditto - - - | Ditto - - - - - | Long piece, 5 27; Short piece, 2 18 | 1 11 | 1 2 | 0 14 6 | Rajahmundry. Bought in Madras. |
| 57 | Ditto - - - | Ditto - - - | - - - - - - | 8 18 | 1 11 | 1 3 | 1 4 6 | Madura. Bought in Madras. |
| 58 | Ditto - - - | Ditto - - - | Badly dyed - - - - | 8 9 | 1 10 | 1 11 | 0 7 0 | Masulipatam, Madras. |
| 59 | Ditto - - - | Ditto - - - | - - - - - - | 4 9 | 1 0 | 0 13 | 0 4 0½ | Mylapore, Madras. |
| 60 | Ditto - - - | Ditto - - - | - - - - - - | 2 9 | 1 9 | 0 10½ | 0 2 3 | Karikal, Madras. |
| 61 | Ditto - - - | Cotton and Silk - | With yellow silk check - - - | 3 27 | 1 2 | 0 10 | 0 4 6 | Mylapore, Madras. |
| 62 | Ditto - - - | Cotton - - - | - - - - - - | 6 0 | 1 4 | 1 5½ | 0 7 9 | Coonathoor, Madras. |
| 63 | Ditto - - - | Ditto - - - | - - - - - - | 3 27 | 1 3 | 0 16½ | 0 3 6 | Ditto. |
| 64 | Ditto - - - | Ditto - - - | Four woven together, with "fags" between. | single piece, 2 9 | single piece, 1 4 | 0 4 | 0 2 6 | Karikal. Bought in Madras. |
| 65 | Ditto - - - | Ditto - - - | - - - - - - | 3 18 | 1 2 | 1 1 | 0 3 0 | Pulicat, Madras. |
| 66 | Ditto - - - | Ditto - - - | - - - - - - | 3 27 | 1 6 | 0 12 | 0 2 9 | Mylapore. Bought in Madras. |
| 67 | Ditto - - - | Ditto - - - | - - - - - - | 4 9 | 1 2 | 0 14 | 0 8 0 | Pulicat. Bought in Madras. |
| 68 | Ditto - - - | Ditto - - - | - - - - - - | 3 27 | 1 2 | 1 3 | 0 5 3 | Pulicat, Madras. |
| 69 | Ditto - - - | Ditto - - - | - - - - - - | 7 12 | 1 2 | 1 6 | 0 7 0 | Mylapore, Madras. |
| 70 | Ditto - - - | Ditto - - - | - - - - - - | 8 9 | 1 0 | 1 9 | 0 7 6 | Mylapore or St. Thomas, Madras. |
| 71 | Ditto - - - | Ditto - - - | - - - - - - | 2 9 | 1 4 | 0 7½ | 0 2 0 | Coonathoor, Madras. |
| 72 | Ditto - - - | Ditto - - - | - - - - - - | 6 27 | 1 3 | 1 6 | 0 8 0 | Ditto. |
| 73 | Ditto - - - | Ditto - - - | - - - - - - | 3 18 | 0 34 | 0 9 | 0 2 7½ | Ditto. |
| 74 | Ditto - - - | Ditto - - - | - - - - - - | 6 18 | 1 0 | 1 11 | 0 2 7½ | Kurnool, Madras. |
| 75 | Ditto - - - | Ditto - - - | - - - - - - | 5 28 | 1 4 | 1 7 | 0 3 3 | Gangam, Madras. |
| 76 | Ditto - - - | Ditto - - - | - - - - - - | 3 0 | 1 3 | 0 8½ | 0 1 3 | Cundapoora, N. Canara. |
| 77 | Ditto - - - | Ditto - - - | Unbleached thread - - - | 8 9 | 1 5 | 1 10 | 0 2 4½ | Vencatagorry, Madras. |
| 78 | Ditto - - - | Ditto - - - | - - - - - - | 2 18 | 0 27 | 0 7 | 0 1 6 | Mangalore S. Canara. |
| 79 | Boy's garment - - | Ditto - - - | Very common - - - - | 1 3 | 0 19 | 0 2 | - - - | Bickul, N. Canara. |
| 80 | Man's garment - - | Ditto - - - | - - - - - - | 5 9 | 1 0 | 3 1 | - - - | Coimbatore, Madras. |

## Vol. 3.

## GARMENTS FOR MEN, &c.

| No. | Description. Name and Use. | Material. | Quality, &c. | Length. | Width. | Weight. | Price. | Whence procured, Place of Manufacture &c. |
|---|---|---|---|---|---|---|---|---|
| | | | | yds. ins. | yds. ins. | lbs. ozs. | £ s. d. | |
| 81 | Man's garment or "Loongee" | Silk - - - | Woven in half widths with gold lace border on one side; two of these widths being sewn together form the complete scarf. | single piece 3 25 | single piece 0 29 | 0 14¼ | - - - | Bhawulpore. |
| 82 | Ditto - - - | Ditto - - - | This, unlike the previous one, is woven in one piece, with a border on each side, same as in pattern. | 3 10 | 1 16 | 1 4¾ | - - - | Jhelum, Punjab. |
| 83 | Ditto - - - | Ditto - - - | With silver thread introduced in ends - | 6 24 | 1 14 | 1 1 | - - - | Rawul Pindee. |
| 84 | Ditto - - - - | Ditto - - | Woven in half widths with gold lace and coloured silk border on one side; the two widths sewn together form the complete scarf. | single piece 4 3 | single piece 0 28½ | 0 9½ | - - - | Bhawulpore. |
| 85 | Ditto - - - | Ditto - - - | Gold lace border and ends - - - | 3 34 | 1 18 | 1 12¾ | 7 19 7½ | Lahore, Punjab. |
| 86 | Ditto - - - | Cotton and silk - | Gold lace border and gold and silk ends | 7 15 | 1 18 | 1 1 | 1 12 0 | Jhelum, Punjab. |
| 87 | Ditto - - - - | Silk - - - | Gold lace border and ends - - - | 3 18 | 1 14 | 1 1½ | 4 0 0 | Goodaspore, Punjab. |
| 88 | Piece to form a scarf or "Loongee." | Ditto - - - | Gold thread in pattern, but no special end or border. | 5 15 | 0 31 | 1 3¾ | - - - | Bhawulpore. |
| 89 | Man's garment or "Loongee" | Ditto - - | Gold border and ends - - - | 4 8 | 1 18 | 1 8½ | - - - | Ditto. |
| 90 | Ditto - - - - | Ditto - - - | Gold thread in ends - - - - | 7 0 | 1 14 | 1 13¼ | 2 6 0 | Buttala, Goodaspore. |
| 91 | Ditto - - - | Ditto - - | Ditto - - - - - - - | 7 5 | 1 20 | 1 14½ | 4 0 0 | Ditto. |
| 92 | Ditto - - - | Silk and Cotton - | Yellow silk border - - - - | 4 7½ | 1 18 | 1 14 | - - - | Hyderabad, Sind. |
| 93 | Ditto - - - | Ditto - - | Silk border and ends - - - - | 4 0 | 1 20 | 2 0 | - - - | Ditto. |
| 94 | Ditto - - - - | Ditto - - - | Silk in ends - - - - | 6 20 | 1 6 | 1 1 | 0 16 0 | Raneepore, Sind. |
| 95 | Ditto - - - | Cotton - - - | Silk borders, and silk in ends - - | 5 24 | 1 8 | 3 4 | - - - | Kohat. |
| 96 | Ditto - - - - | Ditto - - - | Ditto - - - - - - | 4 0 | 1 17 | 1 5½ | 0 12 0 | Leiah, Punjab. |
| 97 | Ditto - - - | Ditto - - | With silk in ends - - - - | 10 0 | 1 1 | 1 12 | - - - | Kohat. |
| 98 | Ditto - - - - | Ditto - - - | With silk in borders and ends - - | 3 0 | 1 8 | 1 8 | 0 11 6 | Nurrapore, Sind. |
| 99 | Ditto - - - | Ditto - - - | With silk in ends - - - | 3 0 | 1 2 | 1 1 | - - - | Kohat, Punjab. |
| 100 | Ditto - - - - | Ditto - - | With coloured border and ends - | 5 28 | 0 32 | 1 2 | 0 4 0 | Shikarpore, Sind. |
| 101 | Ditto - - - - | Ditto - - - | Silk borders and silk in ends - - | 3 7 | 1 8 | 0 11¼ | 0 4 10 | Pind Dadun Khan, Punjab. |
| 102 | Ditto - - - | Ditto - - | Figured coloured borders and ends - | 5 4 | 1 20 | 3 6 | 0 4 7 | Nurrapore, Sind. |
| 103 | Ditto - - - | Ditto - - - | Coloured border and ends - - - | 4 17 | 1 6 | 1 15 | - - - | Kohat. |
| 104 | Ditto - - - | Ditto - - | Silk borders and silk in ends - - | 3 22 | 1 16 | 1 3 | 0 11 6 | Lahore, Punjab. |
| 105 | Ditto - - - | Ditto - - - | Common pattern, coloured border, and ends. | 6 12 | 1 4 | 1 14 | 0 6 0 | Shikarpore, Sind. |
| 106 | Man's garment or "Dhotee" | Ditto - - | Silk figured border - - - - | 3 22 | 1 8 | 0 11½ | 0 5 0 | Surat, Bombay. |
| 107 | Ditto - - - | Ditto - - - | Silk border - - - - - - | 4 6 | 1 2 | 0 13½ | 0 4 0 | Ditto. |
| 108 | Man's garment or "Loongee" | Ditto - - | Silk borders - - - - - - | 2 3 | 1 6 | 0 8 | 0 4 0 | Ditto. |
| 109 | Ditto - - - - | Ditto - - - | Coloured borders - - - - | 2 9 | 1 3 | 0 6½ | 0 1 0 | Ditto. |
| 110 | Ditto - - - | Ditto - - - | Ditto - - - - - - | 4 8 | 1 5 | 0 12½ | 0 1 7½ | Ditto. |
| 111 | Ditto - - - - | Ditto - - - | Coloured borders and ends - - - | 2 30 | 1 18 | 1 7 | 0 7 3½ | Nurrapore, Sind. |
| 112 | Ditto - - | Ditto - - - | Ditto - - - - - | 2 32 | 1 10 | 1 6 | 0 8 0 | Ditto. |
| 113 | Ditto - - - - | Ditto - - - | Ditto - - - - - | 2 27 | 1 14 | 1 7 | 0 4 0 | Shikarpore, Sind. |
| 114 | Ditto - - - - | Ditto - - - | - - - - - - | 2 27 | 1 14 | 1 14 | 0 9 9 | Nurrapore, Sind. |
| 115 | Ditto - - - - | Ditto - - - | - - - - - - | 2 33 | 1 22 | 2 1 | 0 15 4½ | Ditto. |
| 116 | Ditto - - - - | Ditto - - - | - - - - - - | 2 34 | 0 26 | 2 1 | 0 9 9 | Ditto. |
| 117 | Ditto - - - | Ditto - - - | - - - - - - | 4 18 | 1 22 | 1 4 | 0 4 6 | Loodiana, Punjab. |
| 118 | Ditto - - - - | Ditto - - | - - - - - - | 2 13 | 1 4 | 1 12 | 0 5 0 | Raneepore, Sind. |
| 119 | Ditto - - - - | Ditto - - - | Coloured ends - - - - - | 2 27 | 1 20 | 1 5 | 0 12 0 | Ditto. |
| 120 | Ditto - - - | Ditto - - - | - - - - - - | 3 12 | 1 10 | 2 2½ | 0 3 6 | Shikarpore, Sind. |

## Vol. 4.

## GARMENTS FOR MEN, &c.

| No. | Description. Name and Use. | Material. | Quality, &c. | Length. | Width. | Weight. | Price. | Whence procured, Place of Manufacture, &c. |
|---|---|---|---|---|---|---|---|---|
| | | | | yds. ins. | yds. ins. | lbs. ozs. | £ s. d. | |
| 121 | Man's garment - - - | Cotton - - - | - - - - - - | 3 11⅓ | 1 10 | 1 13¼ | 0 2 0 | Shikarpore, Sind. |
| 122 | Ditto - - - | Ditto - - | Coloured borders and ends - - | 2 27 | 1 4 | 1 4 | 0 1 1½ | Ditto. |
| 123 | Man's garment, "Dhotee," | Ditto - - - | Ditto - - - - | 4 21 | 1 1 | 0 12½ | 0 2 6 | Calcutta. |
| 124 | Ditto - - - | Ditto - - | Ditto - - - - | 3 30 | 0 34 | 0 12½ | 0 1 5 | Surat, Bombay. |
| 125 | "Kass" or scarf, man's garment. | Ditto - - - | - - - - | 3 0 | 1 18 | 1 5 | - - - | Sylhet. |
| 126 | Ditto - - - | Ditto - - | - - - - - - | 2 18 | 1 9 | 1 3 | - - - | Cachar. |
| 127 | Ditto - - - | Ditto - - - | Pink striped borders and ends - - | 8 0 | 1 2 | 1 14 | 0 2 0 | Shikarpore, Sind. |
| 128 | Used as a waist cloth, "Dhotee." | Muslin - - - | Pine pattern across each end - | 3 0 | 1 0 | 0 6¼ | - - - | Kathamandoo, Nepal. |
| 129 | "Kass" or scarf, man's garment. | Cotton - - - | - - - - - | 4 30 | 1 8 | 1 0 | 0 6 0 | Shikarpore, Sind. |
| 130 | Ditto - - - - | Ditto - - | Pattern printed on red ground - - | 2 3 | 1 6 | 0 4½ | 0 1 0 | Surat, Bombay. |
| 131 | "Soosee," material used for for trousers for both sexes. | Silk - - - | - - - - - - | 6 17 | 0 28 | 0 12 | 0 13 10½ | Deyra Ishmail Khan, Punjab. |
| 132 | Ditto - - | Cotton - - - | - - - - - - | 2 32 | 0 18 | 0 6½ | 0 3 0 | Shikarpore, Sind. |
| 133 | Ditto - - | Cotton - - - | - - - - - - | 2 35 | 0 17 | 0 4 | 0 2 3 | Surat, Bombay. |
| 134 | Ditto - - - | Ditto - - | With silk border - - - | 9 18 | 0 21 | 1 2 | 0 10 0 | Lahore, Punjab. |
| 135 | Ditto - - - | Ditto - - - | - - - - - | 2 30 | 0 18 | 0 4 | 0 2 0 | Shikarpore, Sind. |
| 136 | Ditto - - - | Ditto - - | - - - - - | 7 31 | 0 21 | 0 14 | 0 2 0 | Surat, Bombay. |
| 137 | Ditto - - - | Ditto - - - | Narrow coloured border - - | 7 0 | 0 22 | 0 14 | 0 2 0 | Ditto. |
| 138 | Ditto - - - | Ditto - - | Ditto - - - - - | 15 29 | 0 20 | 1 5 | 0 5 0 | Ditto. |
| 139 | Ditto - - - | Ditto - - - | - - - - - - | 2 34 | 0 18 | 0 5½ | 0 2 0 | Shikarpore, Sind. |
| 140 | Ditto - - - | Ditto - - | - - - - - - | 3 3 | 0 18 | 0 5¼ | 0 2 0 | Surat, Bombay. |
| 141 | Ditto - - - | Cotton and Silk | With border - - - - | 5 22 | 0 21 | 0 12 | 0 4 0 | Rutul Mudpore, Punjab. |
| 142 | Piece goods - - - | Cotton - - - | In imitation of English moleskin - | 9 20 | 0 26 | 5 5 | 0 12 10½ | Loodiana, Punjab. |
| 143 | Ditto, for pantaloons - | Ditto - - | - - - - - - | 3 0 | 0 28 | 1 5 | 0 1 6 | Ditto. |
| 144 | Ditto - - - | Ditto - - - | - - - - - - | 2 24 | 0 25 | 1 3½ | 0 1 6 | Ditto. |
| 145 | Ditto - - - | Ditto - - | - - - - - - | 3 0 | 0 25 | 1 8 | 0 1 6 | Ditto. |
| 146 | Ditto - - - | Ditto - - - | - - - - - - | 7 0 | 0 27 | 1 10½ | 0 5 0 | Ditto. |
| 147 | Ditto - - - | Ditto - - | - - - - - - | 3 0 | 0 26 | 1 2 | 0 1 6 | Ditto. |
| 148 | Ditto - - - | Ditto - - - | - - - - - - | 3 2 | 0 27 | 1 7½ | 0 3 0 | Ditto. |
| 149 | Ditto - - - | Ditto - | - - - - - - | 3 0 | 0 25 | 0 11½ | 0 2 0 | Ditto. |
| 150 | Ditto - - - | Ditto - - - | - - - - - - | 6 4 | 0 25 | 1 5½ | 0 5 0 | Ditto. |
| 151 | "Palempore" or bed cover | Ditto - - | Printed pattern - - - | 3 13 | 1 24 | 1 3¼ | - - - | Futtygurh, Bengal. |
| 152 | Ditto - - - | Ditto - - - | Ditto - - - | 3 12 | 1 21 | 1 0¼ | - - - | Ditto. |
| 153 | Ditto - - - | Ditto - - | Ditto - - - - | 3 12 | 1 26 | 0 15½ | - - - | Ditto. |
| 154 | Ditto - - - | Ditto - - | Ditto - - - | 6 0 | 1 7 | 1 1½ | - - - | Ditto. |
| 155 | Ditto - - - | Ditto - - | Ditto - - - | 3 9 | 1 24 | 1 1 | - - - | Ditto. |
| 156 | Ditto - - | Ditto - - - | Ditto - - - | 4 21 | 1 18 | 1 4 | 0 4 0 | Shikarpore, Sind. |
| 157 | Ditto - - - | Ditto - - | Ditto - - - - | 5 0 | 1 18 | 1 15 | 0 6 0 | Ditto. |
| 158 | Ditto - - - | Ditto - - - | Diaper pattern with pink borders and ends. | 4 32 | 1 18 | 1 15 | 0 15 0 | Hoshyarpore, Punjab. |
| 159 | Ditto - - - | Ditto - - | Blue borders and ends - - - | 4 7 | 1 13 | 2 8 | - - - | Loodiana, Punjab. |
| 160 | Ditto - - - | Ditto - - - | - - - - - - | 3 8 | 1 22 | 1 8 | 0 2 6 | Hazara, Punjab. |

## Vol. 5.

## GARMENTS FOR WOMEN.

| No. | Description. | | | Length. | Width. | Weight. | Price. | Whence procured, Place of Manufacture, &c. |
|---|---|---|---|---|---|---|---|---|
| | Name and Use. | Material. | Quality, &c. | | | | | |
| | | | | yds. ins. | ds. ins. | lbs. ozs. | £ s. d. | |
| 161 | **Woman's Garment** - - | **Silk and gold thread** - | Deep flowered end, has six small pines at upper part, and four large ones below. Gold thread border extends for only 2 yards 12 inches, the remaining portion and opposite border being of plain silk. | 8 32 | 1 7 | 1 8¾ | 4 10 0 | Tanjore. Bought in Madras. |
| 162 | Ditto - - - | Cotton and silk - | Gold in border extends for 2 yards, the remainder being of plain silk. | 9 0 | 1 2 | 1 3 | 1 5 0 | Ditto. |
| 163 | Ditto - - - | Ditto - - | - - - - - - | 7 0 | 1 0 | 1 5 | 0 4 6 | Madras. |
| 164 | Ditto - - - | Silk - - - | Principal end worked with gold - - | 8 18 | 1 12 | 1 15 | 3 10 4 | Berhampore in Gangam, Madras. |
| 165 | Ditto - - - | Cotton - - | With silk in principal end - - - | 7 27 | 1 2 | 1 2 | 0 12 6 | Madras. |
| 166 | Ditto - - - | Ditto - - | Ditto - - - - - | 6 18 | 1 0 | 1 6 | 0 5 0 | Sydapat, Madras. |
| 167 | Ditto - - - | Ditto - - | With a little silk in principal end - | 6 27 | 1 2 | 1 5½ | 0 4 9 | Madras. |
| 168 | Ditto - - - | Ditto - - | With silk in borders - - - | 8 0 | 1 8 | 1 11 | 1 6 0 | Gangam, Madras. |
| 169 | Ditto - - - | Ditto - - | Silk in principal end. Borders two different colours. | 7 9 | 1 2 | 1 13 | 0 7 6 | Mylapore. Bought in Madras Bazaar. |
| 170 | Ditto - - - | Ditto - - | Ditto. White stripes in body of piece, 4¾ yards in length. | 7 27 | 1 2 | 1 7 | 0 12 0 | Cuddalore. Bought in Madras Bazaar. |
| 171 | Ditto - - - | Ditto - - | Silk in borders and end - - - | 8 0 | 1 9 | 1 9 | 0 13 0 | Mangalore. Bought in Madras Bazaar. |
| 172 | Ditto - - - | Ditto - - | Silk in borders and ends. Gold in principal end. | 7 27 | 1 5 | 1 7½ | 1 1 | Trichinopoly. Bought in Madras Bazaar. |
| 173 | Ditto - - - | Ditto - | With silk and gold in end - - | 7 0 | 1 0 | 1 3 | 0 10 0 | Condapore, S. Canara. |
| 174 | Ditto - - - | Silk - - - | With deep borders and ends - - | 8 0 | 1 3 | 1 6 | 1 5 0 | Tanjore, Madras. |
| 175 | Ditto - - | Ditto - - | Twilled. Ornamental border and end - | 8 0 | 1 7 | 1 4 | 1 10 0 | Combaconum, Madras. |
| 176 | Ditto - - - | Cotton - - - | Silk in end - - - - - - | 7 0 | 1 0 | 0 11 | 0 11 0 | Madras. |
| 177 | Ditto - - - | Ditto - - | Common material - - - | 7 27 | 1 3 | 1 7 | 0 5 0 | Ventapollam. Bought in Madras. |
| 178 | Ditto - - - | Ditto - | Silk stripes in principal end - - | 7 0 | 0 31 | 0 15 | 0 13 0 | Combaconum. Bought in Madras. |
| 179 | Ditto - - - | Ditto - - | Silk in principal end. Stripes in body of piece run about 4¾ yards, and then cease. | 7 27 | 1 2 | 1 7 | 0 12 0 | Cuddalore. Bought in Madras. |
| 180 | Ditto - - | Ditto - - | - - - - - - | 8 9 | 1 6 | 2 0 | - - - | Coimbatore, Madras. |
| 181 | Ditto - | Ditto - - | Borders of different colours - - | 7 9 | 1 4 | 1 8 | 0 5 3 | Pondicherry. Bought in Madras. |
| 182 | Ditto - - - | Ditto - - | Favourite texture - - - | 8 27 | 1 6 | 1 3 | - - - | Arnee. Bought in Madras. |
| 183 | Ditto - - - | Ditto - - | Silk in principal end - - - | 8 0 | 1 4 | 1 8 | 0 5 6 | Sydapat. Bought in Madras. |
| 184 | Ditto - - - | Ditto - - | Common material - - - | 3 0 | 1 3 | 1 12 | 0 3 9 | Ventapollam. Bought in Madras. |
| 185 | Ditto - - - | Ditto - - | Strong and durable; common pattern - | 7 0 | 1 0 | 2 1 | 0 4 3 | Poree Arnee. Bought in Madras. |
| 186 | **Girl's Garment** - - | Ditto - - | Common material; favourite colour - | 3 18 | 0 27 | 0 10 | 0 1 3 | Congeveram. Bought in Madras. |
| 187 | **Woman's Garment** - - | Ditto - - | - - - - | 7 0 | 1 0 | 1 10 | 0 2 3 | Bellary. Bought in Madras. |
| 188 | Ditto - - - | Ditto - - | - - - - | 8 27 | 1 7 | 1 6¾ | 0 3 0 | Ooppaddy. Bought in Madras. |
| 189 | Ditto - - - | Muslin - - - | Narrow stripe of gold worked in end - | 8 18 | 1 9 | 1 4 | 0 6 9 | Gangam. Bought in Madras. |
| 190 | Ditto - - - | Cotton - - - | Light texture - - - - | 7 28 | 1 4 | 1 3 | 0 4 1 | Arnee. Bought in Madras. |
| 191 | Ditto - - - | Ditto - - | Common material - - - | 5 27 | 1 0 | 1 6 | 0 3 0 | Ventapollam. Bought in Madras. |
| 192 | Ditto - - - | Muslin - - - | - - - - - - | 9 0 | 1 9 | 2 0 | 0 5 6 | Gangam. Bought in Madras. |
| 193 | Ditto - - - | Cotton - - - | Common material - - - - | 3 0 | 1 0 | 1 3 | 0 1 0 | Coimbatore. Bought in Madras. |
| 194 | Ditto - - - | Ditto - - | Coarse - - - - - - - | 3 0 | 1 0 | 0 13 | 0 1 6 | Bickul, N. Canara. |
| 195 | Ditto - - - | Ditto - - | Common material - - - | 6 0 | 1 0 | 1 7 | 0 1 9 | Congeveram. Bought in Madras. |
| 196 | Ditto - - - | Ditto - - | Deep pine pattern in end - - - | 8 9 | 1 8 | 1 6 | 0 3 3 | Arcot. Bought in Madras. |
| 197 | Ditto - - - | Muslin - - - | Narrow stripes of gold in principal end | 6 18 | 0 27 | 0 8 | 0 6 0 | Madras. |
| 198 | Ditto - - - | Cotton - - | Coarse - - - - - - | 6 30 | 0 29 | 1 6 | 0 2 1½ | Cuddapah. Bought in Madras. |
| 199 | Ditto - - - | Ditto. Covering for head and shoulders. | Glazed chintz - - - - - | 2 9 | 1 14 | 0 12 | - - - | Poonary. Bought in Madras. |
| 200 | Ditto - - - | Ditto - - | Ditto - - - - - | 2 9 | 1 14 | 0 12 | - - - | Ditto. |

## Vol. 6.

## GARMENTS FOR WOMEN.

| No. | Description. Name and Use. | Material. | Quality, &c. | Length. | Width. | Weight. | Price. | Whence procured, Place of Manufacture, &c. |
|---|---|---|---|---|---|---|---|---|
| | | | | yds. ins. | yds. ins. | lbs. ozs. | £ s. d. | |
| 201 | Employed for making up into bodices or jackets called "cholees," woman's garment. | Silk - - - | With gold border - - - | 4 27 | 1 1½ | 1 1 | 2 16 0 | Sattara, Deccan. |
| 202 | Ditto - - - | Ditto - - | Ditto - - - - - | 4 0 | 0 35½ | 0 11 | 2 16 0 | Ditto. |
| 203 | Ditto - - - | Ditto - - | Ditto - - - - - | 4 23 | 1 1 | 1 0 | 4 0 0 | Ditto. |
| 204 | Ditto - - - | Ditto - - | Ditto - - - - - | 4 21 | 1 0 | 0 14½ | 4 0 0 | Ditto. |
| 205 | Woman's garment - - | Ditto - - | With wide borders and deep gold flowered end. | 8 29 | 1 12½ | 1 4½ | 3 10 0 | Nagpore, Berar. |
| 206 | Ditto - - - | Silk and a little cotton | - - - - - - | 8 32 | 1 9½ | 1 7 | 2 2 0 | Ditto. |
| 207 | Ditto - - - | Silk and cotton gauze | - - - - - - | 9 8 | 1 9 | 1 3½ | 2 18 0 | Ditto. |
| 208 | Ditto - - - | Cotton and silk - | - - - - - - | 4 28 | 0 34 | 0 8½ | - - - | Benares. |
| 209 | Ditto - - - | Silk and cotton | This sample, unlike the majority of such articles of apparel, is without any special ornament in the ends. | 9 26 | 0 30 | 1 9½ | - - - | Ditto. |
| 210 | Ditto - - - | Ditto - - | - - - - - - | 7 30 | 1 6 | 1 15 | 1 6 0 | Belgaum, 42 miles N.W. of Dharwar. |
| 211 | Ditto - - - | Cotton with silk - | - - - - - - | 7 32 | 1 5 | 1 13½ | 0 11 0 | Ditto. |
| 212 | Ditto - - - | Silk - - - | A little gold thread in principal end - | 9 16 | 1 6 | 2 0 | 3 8 0 | Ditto. |
| 213 | Ditto - - - | Cotton - - | Silk in borders and ends - - | 8 17 | 1 8 | 2 3 | 1 0 0 | Ditto. |
| 214 | Ditto - - - | Cotton and silk - | - - - - - - | 8 0 | 1 6 | 1 14 | 1 0 0 | Ditto. |
| 215 | Ditto - - - | Ditto - - | - - - - - - | 4 16 | 1 3 | 0 11 | 0 4 0 | Surat, Bombay. |
| 216 | Ditto - - - | Cotton - - - | Deep silk borders and ends - - | 8 18 | 1 10 | 2 2 | 2 16 0 | Belgaum, 42 miles N. W. of Dharwar. |
| 217 | Ditto - - | Ditto - - | Deep silk borders and silk in ends - | 8 18 | 1 10 | 2 5 | 0 16 0 | Ditto. |
| 218 | Ditto - - | Silk - - - | Gold thread in borders and ends - | 3 4½ | 1 15 | 0 9 | 0 18 0 | Bombay. |
| 219 | Ditto - - | Silk and cotton - | - - - - - - | 7 27 | 1 9 | 2 4 | 1 8 0 | Belgaum, 42 miles N. W. of Dharwar. |
| 220 | Ditto - - - | Cotton - - - | - - - - - - | 5 16 | 1 2 | 1 2 | - - - | Gya, 289 miles N. W. of Calcutta. |
| 221 | Ditto - - | Ditto - - | Borders of different colours, one side being red, the other blue. | 4 22 | 1 22 | 0 11 | 0 3 0 | Calcutta. |
| 222 | Ditto - - - | Ditto - - | Narrow stripe in principal end, pattern inserted "crossways." | 3 0 | 0 23 | 0 3 | 0 2 0 | Ditto. |
| 223 | Ditto - - - | Ditto - - | Narrow white stripe in both ends - | 2 32 | 0 26 | 0 5½ | 0 2 0 | Ditto. |
| 224 | Ditto - - - | Ditto - - | Ditto - - - - | 3 22 | 0 29 | 0 6½ | 0 2 0 | Ditto. |
| 225 | Ditto - - - | Ditto - - | Pattern inserted "crossways," showing full width and borders. | 3 18 | 0 30 | 0 6 | 0 2 0 | Ditto. |
| 226 | Ditto - - - | Ditto - - | Pattern sample inserted crossways, showing one border narrow and the other broad. | 3 18 | 0 29 | 0 6½ | 0 1 9 | Ditto. |
| 227 | Ditto - - - | Ditto - - | Narrow stripe in each end - - | 4 27 | 1 3 | 0 11 | 0 3 0 | Ditto. |
| 228 | Ditto - - - | Ditto - - | - - - - - - | 4 32 | 1 2 | 0 12 | 0 3 0 | Ditto. |
| 229 | Ditto - - - | Ditto - - | Pattern sample inserted crossways. Narrow red stripe in principal end. | 2 27 | 0 25 | 0 | 0 2 0 | Ditto. |
| 230 | Ditto, for petticoat skirts | Ditto - - | The sample extended shows one half of the whole length of piece, which when complete is cut in two at the centre, and joined at the sides to form a skirt. The other half is similar to the one shown. | 2 16 | 0 23 | 0 6½ | - - - | Pegu. |
| 231 | Ditto - - - | Ditto - - | Ditto - - - - | 2 12 | 0 23½ | 0 6½ | - - - | Ditto. |
| 232 | Ditto - - - | Ditto - - | Ditto - - - - | 2 8 | 0 22 | 0 6½ | - - - | Ditto. |
| 233 | Ditto - - - | Ditto - - | Ditto - - - - | 2 8 | 0 24 | 0 6½ | - - - | Ditto. |
| 234 | Ditto - - - | Ditto - - | With embroidered silk borders. The piece is cut at the half length, and joined at sides to form skirt. | 1 29 | 0 26 | 1 1 | - - - | Sylhet. |
| 235 | Ditto - - - | Ditto - - | One border embroidered with yellow, the other with white silk. The piece is cut across at centre and joined at sides to form a skirt. | 1 29 | 0 25 | 1 1 | - - - | Ditto. |
| 236 | Ditto - - - | Ditto - - | - - - - - - | 5 11 | 0 29 | - - | - - - | Kathamandoo, Nepal. |
| 237 | Ditto - - - | Ditto - - | - - - - - - | 6 0 | 0 30 | 2 9 | - - - | Ditto. |
| 238 | Ditto - - - | Ditto - - | - - - - - - | 5 0 | 0 31 | 1 9 | - - - | Ditto. |
| 239 | Ditto - - - | Ditto - - | - - - - - - | 4 25 | 0 28 | 1 11 | - - - | Ditto. |
| 240 | Ditto - - - | Ditto - - | - - - - - - | 5 0 | 0 28 | 1 10 | - - - | Ditto. |

## Vol. 7.

## MUSLINS, PLAIN AND EMBROIDERED.

| No. | Description. | | | Length. | Width. | Weight. | Price. | Whence procured, Place of Manufacture, &c. |
|---|---|---|---|---|---|---|---|---|
| | Name and Use. | Material. | Quality, &c. | | | | | |
| | | | | yds. ins. | yds. ins. | lbs. ozs. | £ s. d. | |
| 241 | "Abrawan" or "Running Water," for dresses. | Muslin - - - | Plain - - - - - - - | 20 0 | 1 0 | 0 7½ | 6 4 0 | Dacca, Bengal. |
| 242 | "Circar Ali," for dresses, &c. | Ditto - - | Ditto. Fine quality - - | 20 0 | 1 0 | 0 6¾ | - - - | Ditto. |
| 243 | "Shubnam" or "Evening Dew," for dresses. | Ditto - - | Ditto. Fine material - - | 19 14 | 0 34 | 0 6½ | 3 4 0 | Ditto. |
| 244 | "Tunzeb," for dresses - | Ditto - - | Ditto. Fine quality - - - | 21 5 | 1 0 | 0 12¼ | 5 0 0 | Ditto. |
| 245 | "Nyansook," for neckerchiefs, &c. | Ditto - - | Ditto. Good quality - - - | 19 18 | 1 7 | 1 2¼ | 4 0 0 | Ditto. |
| 246 | "Jungle Khassa," for dresses, &c. | Ditto - - | Ditto. Ditto - - - - - | 21 6 | 1 5 | 1 9¼ | 5 2 0 | Ditto. |
| 247 | "Dooreea," for children's dresses, &c. | Ditto - - | Striped - - - - - - - | 13 14 | 0 28 | 0 10½ | - - - | Gwalior. |
| 248 | "Dooreea," chiefly for children's dresses. | Ditto - - | Ditto - - - - | 10 6 | 1 0 | 0 12½ | - - - | Radnagore. |
| 249 | "Dooreah," chiefly for children's dresses. | Ditto - - | Ditto. Fine - - - - - | 10 0 | 1 0 | 0 13¾ | 1 4 0 | Dacca, Bengal. |
| 250 | "Charkanu," for dresses, &c. | Ditto - - | Check. Good quality - - - | 9 26 | 0 35½ | 0 15 | 1 0 0 | Ditto. |
| 251 | Ditto - - - | Ditto - - | Ditto - - - - - - - | 9 29 | 1 0 | 0 10½ | 1 0 0 | Ditto. |
| 252 | "Phoolkary," for dresses, &c. | Ditto - - | Stripes and Flowers - - - | 13 13 | 0 28 | 0 14¼ | - - - | Gwalior. |
| 253 | "Jamdanee," for dresses, &c. | Ditto - - | Figured in the loom. Very fine quality | 11 20 | 1 0 | 0 13¾ | 3 18 0 | Dacca, Bengal. |
| 254 | "Jamdanee," for dresses, &c. | Ditto - - | Ditto - - - - - - - | 10 0 | 0 31 | 0 11 | 3 18 0 | Ditto. |
| 255 | "Chikan work," for dresses | Ditto - - | Embroidered in diagonal stripes of flowers. | 10 0 | 0 34 | 1 0¾ | 4 0 0 | Ditto. |
| 256 | Ditto - - - | Ditto - - | Embroidered flower pattern. Good quality. | 10 0 | 0 35 | 0 13¼ | 3 18 0 | Ditto. |
| 257 | Ditto - - - | Ditto - - | Embroidered. Diagonal stripes and flowers. A fine example. | 10 0 | 1 0 | 1 5 | 4 0 0 | Ditto |
| 258 | Ditto - - - | Ditto - - | Embroidered. Of fine quality - - | 10 0 | 1 0 | 0 9½ | 3 18 6 | Ditto. |
| 259 | Ditto - - - | Ditto - - | Ditto. ditto - - | 9 14 | 0 33 | 0 11¼ | 3 18 0 | Ditto. |
| 260 | "Bootee," for dresses - | Ditto - - | Ditto, with crimson spots - - | 10 0 | 1 0 | 0 13¼ | 1 10 0 | Ditto. |
| 261 | - - - - | Gold cloth - - | Plain - - - - - | 2 31 | 0 24 | 0 5 | 1 16 0 | Hyderabad, Deccan |
| 262 | - - - - | Silver cloth - - | Ditto - - - - - - | 2 32 | 0 23½ | 0 5¼ | - - - | Ditto. |
| 263 | - - - - | Gold cloth - - | With red silk stripes - - - | 2 33 | 0 26½ | 0 5¾ | - - - | Ditto. |
| 264 | - - - - | Silver cloth - - | Plain - - - - - - | 1 0 | 0 22½ | 0 1¾ | - - - | Ditto. |
| 265 | - - - - | Gold cloth - - | With green silk stripes - - - | 2 0 | 0 25 | 0 4 | About 1 16 0 | Ditto. |
| 266 | - - - - | Silver cloth - - | With crimson silk stripes - - | 2 33 | 0 24 | 0 5¼ | - - - | Ditto. |
| 267 | - - - - | Ditto - - | Plain - - - - - - - | 1 4 | 0 33½ | 0 4¼ | - - - | Moorshedabad, Bengal. |
| 268 | - - - - | Gold cloth - - | Figured - - - - - - | 1 9 | 0 28 | 0 5¼ | - - - | Ditto. |
| 269 | - - - - | Silver cloth - - | Ditto - - - - - - | 1 8 | 0 31 | 0 5¼ | - - - | Ditto. |
| 270 | - - - - | Gold cloth - - | With gold and beetle wing embroidery - | 2 22 | 0 20 | 0 6¼ | - - - | Madras. |
| 271 | - - - - | Muslin - - - | Printed with gold flowers - - - | 9 27 | 1 25 | 1 0 | - - - | Jeypore, Rajpootana states. |
| 272 | For small scarfs - | Ditto - - | Printed with silver. Piece incomplete - | 0 33 | 1 5 | 0 3 | 0 4 6 | Hyderabad, Deccan. |
| 273 | - - - - | Ditto - - | Ditto Ditto - | 0 33 | 1 7 | 0 3 | 0 4 6 | Ditto. |
| 274 | For making women's bodices | Ditto - - | Worked in gold figures - - - | 1 4 | 1 0 | 0 3 | - - - | Madras. |
| 275 | "Kincob" - - - | Silk gauze and gold - | Diagonal stripes and flowers of gold on a mauve ground. | 4 20 | 0 34 | 2 4½ | - - - | Benares. |
| 276 | To make up into scarfs - | Muslin - - - | Embroidered. Diagonal stripes and flowers in gold and beetle wing. | 9 22 | 1 3 | 1 11½ | - - - | Madras. |
| 277 | - - - - | Ditto - - | Embroidered in gold, &c. - - - | 1 29 | 1 13 | 0 12 | - - - | Ditto. |
| 278 | For scarfs and head coverings. | Ditto - - | Embroidered in gold stars and flowers - | 2 2 | 1 8 | 0 6½ | 5 0 0 | Ditto. |
| 279 | - - - - | Ditto - - | Embroidered in gold, &c. Pine pattern. Very rich. | 3 7 | 1 12 | 0 8¼ | 7 10 0 | Ditto. |
| 280 | - - - - | Ditto - - | Leaf pattern, embroidered in gold - | 3 3 | 1 8 | 0 9½ | - - - | Ditto. |

## Vol. 8.

# MUSLINS, CALICOES, AND OTHER PIECE GOODS.

| No. | Description. Name and Use. | Material. | Quality, &c. | Length. | Width. | Weight. | Price. | Whence procured, Place of Manufacture, &c. |
|---|---|---|---|---|---|---|---|---|
| | | | | yds. ins. | yds. ins. | lbs. ozs. | £ s. d. | |
| 281 | "Doorea" - - | Striped muslin - | Unbleached. Coarse. Four pieces (3 yards 22 inches each) woven in one length and connected by a fag. Plain ends. | 14 18 | 0 30½ | 2 2 | 0 3 6 | Nagpore, Berar. |
| 282 | "Charkana" - - | Muslin - - | Check pattern. Unbleached. Coarse. Four pieces of 3 yards 22 inches each, woven in one length and connected by a fag. Plain ends. | 14 18 | 0 24½ | 2 0¾ | 0 3 6 | Ditto. |
| 283 | "Doorea - - | Ditto - - | Striped. Narrow gold stripe in end - | 14 0 | 0 30½ | 0 10¾ | 1 13 0 | Chundaree. |
| 284 | "Chudder, a covering for the body. | Ditto - - | Plain. Fine quality. Narrow gold stripe in end. | 14 0 | 0 30½ | 0 10¼ | 1 13 0 | Ditto. |
| 285 | "Charkana" - - | Ditto - - | Check pattern. Superior quality. Gold stripe in end. | 14 1 | 0 31½ | 0 10¼ | 1 13 0 | Ditto. |
| 286 | - - - - | Ditto - - | Plain - - - - - | 15 30 | 1 2 | 1 2¾ | 0 4 3 | Shahabad, Patna. |
| 287 | "Chunderkora" - - | Ditto - - | Bordered. Coarse - - - | 4 18 | 1 4½ | 0 6 | 0 2 7½ | Calcutta. |
| 288 | For covering the head and neck. | Ditto - - | Bordered - - - - - | 2 33 | 1 10 | 0 3½ | 0 2 0 | Ditto. |
| 289 | "Santipore dhootee" - | Ditto - - | Very light. Coloured figured borders with tussah silk worked therein. | 5 32 | 1 9 | 0 5¼ | 0 5 6 | Santipore, Bengal. |
| 290 | Ditto - - - - | Ditto - | Very light. Coloured borders and ends - | 4 18 | 0 32 | 0 5¼ | 0 5 6 | Ditto. |
| 291 | Ditto - - - - | Ditto | Very light. Uncommon pattern. One border orange and blue, the opposite border crimson and blue. | 5 20 | 1 10 | 0 6¼ | 0 5 6 | Ditto. |
| 292 | When ends and borders are added, used for shawls and scarfs. | Cotton and silk - | Embroidered with silk flowers - - | 4 9 | 0 33½ | 0 10¾ | - - - | Dacca, Bengal. |
| 293 | For scarfs and dress - | Ditto - | "Moonga" silk. Embroidered - | 4 24 | 1 1½ | 0 12¾ | - - - | Ditto. |
| 294 | Ditto - - - - | Ditto - - | Ditto and cotton. Striped pattern. | 4 16 | 1 0 | 0 8 | - - | Ditto. |
| 295 | Ditto - - - - | Ditto - - | Ditto and cotton, with pattern embroidered in Moonga silk. | 4 17 | 0 33 | 0 13¼ | - - - | Ditto. |
| 296 | - - - - | Ditto - - | "Moonga" silk. Embroidered in coloured cotton. | 4 12½ | 0 33½ | 0 11¼ | - - - | Ditto. |
| 297 | "Gurrah" cloth - - | Cotton - - | Calico. 1st quality - - - | 12 18 | 0 28 | 2 12 | 0 4 0 | Agra, N. W. Provinces. |
| 298 | "Guzzy" cloth - | Ditto - - | Ditto. 2d „ - - - | 17 18 | 0 18 | 1 13 | 0 2 0 | Ditto. |
| 299 | "Gurrah" cloth - | Ditto - - | Ditto. 1st - - - | 16 18 | 0 31 | 3 12 | 0 3 0 | Patna, Bengal. |
| 300 | Ditto - - | Ditto - - | Ditto - - - - - | 12 0 | 0 34 | 3 0 | 0 4 0 | Agra, N. W. Provinces. |
| 301 | "Dhootee" cloth - - | Ditto - - | Coarse calico - - - - | 4 12 | 1 0 | 1 4 | - - - | Bhurtpore, Rajpootana States. |
| 302 | - - - - | Ditto - - | Coarse brown calico. Piece incomplete - | 2 11½ | 0 28 | 0 8½ | - - - | Benares. |
| 303 | "Gurrah cloth - - | Ditto - - | Calico. Unbleached. Cut sample only - | 9 19 | 0 21 | 1 5¾ | - - - | Ditto. |
| 304 | - - - - | Ditto - - | Calico. Coarse. A sample only - - | 2 14 | 1 0 | 0 12 | - - - | Ditto. |
| 305 | For "sarees" (women's garments). | Ditto - - | Coarse gauze, light fabric. A sample only. | 2 12 | 1 1 | 0 6¼ | - - - | Ditto. |
| 306 | "Gurrah" cloth - - | Ditto - - | Coarse. A sample only - - | 2 12 | 0 27 | 0 3¾ | - - - | Ditto. |
| 307 | Sailcloth - - - | Ditto - - | Coloured stripes of orange, green, and red, about one yard from principal end. Sample only. | 5 0 | 0 22½ | 4 12¼ | 0 2 6 | Cutch, Bombay. |
| 308 | - - - - | Cotton piece goods - | Check, woven in colours. Sample only - | 7 25 | 0 29 | 1 0½ | - - - | Benares. |
| 309 | - - - - | Ditto - - | Design, ditto. ditto - | 8 0 | 1 1 | 1 10½ | - - - | Ditto. |
| 310 | - - - - | Ditto - - | Print - - - | 5 28½ | 1 1 | 1 4¾ | - - - | Futtygurh, N. W. Provinces. |
| 311 | - - - - | Ditto - - | Ditto - - - - - | 5 30½ | 1 1½ | 1 4½ | - - - | Ditto. |
| 312 | - - - - | Ditto - - | Ditto - - - - - | 5 31½ | 1 11½ | 1 5½ | - - - | Ditto. |
| 313 | - - - - | Ditto - - | Woven in colours. Imitation of English | 6 18 | 0 23 | 1 5½ | 0 3 0 | Broach, Bombay. |
| 314 | - - - - | Ditto - - | Ditto (plaid). Ditto | 12 0 | 0 22½ | 2 11¼ | 0 6 0 | Ditto. |
| 315 | "Peshgeer," for petticoats of poorer classes. | Ditto - - | Print. Fabric of English thread - | 5 0 | 0 32 | 1 2½ | 0 4 0 | Shikarpore, Sind. |
| 316 | - - - - | Ditto - - | Plaid, woven in colours. Twilled cotton | 8 15 | 0 25 | 1 12 | 0 6 0 | Loodiana, Punjab. |
| 317 | - - - | Ditto - - | Check. Red on yellow ground - - | 5 26 | 0 25 | 0 12½ | 0 3 0 | Ditto. |
| 318 | - - - | Ditto - - | Check or Plaid - - - - | 8 33 | 0 26 | 1 1 | 0 3 0 | Ditto. |
| 319 | - - | Ditto - - | Print - - - - | 5 26 | 1 1½ | 1 5½ | - - - | Futtygurh, N. W. Provinces. |
| 320 | - - - - | Ditto - - | Plain cloth dyed with indigo - - | 8 6 | 0 34 | 3 1½ | 0 3 6 | Beejapoor, Deccan. |

## Vol. 9.

## MUSLIN, SILK, AND OTHER PIECE GOODS.

| No. | Description. | | | Length. | Width. | Weight. | Price. | Whence procured, Place of Manufacture, &c. |
|---|---|---|---|---|---|---|---|---|
| | Name and Use. | Material. | Quality, &c. | yds. ins. | yds. ins. | lbs. ozs. | £ s. d. | |
| 321 | "Sullah" - - - | Muslin - - - | Plain. Fine quality - - - | 13 0 | 1 0 | 0 9 | 4 4 0 | Cuddapah, Madras. |
| 322 | Ditto - - - - | Ditto - - | Ditto. Superfine quality - - | 15 18 | 1 13 | 0 13 | 12 5 0 | Arnee, Madras. |
| 323 | "Dooreea Sullah" - - | Ditto - - | Striped - - - - | 10 18 | 0 27 | 0 15 | 0 6 0 | Hyderabad, Deccan. Bought in Madras. |
| 324 | - - - - | Ditto - - | Ditto. Good quality - - | 14 0 | 1 4 | 1 4 | 0 15 0 | Arnee, Madras. |
| 325 | "Charkhana Sullah" for children's dresses. | Ditto - - | Check - - - - | 7 0 | 0 33 | 1 4 | 0 5 10 | Ditto. |
| 326 | Ditto - - - | Ditto - - | Ditto - - - - | 7 0 | 0 34 | 1 1 | 0 5 10 | Ditto. |
| 327 | Ditto - - | Ditto - - | Ditto. Fine quality - - | 10 0 | 1 4 | 0 9 | 1 4 6 | Ditto. |
| 328 | Ditto - - - | Ditto - - | Ditto - - - - | 13 0 | 1 2 | 1 14 | 0 8 0 | Nellore, Madras. |
| 329 | Ditto - - - | Ditto - - | Ditto. Finest quality - - | 15 18 | 1 4 | 1 2 | 4 11 0 | Arnee, Madras. |
| 330 | - - - - | Ditto - - | Fine quality. Pattern worked in loom - | 15 0 | 0 32 | 1 0 | 1 8 0 | Chicacole, Madras. |
| 331 | - - - - | Ditto - - | Good quality. Flower pattern loom wrought. | 16 0 | 0 31 | 1 3 | 0 14 0 | Ditto. |
| 332 | - - - - | Ditto - - | Coloured check - - - | 15 0 | 0 39 | 1 0½ | 0 6 1½ | Arnee, Madras. |
| 333 | - - - - | Ditto - - | Ditto - - - - | 10 0 | 0 32 | 0 12½ | 0 10 0 | Ditto. |
| 334 | - - - - | Ditto - | Ditto - - - - | 15 0 | 1 2 | 1 3½ | 0 15 0 | Ditto. |
| 335 | - - - - | Ditto - - | Ditto - - - - | 7 0 | 0 30 | 1 0 | 0 4 0 | Chicacole, Madras. |
| 336 | - - - - | Ditto - | Ditto - - - - | 7 0 | 0 32 | 1 0 | 0 4 0 | Ditto. |
| 337 | - - - - | Ditto - - | Ditto - - - - | 7 0 | 0 32 | 0 9 | 0 3 0 | Arnee, Madras |
| 338 | - - - - | Ditto - - | Ditto - - - - | 7 18 | 0 37 | 0 10 | 0 3 0 | Ditto. |
| 339 | - - - - | Ditto - - | Ditto - - - - | 7 0 | 0 32 | 0 15 | 0 4 0 | Chicacole, Madras. |
| 340 | - - - - | Ditto - - | Ditto - - - - | 7 0 | 0 32 | 0 15½ | 0 4 0 | Ditto. |
| 341 | - - - - | Ditto - - | Ditto. Fine quality - - | 15 0 | 1 2 | 1 5 | 0 15 0 | Arnee, Madras. |
| 342 | - - - - | Ditto - - | Ditto - - - - | 15 0 | 0 30 | 1 3 | 0 6 0 | Chicacole, Madras. |
| 343 | - - - - | Ditto - - | Coloured stripes. Very light texture - | 13 0 | 1 2 | 1 4½ | 0 11 0 | Nellore, Madras. |
| 344 | Scarf, worn by Hindoo women. | Ditto - - | Printed - - - - | 4 9 | 1 0 | 0 7 | 0 4 0 | Trichinopoly, Madras. |
| 345 | Ditto - - - | Ditto - - | Ditto - - - - | 4 18 | 1 0 | 0 7 | 0 4 0 | Ditto. |
| 346 | Ditto - - - | Ditto - - | Ditto - - - - | 4 18 | 1 0 | 0 7½ | 0 4 0 | Ditto. |
| 347 | Ditto - - - | Ditto - - | Ditto - - - - | 4 18 | 1 0 | 0 6½ | 0 4 0 | Madras. |
| 348 | Ditto - - - | Ditto - - | Ditto - - - - | 4 18 | 1 0 | 0 7½ | 0 5 0 | Ditto. |
| 349 | Ditto - - - | Ditto - - | Ditto - - - - | 4 27 | 0 38 | 0 6 | 0 4 0 | Ditto. |
| 350 | Ditto - - - | Ditto - - | Ditto - - - - | 4 18 | 1 2 | 0 6½ | 0 4 0 | Cuddapah, Madras. |
| 351 | - - - - | Silk - - - | Tartan - - - - | 9 0 | 0 22 | 0 15 | 1 2 0 | Tanjore, Madras. |
| 352 | - - - - | Silk and cotton - | Check - - - - - | 11 27 | 0 22 | 1 0 | 0 7 0 | Ditto. |
| 353 | Worn by women and children. | Ditto - - | Ditto - - - - | 11 27 | 0 22 | 1 0 | 0 7 6 | Ditto. |
| 354 | - - - - | Silk - - - | Fine cross stripes - - - | 9 0 | 0 30 | 0 10 | 0 18 0 | Ditto. |
| 355 | - - - - | Silk and cotton - | Striped - - - - | 11 27 | 0 22 | 1 10 | 0 8 6 | Ditto. |
| 356 | - - - - | Ditto - - | Check - - - - | 12 0 | 0 22 | 1 0 | 0 9 6 | Ditto. |
| 357 | - - - - | Cotton - - - | Dyed. Plain - - - | 6 9 | 0 25 | 0 10½ | 0 3 0 | Coonatoor, Madras. |
| 358 | - - - - | Silk and cotton - | Check - - - - - | 11 27 | 0 22 | 1 0 | 0 9 0 | Tanjore, Madras. |
| 359 | - - - - | Cotton - - | Plaid. Imitation of English pattern - | 6 0 | 21 | 0 14 | 0 4 0 | Pulicat, Madras. |
| 360 | - - - - | Ditto - - | Ditto - - - - | 6 0 | 0 22 | 0 14 | 0 4 0 | Mylapore, Madras. |

## Vol. 10.

## COTTON PIECE GOODS, DYED AND PRINTED.

| No. | Description. Name and Use. | Material. | Quality, &c. | Length | Width. | Weight. | Price. | Whence procured, Place of Manufacture, &c. |
|---|---|---|---|---|---|---|---|---|
| | | | | yds. ins. | yds. ins. | lbs. ozs. | £ s. d. | |
| 361 | Kerchief, worn on head and shoulders. | Cotton - - - | Half dye. Eight woven in a piece - | Each, 0 35 | Each, 0 33 | Each, 0 2½ | Each, 0 0 8 | Coonathoor, Madras. |
| 362 | Ditto - - - | Ditto - - | Fast colours, ditto - - - - | Each, 0 30 | Each, 0 28 | Each, 0 3¾ | Each, 0 0 7½ | Ditto. |
| 363 | Ditto - - - | Ditto - - - | The glaze by a chank shell rubbed over the surface. Eight woven in a piece. | Each, 1 0 | Each, 1 0 | Each, 0 3 | Each, 0 0 7½ | Ventapollum, Madras. |
| 364 | Ditto - - - | Ditto - - | Ditto - - - - - | Each, 1 0 | Each, 1 0 | Each, 0 3⅜ | Each, 0 0 7½ | Ditto. |
| 365 | Ditto - - - | Ditto - - | Ditto - - - - - | Each, 1 0 | Each, 1 0 | Each, 0 3½ | Each, 0 0 7½ | Ditto. |
| 366 | Ditto - - - | Ditto - - | Ditto - - - - - | Each, 1 0 | Each, 1 0 | Each, 0 3½ | 0 1 1½ | Ditto. |
| 367 | Chintz, with an end for covering the head and shoulders. | Ditto - - - | Printed and glazed - - - | 3 0 | 1 0 | 0 12 | 0 1 6 | Arcot, Madras. |
| 368 | Piece goods - - - | Ditto - - | Print - - - - - | 3 24 | 1 5 | 0 15½ | 0 2 0 | Masulipatam, Madras. |
| 369 | Ditto - - - | Ditto - - - | Print; coarse - - - - | 5 26 | 1 1 | 1 5 | 0 3 9 | Ditto. |
| 370 | Chintz - - - | Ditto - - | Printed and glazed; good pattern and material. | 3 27 | 1 2 | - - | 0 8 0 | Ditto. |
| 371 | - - - - | Ditto - - - | Printed, with end pattern - - | 4 18 | 1 0 | 0 15 | 0 4 0 | Madras. |
| 372 | For petticoats - - | Ditto - - | Print - - - - - - | 7 18 | 1 0 | 1 12 | 0 3 1½ | Bellary, Madras. |
| 373 | Piece goods - - - | Ditto - - - | Print; good pattern - - - | 4 0 | 1 6 | 1 1 | 0 2 7½ | Ponnary, Madras. |
| 374 | Ditto, "chetee," chintz - | Ditto - - | Print; coarse fabric - - - | 7 0 | 0 30 | 1 7 | 0 2 0 | Arcot, Madras. |
| 375 | Ditto ditto - - | Ditto - - - | Ditto - - - - - | 9 0 | 1 0 | 2 10 | 0 4 1½ | Ponnary, Madras. |
| 376 | Ditto ditto - - | Ditto - - | Ditto - - - - - | 3 18 | 1 6 | 0 14 | 0 2 1½ | Ditto. |
| 377 | Ditto ditto - - | Ditto - - - | Print - - - - - | 3 18 | 1 8 | 0 14 | 0 2 0 | Arcot, Madras. |
| 378 | Ditto ditto - - | Ditto - - | Ditto - - - - - | 3 18 | 1 8 | 0 14 | 0 2 0 | Ditto. |
| 379 | Piece goods - - - | Ditto - - | Ditto (imperfectly printed) - - | 3 18 | 1 2 | 0 12 | 0 2 0 | Ditto. |
| 380 | Ditto - - - | Ditto - - | Ditto - - - - | 4 18 | 1 4 | 1 3 | 0 3 1½ | Ponnary, Madras. |
| 381 | Ditto, "chetee," chintz - | Ditto - - | Ditto - - - - | 3 18 | 1 5 | 1 0 | 0 2 0 | Arcot, Madras. |
| 382 | Piece goods - - - | Ditto - - | Ditto - - - - | 3 18 | 1 0 | 0 12 | 0 2 0 | Ditto. |
| 383 | Ditto, "chetee," chintz - | Ditto - - - | Ditto - - - - | 9 18 | 1 0 | 2 12 | 0 4 1½ | Ponnary, Madras. |
| 384 | Ditto ditto - - | Ditto - - | Ditto - - - - | 6 18 | 1 7 | 1 12 | 0 3 10½ | Ditto. |
| 385 | Piece goods - - - | Ditto - - - | Ditto - - - - | 7 0 | 0 19 | 1 9 | 0 3 3 | Bellary, Madras. |
| 386 | Ditto - - - | Ditto - - | Ditto - - - - | 4 0 | 1 6 | 1 1 | 0 2 7½ | Ponnary, Madras. |
| 387 | Ditto, "chetee," chintz - | Ditto - - - | Ditto - - - - | 5 0 | 1 0 | 0 15 | 0 2 0 | Sydapat, Madras. |
| 388 | Ditto ditto - - | Ditto - - | Ditto - - - - | 6 0 | 1 0 | 1 5 | 0 4 6 | Masulipatam, Madras. |
| 389 | Piece goods - - - | Ditto - - - | Ditto - - - - | 5 18 | 1 6 | 1 8 | 0 3 4½ | Ponnary, Madras. |
| 390 | Ditto - - - | Ditto - - | Ditto; coarse - - - | 5 27 | 1 0 | 1 12 | 0 3 1½ | Masulipatam, Madras. |
| 391 | Ditto - - - | Ditto - - - | Ditto - - - - | 6 0 | 1 0 | 1 12 | 0 3 1½ | Ditto. |
| 392 | Ditto, "chetee," chintz - | Ditto - - | Ditto - - - - | 7 0 | 0 29 | 1 9 | 0 2 0 | Arcot, Madras. |
| 393 | Ditto ditto - - | Ditto - - - | Ditto - - - - | 9 0 | 1 2 | 2 8 | 0 4 1½ | Ponnary, Madras. |
| 394 | Piece Goods - - | Ditto - - | Ditto - - - - | 7 0 | 0 31 | 1 12 | 0 2 3 | Ditto. |
| 395 | Ditto - - - | Ditto - - - | Ditto; coarse - - - - | 9 0 | 1 0 | 2 10 | 0 4 1½ | Ditto. |
| 396 | Ditto - - - | Ditto - - | Ditto - - - - | 7 9 | 0 32 | 1 10 | 0 2 3 | Arcot, Madras. |
| 397 | Ditto, "gudkacheet" for petticoats. | Ditto - - - | - - - - - | 4 18 | 0 31 | - - | 0 2 0 | Agra, N. W. Provinces. |
| 398 | "Chetee," chintz for lining tents. | Ditto - - | Print; coarse - - - - | 5 0 | 1 4 | 0 9 | 0 2 7½ | Arcot, Madras. |
| 399 | Ditto - - - | Ditto - - - | Ditto - - - - | 5 0 | 1 4 | 1 3 | 0 2 1½ | Ditto. |
| 400 | Ditto - - - | Ditto - - | Ditto - - - - - | 5 0 | 1 4 | 1 7 | 0 2 7½ | Ditto. |

## Vol. 11.

## COTTON PIECE GOODS, TOWELLINGS, &c.

| No. | Description. | | | Length. | Width. | Weight. | Price. | Whence procured, Place of Manufacture, &c. |
|---|---|---|---|---|---|---|---|---|
| | Name and Use. | Material. | Quality, &c. | yds. ins. | yds. ins. | lbs. ozs. | £ s. d. | |
| 401 | Gown-piece - - - | Cotton - - - | Plaid pattern, imitation English - | 6 0 | 0 21 | 0 13 | 0 3 10½ | Mylapore, Madras. |
| 402 | Ditto - - - | Ditto - - - | Ditto - - - - | 5 27 | 0 21 | 0 13 | 0 3 0 | Coonathoor, Madras. |
| 403 | Ditto - - - | Ditto - - - | - - - - - - | 11 21 | 0 22 | 1 3 | 0 5 6 | Tanjore, Madras. |
| 404 | Ditto - - - | Ditto - - | - - - - - - | 6 0 | 0 31 | 0 12 | 0 5 0 | Cuddalore, Madras. |
| 405 | Ditto - - - - | Ditto - - | Check pattern - - - - | 6 0 | 0 31 | 0 14 | 0 4 6 | Ditto. |
| 406 | Ditto - - - | Ditto - - - | Ditto - - - - | 5 20 | 0 26 | 0 11 | 0 2 0 | Pulicat, Madras. |
| 407 | Ditto - - - | Ditto - - - | Ditto - - - - | 5 23 | 0 22 | 0 14 | 0 4 0 | Mylapore, Madras. |
| 408 | Ditto - - - | Ditto - - | - - - - - - | 6 13 | 0 25 | 0 12 8/16 | 0 2 6 | Coonathoor, Madras. |
| 409 | Ditto - - - | Ditto - - - | Small check pattern - - - | 6 8 | 0 25 | 0 12½ | 0 2 6 | Ditto. |
| 410 | Ditto - - - | Ditto - - - | - - - - - - | 7 6 | 0 26 | 0 12 | 0 2 6 | Ditto. |
| 411 | Ditto - - - | Ditto - - | Check pattern - - - - | 6 30 | 0 26 | 0 11 | 0 2 6 | Ditto. |
| 412 | Ditto - - - | Ditto - - - | Ditto - - - - | 6 0 | 0 28 | 0 14 | 0 3 0 | Pulicat, Madras. |
| 413 | Ditto - - - | Ditto - - | Ditto - - - - - | 6 26 | 0 26 | 0 15 | 0 4 6 | Teroomaly, Madras. |
| 414 | Ditto - - - | Ditto - - - | Ditto - - - - | 7 0 | 0 26 | 0 15 | 0 3 9 | Coonathoor, Madras. |
| 415 | Ditto - - - - | Ditto - - | Ditto, English pattern - - - | 6 9 | 0 18 | 1 0 | 0 3 6 | Masulipatam, Madras. |
| 416 | - - - - | Ditto - - - | Small check gingham - - - | 10 27 | 0 20 | 1 10 | 0 3 6 | Cuddalore, Madras. |
| 417 | - - - - | Ditto - - | Ditto, good quality - - - - | 6 0 | 0 27 | 1 10 | 0 6 0 | Ditto. |
| 418 | - - - - | Ditto - - - | Striped gingham - - - - | 10 0 | 0 20 | 2 2 | 0 3 0 | Palamcottah, Madras. |
| 419 | Table napkins - - - | Ditto - - - | Unbleached damask - - - | 0 21 | 0 21 | - - | Per dozen 0 7 0 | Madras. |
| 420 | Ditto - - - - | Ditto - - - | Ditto - - - - | 0 19 | 0 19 | - - | Per dozen 0 8 0 | Cuddalore, Madras. |
| 421 | Ditto - - - | Ditto - - - | Unbleached diaper - - - | 0 22 | 0 22 | - - | Per dozen 0 8 6 | Ditto. |
| 422 | Towels - - - - | Ditto - - - | Unbleached huckaback - - - | 0 35 | 0 35 | - - | Per dozen 0 13 0 | Ditto. |
| 423 | Ditto - - - | Ditto - - - | Bleached dungary - - - | 0 33 | 0 22 | - - | Per dozen 0 4 0 | Ditto. |
| 424 | Table napkins - - - | Ditto - - - | Unbleached damask - - - | 0 30 | 0 29 | - - | Per dozen 0 13 0 | Masulipatam, Madras. |
| 425 | Towels - - - | Ditto - - - | Unbleached diaper - - - | 1 0 | 0 31 | - - | Per dozen 0 8 0 | Chingleput, Madras. |
| 426 | Table napkins - - - | Ditto - - - | Bleached diaper - - - - | 0 17 | 0 17 | - - | Per dozen 0 2 3 | Masulipatam, Madras. |
| 427 | Towels - - - | Ditto - - | Unbleached dungary - - - | 0 32 | 0 31 | - - | Per dozen 0 4 0 | Salem, Madras. |
| 428 | Table napkins - - - | Ditto - - - | Unbleached damask - - - | 0 23 | 0 23 | - - | Per dozen 0 3 0 | Broach, Bombay. |
| 429 | Towels - - - | Ditto - - | Coarse unbleached huckaback - - | 0 33 | 0 33 | - - | Per dozen 0 2 3 | Ditto. |
| 430 | Ditto (Hand) - - | Ditto - - - | (Like diaper) coloured borders - - | 0 27 | 0 25 | - - | Per dozen 0 3 0 | Goa, sent from Madras. |
| 431 | D'Oyleys - - - - | Ditto - - | In colours - - - - | 0 13 | 0 13 | - - | Per dozen 0 9 0 | Madras. |
| 432 | Ditto - - - | Ditto - - | Ditto - - - - - | 0 13 | 0 13 | - - | Per dozen 0 8 3 | Cuddalore, Madras. |
| 433 | "Soojnee" or counterpane - | Ditto - - | Quilted - - - - | 2 6 | 1 10 | 2 4 | 0 8 0 | Hyderabad, Deccan. |
| 434 | Rug for sleeping on - - | Ditto - - - | Sewn together in centre - - - | 2 8 | 1 24 | 6 2 | - - - | Upper Assam. |
| 435 | Rug "suttringee" - - | Ditto - - | - - - - - - | 1 32 | 0 32 | 2 4 | 0 3 0 | Mangalore, Madras. |
| 436 | Ditto - - - | Ditto - - - | - - - - - - | 5 13 | 2 20 | 15 3 | 0 2 0 | Ditto. |
| 437 | Ditto - - - | Ditto - - - | Sepoy regulation rug - - - | 2 14 | 1 4 | 2 5 | 0 2 0 | Palamcottah, Madras. |
| 438 | Ditto - - | Ditto - - - | - - - - - - | 2 16 | 1 6½ | 2 14 | 0 2 0 | Ditto. |
| 439 | Ditto - - - | Ditto - - | Very durable fabric - - - | 2 30 | 1 24 | 8 11 | - - - | Agra, N. W. Provinces. |
| 440 | Ditto - - - | Ditto - - - | Ditto - - - | 2 30 | 1 19 | 8 13 | - - - | Ditto. |

## Vol. 12.

## SILK AND COTTON PIECE GOODS.

| No. | Description. Name and Use. | Description. Material. | Description. Quality, &c. | Length. | Width. | Weight. | Price. | Whence procured, Place of Manufacture, &c. |
|---|---|---|---|---|---|---|---|---|
| | | | | yds. ins. Each piece, | yds. ins. Each piece, | lbs. ozs. Each piece, | £ s. d. Per piece, | |
| 441 | Piece goods for making up into "Cholees" or close fitting bodices for women. | Silk | With gold stripes. The piece includes material for six "cholees," separated by a "fag" woven between. | 0 17 | 0 29 | 0 1¼ | 0 1 9 | Tanjore, Madras. |
| 442 | Ditto | Ditto | With silver stripes. Six in a piece | 0 17 | 0 29 | 0 1¼ | 0 1 9 | Ditto. |
| 443 | Ditto | Ditto | Ditto. ditto | 0 17 | 0 29 | 0 1¼ | 0 1 9 | Ditto. |
| 444 | Ditto | Ditto and Cotton | Coloured stripes. ditto | 0 24 | 0 19 | 0 1¼ | 0 1 9 | Trichinopoly, Madras. |
| 445 | Ditto | Silk gauze | With gold flowers and borders | 0 22 | 1 7 | - - | 0 13 0 | Hyderabad. Bought in Madras. |
| 446 | For petticoats | Cotton and silk gauze | - | 7 0 | 0 23 | 0 13 | 0 14 0 | Trichinopoly, Madras. |
| 447 | Ditto | Cotton and silk | - | 11 15 | 0 23 | 0 14½ | 0 10 0 | Tanjore, Madras. |
| 448 | "Soosee" for trouserings | Ditto | - | 7 0 | 0 33 | 0 14 | 0 8 0 | Trichinopoly, Madras |
| 449 | "Soosee" for trouserings and petticoats. | Ditto | - | 8 0 | 1 0 | 0 15 | 0 8 0 | Syempettah, Madras. |
| 450 | Ditto | Cotton | - | 6 0 | 0 26 | 0 10 | 0 3 0 | Ditto. |
| 451 | Ditto | Cotton and silk | - | 7 0 | 0 33 | 0 12 | 0 8 0 | Trichinopoly, Madras. |
| 452 | "Soosee," used for trouserings. | Silk and cotton | - | 11 0 | 0 27 | 1 9 | 0 8 0 | Ditto. |
| 453 | "Soosee," for trousering and petticoats. | Cotton | - | 6 0 | 0 29 | 0 15 | 0 2 4½ | Coonatoor, Madras. |
| 454 | - | Ditto | Check. English pattern | 8 0 | 0 32 | 2 5 | 0 5 3 | Masulipatam, Madras. |
| 455 | Twill for trousering | Ditto | Twill | 5 11 | 0 25 | 1 10 | 0 4 1½ | Cuddalore, Madras. |
| 456 | Ditto | Ditto | Ditto | 5 12 | 0 22 | 1 10 | 0 2 6 | Ditto. |
| 457 | Pocket handkerchief | Ditto | Plain, deep borders | 0 20 | 0 20 | - - | Per dozen, 0 4 6 | Nellore, Madras. |
| 458 | Ditto | Ditto | Ditto | 0 20 | 0 20 | - - | Per dozen, 0 8 0 | Ditto. |
| 459 | "Chunderkana," muslin for handkerchiefs. | Ditto | Without borders; Second sort of good quality | 8 0 | 1 2 | 0 12 | 0 18 0 | Arnee, Madras. |
| 460 | Muslin | Ditto | Plain; similar to Dacca muslin in its softness of texture. | 12 0 | 1 3 | 0 11½ | 0 12 0 | Hyderabad, Deccan. Bought in Madras. |
| 461 | Kerchiefs | Ditto | Coloured. Coarse | 1st size, 0 23; 2d size, 0 27 | 1st size, 0 23; 2d size, 0 27 | - - | Largest size, 0 1 6 | Cundapoor, S. Canara. |
| 462 | Ditto | Ditto | Coloured borders | 0 29 | 0 29 | Weight of eight, 1 1 | Price of eight, 0 4 6 | Masulipatam, Madras. |
| 463 | Long cloth | Ditto | Fine quality. Made to order | 33 0 | 1 0 | 4 14 | 9 0 0 | Rajahmundry, Madras. |
| 464 | Long cloth. Watered "Isree." | Ditto | Calico of good quality | 11 24 | 1 0 | 2 4 | 1 6 0 | Nellore, Madras. |
| 465 | Watered "Isree" | Ditto | Plain. Coarse | 6 18 | 0 31 | 1 12 | 0 4 0 | Vizagapatam, Madras. |
| 466 | "Punjum" cloth | Ditto | Calico. Coarse quality. "22s." | 10 9 | 1 4 | 2 5 | 0 7 0 | Nellore, Madras. |
| 467 | Ditto | Ditto | Ditto. ditto "26s." | 18 18 | 1 2 | 4 14 | 0 18 0 | Vizagapatam, Madras. |
| 468 | Canvas | Ditto | Bleached | 12 0 | 0 30 | 5 0 | 0 7 0 | Nellore, Madras. |
| 469 | "Soojney," used for sheeting | Ditto | Figured dimity, unbleached | 3 0 | 1 17 | 1 14 | 0 6 3 | Madras. |
| 470 | "Punjum" cloth | Ditto | Coarse. Unbleached (Incomplete piece) | 35 0 | 1 0 | - - | 0 9 6 | Vizagapatam, Madras. |
| 471 | "Dungary" cloth | Ditto | Unbleached ditto | - - | 0 15½ | - - | - - - | Salem, Madras. |
| 472 | Country canvas | Ditto | Ditto | 19 0 | 0 23 | 10 11 | 0 9 6 | Rajahmundry, Madras. |
| 473 | "Dungary" cloth, used as sailcloth. | Ditto | - | 16 0 | 0 23 | 6 10 | 0 6 0 | Salem, Madras. |
| 474 | Ditto | Ditto | Coarse | 11 0 | 0 23 | 2 6 | 0 2 0 | Ditto. |
| 475 | "Palempores," or bed covers. | Ditto | Chintz, glazed. Four woven in one piece. | 1 12 | 1 12 | Of four, 1 7 | Of four, 0 14 0 | Masulipatam, Madras. |
| 476 | Ditto | Ditto | Chintz, unglazed. Printed pine pattern ends. Sewn together in centre. | 2 9 | 1 23 | 0 13 | 0 1 5 | Paumodee, Madras. |
| 477 | Ditto | Ditto | Chintzes, unglazed. Printed cotton | 2 0 | 1 0 | 0 8 | 0 1 3 | Masulipatam, Madras. |
| 478 | Ditto | Ditto | Ditto. Printed border. Seam 14 inches from the edge. | 2 14 | 1 14 | 0 13 | 0 2 0 | Ditto. |
| 479 | "Soojney," used as a counterpane. | Ditto | - | 2 9 | 1 4 | 2 0 | 0 4 6 | Kurnool, Madras. |
| 480 | Ditto | Ditto | Coloured thread | 2 9 | 1 4 | 2 0 | 0 4 6 | Ditto. |

## Vol. 13.

## KINCOBS, SATINS, AND SILKS.

| No. | Description. | | | Length. | Width. | Weight. | Price. | Whence procured, Place of Manufacture, &c. |
|---|---|---|---|---|---|---|---|---|
| | Name and Use. | Material. | Quality, &c. | yds. ins. | yds. ins. | lbs. ozs. | £ s. d. | |
| 481 | "Kincob," made up into garments. | Silk - - - | With gold flowers - - - - - | 5 0 | 0 26 | 0 11 | 2 16 0 | Trichinopoly, Madras. |
| 482 | Ditto - - - | Satin - - - | With stripes and flowers of gold and silver. | 5 9 | 0 34 | 0 15 | 1 11 0 | Tanjore, Madras. |
| 483 | Ditto - - - | Ditto - - | With gold flowers - - - - | 4 27 | 0 24 | 0 14 | 3 0 0 | Trichinopoly, Madras. |
| 484 | Ditto. Used for petticoats. | Silk - - - | Ditto - - - - - - | 5 0 | 0 27 | 0 11 | 2 10 0 | Ditto. |
| 485 | Brocade - - - | Ditto - - | With flowers of white silk - - | 5 14 | 0 31 | 1 8 | - - - | Hyderabad, Deccan. Bought in Madras. |
| 486 | "Mushroo" - - - | Satin, silk surface, cotton back. | Flowers embroidered in loom - - | 5 9 | 0 32 | 1 10½ | 2 0 0 | Ditto. |
| 487 | Ditto - - - | Ditto - - | Ditto - - - - - | 5 0 | 0 30½ | 1 7 | 2 0 0 | Ditto. |
| 488 | Ditto - - - | Ditto - - | Flowered with gold and silk - - | 4 18 | 0 35 | 1 12 | 2 2 0 | Trichinopoly, Madras. |
| 489 | Ditto - - - | Ditto - - | Flowered in gold, with silk stripes - | 4 27 | 0 24 | 0 14 | 2 4 0 | Ditto. |
| 490 | Ditto - - - | Ditto - - | Gold stripes - - - - - | 6 0 | 0 28 | 1 5 | - - - | Hyderabad, Deccan. |
| 491 | Ditto - - - | Ditto - - | Dotted with gold. Striped silk - - | 4 18 | 0 24 | 0 14 | 2 4 0 | Tanjore, Madras. |
| 492 | Ditto - - - | Ditto - - | Flowered stripe in silk - - - | 4 24 | 0 29 | 0 11 | 0 11 6 | Ditto. |
| 493 | Ditto - - - | Ditto - - | Coloured stripes - - - - | 6 15 | 1 0 | 1 10½ | 0 16 0 | Ditto. |
| 494 | Ditto - - - | Ditto - - | Flowered stripes - - - - | 6 30 | 1 0 | 1 2 | 1 16 0 | Hyderabad, Deccan. Bought in Madras. |
| 495 | Ditto - - - | Ditto - - | - - - - - | 6 9 | 0 33 | 1 7 | 0 16 0 | Tanjore, Madras. |
| 496 | Ditto - - - | Ditto - - | Coloured stripes and flowers - - | 5 0 | 1 0 | 1 10 | 0 17 0 | Trichinopoly, Madras. |
| 497 | Ditto - - - | Ditto - - | - - - - - | 6 0 | 0 31 | 1 4½ | 1 7 0 | Hyderabad, Deccan. |
| 498 | Ditto - - - | Ditto - - | Parti-coloured and figured stripes - | 5 0 | 1 0 | 1 5 | 0 17 0 | Trichinopoly, Madras. |
| 499 | Ditto - - - | Ditto - - | Flowered stripes - - - | 5 32 | 0 30½ | 1 4 | 1 18 0 | Hyderabad, Deccan. |
| 500 | Ditto - - - | Ditto - - | Plain. Pink - - - - - | 5 31 | 0 31 | 1 2 | 1 18 0 | Ditto. |
| 501 | Ditto - - - | Ditto - - | Crimson, with zigzag cross stripes of a lighter shade. | 6 0 | 0 32 | 1 3½ | 1 16 0 | Ditto. Bought in Madras. |
| 502 | Ditto - - - | Ditto - - | Plain purple - - - - - | 3 20 | 0 34 | 0 13 | 0 11 0 | Trichinopoly, Madras. |
| 503 | Ditto - - - | Ditto - - | Crimson, white zigzag stripes across; same pattern as No. 501. | 6 9 | 0 33 | 1 9 | 0 17 0 | Ditto. |
| 504 | Ditto - - - | Ditto - - | Red, with yellow dotted cross stripe - | 5 31 | 0 26 | 1 2 | 1 18 0 | Hyderabad, Deccan. |
| 505 | Ditto - - - | Ditto - - | Zigzag cross stripes, intersected by variegated stripes lengthwise. | 6 14 | 0 34½ | 1 11½ | 1 0 0 | Tanjore, Madras. |
| 506 | Ditto - - - | Ditto - - | Zigzag stripes in white, with red tinted edges, on a puce ground. | 4 27 | 0 35 | 1 6 | 0 17 0 | Trichinopoly, Madras. |
| 507 | Ditto - - - | Ditto - - | Plain green - - - - | 5 37 | 0 30½ | 1 2½ | 1 16 0 | Hyderabad, Deccan. |
| 508 | Ditto - - - | Ditto - - | Crimson, with narrow white stripes one inch apart. | 5 0 | 1 0 | 1 5 | 0 17 0 | Trichinopoly, Madras. |
| 509 | Ditto - - - | Ditto - - | Orange, with white stripes - - | 6 15 | 1 0 | 2 7 | 0 18 0 | Tanjore, Madras. |
| 510 | Ditto - - - | Ditto - - | Plain crimson - - - - - | 6 0 | 0 32 | 1 4 | 1 16 0 | Hyderabad, Deccan. |
| 511 | Ditto - - - | Ditto - - | Bright yellow and coloured stripes and spots. | 5 27 | 0 27 | 1 6 | 1 16 0 | Ditto. |
| 512 | Ditto - - - | Ditto - - | Pink flowered stripes - - - | 5 33 | 0 30 | 1 1 | 1 15 0 | Ditto. Bought in Madras. |
| 513 | Ditto - - - | Ditto - - | Broad coloured stripes on dark amber ground. | 6 14 | 1 0 | 1 6 | 0 14 0 | Trichinopoly, Madras. |
| 514 | Ditto - - - | Ditto - - | Plain red - - - - - | 4 22 | 0 31 | 0 10½ | 1 18 0 | Hyderabad, Deccan. Bought in Madras. |
| 515 | Ditto - - - | Ditto - - | Plain white - - - - - | 4 16 | 0 32½ | 0 15 | 1 9 0 | Hyderabad, Deccan. |
| 516 | Used for trowserings - | Silk - - - | Figured stripes. Thin and light material | 9 4 | 0 37 | 0 14 | 1 10 0 | Trichinopoly, Madras. |
| 517 | Ditto - - - | Ditto - - | Plain and flowered (coloured) stripes - | 8 27 | 0 35 | 1 2 | 2 2 0 | Ditto. |
| 518 | Used for bodices, petticoats, and trowserings. | Ditto - - | Gauze-like fabric. Green and yellow dotted cross stripes. | 11 0 | 0 33 | 0 14½ | 2 0 0 | Ditto. |
| 519 | Used for trowsering and under garments. | Ditto - - | Gauze-like fabric, coloured stripes - | 9 0 | 0 34 | 0 12 | 0 17 0 | Ditto. |
| 520 | Used for trowserings - | Ditto - - | Gauze-like fabric. Amber and faint white stripe. | 9 6 | 0 34 | 0 11½ | 0 19 0 | Tanjore, Madras. |

## Vol. 14.

## SILK PIECE GOODS.

| No. | Description: Name and Use. | Material. | Quality, &c. | Length. yds. ins. | Width. yds. ins. | Weight. lbs. ozs. | Price. £ s. d. | Whence procured, Place of Manufacture, &c. |
|---|---|---|---|---|---|---|---|---|
| 521 | Piece goods | Silk | Plain, red | 17 15 | 0 21½ | 2 9¾ | 3 0 0 | Lahore. |
| 522 | Ditto | Ditto | Plain, purple shot with red | 13 9 | 0 21½ | 1 8½ | 1 16 0 | Ditto. |
| 523 | Ditto | Ditto | Plain, light green | 15 31 | 0 20½ | 2 1 | 3 0 0 | Ditto. |
| 524 | Ditto | Ditto | Plain, red (shot) | 24 0 | 0 20½ | 2 8½ | 3 9 0 | Ditto. |
| 525 | Ditto | Ditto | Crimson, with small green stripes | 17 33 | 0 21½ | 2 7 | 3 0 0 | Ditto. |
| 526 | Ditto | Ditto | Yellow, with red stripes | 15 0 | 0 22 | 2 3 | 4 6 0 | Ditto. |
| 527 | Ditto | Ditto | Crimson, with white stripes | 18 0 | 0 21½ | 2 8 | 3 6 0 | Ditto. |
| 528 | Ditto | Ditto | Green, with red stripes | 16 15 | 0 21 | 2 2¼ | 3 0 0 | Ditto. |
| 529 | Ditto | Ditto | Crimson, with yellow stripes | 15 26 | 0 21½ | 2 5 | 2 16 0 | Ditto. |
| 530 | Ditto | Ditto | Puce, with red stripes (shot) | 16 18 | 0 21 | 1 13¼ | 2 6 0 | Ditto. |
| 531 | Ditto | Ditto | Purple, with yellow stripes (shot) | 8 0 | 0 19 | 0 10¾ | 1 2 6 | Dera Ishmael Khan. |
| 532 | "Golabee Durreeaee" | Ditto | Red | 6 11 | 0 13 | 0 4 | 0 10 6 | Agra, N. W. Provinces. |
| 533 | "Sungee Charkhanah" | Ditto | Coloured check | 4 33 | 0 27 | 0 7¾ | 1 10 0 | Benares. |
| 534 | - - - | Ditto | Flowered and striped | 5 32 | 0 28½ | 0 15½ | - - - | Bhawulpore. |
| 535 | For dresses | Ditto | Purple check | 15 0 | 1 0 | 1 10½ | - - - | Bhagulpore, Bengal. |
| 536 | Ditto | Ditto | Ditto, good quality | 15 0 | 1 0 | 1 10 | - - - | Berhampore. |
| 537 | - - | Ditto | Coloured stripes | 5 18 | 0 31½ | 0 11½ | - - - | Bhawulpore. |
| 538 | "Elaiche" | Ditto | Red, with small white stripes | 19 11 | 0 19 | 1 5 | 1 14 0 | Agra, N. W. Provinces. |
| 539 | "Durreeaee" | Ditto | Coloured stripes | 14 14 | 0 11 | 0 6¼ | 0 10 6 | Ditto. |
| 540 | "Yeolah" | Ditto | Plain pink, thin texture, extra wide | 11 0 | 1 5 | 1 3 | 5 7 3 | Ahmednugger, Bombay. |
| 541 | "Durreeaee" | Ditto | Yellow, very narrow | 39 18 | 0 11½ | 1 0¼ | 1 9 8½ | Agra, N. W. Provinces. |
| 542 | - - - | Silk and Cotton | Small check | 10 18 | 0 28 | 1 6¼ | - - - | Ditto. |
| 543 | For garments for men and women. | Silk | A peculiar fabric, woven with stripes at centre and ends. To be cut in two, and sewn together at sides to form a garment. | 8 28 | 0 24½ | 1 1¾ | - - - | Pegu, Burmah. |
| 544 | Ditto | Ditto | For wear, cut in two and sewn together at sides. | 8 28 | 0 25½ | 1 2¼ | - - - | Ditto. |
| 545 | Ditto | Ditto | Ditto | 8 30 | 0 25 | 1 4 | - - - | Ditto. |
| 546 | Ditto | Ditto | Ditto, with coloured stripes | 8 26 | 0 27½ | 1 1½ | - - - | Ditto. |
| 547 | Ditto | Ditto | White and green stripes | 9 0 | 0 24 | 1 13½ | - - - | Ditto. |
| 548 | "Lahemeenia" kerchiefs | Ditto | Black, with dull yellow figures and spots, red dotted border. | 1 11 | 1 21 | 0 5¼ | 0 6 0 | Surat, Bombay. |
| 549 | "Lahe" kerchiefs | Ditto | Black, with red tinted spots, red border | 1 10 | 0 29 | 0 1¾ | 0 6 0 | Ditto. |
| 550 | Handkerchief | Ditto | Red, white spots. Black border, spotted pattern. | 0 31½ | 0 30 | 0 2 | 0 3 0 | Ditto. |
| 551 | Ditto "Printed Lahe" | Ditto | Black, red figured pattern and spotted border. | 0 32 | 0 31 | 0 2 | 0 5 3 | Ditto. |
| 552 | Gauze | Ditto | With gold flowers | 8 0 | 1 0 | 0 6½ | 0 19 0 | Trichinopoly, Madras. |
| 553 | Ditto | Ditto | Ditto | 8 0 | 0 34 | 0 6½ | 0 19 0 | Ditto. |
| 554 | Ditto | Ditto | Ditto | 8 0 | 1 0 | 0 5¼ | 0 19 0 | Ditto. |
| 555 | Ditto, for Mosquito curtains. | Ditto | - - - - | 11 0 | 0 31 | 0 5¾ | 1 12 0 | Bhagulpore, Bengal. |
| 556 | "Tussur" | Ditto | Plain | 10 18 | 1 1 | 1 15¼ | 0 15 10½ | Warungul, Hyderabad, Deccan. |
| 557 | Ditto | Ditto | Twilled, dyed | 11 0 | 0 26 | 1 7½ | 0 13 0 | Bhagulpore, Bengal. |
| 558 | Ditto | Ditto | Large check, dyed | 9 18 | 0 25½ | 1 4 | 0 13 0 | Ditto. |
| 559 | Eria "Dooklee" | Ditto | Coarse | 4 0 | 0 34 | 1 6 | 0 4 0 | Cachar, Bengal. |
| 560 | Ditto, "Endi" used for garments by both sexes. | Ditto | - - - - | 3 2 | 1 4 | 1 4 | - - - | Darjeeling. |

## Vol. 15.

## FABRICS FROM CENTRAL ASIA AND RUSSIA.

| No. | Description. Name and Use. | Material. | Quality, &c. | Length. | Width. | Weight. | Price. | Whence procured, Place of Manufacture, &c. |
|---|---|---|---|---|---|---|---|---|
| | | | | yds. ins. | yds. ins. | lbs. ozs. | £ s. d. | |
| 561 | "Uddrussa" | Silk and cotton | Coloured stripes | 7 0 | 0 11½ | - | 0 8 0 | Bokhara. |
| 562 | - | Silk | Yellow borders and ends | - | 0 25 | - | - | |
| 563 | "Uddrussa" and "Elacha." For coat linings. | Cotton and silk | (Full pattern shown in half piece) | 7 9 | 0 12 | - | 0 11 0 | Ditto. |
| 564 | Ditto | Ditto | (Cut crossways to show full pattern) | 3 16 | 0 19½ | - | 0 13 0 | Ditto. |
| 565 | "Ulukh" | Ditto | Sample (one third of full width), shows full pattern. | 3 6 | 0 20½ | - | 0 10 0 | Ditto. |
| 566 | "Goolbuddan" | Silk | Striped | 0 32 | 0 29 | - | about 0 2 10 | Ditto. |
| 567 | For garments | Ditto | Bordered piece | - | 0 26 | - | - | |
| 568 | - | Silk and cotton | Coloured stripes. Full pattern in sample. | about 5 0 | 0 12½ | - | about 0 12 0 | Ditto. |
| 569 | "Kootnee" | Cotton chintz | Glazed. Coloured stripes. Full pattern in sample. In pretty general use. | 3 18 | 0 21½ | - | 0 8 0 | Ditto ? |
| 570 | - | Cotton | Glazed. Coloured stripes. Cut crossways. | - | 0 11 | - | - | |
| 571 | "Khoodbauf" | Silk | Same pattern in two colours (A. B.) | 1 0 | 0 29 | - | 0 4 6 | Made at Bokhara. Obtained in Sind. |
| 572 | - | Cotton chintz | Glazed. Striped. (Two samples) (A. B.) | - | 0 20 | - | - | Bokhara. |
| 573 | "Nauker" | Cotton | Plain green | - | 0 14 | - | - | |
| 574 | "Goolbuddan" | Silk | Striped with border. Cut crossways to exhibit full pattern. | 0 32 | 0 25 | - | 0 3 11 | Ditto. |
| 575 | "Kunawey" | Ditto | Plain primrose colour } each | 0 30 | 0 27½ | - | 0 2 7½ | Ditto. |
| 576 | Ditto | Ditto | Plain cinnamon colour | | | | | |
| 577 | Ditto | Ditto | Plain red shot with blue } each | 0 30 | 0 27½ | - | 0 2 7½ | Ditto. |
| 578 | Ditto | Ditto | Plain green | | | | | |
| 579 | Ditto | Ditto | Plain pink } each | 0 30 | 0 27½ | - | 0 2 7½ | Ditto. |
| 580 | Ditto | Ditto | Plain green shot with red | | | | | |
| 581 | Ditto | Ditto | Plain green shot with yellow } each | 0 30 | 0 27½ | - | 0 2 7½ | Ditto. |
| 582 | Ditto | Ditto | Plain blue shot with red | | | | | |
| 583 | "Boolbool Chrshum" | Ditto | Figured red and yellow | - | 0 28 | - | - | Meshed. |
| 584 | Ditto | Ditto | Ditto White | - | 0 21 | - | - | Ditto |
| 585 | Ditto | Ditto | Ditto Green shot with red and green figure. | - | 0 16 | - | about 0 5 6 per yard | Ditto. |
| 586 | Ditto | Ditto | Ditto Pink, white figure | - | 0 24 | - | | |
| 587 | - | Ditto | Crimson ground, blue figure | - | 0 16 | - | - | Ditto. |
| 588 | - | Ditto | Coloured and figured stripes | - | 0 20 | - | - | Ditto. |
| 589 | - | Ditto | Yellow ground, red figure | - | 0 18 | - | - | Ditto. |
| 590 | "Musjoor" | Ditto | Yellow, figured } each | - | 0 18 | - | - | Ditto. |
| 591 | Ditto | Ditto | Crimson, ditto | | | | | |
| 592 | - | Silk gauze | Flowered stripes on yellow ground | - | 0 24 | - | - | Ditto. |
| 593 | - | Ditto | Ditto on white ground | - | 0 24 | - | - | |
| 594 | "Ubra" or "Shalwal," for Choga, &c. Shawl pattern. | Silk cloth | Shawl pattern | - | 0 25½ | - | per yard 0 10 0 | Herat. |
| 595 | Ditto | Ditto | Ditto | - | 0 25½ | - | per yard 0 10 0 | Ditto. |
| 596 | Ditto | Ditto | Ditto | - | 0 25½ | - | per yard 0 10 0 | Ditto. |
| 597 | Ditto | Ditto | Ditto | - | 0 25½ | - | per yard 0 10 0 | Ditto. |
| 598 | Ditto | Ditto | Ditto | - | 0 25½ | - | per yard 0 10 0 | Ditto. |
| 599 | "Atlas" | Cotton and silk | Plain red | - | 0 29 | - | - | Ditto. |
| 600 | Ditto | Ditto | Plain black | - | 0 17½ | - | - | |
| 601 | "Naukrr" | Cotton | Plain brown | - | 0 17 | - | - | Ditto. |
| 602 | "Atlas" (Satin) | Silk face, cotton back | Plain yellow | - | 0 28 | - | - | |
| 603 | "Goolbuddun" | Silk | Narrow stripes on a deep red ground | - | 0 18 | - | - | Yezd. |
| 604 | - | Ditto | Brocade. Crimson flower on yellow ground. | - | 0 29 | - | about 0 4 0 per yard | Balk. |
| 605 | - | Ditto | Ditto | - | 0 29½ | - | about 0 4 0 per yard | Ditto. |
| 606 | "Boodul" | Ditto | Shaded figure, yellow } Each piece varies from | - | 0 9 to 0 17 | - | about 0 2 0 per yard | Ditto. |
| 607 | Ditto | Ditto | Ditto crimson | | | | | |
| 608 | Ditto | Ditto | Shaded figure. Deep blue. (Flimsy) | - | 0 17 | - | about 0 2 0 per yard | Ditto. |
| 609 | Ditto | Ditto | Ditto. Light blue. (Harsh surface) | - | 0 19 | - | - | |
| 610 | - | Ditto | Figured. Peculiar design. Pattern complete in sample. | 6 0 | 0 25 | - | 0 13 0 | Ditto. |
| 611 | - | Gauze, silk, and a little cotton. | White. Striped in material } each | - | 0 28 | - | - | Kokan. |
| 612 | - | Gauze; silk only | Crimson, ditto | | | | | |
| 613 | "Dasija" | Silk gauze | White silk stripe on yellow ground } each | 0 30 | 0 26 | - | per piece 0 1 1½ | Ditto. |
| 614 | Ditto | Ditto | Ditto on crimson ground | | | | | |
| 615 | "Saujoo gool goshen" | Silk | Deep blue, shaded figure | - | 0 30 | - | - | Bokhara. |
| 616 | - | Satin | Yellow figure on purple, crimson, and green stripes. | 0 31 | 0 20 | - | 0 7 0 | Obtained in Bokhara. Manufactured in Russia. |
| 617 | - | Ditto | Yellow figure on light blue, red, and green stripes. | 0 31 | 0 20 | - | 0 7 0 | Ditto. |
| 618 | Satin | Silk | Yellow flowered figure on variegated stripes. | 0 31 | 0 20 | - | 0 7 0 | Ditto. |
| 619 | Ditto | Ditto | Ditto on crimson and green stripes | 0 31 | 0 20 | - | 0 7 0 | |
| 620 | Ditto | Ditto | Ditto on variegated stripes | 0 31 | 0 20 | - | 0 7 0 | Ditto. |
| 621 | Ditto | Ditto | Ditto | 0 31 | 0 20 | - | 0 7 0 | |
| 622 | - | Woollen | Striped and flowered in printed colours | - | 0 33 | - | - | Obtained in Bokhara. Manufactured at [illegible] in Russia. |
| 623 | "Naukrr" | Cotton | Blue striped | - | 0 13 | - | - | |

## Vol. 16.

## WOOLLENS.

| No. | Description. | | | Length. | Width. | Weight. | Price. | Whence procured, Place of Manufacture, &c. |
|---|---|---|---|---|---|---|---|---|
| | Name and Use. | Material. | Quality, &c. | | | | | |
| | | | | yds. ins. | yds. ins. | lbs. ozs. | £ s. d. | |
| 624 | "Kooroon" or Sulung" cloth. | Woollen - - - | Fine quality - - - - - | 20 0 | 0 16½ | 3 2 | Per yard. 0 2 3* | Sulung, between Lassa and China. |
| 625 | Ditto | Ditto - - - | Ditto - - - - - | 20 0 | 0 16½ | 3 2 | 0 2 3* | Ditto. |
| 626 | Ditto | Ditto - - - | Ditto - - - - - | 20 0 | 0 17 | 3 2 | 0 2 3* | Ditto. |
| 627 | Ditto - - - | Ditto - - - | Ditto - - - - - | 20 0 | 0 16½ | 2 3 | 0 2 3* | Ditto. |
| 628 | "Cummerbund" or "Ezar-bund" (waistband). | Ditto - - - | Deep ends generally - - - | 6 12 | 0 30 | 1 11 | - - - | Hyderabad, Sind. |
| 629 | Ditto - - - | Ditto - - - | Narrow and coarse - - - | 5 0 | 0 10 | 1 7½ | - - - | Beloochistan. |
| 630 | Ditto - - - | Ditto - - - | Coarse, but strong in texture - - | 6 33 | 0 12 | 1 7 | - - - | Nepal. |
| 631 | "Cumblee" or blanket - | Ditto - - - | Sewn together in centre to form one - | 7 18 | 1 22 | 7 0 | 0 18 6 | Made at Dharwar. Sent from Madras. |
| 632 | "Cummerbund" (waistband) | Ditto - - - | - - - - - - | 5 18 | 0 9½ | 1 0 | - - - | Thibet. |
| 633 | Blanket, worn as a scarf by men. | Ditto - - - | Fair quality. Indifferent colour - - | 3 3 | 0 12 | 2 9 | - - - | Darjeeling. |
| 634 | For men's trouserings - | Ditto - - - | - - - - - - | - - | - - | - - | 0 2 6† | Kangra, Punjab. |
| 635 | For clothing - - - | Ditto - - - | Coarse cloth - - - - - | 5 18 | 0 15 | 2 2 | - - - | Ditto. |
| 636 | "Kulloo" (blanket) - - | Ditto - - - | - - - - - - | 3 13 | 0 28 | 4 0 | - - - | Made at Kooloo. Obtained from Kangra, Punjab. |
| 637 | "Cumblee" (blanket) - | Ditto - - - | Bordered. Two sewn together in centre to form one. | 3 0 | 1 14 | 2 4 | 0 3 0 | Bangalore. Sent from Madras. |
| 638 | "Kumblee" (blanket) - | Ditto - - - | Strong. Coarse material - - | 7 0 | 2 3 | 7 15 | 0 11 3 | Sattara, Mahratta country. |
| 639 | Used principally for making shawls for the "lamas." | Ditto - - - | - - - - - - | 14 0 | 0 9 | 2 0 | - - - | Made at Thibet. From Darjeeling. |
| 640 | "Cumblee" or blanket - | Ditto - - - | - - - - - - | 5 5 | 1 29 | 5 9 | 0 18 0 | Delhi. |
| 641 | Ditto - - - | Ditto - - - | Coarse, but strong. Ends fringed - | 3 14 | 1 13 | 2 15 | 0 6 0 | Made at Beejapoor. Obtained from Sattara. |
| 642 | Ditto - - - | Ditto - - - | Coarse - - - - - | 3 19 | 1 16 | 3 4 | 0 5 3 | Ditto. |
| 643 | Ditto - - - | Ditto - - - | Black. Fringed ends - - - | 7 22 | 2 6 | 8 8 | - - - | Beckaneer. |

* The value here named is the price in Cashmere.

† 2*s.* 6*d.* is the price for material sufficient for one pair of trowsers.

# VOL. 17.

## WOOLLENS.

| No. | Description: Name and Use. | Description: Material. | Description: Quality, &c. | Length. | Width. | Weight. | Price. | Whence procured. Place of Manufacture, &c. |
|---|---|---|---|---|---|---|---|---|
| | | | | yds. ins. | yds. ins. | lbs. ozs. | £ s. d. | |
| 644 | "Cumblee" or blanket - | Woollen - - - | Coloured border, coarse texture. Sewn together in centre when complete. | 3 0 | 1 14 | 2 5 | 0 3 7½ | Made at Bangalore. Obtained in Madras. |
| 645 | Ditto - - - | Ditto - - - | Coarse. Fringed ends. White thread runs down one edge. | 3 6 | 1 8 | 3 4 | 0 10 0 | Made in Bellary. From Madras. |
| 646 | Used for making cloaks - | Ditto - - - | Colours good - - - - | - - | - - | - - | - - - | From Sikim. Obtained from Thibet. |
| 647 | Ditto - - - | Ditto - - - | Ditto, very strong - - | 19 0 | 0 9½ | 6 14 | - - - | Thibet. |
| 648 | "Foorook" and "Puttoo" - | Ditto - - - | Superior quality - - - | 11 0 | 0 15 | 9 11 | 0 12 0 | From Lassa, Thibet. Obtained in Kangra. |
| 649 | "Puttoo" - - - | Ditto - - - | - - - - - | 6 29 | 0 12 | 3 7 | 0 18 0 | Ditto. |
| 650 | Used for making coats and cloaks. | Ditto - - - | Very coarse* - - - - | - - | - - | - - | - - - | Kohat. |
| 651 | - - - - - - | Ditto - - - | Coarse material - - - - | 7 18 | 0 12 | 3 8 | - - | Thibet. |
| 652 | "Loongee" or scarf, used for body clothing during cold weather, also for bed covers and saddle cloths. | Ditto - - - | Silk borders and ends. Sewn together in centre to form one. | 5 12 | 0 25 | 3 14 | About 0 4 0 | Hyderabad, Sind. |
| 653 | For blankets - | Ditto - - - | - - - - - | 7 9 | 0 14 | 5 10 | - - - | Thibet. |
| 654 | "Cumblee" or blanket - | Ditto - - - | Coarse quality. Fringed ends - | 2 27 | 1 2 | 2 10 | 0 1 0 | From Bangalore. Obtained in Madras. |
| 655 | Ditto - - - | Ditto - - - | Mixed with camel hair. Fringed ends. Coarse. Sewn together in centre when complete. | 2 20 | 1 18 | 5 0 | 0 1 6 | Ditto. |
| 656 | Ditto - - - | Ditto - - - | Coarse. Sewn together to form any desired width.† | 2 9 | 0 15 | 2 0 | - - - | Kathmandoo, Nepal. |
| 657 | Used for rugs, &c. - - | Wool and Horsehair - | Coarse - - - - - | 18 14 | 0 16 | 10 13 | - - - | Kangra, Punjab. |
| 658 | For blankets - - - | Woollen - - - | - - - - - | 2 15 | 1 26 | 5 0 | - - - | Odypore, Rajpootana States. |
| 659 | Horse cloth - - - | Ditto - - | English pattern. Large dark check - | 4 0 | 2 21 | 15 15 | 1 0 0 | Delhi. |
| 660 | Felt material used for leggings, &c. | Ditto - - | - - - - - | 0 31 | 0 18 | 0 9 | 0 1 0 | Ladak. |
| 661 | Felted blanket or cloak to cover the head and body. | Ditto - - | - - - - - | 1 21 | 2 21 | 3 13 | - - - | Jeypore, Rajpootana States. |
| 662 | Felt blanket - - - - | Ditto - - | Rough - - - - - | 3 0 | 1 20 | 4 8 | - - - | Ditto. |
| 663 | For blankets - - - | Ditto - - | Coarse - - - - - | 3 16 | 2 9 | 9 14 | - - - | Ditto. |

* Used by peasants of Kohat.
† Made and used by the Hill Tribes.

## WOOLLENS, CASHMERE SHAWL CLOTHS, &c.

| No. | Description. Name and Use. | Material. | Quality, &c. | Length. | Width. | Weight. | Price. | Whence procured, Place of Manufacture, &c. |
|---|---|---|---|---|---|---|---|---|
| | | | | yds. ins. | yds. ins. | lbs. ozs. | £ s. d. | |
| 664 | "Jamewar," cashmere shawl; worn by both sexes. | Cashmere wool | Striped pattern. Figured. Fine quality | 3 14 | 1 19 | 2 8 | 7 0 0 | Kangra, Punjab. |
| 665 | Shawl | Ditto | Pine pattern throughout | 3 9 | 1 15 | 2 2 | - - - | Cashmere. |
| 666 | Shawl cloth | Ditto | Pine pattern | 3 0 | 1 6 | 2 7 | - - - | Ditto. |
| 667 | Ditto, worn by both sexes | Ditto | Plain crimson. Very fine. Good colour | 7 0 | 1 10 | 2 4 | 3 0 0 | Loodiana, Punjab. |
| 668 | Shawl cloth, chiefly used for chogas. | Ditto | Plain black. First quality | 4 10 | 0 19 | 0 12 | - - - | Cashmere. |
| 669 | Shawl cloth | Ditto | Plain white. Very fine | 7 0 | 1 19 | 2 12 | 4 0 0 | Loodiana, Punjab. |
| 670 | Ditto, worn by both sexes | Ditto | Plain. First quality | 5 0 | 0 28 | 1 1¼ | 2 15 0 | Cashmere. |
| 671 | Ditto | Ditto | Plain black. Second quality | 5 0 | 0 26 | 1 0 | - - - | Ditto. |
| 672 | Ditto | Ditto | Plain grey. Second quality | 5 8 | 0 26 | 0 14½ | 3 0 0 | Ditto. |
| 673 | Ditto | Ditto | Plain green. Fine texture | 6 20 | 1 6 | 0 15 | 3 10 0 | Ditto. |
| 674 | Ditto | Ditto | Plain purple. Fine texture | 5 0 | 0 26 | 0 14 | - - - | Ditto. |
| 675 | Ditto | Ditto | Plain crimson. Second quality. Fine colour. | 5 10 | 0 25 | 0 15 | - - - | Ditto. |
| 676 | "Dooputtah" or scarf (incomplete). | Ditto | Deep buff. Silver and silk figured border sewn on. Broad figured stripe in gold thread across end of scarf. | - - | - - | - - | - - - | Ditto. |
| 677 | "Loongee" or scarf | Ditto | Small red and yellow check. Figured narrow border sewn on. | 5 9 | 1 34 | 2 0 | 5 4 0 | Ditto. |
| 678 | Shawl cloth | Woollen | Plain red. Coarse | 6 21 | 0 27 | 1 7 | - - - | Lahore, Punjab. |
| 679 | Cloth for chogas | Ditto | Plain purple | - - | - - | - - | 2 0 0* | Cabool. |
| 680 | "Kid cloth" "puttoo," a wrapper. | Ditto | Plain white. Fine quality. Woven in half width of 31½ inches. Two pieces sewn together in centre forms one complete. | 4 29 | 1 27 | 4 1 | 3 4 0 | Lahore. |
| 681 | Kid cloth "puttoo" or wrapper. | Ditto | Plain brown. Fine quality. | 3 24 | 1 10 | 2 9 | 1 3 3 | Ditto. |
| 682 | Ditto | Ditto | Ditto | 9 22 | 0 27 | 3 15 | - - - | Thibet. |
| 683 | Kid cloth "toosee" or "tose" cloth. | Ditto | Plain grey | 12 27 | 0 13 | 2 15 | 3 0 0 | Baltistan, obtained at Kangra. |
| 684 | Used as a wrapper | Ditto | Ditto, sewn together in centre forms a garment. | 2 18 | 1 20 | 1 12 | - - - | Lahore. |
| 685 | "Burruch" cloth for chogas, &c. | Camel's hair | Plain grey | - - | - - | - - | - - - | Hyderabad, Sind. |
| 686 | Ditto | Ditto | Plain brown | 8 13 | 0 13 | 1 14 | 0 9 0 | Meshed. |
| 687 | "Dhoosa" or wrapper | Woollen | Greyish white, with green, crimson, and yellow striped silk border. | 3 6 | 1 9 | 1 2 | 1 14 0 | Lahore. |
| 688 | Ditto | Ditto | With striped silk borders. Woven in two lengths with a fag between. | Single length 3 4 | 1 17 | 1 12½ | 1 14 0 | Ditto. |
| 689 | Ditto | Ditto | With red silk border. Woven in two lengths with a fag between. | 3 14 | 1 9 | 1 1½ | 1 6 0 | Ditto. |
| 690 | Ditto | Ditto | With red, white, and green silk borders | 2 30 | 1 6 | 0 14½ | 1 6 0 | Ditto. |
| 691 | Ditto | Ditto | With green, red, and yellow silk borders | 3 5 | 1 12 | 1 5¼ | 1 15 0 | Ditto. |
| 692 | Used as a wrapper | Ditto | Inferior quality. Two sewn together form one. | 4 18 | 2 12 | 3 7¼ | 1 6 0 | Ditto. |
| 693 | "Loee" or wrapper | Ditto | Good quality. White | 6 28 | 1 23 | 4 6 | - - - | Beckaneer, N.W. India. |
| 695 | Carpet | Ditto | Deep pile | - - | - - | - - | - - - | Ellore, Madras. |
| 696 | Ditto | Ditto | Short pile | 2 16 | 1 18 | - - | - - - | Wurrungul, Deccan. |
| 697 | Ditto | Ditto | Short, close pile | - - | - - | - - | - - - | Bokhara. |
| 698 | Suttringee or Rug | Cotton | Short pile | 3 12 | 1 24 | - - | - - - | Wurrungul, Deccan. |
| 699 | Ditto | Ditto | Coloured stripes | 2 30 | 1 24 | - - | - - - | Agra, N. W. Provinces. |
| 700 | Carpet | Silk | Short pile | 2 20 | 1 18 | - - | - - - | Wurrungul, Deccan. |

* This is the price of a cloak made from this material. Worn by the higher classes of Northern India.

## PLACES OF MANUFACTURE OR MARTS FROM WHICH THE SPECIMENS WERE OBTAINED.

| Name of Place. | District, &c. | Presidency or Country. | Latitude. | Longitude. |
|---|---|---|---|---|
| | | | ° ′ | ° ′ |
| Agra | Agra | N.W. Provinces | 27 10 | 78 5 |
| Ahmednugger | Ahmednugger | Bombay | 19 6 | 74 46 |
| Arcot | North Arcot | Madras | 12 54 | 79 24 |
| Arnee | Ditto | Ditto | 12 40 | 79 21 |
| Arracan | Arracan | Under Lieut.-Governor, Bengal. | Between 18 0 and 21 33 | Between 92 10 and 94 50 |
| Assam | Assam | Ditto | 25 49 to 28 17 | 90 40 to 97 1 |
| Balk | - | Turkestan | 36 48 | 67 3 |
| Baltistan | - | Thibet | 34 50 to 36 0 | 75 0 to 77 0 |
| Bangalore | Mysore | Native state | 12 58 | 77 38 |
| Beckaneer | Rajpootana | Ditto | 28 0 | 73 22 |
| Beejapoor | Sattara | Bombay | 16 50 | 75 48 |
| Belgaum | Belgaum | Ditto | 15 50 | 74 36 |
| Bellary | Bellary | Madras | 15 8 | 76 59 |
| Beloochistan | - | - | 24 50 to 30 20 | 57 50 to 68 50 |
| Benares | Benares | N.W. Provinces | 25 17 | 83 4 |
| Berhampore | Ganjam | Madras | 19 20 | 84 50 |
| Berhampore | Moorshedabad | Bengal | 24 5 | 88 17 |
| Bhagulpore | Bhagulpore | Ditto | 25 11 | 87 0 |
| Bhawulpore | - | Native State | 29 24 | 71 47 |
| Bhurtpore | Bhurtpore | Ditto | 27 12 | 77 33 |
| Biekul | North Canara | Bombay | 12 23 | 75 5 |
| Bokhara | - | Turkestan | 39 46 | 64 23 |
| Bombay | Bombay | Bombay | 18 57 | 72 52 |
| Broach | Broach | Ditto | 21 42 | 73 2 |
| Buttala | Goodaspore | Punjab | 31 49 | 75 14 |
| Cabool | - | Afghanistan | 34 30 | 69 6 |
| Cachar | Cachar | Bengal | 24 13 to 25 50 | 92 54 to 93 28 |
| Calcutta | Nuddea | Ditto | 22 34 | 88 25 |
| Cashmere | Cashmere | Native State | 32 17 to 36 0 | 73 20 to 79 40 |
| Chicacole | Gangam | Madras | 18 18 | 83 58 |
| Chingleput | Chingleput | Ditto | 12 41 | 80 2 |
| Chundree | Gwalior | Native State | 24 41 | 78 12 |
| Coimbatore | Coimbatore | Madras | 11 0 | 77 1 |
| Combaconum | Tanjore | Ditto | 10 58 | 79 26 |
| Congeveram | Chingleput | Ditto | 12 50 | 79 46 |
| Coonathoor | Chingleput | Ditto | 12 59 | 80 10 |
| Cuddalore | Arcot | Ditto | 11 43 | 79 50 |
| Cuddapah | Cuddapah | Ditto | 14 28 | 78 52 |
| Cundapoora, Cundapoor, or Condapore | South Canara | Ditto | 13 38 | 74 45 |
| Cutch | Cutch | Native State | 22 47 to 24 40 | 68 26 to 71 45 |
| Dacca | Dacca | Bengal | 23 43 | 90 25 |
| Darjeeling | Darjeeling | Ditto | 27 2 | 88 19 |
| Delhi | Delhi | N.W. Provinces | 28 39 | 77 18 |
| DeyraIshmailKhan | Derajat | Punjab | 31 50 | 70 58 |
| Dharwar | Dharwar | Bombay | 15 28 | 75 4 |
| Futtygurh | Furruckabad | N.W. Provinces | 27 22 | 79 41 |
| Gangam | Gangam | Madras | 19 23 | 85 7 |
| Goa | - | Former capital of Portuguese possessions. | 15 30 | 74 0 |
| Goodaspore | - | Punjab. | — | — |
| Gwalior | - | Native State | 21 8 to 26 50 | 74 45 to 79 21 |
| Gya | - | Bengal | 24 18 | 85 4 |
| Hazara | - | Punjab | 33 50 to 35 0 | 72 30 to 73 0 |
| Herat | - | Afghanistan | 34 26 | 62 8 |
| Hoshiarpore | Trans Sutlej States | Punjab | 31 33 | 75 57 |
| Hyderabad | Sind | Bombay | 25 22 | 68 28 |
| Hyderabad | Deccan | The Nizam's territory. | 17 22 | 78 32 |
| Jeypoor | Jeypoor | Native State | 26 56 | 75 55 |
| Jhelum | - | Punjab | 32 56 | 73 47 |
| Kangra | Trans Sutlej States | Ditto | 32 5 | 76 18 |
| Karikal | Tanjore | Madras. A French settlement. | 10 55 | [illegible] |
| Kathamandoo | Nepaul | Independent State | 27 42 | 85 18 |
| Kohat | - | Punjab | 33 32 | 71 27 |
| Kokan | — | — | — | — |
| Kooloo or Kulu | - | - | Between 31 20 and 32 33 | Between 76 45 and 77 50 |
| Kurnool | Kurnool | Madras | 15 50 | 78 5 |
| Ladak | Ladak | Thibet | 32 20 to 35 0 | 75 30 to 79 30 |
| Lahore | Lahore | Punjab | 31 36 | 74 21 |
| Lassa | - | Thibet | 29 30 | 91 6 |
| Leiah | Leiah | Punjab | 30 57 | 71 4 |
| Loodiana | - | Ditto | 30 55 | 75 54 |
| Madras | - | Madras | 13 5 | 80 21 |
| Madura | Madura | Ditto | 9 55 | 78 10 |
| Mangalore | South Canara | Ditto | 12 52 | 74 54 |
| Masulipatam | Masulipatam | Ditto | 16 10 | 81 13 |
| Meshed | - | Persia | 36 17 | 59 42 |
| Moorshedabad | Rajshahye | Bengal | 24 12 | 88 17 |
| Mylapore | Chingleput | Madras | 13 1 | 80 20 |
| Nagang | - | Ditto. | — | — |
| Nagpore | Nagpore | - Dist. | 17 50 to 23 5 | 78 3 to 83 10 |
| | | Town | 21 10 | 79 10 |
| Nellore | Nellore | Madras | 14 27 | 80 2 |
| Nepal | - | IndependentState | 26 25 to 30 17 | 80 15 to 88 15 |
| Nurrapore | - | Sind | 26 0 | 68 16 |
| Oodeypore | Rajpootana States | - | 24 37 | 73 49 |
| Ooppaddy | (*See* Woopparaddy) | Madras. | — | — |
| Palamcottah | Tinnevelly | Ditto | 8 43 | 77 18 |
| Patna | Patna | Bengal | 25 35 | 85 15 |
| Pegu | Pegu | Bengal, Gov. Gen. Administ. | 15 49 to 19 30 | 94 11 to 93 55 |
| Pind Dadun Khan | Sind Sagur Doab | Punjab | 32 36 | 73 5 |
| Pomady or Paumodee. | - | Madras. | — | — |
| Pondicherry | S. Arcot | Madras, a French settlement. | 11 56 | 79 54 |
| Poonary | - | Madras | 13 20 | 80 13 |
| Pulicat | Chingleput | Ditto | 13 25 | 80 22 |
| Radnagore. | — | — | — | — |
| Rajahmundry | Rajahmundry | Madras | 17 0 | 81 50 |
| Raneepore | - | Sind | 27 18 | 68 40 |
| Rawul Pindee | Rawul Pindee | Punjab | 33 37 | 73 6 |
| Runeeporeim | (*See* Raneepore) | Sind. | — | — |
| Rutul Mudpore | - | Punjab. | — | — |
| Salem | Salem | Madras | 11 39 | 78 12 |
| Santipore | Nuddea | Bengal | 23 14 | 88 26 |
| Sattara | Sattara | Bombay | 17 45 | 74 4 |
| Shahabad | Patna | Bengal | 24 30 to 25 46 | 83 20 to 84 56 |
| Shikarpore | Shikarpore | Sind | 28 0 | 68 39 |
| Sikkim | - | Native State | 27 5 to 28 3 | 88 2 to 89 0 |
| Sind | - | - | 23 37 to 28 32 | 66 43 to 71 3 |
| Sulung | Thibet. | — | — | — |
| Surat | Surat | Bombay | 21 10 | 72 52 |
| Sydapet | Chingleput | Madras. | — | — |
| Syempettah | - | Ditto. | — | — |
| Sylhet | Dacca | Bengal | 24 54 | 91 50 |
| Tanjore | Tanjore | Madras | 10 47 | 79 12 |
| Teroomaly | - | Ditto. | — | — |
| Thibet | - | - | 28 0 to 36 0 | 79 0 to 103 0 |
| Trichinopoly | Trichinopoly | Madras | 10 50 | 78 46 |
| Vencatagorry | N. Arcot | Ditto | 13 0 | 78 32 |
| Ventapollam | Guntoor | Ditto | 15 47 | 80 22 |
| Vizagapatam | Vizagapatam | Ditto | 17 41 | 83 21 |
| Warungul | Hyderabad | The Deccan, Nizam's Territories. | 17 58 | 79 40 |
| Woopparaddy | - | Madras | 17 5 | 82 23 |
| Woozzoor or Oosoor | Salem | Ditto | 12 46 | 77 51 |
| Yezd | - | - | 31 45 | 54 50 |

# TABLE SHOWING WHERE THE SAMPLES IN THE FABRIC BOOKS ARE REFERRED TO IN THIS WORK.

| No. of Sample in Vol. I. | Vide Text, page | No. of Sample in Vol. II. | Vide Text, page | No. of Sample in Vol. III. | Vide Text, page | No. of Sample in Vol. IV. | Vide Text, page | No. of Sample in Vol. V. | Vide Text, page | No. of Sample in Vol. VI. | Vide Text, page | No. of Sample in Vol. VII. | Vide Text, page | No. of Sample in Vol. VIII. | Vide Text, page | No. of Sample in Vol. IX. | Vide Text, page |
|---|---|---|---|---|---|---|---|---|---|---|---|---|---|---|---|---|---|
| 1 | 15 | 41 | 26 | 81 | 34 | 121 | 30 | 161 | 52 | 201 | 111 | 241 | 75, 76 | 281 | 77 | 321 | 76 |
| 2 | 16 | 42 | 26 | 82 | 34 | 122 | 30 | 162 | 40 | 202 | 111 | 242 | 76 | 282 | 78 | 322 | 74, 76 |
| 3 | 15 | 43 | 20 | 83 | 35 | 123 | 37 | 163 | 49 | 203 | 111 | 243 | 76 | 283 | 42 | 323 | 77 |
| 4 | 15 | 44 | 24,25 | 84 | 34 | 124 | 37 | 164 | 51 | 204 | 111 | 244 | 76 | 284 | 42, 74 | 324 | 77 |
| 5 | 16 | 45 | 24,25 | 85 | 34 | 125 | 30 | 165 | 45 | 205 | 52 | 245 | 76 | 285 | 42 | 325 | 74, 78 |
| 6 | 16 | 46 | 23,24 | 86 | 33 | 126 | 29, 30 | 166 | 45 | 206 | 50 | 246 | 76 | 286 | 76 | 326 | 78 |
| 7 | 15 | 47 | 23,24 | 87 | 34 | 127 | 29, 30 | 167 | 45, 74 | 207 | 50 | 247 | 77 | 287 | 41 | 327 | 78 |
| 8 | 16 | 49 | 24, 25 | 88 | 35 | 128 | 37 | 168 | 47, 74 | 208 | 48 | 248 | 77 | 288 | 41 | 328 | 74, 78 |
| 9 | 15 | 48 | 25 | 89 | 34 | 129 | 27, 28 | 169 | 45 | 209 | 50 | 249 | 77 | 289 | 37 | 329 | 74, 78 |
| 10 | 16 | 50 | 23, 24, 74 | 90 | 34 | 130 | 31 | 170 | 45, 74 | 210 | 50 | 250 | 78 | 290 | 37 | 330 | 74, 80 |
| 11 | 16 | 51 | 25 | 91 | 34 | 131 | 104 | 171 | 46, 74 | 211 | 49 | 251 | 78 | 291 | 37 | 331 | 74, 80 |
| 12 | 16 | 52 | 23, 24, 74 | 92 | 33 | 132 | 86 | 172 | 49 | 212 | 52 | 252 | 115 | 292 | 115 | 332 | 80 |
| 13 | 16 | 53 | 25 | 93 | 33 | 133 | 86 | 173 | 42 | 213 | 46 | 253 | 79 | 293 | 115 | 333 | 80 |
| 14 | 15 | 54 | 23, 24 | 94 | 33 | 134 | 101 | 174 | 50 | 214 | 49 | 254 | 79 | 294 | 106, 107 | 334 | 80 |
| 15 | 16 | 55 | 25 | 95 | 32 | 135 | 86 | 175 | 52 | 215 | 46 | 255 | 115 | 295 | 115 | 335 | 80 |
| 16 | 16 | 56 | 32 | 96 | 32 | 136 | 86 | 176 | 45 | 216 | 47 | 256 | 115 | 296 | 115 | 336 | 80 |
| 17 | 16 | 57 | 33 | 97 | 31 | 137 | 86 | 177 | 45 | 217 | 46 | 257 | 115 | 297 | 84 | 337 | 80 |
| 18 | 16 | 58 | 31 | 98 | 32 | 138 | 86 | 178 | 45 | 218 | 34 | 258 | 115 | 298 | 84 | 338 | 80 |
| 19 | 19 | 59 | 29, 74 | 99 | 31 | 139 | 86 | 179 | 46 | 219 | 49 | 259 | 79 | 299 | 84 | 339 | 80 |
| 20 | 17 | 60 | 29 | 100 | 29 | 140 | 86 | 180 | 43 | 220 | 44 | 260 | 115 | 300 | 84 | 340 | 80 |
| 21 | 19 | 61 | 33 | 101 | 32 | 141 | 101 | 181 | 43 | 221 | 41 | 261 | 113 | 301 | 84 | 341 | 80 |
| 22 | 19 | 62 | 29, 74 | 102 | 30 | 142 | 84 | 182 | 44 | 222 | 43 | 262 | 113 | 302 | 84 | 342 | 80 |
| 23 | 18 | 63 | 28 | 103 | 31 | 143 | 86 | 183 | 46 | 223 | 43 | 263 | 113 | 303 | 84 | 343 | 80 |
| 24 | 18 | 64 | 29 | 104 | 32 | 144 | 86 | 184 | 46 | 224 | 43 | 264 | 113 | 304 | 84 | 344 | 81 |
| 25 | 18 | 65 | 28 | 105 | 29 | 145 | 86 | 185 | 44 | 225 | 43 | 265 | 113 | 305 | 84 | 345 | 74, 81 |
| 26 | 18 | 66 | 28 | 106 | 37 | 146 | 86 | 186 | 44, 74 | 226 | 43 | 266 | 113 | 306 | 84 | 346 | 81 |
| 27 | 18 | 67 | 28 | 107 | 37 | 147 | 86 | 187 | 44, 74 | 227 | 41 | 267 | 113 | 307 | 85 | 347 | 74, 81 |
| 28 | 18 | 68 | 28 | 108 | 31 | 148 | 86 | 188 | 41 | 228 | 41 | 268 | 113 | 308 | 80 | 348 | 81 |
| 29 | 18 | 69 | 28 | 109 | 23, 24 | 149 | 86 | 189 | 42 | 229 | 43 | 269 | 113 | 309 | 80 | 349 | 81 |
| 30 | 17 | 70 | 74, 86 | 110 | 23, 24 | 150 | 86 | 190 | 44 | 230 | 87 | 270 | 116 | 310 | 91 | 350 | 81 |
| 31 | 17 | 71 | 28 | 111 | 28, 29 | 151 | 90, 94 | 191 | 44 | 231 | 87 | 271 | 81 | 311 | 91 | 351 | 105 |
| 32 | 17 | 72 | 28 | 112 | 30 | 152 | 90, 94 | 192 | 44 | 232 | 87 | 272 | 81 | 312 | 91 | 352 | 101 |
| 33 | 18 | 73 | 28 | 113 | 29 | 153 | 90, 94 | 193 | 41 | 233 | 88 | 273 | 81 | 313 | 88 | 353 | 101 |
| 34 | 17 | 74 | 74, 86 | 114 | 30 | 154 | 90, 94 | 194 | 41, 74 | 234 | 115 | 274 | 116 | 314 | 88 | 354 | 104 |
| 35 | 20 | 75 | 23, 24, 74 | 115 | 30 | 155 | 90, 94 | 195 | 41 | 235 | 115 | 275 | 112 | 315 | 92 | 355 | 101 |
| 36 | 19 | 76 | 23, 24 | 116 | 30 | 156 | 90, 94 | 196 | 48 | 236 | 87 | 276 | 116 | 316 | 88 | 356 | 101 |
| 37 | 19 | 77 | 23, 24 | 117 | 27, 28 | 157 | 90, 94 | 197 | 48, 74 | 237 | 87 | 277 | 116 | 317 | 88 | 357 | 86 |
| 38 | 20 | 78 | 23, 24, 74 | 118 | 30 | 158 | 96 | 198 | 48, 74 | 238 | 87 | 278 | 116 | 318 | 88 | 358 | 101 |
| 39 | 20 | 79 | 23 | 119 | 29,30 | 159 | 96 | 199 | 48 | 239 | 87 | 279 | 116 | 319 | 92 | 359 | 88 |
| 40 | 20 | 80 | 23, 74 | 120 | 30 | 160 | 94 | 200 | 48 | 240 | 87 | 280 | 116 | 320 | 90, 93 | 360 | 88 |

## TABLE SHOWING WHERE THE SAMPLES IN THE FABRIC BOOKS ARE REFERRED TO IN THIS WORK.—*continued.*

| No. of Sample in Vol. X. | Vide Text, page | No. of Sample in Vol. XI. | Vide Text, page | No. of Sample in Vol. XII. | Vide Text, page | No. of Sample in Vol. XIII. | Vide Text, page | No. of Sample in Vol. XIV. | Vide Text, page | No. of Sample in Vol. XV. | Vide Text, page | No. of Sample in Vol. XVI. | Vide Text, page | No. of Sample in Vol. XVII. | Vide Text, page | No. of Sample in Vol. XVIII. | Vide Text, page |
|---|---|---|---|---|---|---|---|---|---|---|---|---|---|---|---|---|---|
| 361 | 53 | 401 | 88 | 441 | 111 | 481 | 112 | 521 | 104 | 561, 562 | | 624 | 136 | 644 | 35 | 664 | 134 |
| 362 | 53 | 402 | 88 | 442 | 111 | 482 | 112 | 522 | 104 | 563 | | 625 | 136 | 645 | 139 | 665 | 134 |
| 363 | 53 | 403 | 88 | 443 | 111 | 483 | 112 | 523 | 104 | 564, 565 | | 626 | 136 | 646 | 139, 140 | 666 | 134 |
| 364 | 53 | 404 | 89 | 444 | 101 | 484 | 112 | 524 | 104 | 566 | | 627 | 136 | 647 | 139, 140 | 667 | 134 |
| 365 | 53 | 405 | 89 | 445 | 116 | 485 | 105 | 525 | 104 | 567, 568 | | 628 | 35 | 648 | 135 | 668 | 134 |
| 366 | 53 | 406 | 89 | 446 | 101 | 486 | 102 | 526 | 104 | 569, 570 | | 629 | 38 | 649 | 135 | 669 | 134 |
| 367 | 47 | 407 | 89 | 447 | 101 | 487 | 102 | 527 | 104 | 571 | 146 | 630 | 38 | 650 | 139 | 670 | 134 |
| 368 | 91 | 408 | 89 | 448 | 101 | 488 | 112 | 528 | 104 | 572, 573 | | 631 | 136 | 651 | 139 | 671 | 134 |
| 369 | 91 | 409 | 89 | 449 | 101 | 489 | 112 | 529 | 105 | 574 | | 632 | 38 | 652 | 36 | 672 | 134 |
| 370 | 91 | 410 | 89 | 450 | 86 | 490 | 112 | 530 | 105 | 575, 576 | | 633 | 38 | 653 | 139 | 673 | 134 |
| 371 | 47 | 411 | 89 | 451 | 101 | 491 | 112 | 531 | 105 | 577 | | 634 | 139 | 654 | 139 | 674 | 134 |
| 372 | 92 | 412 | 89 | 452 | 101 | 492 | 102 | 532 | 104 | 578, 579 | | 635 | 38 | 655 | 139 | 675 | 134 |
| 373 | 92 | 413 | 89 | 453 | 86 | 493 | 102 | 533 | 105 | 580, 581 | | 636 | 35 | 656 | 139, 140 | 676 | 36 |
| 374 | 92 | 414 | 89 | 454 | 89 | 494 | 102 | 534 | 105 | 582 | | 637 | 35 | 657 | 139 | 677 | 35 |
| 375 | 93 | 415 | 89 | 455 | 86 | 495 | 102 | 535 | 105 | 583, 584 | | 638 | 139 | 658 | 139 | 678 | 134 |
| 376 | 91 | 416 | 89 | 456 | 86 | 496 | 102 | 536 | 105 | 585, 586 | | 639 | 139 | 659 | 139 | 679 | 136 |
| 377 | 91 | 417 | 89 | 457 | 95 | 497 | 102 | 537 | 105 | 587 | | 640 | 139 | 660 | 140, 141 | 680 | 135 |
| 378 | 91 | 418 | 86 | 458 | 95 | 498 | 102 | 538 | 105 | 588, 589 | | 641 | 139 | 661 | 140, 141 | 681 | 135 |
| 379 | 91 | 419 | 95 | 459 | 76 | 499 | 103 | 539 | 105 | 590 | | 642 | 35 | 662 | 140, 141 | 682 | 135 |
| 380 | 93 | 420 | 95 | 460 | 76 | 500 | 102 | 540 | 104 | 591, 592 | | 643 | 139 | 663 | 139 | 683 | 135 |
| 381 | 91 | 421 | 95 | 461 | 53 | 501 | 103 | 541 | 104 | 593 | | | | | | 684 | 135 |
| 382 | 91 | 422 | 95 | 462 | 53 | 502 | 103 | 542 | 101 | 594, 595 | | | | | | 685 | 135 |
| 383 | 91 | 423 | 95 | 463 | 74, 84 | 503 | 103 | 543 | 51 | 596, 597 | 147 | | | | | 686 | 135 |
| 384 | 93 | 424 | 95 | 464 | 74, 84 | 504 | 103 | 544 | 51 | 598 | | | | | | 687 | 36 |
| 385 | 93 | 425 | 95 | 465 | 84 | 505 | 103 | 545 | 51 | 599, 600 | | | | | | 688 | 36 |
| 386 | 93 | 426 | 95 | 466 | 84 | 506 | 103 | 546 | 105 | 601, 602 | | | | | | 689 | 36 |
| 387 | 92 | 427 | 95 | 467 | 84 | 507 | 102 | 547 | 51 | 603 | | | | | | 690 | 36 |
| 388 | 91 | 428 | 95 | 468 | 74, 84 | 508 | 103 | 548 | 106 | 604, 605 | | | | | | 691 | 36 |
| 389 | 93 | 429 | 95 | 469 | 84 | 509 | 103 | 549 | 97, 106 | 606 | | | | | | 692 | 135 |
| 390 | 92 | 430 | 95 | 470 | 84 | 510 | 102 | 550 | 106 | 607, 608 | | | | | | 693 | 136 |
| 391 | 92 | 431 | 96 | 471 | 74, 85 | 511 | 103 | 551 | 106 | 609, 610 | | | | | | 694 | Cancelled. |
| 392 | 93 | 432 | 96 | 471 A | 85 | 512 | 103 | 552 | 116 | 611 | | | | | | 695 | 142, 144 |
| 393 | 93 | 433 | 96 | 472 | 85 | 513 | 103 | 553 | 116 | 612, 613 | | | | | | 696 | 142, 144 |
| 394 | 93 | 434 | 142 | 473 | 74, 85 | 514 | 102 | 554 | 116 | 614 | | | | | | 397 | 142, 144 |
| 395 | 93 | 435 | 142 | 474 | 85 | 515 | 102 | 555 | 98 | 615, 616 | | | | | | 698 | 142, 143 |
| 396 | 93 | 436 | 142 | 475 | 94 | 516 | 104 | 556 | 107 | 617 | 148 | | | | | 699 | 142 |
| 397 | 93 | 437 | 142 | 476 | 94 | 517 | 104 | 557 | 107 | 618, 619 | | | | | | 700 | 142, 144 |
| 398 | 92 | 438 | 142 | 477 | 94 | 518 | 104 | 558 | 107 | 620 | | | | | | | |
| 399 | 92 | 439 | 142 | 478 | 94 | 519 | 104 | 559 | 107 | 621, 622 | | | | | | | |
| 400 | 92 | 440 | 142, 143 | 479 | 29,30,96 | 520 | 104 | 560 | 107 | 623 | | | | | | | |
| | | | | 480 | 29,30,96 | | | | | | | | | | | | |

THE END.

LONDON:
Printed by GEORGE E. EYRE and WILLIAM SPOTTISWOODE,
Printers to the Queen's most Excellent Majesty.